ILLUSTRATED MONOGRAPHS

No. XVI

Printers' & Publishers' Devices
in England & Scotland
1485—1640

BY

RONALD B. McKERROW

LONDON
THE BIBLIOGRAPHICAL SOCIETY
1949

FIRST PRINTED 1913
AT THE CHISWICK PRESS
REPRINTED PHOTOGRAPHICALLY 1949
IN GREAT BRITAIN
AT THE UNIVERSITY PRESS, OXFORD
BY CHARLES BATEY
PRINTER TO THE UNIVERSITY

PRINTED IN GREAT BRITAIN

FOREWORD

'McKERROW'S DEVICES' is the third of the Bibliographical Society's publications to be reprinted by photo-offset-lithography for sale to the public as well as to members of the Society. Like its two companions, the *Short-title Catalogue* and Duff's *Century*, it has become an indispensable work of reference for students of early English books. Although it is over 35 years since it first appeared and although much additional information about the use of the various devices has been accumulated, it remains a remarkably complete survey of the field, very few additions having been found. The appearance of this reprint does not mean that the Council of the Bibliographical Society has abandoned the intention of bringing out a revised edition at the appropriate time. Corrections and additions are always gratefully received and carefully filed for future use.

November 1948   F. C. F.

PREFACE

HE present volume is intended to contain an account of all marks and devices used by printers and publishers resident in England and Scotland from the time of the introduction of printing until 1640, and also of all wood-cut borders and ornaments containing the owner's device or initials used here during the period. The devices of foreign printers of books for the English market are not included, nor are those of one or two foreign firms trading in England, such as the Birckmans, whose business seems rather to have been of the nature of an agency than independent, and who used the device of their principal establishment on the Continent.

That the collection should be complete will not, I hope, be expected, for though much work bearing upon the subject has already been done, this is the first attempt to deal with it as a whole. Several devices are only known from their occurrence in a single book, and it is probable that there still remain a number which have not been recorded. Even approximate completeness in work of this kind can only be arrived at in the course of time and by the assistance of collectors and librarians.

Indeed, the task is one that should properly have been attempted by a librarian. It is, I confess, a source of regret to me that the work could have been far more adequately performed, in perhaps a tenth of the time that I have spent upon it, by any one having direct access to a large collection of books of the period, and able to make a systematic search for unrecorded devices in those less important books and pamphlets which have never been fully described. Were it not for a short period of office as Deputy Librarian at Trinity College, Cambridge, during the course of the work, it would be yet more imperfect than it is; and the great amount of new material which I was then able to add in the comparatively few hours that I was able to devote to the search, has made me realize very clearly how much still remains to be done. The book is indeed but a beginning, something for those with better opportunities to complete.

What rendered it possible for me to attempt this work at all was the existence at the British Museum of the two great collections of title-pages and fragments known as the Bagford and Ames Collections, and I gladly record my debt to the much-abused worthies who gathered them together. The Bagford Collection is the larger and the better known, by reason of the number and interest of the fragments from rare books which it contains, but for the purpose of the present work that of Ames has proved by far the more useful. The title-pages in this collection are as a rule complete, most of them are in good condition, and most important of all for work of this kind, they are arranged in chronological order. The Bagford Collection, on the other hand, is almost entirely without arrangement, though traces of a plan—indeed, of several different plans—may be discerned here and there; in a great number of cases the device or imprint alone is preserved and there is no means of discovering from what book it was taken, and the fragments are mutilated in every way and often so badly or carelessly stuck into the scrapbooks that even the whole information that they might afford is not available.

Between them these two collections have supplied a large part of my material. Next to these in usefulness have been, for the earlier part, Herbert's edition of Ames' *Typographical Antiquities* and, for the later, Mr. Sayle's *Catalogue of English Books in the Cambridge University Library*. Both these books have proved in different ways of the highest value. Herbert does not always give the precise details desired, but he had the rare virtue of not saying more than he knew; and so is never misleading. His work, of course, stops at 1600 and it is from this point that Mr. Sayle's *Catalogue*, in the earlier portion of which—to about 1570—devices are only occasionally mentioned, has been of the greatest help.

In the course of the work I have been compelled to trouble many, both friends and strangers, with inquiries and requests for assistance, and I may say that in no single instance have I met with anything but the promptest and most courteous reply. All information for which I asked has been given me, and every request for permission to reproduce a device has been granted. To all who have helped me I offer my sincere thanks.

The Society is indebted to Lord Newton for permission to reproduce the earliest known print of Caxton's mark (No. 1); to Viscount Clifden for the device used by James Gaver (No. 90); to Mr. Christie-Miller for Nos. 172, 176; to Mr. E. F. Bosanquet for Nos. 74β, 218; to the Master and Fellows of Trinity College, Cambridge, for Nos. 45, 46β, 57, 73, 200, 235, 267, 276, 307, 343, 350; to the Warden and Fellows of New College, Oxford, for No. 34α; to the Dean and Chapter of St. Paul's Cathedral for No. 83α; to the Advocates' Library, Edinburgh, for No. 29; to the Bodleian Library for Nos. 7, 12, 56, 58, 64, 72, 130, 136, 137, 144α, 161, 171, 173, 178, 201, 205, 209, 224, 319, 331; to Cambridge University Library for Nos. 8γ, 131, 135, 162, 255, 386; to the John Rylands Library for Nos. 42, 84β, 115, 144β, 158; and to the New York Public Library for No. 120.

Most of the other blocks in the volume—about seven-eighths

of the whole number—have been reproduced from books in the British Museum, to the Trustees and Staff of which the Society are under great obligation.

In this connection special thanks are due for information and assistance to the Librarians of the several Libraries mentioned and more particularly to Dr. W. W. Greg at Trinity College, Cambridge, Mr. R. S. Rait at New College, Oxford, the Revd. W. P. Besley of St. Paul's Cathedral Library, Mr. W. K. Dickson, Keeper of the Advocates' Library, Mr. F. Madan of the Bodleian, Mr. C. Sayle at the University Library, Cambridge, Mr. H. Guppy of the John Rylands Library, Mr. W. Eames of the Public Library, New York, and Mr. H. Collmann, Librarian to Mr. Christie-Miller.

The proofs of the early part of the work—to 1557—have been read, to their very great advantage, by Mr. E. Gordon Duff, who also gave me a large number of notes on the early devices and has at all times been ready with his help. Indeed, taking into consideration the great amount of assistance that I have derived from Mr. Duff's work in the *Handlists of English Printers* and elsewhere, it is not too much to say that the bulk of the information which I have collected as to the devices of the earlier printers is directly due to him.

Mr. H. G. Aldis very kindly looked through the devices of the Scottish Printers and sent me a number of most useful notes.

I am also indebted for information as to particular devices to Mr. G. J. Gray, Mr. H. R. Plomer, and Mr. R. Steele. More particularly I owe gratitude to Mr. A. W. Pollard, who has read the proofs of the whole book, and helped me with many valuable suggestions.

R. B. McK.

1 *July* 1913.

CONTENTS

PAGE

PREFACE V

INTRODUCTION xi
    Explanatory Note on Arrangement, etc. . . . xlix
    List of some Books referred to lii
    Collections and Libraries liv

PRINTERS' DEVICES I

APPENDIX OF UNTRACED DEVICES, ETC. 160

NOTES ON THE TRANSFER OF DEVICES 164
    Reversed list of Transfers 188

FACSIMILES

INDEXES:
    I. Devices and Compartments according to size . . 195
    II. Printers, Booksellers, etc. 201
    III. Mottoes and Inscriptions 209
    IV. Initials of Designers or Engravers 211
    V. Devices and Compartments according to Subjects
        represented 212

INTRODUCTION

NTERESTING as it might be to investigate the early history of the use by printers and publishers of special ornaments or designs in order to distinguish their work from that of others, the task would be by no means an easy or a brief one, and it is fortunate that there is no need to embark upon it here. So far as the English printing trade is concerned the origin of the practice is clear enough: it came from the Continent, where devices had been employed by many printers since the first appearance of the Fust-Schoeffer mark in the Bible of 1462. The earliest device used in England, that of the St. Albans Press, does not date from before 1485, the second, Caxton's, was first used in 1487 or 1488, and up to the end of the fifteenth century we have only eleven separate devices in all.

Leaving, then, to the expert in foreign incunabula the question of how and why devices came into use in printed books, we may turn at once to the matter which more immediately concerns us, the devices of our native printers. And first it would be well if we could form a clear idea of what a device is. It may at least be expected that I should offer some definition by which we may decide what may fairly be admitted into a book upon the subject. But of all problems with which one meets in the study of devices, it is surely the most difficult to say what a device is. I confess to some envy of those who can distinguish at a glance between a device and a mere ornament, or an emblem, or a cut, as the case may be; for I certainly have not yet learnt to do so. There are, of course, things which no one would hesitate to class as devices, for example a block representing a printer's sign or his mark; while certain of the commoner metal ornaments can at once be dismissed as nothing more than ornaments, though even some of these may at times have a claim to the rank of devices when they happen to be used by a printer who had as his sign the object that they represent. But unfortunately a great number of blocks found on title-pages or in colophons do not belong to either of the two classes, and it is with these that the difficulty arises.

So far as I am aware, only one definition of a device has been attempted. This is to be found in Mr. F. Madan's memorandum on *Degressive Bibliography* printed in the Society's *Transactions*, vol. ix. Unfortunately, however, this is intended as a definition of devices in general, not of those of printers or publishers alone, and is therefore too widely inclusive for our purpose, while on the other hand it would exclude many things that are customarily regarded as falling within our subject. We must therefore attempt a definition for ourselves.

As I have said, the matter is a difficult one, and it will, I think, be best dealt with by taking first a somewhat narrow definition and afterwards adding certain classes of objects which are not covered by it but are used in a similar way. Let us say, then, in the first place that any picture, design, or ornament (not being an initial letter) found on a title-page, final leaf, or in any other conspicuous place in a book, and having an obvious reference to the sign at which the printer or publisher of the book carried on business, or to the name of either of them, or including the arms or crest of either of them, is—whatever its origin—that printer's or publisher's device.

I say 'whatever its origin' because I do not see how we can logically exclude things that were not originally intended as devices. Thus if a man who works at the sign of the Sun uses a cut of the sun in his title-pages or at the end of his books, that seems to be certainly his device, even though it may be merely an old wood-cut, perhaps out of some work on astronomy, which he happened to have in his possession, and even though if this same cut had been used by a man with a different sign, no one would ever dream of counting it. Thus the cut of the sun used by James Gaver (No. 90) should, I think, rank as a device though it first appeared as an illustration in the work of another printer. Similarly the little swan (No. 303) must be included on the strength of its appearance on the title-page of books printed by Valentine Symmes at a time when he was trading at the sign of the White Swan, though it seems hardly likely that such an insignificant ornament would have been specially cut for use as a device.

If we had to deal with printers up to 1557 alone the rough definition that I have given would cover almost, if not quite, all cases. But when we pass that date there is a great change. The emblematic form of device begins to predominate largely over that which had reference to the sign, and the emblem chosen evidently depended on the mere fancy of the printer or publisher who chose it. Thus to take one or two of the best known devices, Vautrollier and, after him, Field used an anchor with the motto 'Anchora Spei,' but there seems no indication that Vautrollier ever used an anchor as his sign, and Field's was the Splayed Eagle. Reyner Wolfe, who worked at the sign of the Brazen Serpent, often used this as a device, but in many of his books had the Tree of Charity, which had nothing whatever to do with his sign. John Wolfe commonly used a fleur-de-lis, but it is not stated that this was ever his sign. William Leake dwelt successively at the Crane, the

White Greyhound, and the Holy Ghost, but the device that he used represented a winged death-head (No. 341). Many more examples could of course be given, but these will suffice to show that a connection between the sign and the device is not always to be looked for, and we must enlarge our definition so that it includes any emblematic cut commonly used by a printer or publisher, provided that it has no apparent reference to the subject-matter or author of the book in which it appears. Here of course we are at once in another difficulty, for we have to interpret the word ' commonly,' and may be asked whether a device is any less a device because it only happens to occur once or twice. But, as I have said, it is hard to draw up a satisfactory definition; we must be content to regard certain blocks as lying on the border line and include or reject them as we please.

There is, however, one troublesome question which must be referred to in passing. Some printers and publishers, including several of the smaller houses, instead of having a device specially cut for them, made common use of what cannot properly be regarded as more than an ornament, such as a rose, a mermaid, a monster's mask, a cherub's head or the like. Most of these were probably metal, and may have been cast, and it is therefore impossible to tell whether there was one block or several. There is at any rate no reason for denying that two or more printers *may* have possessed similar casts.

As examples of such ornament-devices we may take Nos. 259, 332, and 333. The first of these, a two-tailed mermaid blowing a pair of trumpets at the same time, was used at Cambridge by the elder John Legate from 1590 to 1598 and afterwards at London from 1615 to 1632. The others are a crowned rose used in two sizes from about 1598 to 1603 by Valentine Symmes. In neither case has the object represented anything to do with the sign of the house, and either of them may be simply a common ornament bought from a type-founder—the mermaid perhaps a foreign one. That I do not happen to have found either of these in simultaneous use by two or more printers is no evidence that they were not.

What is to be done with things like these? Should we include them in a book of devices or should we omit them? I have little hesitation in saying that if we are considering devices in the abstract, such blocks cannot properly be counted among them; but at the same time it seems to me quite certain that as a matter of convenience and utility, the more of them that we include in a collection of facsimiles the more useful it will be. It is just the books issued from the smaller printing and publishing houses that as a rule offer the greatest difficulties when we wish to trace their origin, and though the presence of an ornament such as those to which I refer cannot alone prove from what house the book came, yet the knowledge that such and such a printer was using that block—or at least one exactly similar—at a particular date may often put us on the right track.

The chief objects which we find on title-pages, and which clearly ought *not* to be considered as printers' devices are cuts or emblems appropriate to the particular book in which they appear, or referring to the author of it: though as we shall see presently there are a few cases of emblems cut for a particular book being afterwards used by the printer of the book or by a later owner as his own device.

Secondly, coats of arms and crests of the author or his patron are not to be regarded as printers' devices, though here again we must be careful that the arms are not used as being those of the *printer's* patron. For example, during the last two or three years of his life Bynneman frequently used as his device a small cut of Sir Christopher Hatton's crest, a hind (No. 229). He, however, also possessed a larger cut of the same crest, which is used, so far as I know, only in a single book of Gabriel Harvey's printed by him. As this book consists of several parts, each dedicated to a different nobleman, and as each part has the nobleman's arms upon it, we must in this case regard Sir Christopher Hatton's crest as a dedication cut and not as the printer's device. Thus two cuts exactly similar except in size may be, one a printer's device, the other not.

Cuts of the royal arms present a difficulty. It is hard to see why, in the case of a printer under royal patronage, the royal arms are not as much his device as the arms of any other patron would be; and it has certainly been customary to consider, for example, the tiger's head, the crest of Sir Francis Walsingham, as Barker's device, and the wyvern, the Earl of Cumberland's, as that of Aggas. There would therefore, I think, be some justification for counting these arms as a device in the case of the royal printers, but not otherwise. In practice, however, there is considerable difficulty in doing this, on account of the men who had privileges for particular classes of books, and used the royal arms in these. It seemed so difficult to know where to draw the line between inclusion and omission that I have thought it better to omit them all, more especially as most of them have recently been reproduced in the Catalogue of Proclamations in the *Bibliotheca Lindesiana*.

It will be readily understood that it is not always an easy task to distinguish between emblems of the author of a book, or referring to the work itself, and those of a publisher. If we can find a particular block on several works by the same writer, but issued by different houses, we of course can at once conclude that it is the author's, and need trouble no more about it; but only rarely can we do this. As an example of devices which certainly at first sight might be thought to belong to the printer or publisher, we may take the goat's head which appears on the title-page of the surgeon Walter Cary's *Hammer for the Stone*. This, however, seems to refer to the fact that the quintessence in praise of which his book was written was manufactured from the blood of a goat. Two devices which have every appearance of being those of a bookseller were used by John Hester, a physician or apothecary, in his translation from J. Du Chesne, entitled *A Brief Answer of Joseph*

xvi

Quercetanus, 1591, with a second part, *The True and Perfect Spagerike Preparation of Minerals*.[1] These consist of Hester's monogram in a frame, the larger one with his initials I. H. at the sides. There seems no evidence that John Hester was a bookseller, for what has sometimes been read as a statement that the book is to be sold by him, evidently refers not to the book, but to certain drugs described in it, and we must therefore treat these as author's devices and exclude them.

Some devices indeed that I have admitted into this collection may be of the same class. I have great doubts about two which are found chiefly in song-books (Nos. 305, 322), and also about one in Selden's *Duello* (No. 369), and I should not be surprised to learn that one or two others belong to the authors, not to the 'mechanical producers' of the books in which they occur. But enough has been said to warn readers of the difficulty of drawing up a satisfactory definition of printer's devices, or even, if we could do so, of holding to it consistently. We may now pass to the subject of the devices themselves.

The devices used in this country are so various in origin and in quality of workmanship that it seems useless to attempt any historical treatment of them. To anyone who glances through the facsimiles given in this volume a certain more or less gradual change in character in the devices, both in design and execution, will be evident. It cannot, however, be called a development, for in artistic qualities the later ones are by no means superior to the earlier; it is rather the abandonment of one set of models for another, a mere change of fashion. Here and there at all periods we may find a design that is not without merit, but it must be confessed with regret that in this, as in most other respects, our printers, during the period with which we have to deal, were as a rule far behind those of the Continent. Instead, therefore, of treating our devices historically, it will be more convenient to attempt a

---

[1] See No. 4 in the Appendix.

xvii

rough classification of them, which, however imperfect, will serve to give some idea of the subject as a whole.

In the first place we have the large group of devices which represent or include the sign at which the printer or publisher worked. With some notable exceptions, such as those of Wynkyn de Worde and Pynson, most of the early devices are of this type. Several even of de Worde's fall within this class, or at least on the border line of it, inasmuch as they include his sign of the Sun, though with so many other objects besides that it would be difficult indeed to infer from them the name of his place of business. Of this class may be mentioned the Trinity devices of Jacobi and Pepwell (Nos. 16, 33, 34, 52), the Maiden's Head of Richard Faques (No. 31), and the Mermaid of Rastell (No. 37). Peter Treveris, who traded at the ' Wodows ' or ' Woodwoses,' a kind of wild men of the woods, common in heraldry as ' supporters,' had a male and female figure covered with long hair and bearing bows and arrows (No. 60): Berthelet had the well-known figure of Lucrece (No. 80), which was also his sign: Wyer a cut of St. John the Evangelist (Nos. 67, 68, 70): the Coplands' devices included their sign of the Rose Garland (Nos. 71 and 73), and so on. In later times we find other examples of the same class, such as the Mermaid of Bynneman (Nos. 149, 155), the Star of Denham (Nos. 150, 211, 214), and the Lucrece of Thomas Purfoot (Nos. 151, 161, 173); but relatively they are far less numerous than during the first century of printing.

The next class in importance consists of those devices which represent a rebus or pun upon the owner's name, such as those of Grafton, a tun with a graft or shoot growing in or through it. Most printers whose name happened to end in -ton seem to have used a device of this kind.[1] Thus William Norton had a tun with the word ' Nor ' on it, and a sweet-william growing out of it

---

[1] As did many who were not printers. Camden in his *Remains*, ed. 1870, p. 180, instances the rebuses of Morton, Luton, Thorneton and Ashton.

(Nos. 174, 175). Seton had a tun floating in the sea, and William Middleton and Singleton had tuns with their initials (Nos. 102, 106, 127, 198, 250). Those whose names included names of birds or beasts punned upon them in a similar way. Thomas Woodcock used a cock on a wood-pile (No. 247); Thomas Fisher a kingfisher (No. 321). Hugo Goes is said to have used a great H and a goose (No. 1 in the Appendix), though unluckily no book bearing it is now to be found. Oxenbridge used an ox on a bridge (Nos. 288, 289); Henry Bell a hen, rye, and a bell (Nos. 386, 388); and the Harrisons a hare, rye, and the sun (Nos. 143, 169, etc.). Reyner Wolfe in one of his borders had a fox (for Renard) and a wolf (No. 120). Pavier used a man paving (No. 345); Christopher Barker a man barking logs (Nos. 169, 171, 190); Dexter a right hand pointing to a star (Nos. 257, 260); Richard Watkins a hare, because it was familiarly called 'Wat' (Nos. 169, 171); and Jugge a nightingale, because the word 'jug' was commonly used to represent the nightingale's song (Nos. 181, 182). Devices of this type seem indeed to have been the favourite ones with all those upon whose name a pun, however far-fetched, was possible. Some are very far-fetched indeed, such as that of Gerard or Garrat Dewes, which is found in a border of the devices of the assigns of Francis Flower (Nos. 169, 171), though, like that of Watkins, it does not seem to occur alone. It takes the form of a little picture of two men playing dice in a garret, and casting a 'deuce,' or two, and is referred to by William Camden, not without irony, as 'most memorable.'[1] It is indeed possible that some are so far-fetched that the lapse of time and changes in pronunciation have obscured their meaning; for example, the figure of Mars used by Thomas Marshe (No. 180) may have been intended as an allusion to his name, for there is some evidence in contemporary puns that the pronunciation of final *sh* and *s* were not very clearly distinguished.

[1] *Remains*, ed. 1870, p. 181.

Possibly a few devices for which no simple explanation offers itself may be personal in the sense of referring to some incident in their owner's career, but I do not know of any case in which we can prove this. Two devices which may be suspected of some such hidden meaning may, however, be referred to in passing. I have already mentioned Dexter's device of a right hand pointing to a star. The meaning of the hand is of course clear enough, but what about the star? It is no common star, but evidently what was known as a 'blazing star.' Now is it a mere coincidence that the most famous 'blazing star' of the Elizabethan period was that which appeared on 8th October 1580, and that it was at Michaelmas of the same year that Dexter began his nine years' apprenticeship to Francis Coldock? May not the sailor's son from Ipswich have seen in this strange portent an omen of good luck for his future career, and when he came to set up in business for himself, have remembered his star and used it in his device? This is of course a mere guess, but the explanation is not, I think, an impossible one.

Another device which may perhaps be explained in a somewhat similar way is the well-known swan in a border of intertwined serpents used by Robert Waldegrave, the puritan printer, with the motto, "God is my Helper" (No. 227). It so happens that in the Marprelate tract *Hay any Work for Cooper*, in the printing of which Waldegrave assisted, there is a list of the very numerous occasions upon which he had been in prison. Among these was one when he had been 'strangely released' by one of the Bishop of London's swans. Unfortunately we have no further information about this remarkable incident, but it seems not altogether impossible that the swan with "God is my Helper," which Waldegrave took for his device, so far as can be made out, at about the same date, was an allusion to it.

Another group of devices consists of monograms or initials, with or without a "mark." Of simple monograms we have among the earliest devices one of Pynson's (No. 3), the G. F.

monogram of William Faques (No. 15), and a J. R. of John Rastell (No. 40); among the later those of Francis Burton (No. 364), and Thomas Langley (No. 387). Monograms are, however, much more frequently found as parts of ornamental borders than standing alone. Among monograms or initials combined with or accompanied by a mark are those of Caxton, Egmont and Barrevelt, Notary, Grafton, Cawood, and others, among which may be noticed that of Michael Sparke (No. 406) used in 1628, and noteworthy, with No. 417, as a throw-back to the usage of the preceding century, for the early form of the printer's mark with a top shaped like a reversed "4," seems, except for an occasional appearance in a border, to have passed out of use in England by about 1560.

The most personal kind of device which it would be possible to use would be a portrait. Two printers made use of this: John Day, whose large portrait-device (No. 145) is well known, and John Wight (No. 205), if indeed, as is most probable, the picture of an old man in a gown, holding a book labelled "Scientia," and surrounded by the words "Welcome the wight that bringeth such light," is meant to represent the printer himself. Several other portraits are to be found in Ames' *Typographical Antiquities*, but unfortunately none of them seems to be authentic. They are stated to have been mostly the work of the engraver William Faithorne, and some are known to be copies of foreign prints; that, for example, which stands for Wynkyn de Worde being taken from a portrait of Joachim Ringelberg, an Antwerp scholar of the early part of the sixteenth century.

Heraldic devices form a larger group. They sometimes represent the printer's or publisher's own arms, and sometimes those of his patron. Among the former we have the arms of Richard Pynson, William Bretton (?), William Marshall, John Day, Richard Day, Christopher Barker, Thomas East, and John Beale, while other printers made use of some part of their family arms in their devices, such as Thomas Davidson (No. 65). Of the second kind

xxi

we have the tiger's head crest of Walsingham, used by Christopher Barker, the wyvern rising from a ducal coronet, the crest of George Clifford, Earl of Cumberland, used by Edward Aggas, Sir Christopher Hatton's hind, used by Bynneman, and several others. The arms of other noble families frequently appear in ornaments, the wheatsheaf or garb of Lord Burghley being especially common, but most of these seem to have been originally cut for use in works dedicated to the particular noblemen, and do not indicate that the printer or publisher was under his patronage. We therefore need not concern ourselves with them further.

We now come to what is on the whole the most interesting group of devices, or at any rate the most varied, namely those which represent not the owner's sign or a pun on his name, but an emblem of some sort. This may be of any degree of elaboration from a simple object such as an anchor or a caduceus, to a complicated picture borrowed from one of the emblem books. With these designs we may include such things as the Good Shepherd device, and that of Christ rising from the Tomb, though these are hardly, I suppose, to be called emblems in the ordinary sense.

Many of the emblematic devices require, of course, no explanation. The Anchor of Hope, the figure of Time mowing, the man looking into a mirror and seeing not his own face, but that of Death who stands at his shoulder; all these and many more can be understood at a glance. Others, however, including most of those copied directly from the emblem books, are hardly to be understood without a knowledge of the explanations there given. For example, to take one of the simpler ones: there is a device (No. 341) which was used from 1602 to 1609 by William Leake, and is perhaps a good deal older than this, for even in 1602 the border was badly broken. It represents a winged and laureated skull, resting upon the globe, with, above it, an hour-glass and an open book, on which are the words, 'I live to die, I die to live.'

This is copied from a design of the Hungarian scholar, John Sambucus, of whose *Emblemata* there were several editions from 1564 onwards. The motto on the book is there *In morte vita*, and the emblem is explained as meaning that if a man gives his life to the pursuit of learning his fame will fly all over the world even when he himself is dead.

Another emblem was used by Thomas Millington in the years 1595-7 (No. 302). This represents a tree broken by a storm, before which reeds bend uninjured. It is taken from Whitney's *Choice of Emblems*, and comes originally, I believe, from Adrianus Junius. The meaning is that Envy, Hatred, and Contempt, which are the storms and tempests of this life, are to be suffered with patience and not resisted.

The meaning of the winged skull and of the broken tree could probably be guessed without much difficulty. One would at any rate not go far wrong in the interpretation; but others are less easy. For example, take the well-known oval device (No. 142), first used by Rowland Hall in 1563, and later by William Howe and others. It depicts a fat boy with wings on one arm, and (apparently) trying with the other to lift a heavy bag. Would it not be a reasonable guess to say that it represents the soul aspiring after excellence, but held down by its reluctance to abandon its earthly possessions—a hint, perhaps, to a hesitating purchaser? But the true meaning, as we know from the *Emblemata* of Alciat, is quite different. The emblem represents a man ambitious to rise in the world, but kept down by his poverty. Surely a strange symbol for poverty, this well-filled bag!

Or take another, the device that was first used by Thomas Scarlet, and afterwards by Richard Bradock (No. 280, and in a smaller form, No. 277). This is described by Herbert as representing 'a kite, or some bird of prey, with a small bird in his talons, flying over a castle on a hill; the sun in full blaze; in a compartment with this motto, *Sic crede.*' The description is quite accurate, but when we turn to the *Symbola* of Joachim Camerarius the younger we find that the meaning is something very different from what this description implies. The device does not, as one perhaps might fancy, symbolize the relations between the publisher and the too credulous author, but alludes to the story that the eagle in order to see whether its young is worthy to be reared, takes up the newly hatched eaglet in its talons and compels it to gaze at the sun. If it can do so without blinking, it is looked on as satisfactory, if not the eagle dashes it to the ground. Scarlet perhaps meant to imply that he printed nothing but first-rate work.

An emblem which is still more difficult to interpret was used by Islip in 1598 and 1613, and I am sorry to say that I can give no explanation of it. The device (No. 309) is, save for some simplification of detail, a close copy of an emblem of the Hungarian Sambucus whom I have already mentioned, and, as is evident from its motto, represents the things which are necessary to the stability of a commonwealth. Sambucus accompanied it by a Latin poem in which he gives a great deal of excellent advice to persons about to establish a government, but unfortunately omits to explain the details of his picture. The meaning of parts of the design may of course be guessed. The pillar, as will be seen, stands on a shield and helmet; this may symbolize the need for military power. The goose or gull at the top has a ring round its beak which prevents it from using the quill which it holds—hinting, I suppose, at the necessity of a literary censorship. The cornucopia perhaps means that liberality is requisite in the rulers, or it may mean that plenty will be the result of such a government; but what is implied by the balance, the scales of which contain one a snake and the other a cat—or why the cat seems so anxious to get away—I cannot even guess. So far, no rational explanation has occurred to me, and unfortunately, though there is said to be an edition of Sambucus with notes by Don John of Austria, I have been unable to find a copy of this, or any other annotated edition, if such there be.

If we were to go through the whole number of the devices used during the second half of our period, we should find that a very considerable proportion, perhaps the majority, are based ultimately upon emblems. But it does not follow that they were in all cases taken directly from the emblem books. Many of them came to England through the medium of the device of a foreign printer. And this brings us to the next part of our subject, the borrowing of devices from abroad.

It has long been recognized that some of the earlier devices were adapted by English printers from continental models. In a paper on *Illustrated Books* read before the Bibliographical Society in 1900, Mr. Pollard gave several instances of this borrowing. Thus the earlier device used by Pynson was modelled on that of the Rouen printer Guillaume Le Talleur, from whom Pynson appears to have learnt his trade. That of Richard Faques is an altered copy of the elder Thielman Kerver's, who printed at Paris in the early years of the century, and the ungainly female used by John Byddell to represent Virtue or Pity is copied, and very badly copied, from a device used by Jaques Sacon, a printer at Lyons. I need only refer in passing to the history of the Brazen Serpent used by Reyner Wolfe and later by Peter Short, for this has been the subject of a special study which is printed in the Society's *Transactions*.

Later, the copying of foreign devices by English printers seems to have become even more common. The famous Estienne device of the olive-tree with ' Noli altum sapere' was used in 1599 by John Wolfe (No. 310), and re-cut (No. 311), from 1618 to about 1640 by George and Elizabeth Purslowe. In another form it was used from 1605 to 1624 or later by John Norton and John Bill, who had at least two, and probably three, blocks of it (Nos. 348-50). It was stated by T. B. Reed in his *Old English Letter*

Foundries, that permission to use this device was granted to John Norton by Paul Estienne, son of Henry Estienne the younger, while on a visit to England in 1594, as a mark of admiration for his printing. Paul Estienne did indeed visit England in 1594, but I am sorry to say I have been unable to discover any ground for the rest of the story. The authority referred to by Reed, the *Histoire de l'Imprimerie* of Paul Dupont, 1854, gives no evidence in support of it, and I have been unable to trace it further back.

Another famous foreign device, the Pegasus over a caduceus and crossed cornucopias used by Andreas Wechel at Paris in the middle of the sixteenth century was closely copied in or before 1600, probably by John Harrison III (No. 316; cf. Nos. 317, 318). There were several blocks of this also, one of which was in use at least until 1684.

The Plantin device of a pair of compasses with the motto *Labore et Constantiâ* was used here in two forms, both closely copied from foreign originals, one upright (No. 334) used from 1601 to 1608 by John Harrison and Nicholas Okes; the other, lengthways (No 411), used about 1630 and, re-cut, from 1649 to 1658 or later. The device of Sébastien and Antoine Gryphius, a griffin squatting on a stone, or perhaps a book, underneath which is a ball with wings, was used in 1587 by Vautrollier and in a larger form in 1602 by Thomas Creede (Nos. 246, 339). Of this also there appear to have been other blocks later.

It is not my purpose to give a list of the devices modelled on those of foreign printers; but one group, namely the imitations of the devices of the Gioliti brothers of Venice, seems to deserve especial mention.

The earliest of the Giolito devices to be copied was that of a phoenix looking at the sun, which is found in books printed at Venice in 1562. This was used by Henry Bynneman in 1578-9 (No. 203). He does not seem, however, to have regarded it as one of his regular devices, and two years later, when Newbery printed by

xxvi

his assignment Stephen Bateman's *Doom warning all men to the Judgement*, the printer used this device to illustrate a description of the phoenix, for which purpose its emblematic character renders it of course quite unsuitable. Newbery is said to have used it in another book also printed in 1581, but after this date it does not seem to be met with.

Another of the Giolito devices, the best known, represents an urn upheld by two satyrs; from the mouth of the urn flames issue and from these a phoenix is rising. In England this device is found in two forms. The larger (No. 254) is rather roughly imitated from the foreign design, and was, so far as I have seen, only used in three books printed in the year 1589 by Thomas Orwin. The smaller (No. 252) has, however, a longer and more interesting history.

It seems to be generally held, though I cannot recall having seen the statement in print, that some of the foreign devices used by English printers were the actual foreign blocks; and if there ever was a device which might well give rise to such a belief, it is certainly this smaller Giolito one, for not only does it appear at first sight to be absolutely identical with the Venetian block, but it even bears the letters G.G.F., standing for Gabriele Giolito de' Ferrari, as does the original. Careful examination of clear prints from the English and foreign blocks puts it, however, beyond doubt that they were not identical, and that the English one is simply a very careful copy.

But the interesting point about this block is the use to which it was put. As is well known, in the years 1587-1591, or thereabouts, John Wolfe printed a number of Italian books.[1] To a few of these he put his own imprint, but several have the imprint of

[1] It may be noted that the English editions of Italian books may generally be distinguished by the occurrence here and there of black-letter punctuation marks, especially full stops and colons, which would of course not be met with in genuine Italian books of this date.

an Italian printer and a device copied from an Italian one, though not necessarily from that of the man by whom the book purported to be printed. Why Wolfe did this is not altogether clear. It can hardly have been in order to evade any prohibition against printing these books in England, as most of them, including the *Ragionamenti* of Pietro Aretino, the *Decamerone*, and several works of Macchiavelli were entered to Wolfe in the Stationers' Register. I suspect that the purpose of the deception was merely because genuine Italian editions would fetch a better price than English, as being more correct; and it is by no means impossible that Wolfe exported these books to Holland and Germany, where an English print of an Italian book could hardly be expected, if known for what it was, to find much favour. In any case Wolfe evidently found it worth while to take a good deal of trouble to get careful copies made of some of the foreign devices.

The one which we are now considering is first found in the *Historie* of Macchiavelli ' In Piacenza appresso gli heredi de Gabriel Giolito de Ferrari,' 1587, after which date, so far as I am aware, it disappears from view for several years. It turns up again in 1600, when it was used in the *Palestina* of Robert Chambers, which bears the imprint of ' Bartelmew Sermartelli ' of Florence. The work is in English, and taking into account the appearance of the workmanship and the fact that the book is a curious allegorical romance dealing with biblical characters to which objection might easily be taken on religious grounds, it seems highly probable that it was secretly printed in England, but the printer has not been identified.[1]

The later history of this device is not very clear. After its use in *Palestina* we lose sight of it for several years. In 1611, however, it turns up again in a book said to have been printed at

---

[1] Wolfe was still printing, and it is possible that it may be his. It may be remarked that Sermatelli [*sic*] was a real person, but there seems no reason for thinking that he ever used the Giolito device.

Britain's Burse for John Budge, and in 1612 is used in one bearing merely a date with no place or printer's name. In 1613 it appears in a book printed by Stansby for John Budge, and later in one with the imprint of Cantrell Legge of Cambridge.

But this Giolito device was not by any means the only block of foreign design used by Wolfe in his Italian books. In Macchiavelli's *Asino d'Oro* and *Clitia*, printed in 1588, we find a close copy of the lower part of a device used by Domenico Giglio at Venice in 1552 (No. 249), which is, as A. J. Butler pointed out in his paper on the Giolito Press, read before the Bibliographical Society in 1909 (*Transactions*, x. 98), itself imitated from the Giolito device. In this case also he kept the initials of the foreign printer (D. G. F.). This block also had a long history, not the least remarkable feature of which is its appearance in a book purporting to have been printed by Robert Waldegrave at Edinburgh in 1603. It came eventually into the hands of Augustine Mathewes, who used it until at least 1633.

Another device used by Wolfe in his Italian books, an emblematic device of serpents and toads at the base of a palm tree, is also probably copied from a foreign one, but though the same general design is to be found in the emblem-books I have not traced any direct original for this block.

Wolfe had, as is well known, a connection with Italy, and is supposed to have passed some time at Florence about 1576.[1] It is perhaps for this reason that as his regular device he used the fleur-de-lis of the Junta family. Most if not all of his numerous fleur-de-lis devices are more or less closely copied from those of one or other branch of this family, who had printing establishments at Florence, Venice, and Lyons. Information about the later Italian devices is, however, as a rule, not easy to obtain, and I have been unable to discover whether Wolfe's blocks were exact

[1] Two Italian *Rappresentazioni* were printed at Florence in that year, 'ad instanzia di Giouanni Vuolfio, Inglese' (*Dictionary I*, p. 296).

copies of particular foreign ones, or mere imitations of a general design.

We must, I think, confess that what with devices borrowed from those of foreign printers, and devices taken from foreign books of emblems, the native powers of invention and design make a very poor show. Indeed, with the exception of the heraldic cuts, and these are not numerous, hardly a single one of the later devices can be claimed as genuinely English in origin. Such native work as there was is rather to be found in the woodcut borders than in the devices, though even here there are, throughout the period, innumerable signs of foreign influence. If we should seek for a reason for the comparative inferiority of the English work we should probably find it in the rise of copper-plate engraving, which came much into vogue about the middle of Elizabeth's reign, to the neglect of the better kinds of wood-cutting. But this is an inquiry which would lead us too far from our subject.

Before passing to consider some points of interest in the particular history of one or two devices, it may be well to draw attention to a small group of designs which, if one may be permitted the expression, were not born devices, but had deviceship thrust upon them. I do not mean simple cuts such as those of the Trinity and of the Infant Christ, occasionally found in Robert Redman's productions; nor the two depicting the expulsion of Adam and Eve from the Garden of Eden, and the Sacrifice of Isaac, which Herbert called devices on the ground that Tisdale made frequent use of them; nor yet that abominable little cut reputed to represent Hercules striking a Centaur with a club, which occurs in many books of John Skot of Edinburgh, for none of these has been included in the present volume; but those more elaborate pictures which from the frame in which they are set, and the general character of their design, would naturally be regarded as devices, and which yet seem to have been originally intended as embellishments for particular books.

xxx

Among these we may perhaps class one of the devices commonly used by John Day (No. 208). It depicts Christ with a palm in His right hand, trampling upon a skeleton, evidently intended to represent death, and on a dragon intended to represent sin. The earliest print of this block that I have been able to find is on the title-page of a tract, *Contra Missae Sacrificium*, appended to Peter Baro's *Praelectiones in Jonam Prophetam*, 1579. The title-page of the tract which bears this device is dated 1578, but the end is dated 1579. It is thus probable that it was printed late in 1578. Now also in 1579 John and Richard Day issued a work of John Foxe translated into English under the title of *Christ Jesus Triumphant. A fruitful Treatise wherein is described the most glorious Triumph and Conquest of Christ Jesus, our Saviour, over Sin, Death, the Law, the strength and pride of Satan and the World, with all other enemies whatsoever against the poor Soul of Man.* This work was entered in the Stationers' Register on 28th May 1578 (Arber, ii. 327), and hence was probably in preparation, and at least partly in type before the tract mentioned above.[1] When, therefore, we consider how closely this block accords with the subject of *Christ Jesus Triumphant*, it is difficult, in spite of its apparent use a few months earlier, to resist the idea that it was originally cut for Foxe's work. Once having obtained it, however, the printer probably thought it a pity to make no further use of it, and employed it in the title-pages of several of his other productions, and in fact it came to be one of his regular devices.

Another case of the same kind is a certain cut of an old man praying and an angel blessing him (No. 308). This seems first to occur in the 1597 edition of a work entitled *Daniel his Chaldee Visions*, printed by Gabriel Simson, and I think there can be little doubt that it was designed for that particular work. So far as I

---

[1] The tract *Contra Missae Sacrificium* does not seem to have been entered in the Register, but *Baro in Jonam* was entered 26th March 1579 (Arber, ii. 350).

can discover, it was never again used by Simson, but from 1606 to 1620 it frequently occurs in books printed by George Eld, who had succeeded to Simson's business, and is indeed regarded as one of Eld's usual devices.

An even clearer case than these can be found in a device which was used on the title-page of Healey's translation of St. Augustine's *De Civitate Dei* (No. 375). This represents the sun breaking through clouds, and has a motto, evidently cut in the block itself, '*Sic Augustinus dissipabit*.' This motto was afterwards removed, and the block was used, either with or without a motto inserted in type, as a regular printer's device.

Even the well-known half-eagle and key—the arms of the city of Geneva—used by Rowland Hall, and many others after him, may be of this class, for it seems first to occur in Hall's *Laws and Statutes of Geneva*, 1562. As, however, Hall in the same year took the Geneva Arms as his device, we cannot say whether the sign was suggested by the cut or the cut by the sign. I have been unable to ascertain whether the French original of the *Laws and Statutes* has a similar cut of the arms or not. This would perhaps settle the point.

To the bibliographer the important part of the study of devices is, as a rule, the history of the blocks considered singly, for a knowledge of the ownership of them at different times, of the alterations made in them, and of the accidents that befell them, is often of the greatest service in aiding us to date books in which they occur, or to assign them to their true printers. But such a detailed history of the blocks is of course the main purpose of the present volume, and it is not necessary to dwell upon it here. It may, however, perhaps not be out of place to bring together a few notes on the subject.

First, as illustrating the long life of some of these blocks, it may be remarked that the half-eagle and key (No. 136) can be traced in use from 1562 to 1637. The palm tree with snakes and toads about its roots (No. 226), used by John Wolfe in 1584, is found as late as 1681.[1] An insignificant little fleur-de-lis device (No. 263) which I have not met with before 1602, when it had already been mutilated by the excision of the motto, but which probably dates from some ten years earlier, is found in 1685 on the title-page of the 'Fourth Folio' of Shakespeare's works. Lastly, the caduceus device (No. 112) used by William Baldwin in 1549 is met with as late as 1674. It had thus a life of 125 years, not bad for a woodcut, though not indeed to be compared with the life of some of the cuts used to illustrate ballads.

Cases such as these are of course exceptional, but a very large number of devices occur at intervals extending over a period of thirty or forty years, though it need hardly be said that a woodcut in regular use would generally be worn out in a very much shorter time than this. For example, a device of Pynson's (No. 6) began to crack in the second or third year of use, and was shortly afterwards practically discarded. Some are found for only a year or two; others seem only to occur in a single book, whether because they broke, or for what other reason, we cannot say. The life of a device no doubt depended greatly on its owner; the less he cared about the appearance of his books the longer he made his devices last.

A life of a hundred years or more must naturally imply a succession of owners, and some of the devices passed through the hands of a surprising number. The eagle and key device, which has just been mentioned, was used in turn by Rowland Hall, Richard Serle, John Charlewood, Richard Jones, James Roberts, William Jaggard, and Thomas Cotes. The devices of Henry Denham, together probably with Bynneman's, passed through the hands of Richard Yardley and Peter Short, Henry Lownes, and Robert Young. The anchor devices, originally owned by Vautrollier, passed later to Richard Field, George Miller and Richard Badger in partnership, and Abraham Miller. A device of a

---

[1] For my knowledge of this I am indebted to Mr. Sayle.

xxxiii

swan in a border of intertwined serpents (No. 227), originally cut for Robert Waldegrave about 1583, was afterwards used in succession by East, Snodham, and Harper, in whose possession it was certainly as late as 1639, and perhaps later. Some of the title-page borders were used by a greater number of printers than even these devices, but, as we shall see later, it is doubtful if a border was always the property of the printer in whose work it appears.

Most of these devices passed from one owner to another with little change save for cracks and other accidental damage, but others were more or less altered in the course of time, and exist therefore in two or more 'states.' The reasons for such changes were various, but as we should expect, by far the most frequent was the desire to get rid of such details as identified the block with a former owner. A large number bore the initials of the person for whom they were originally cut, and in many cases, but not all, later owners removed these or altered them. For example, one of Vautrollier's anchors (No. 210) had the initials T. V. When this passed into the hands of Field, he had them removed. The Fortune device of Thomas Marshe had the letters T. M., which were excised when the block became Kingston's. And so in many other cases, both of devices and ornamental borders. The practice obtained from quite early times, as may be seen in the devices of Notary (No. 8), de Worde (No. 50), Pepwell (No. 48), Hertford (No. 84), and Gibson (No. 83). The last is a somewhat curious example, for in addition to having at the sides the letters T. G., the initials of its first owner, it had also a G on the forehead of the sun which forms the lower part of the design. John Day, into whose hands the block afterwards came, removed the T. G. from the sides, replacing them by his own initials in type; but apparently thinking that it would be troublesome to insert new letters into the forehead of the sun, he carefully cut away part of the G, so that what remains might serve as the initial of his Christian name —the sun itself perhaps representing Day. Robert Waldegrave, into whose possession the block next passed, perhaps did not identify this I with John Day, for while sometimes using his own initials at the sides, he let it remain.

In one early case, where a device passed from Henry Jacobi to Henry Pepwell, the later printer cut out Jacobi's surname, but kept the 'Henry,' as it was applicable to himself also (No. 34). We may surmise that he meant to insert his own name in type in the vacant space, but found—as indeed is apparent—that there was not room.

We find also a certain number of alterations of name made for other reasons. Richard Faques, who seems never to have been able to decide upon the most satisfactory spelling of his name, had it first cut as Faques (No. 31), but later removed the 'ques' and inserted 'kes' in type. John Skot had his mark and initials removed from one of his devices (No. 59) and replaced by a monogram. Why he did this we cannot guess.

Alterations made for the purpose of improving the design are, as we should expect, few in number. There is, however, at least one case of the rectification of a verbal error which is sufficiently curious to be worth mentioning, especially as it concerns a somewhat elaborate device, Christopher Barker's tiger's head and lamb. The greater part of this device, which Barker possessed in two sizes (Nos. 191, 194), is occupied by a folded scroll, bearing an inscription in Italian. This inscription is an odd one, and I cannot think that the Italian is altogether satisfactory. It appears to mean—or to have been intended to mean—'The tiger, a wicked animal, son of the old Adam, by the grace of the gospel has become a lamb.' Unfortunately, however, Barker, or his engraver, was not a good Italian scholar, and instead of cutting the word 'agnello,' meaning a lamb, he cut 'agnolo,' a variant form of the word *angelo*, 'angel,' and the inscription accordingly declared that by the grace of the gospel the tiger had become an angel. Someone perhaps pointed out to Barker that this was ridiculous, and might even savour of heresy, so he went to the expense of having the offending word cut out and the correct 'agnello' inserted. Of two Bibles which he printed in 1576 one has 'agnolo,' the other 'agnello.' The smaller device does not seem to have been used after the discovery of the error, and perhaps was never corrected.

There was, however, one group of devices which appear to have been altered for æsthetic reasons—at least I can suggest no other reason for the changes that were made in them. These are the well-known group showing Christ as the 'Good Shepherd' carrying the lost sheep, and having the motto, 'Periit et inventa est.' There were three sizes of this device, respectively 91, 64, and 30.5 mm. in height (Nos. 153, 202, 207). With the smallest we are not concerned, as during the twenty or so years for which we can trace it, none of its owners seems to have made any change in it, but the history of the other two is somewhat curious. They have, it may be said, every appearance of belonging together, and of having been designed and cut by the same hand, but are first found in the work of different printers.

The largest (No. 153) in its original state was first used by Henry Wykes from 1567 to 1571. It had then a face at the top of the border, other faces on each side, and, below, a rampant lion and an elephant, the latter evidently representing Wykes's sign of the Oliphaunt or Black Elephant. When Wykes gave up printing in, or soon after, 1571, the device seems to have passed to Ralph Newbery, who used it in 1577. In the next year, however, it is found in a book printed by Henry Middleton, in whose hands it apparently remained for the rest of its existence. Ralph Newbery, though he did not use the sign of the Elephant, had kept the device unchanged, and so did Middleton until 1579. In that year, however, he seems to have taken a sudden dislike to the faces which appear in the border, for he had all three of them cut out and harmless ornaments inserted in their places. He also removed the lion and elephant below and inserted ornaments there also.

The work was very neatly done and must have cost a good deal of trouble; but in most prints it is possible to see the joins. In its amended form the block was used by Middleton until 1585.

The middle-sized block (No. 202) also passed through the hands of two or three owners, but I have not, so far, been able to discover that Wykes had it, or indeed to find it earlier than 1578, when it was used by Middleton. This block also had a face at the top, and in 1579 Middleton had similar alterations made in it to those which were made in the larger block, the face being cut out and a kind of bunch of leaves substituted. In this form he used it in three parts of the Latin Bible printed in 1579-80. Even so, however, he was not satisfied, and before printing the fourth part of the Bible he made another alteration, cutting away a large part of the ornament which he had inserted, so as to leave merely a little point in the centre instead of the bunch of leaves. From this date the history of the device becomes somewhat obscure, for it seems to have been used jointly by Newbery and Middleton. What, if anything, is the significance of this fact, I have been unable to discover; for though Newbery printed one or two books at various times for Middleton, there does not seem to be any trace of a regular connection between the two firms. However this may be, we certainly find the block used in 1580 by Middleton; in 1582 and 1583 by Newbery; in 1583 again by Middleton; in 1584 by Newbery; and in 1585 by Middleton, in whose hands it apparently was at his death; for the block then passed to Robert Robinson, who bought Middleton's printing material. It is uncertain who had it after Robinson, but it was still in existence in 1635, when it occurs in a book printed for John Legate II and Ralph Mab. By this time the piece inserted by Middleton had fallen out and been lost, leaving a square gap at the top. It was perhaps not considered worth while to patch it up by the insertion of a new piece, and it seems to have been discarded.

Though this is the only example known to me of an important change, involving recutting of part of the design, being made apparently for æsthetic reasons, there are several examples of smaller changes which were perhaps due to a similar intention, as, for example, the white dots cut in Nos. 3 and 74, and the clearing away of the background in Nos. 46, 188, and 262. In the last three cases it may have been found difficult to get reasonably clean prints from the blocks in their original state.

These will suffice for examples of alteration, and in this connection I may say that I have not come across a single instance of an attempt being made to repair a broken block by the insertion of new pieces, though one would have thought that such trifling defects at least as broken rule borders might easily have been put right. When a border broke the printers seem usually to have cut it away altogether, as in the case of Nos. 3, 144, and 354, or if this did not satisfy them, to have had a new block made and discarded the old one altogether.

There are a good many instances of a design being re-cut, whether for the original owner or a later imitator, the earliest being the well-known large 'tripartite device' of Wynkyn de Worde, of which there were three blocks (Nos. 19, 20, 21). Later were William Norton's device of a tun with the word 'nor' and a sweet-william (No. 174); two forms of the Estienne device (Nos. 310 and 348); the Pegasus device of Wechel (No. 316); and, most troublesome of all, the small fleur-de-lis devices, of which there were two main forms, with a plain background and with a dotted one, each of these forms being recut a number of times. I have given ten blocks of these fleurs-de-lis (Nos. 263-272), but even now cannot hope that I have got them all.

A device the re-cutting of which seems to have passed unnoticed is No. 273. This, which represents clasped hands and cornucopias, was used by Thomas Orwin in 1590, and later by his widow, and by Felix Kingston, until about 1607, by which time it was badly cracked. It was then replaced by No. 274, which differs from it in having a cross as ornament at the top of the frame, instead of a rivet-head as the earlier block.

In connection with this recutting of blocks, there is one point to which I must briefly refer, though indeed I cannot throw any fresh light upon it, namely, the material of which the blocks themselves of the devices were made. It is of course evident that many, indeed most of them, were of wood, for we find cracks and wormholes that cannot be explained on any other assumption, but it is at least highly probable that several of the later ones, as well as a few of the earlier, were of metal. It is not only that they have finer lines than we generally associate with sixteenth and early seventeenth century wood-cutting, but that they remain in good condition for a far longer period than a wood block can be expected to do. Some indeed give as good prints after twenty or thirty years of service as when new.

Now it matters to us very little whether a block is of metal or of wood; but if it is of metal, it matters a great deal whether it is cast, or cut from a solid block as a wood-cut is. For if it is cast, there is no reason why there should not have been in existence several blocks giving prints indistinguishable from one another, and hence rendering untrustworthy any inference as to the order in which books were printed, based on the apparent condition of the device.

Small metal ornaments cast from matrices were, I believe, in use in England from quite early times in the history of printing, but the earliest certain evidence of the casting of anything large and elaborate that I have come across dates from 1583, when on the title-page of Day's quarto edition of Sternhold and Hopkins's *Psalms* we find two blocks of the well-known ornament of archers with dogs, etc., at the head and at the foot of the page. The blocks are so exactly similar that I think there can be no doubt that they were cast, and hardly touched up at all by the graver afterwards.

If it was possible to cast ornaments of this size—they measure 34 by 139 mm. (about $1\frac{3}{8}$ by $5\frac{1}{2}$ inches)—it must have been possible to cast devices, and I have therefore been for some time on the look out for any evidence of such casting. I refer of course to devices properly so called, and not to the smaller ornaments sometimes used as substitutes for them. Up to the present I am glad to say that I have found no indication whatever that any device was cast. Such evidence as there is seems all to point to there being only one block of each in use at a time.

If a printer regarded a device as of any practical service in distinguishing his books, he would surely have preferred always to use the same one. As I shall attempt to show later, in order to do this conveniently, he would have needed a number of blocks, but if they were cast there would have been no difficulty in obtaining as many as he required. Yet we find that without exception the printers either used a number of quite different devices, or issued some of their books with no device at all. Further, if devices were cast, it would probably have been an easy matter to produce new blocks by using the old as a pattern—provided of course that this was done before they were too badly worn or broken—and going over the result with a graver. I have, however, found no re-cutting of a block sufficiently close to the original for it to have been produced in this manner.

Though casting must have been possible, it may not have been easy. A satisfactory cast cannot be produced by simply pouring type metal on an impression of a pattern in sand or clay, and the expense of making a mould of the right shape for the particular block, in which the cooling metal would by its own expansion be forced into the interstices of the matrix, might easily have been more than that of procuring a new cut, when wood-cutting, and old devices of other printers, were cheap. It may have been quite worth while for the type-founders to make such moulds for casting ornaments and initial letters of which a number of blocks would

xl

be wanted for sale to several printers, and which of course tend to standard sizes, but it would be a different matter when at most half-a-dozen copies of a particular device were required. The question cannot, however, be regarded as by any means settled, and I hope that anyone who has evidence of the casting of any device will not fail to call attention to it.

In conclusion it may be well to say something about the use of devices as a whole, and here the most noteworthy fact is the way in which the frequency of their occurrence varied at different times. The fashions changed, no doubt, in this as in other things, and what at one period was a necessity to every respectable printing house and to every well printed book, at others was a thing of no moment at all. It would be interesting to know at what time the percentage of the whole output of books which bore a device was greatest, but to discover this would need a long and complicated inquiry. My impression is that the percentage was highest in the first quarter of the fifteenth century, but this is merely a guess. A much easier task is to determine the number of *new* devices cut at different times, and of this the following list (which includes signed borders) will give some idea. It must, however, be understood that the numbers are only approximate, for in a large proportion of cases the date when a device first came into use is not precisely known. Some devices of which the date is specially uncertain have been omitted from the count.

To 1500	11	1576-1600	128
1501-25	46	1601-25	76
1526-50	60	1626-40	34
1551-75	66		

It will be seen that the period most prolific in new devices and signed borders was the last quarter of the sixteenth century. It coincides therefore almost exactly with the decline of wood-cutting for purposes of book-illustration. Perhaps the woodcut artists found in work of this kind a partial substitute for their lost employment.

In a list of devices arranged according to the year in which they make their first appearance, the most striking thing is the sudden outburst of new devices in the years 1574-6. The preceding three years 1571-3 had produced only five devices, a fair average for some time back. Against this we find in the years 1574-6 no less than twenty-eight, nearly six times as many. For several years after 1574 the number is high, the period 1574-81 producing fifty-seven, an average of over seven per annum. Thereafter the numbers become irregular again, but are on the whole high, the year 1592 being a record year with fourteen. After the beginning of the seventeenth century there is a considerable drop in numbers, especially in 1620-6, when only nine make their appearance, and there are several years when we find no new ones at all.

If the English printers and publishers had been as consistent in the use of their devices as most of the more important foreign ones were, the study of the subject would be a far simpler matter than it is. On the other hand, the value of such study for the identification of the printer or publisher of books issued without an imprint, would probably have been much less. Had an Aldus or an Estienne thought it unwise to make public his share in a work which had issued from his press, we may be sure that he would not have put his device upon it, for who, seeing the dolphin and anchor, or the old man and the olive tree, would have failed to recognize the house from which the book came? But an English printer with half-a-dozen devices of various designs and origins might safely give his work a finish by using one of those he employed infrequently, for no one, save perhaps another printer, would be at all likely to connect it with him. No doubt in cases where it was very important to conceal the origin of a book, the printer would attempt to eliminate all traces whatever of his work, but a comparatively large number of books are to be found in which the printer seems not to have wished to advertise his share, and yet not particularly anxious to conceal it. Thus the printer of the three 'Pasquil' tracts against the Martinists in 1589-90 refrained from putting his name on them, using such fantastic imprints as ' printed between the sky and the ground within a mile of an oak,' ' printed by Pepper Alley,' and ' printed where I was,' but nevertheless placed on these tracts a device (No. 112β) which must surely have revealed to those in the trade from whose press they came.

By the later printers, at all events, their device seems seldom to have been regarded as a thing of importance. They used it or not, and they used their own or an old one of some other printer's, as suited their convenience at the moment. Of all those who after 1550 produced any considerable body of work, there is, I think, only Vautrollier and his successor, Field, who were absolutely consistent in always using a form of the same design, in their case the well-known anchor. Every other printer seems at one time or another to have either varied his device or to have used old blocks of another house. And of course even Vautrollier and Field issued books with no device at all.

It may be thought strange that a printer who had his device in two or three sizes, suitable for a folio, a quarto, and an octavo, as many did, should not have used it in *all* his books. Considering how few presses these printers had, it would seem unlikely that they should be printing off the title-sheet or colophon of more than one book at a time, and one would therefore have expected a device-block always to be available. There is, however, I think, a simple explanation of this in the custom of keeping the type of a title-page standing after the rest of the book had been distributed. A good many stray pieces of evidence, which taken together have considerable cumulative value, point to this being a common practice,[1] and the reason for it is almost certainly that prints of a

[1] As to plays of different editions in which the title-page is from the same setting-

xliii

title-page were the common form of book-advertisements. We know that even in the time of Martial the titles of books were posted up on the booksellers' shops, and the custom probably continued until it was replaced by more modern methods of advertising. There are numerous allusions to the posting-up of title-pages in the Elizabethan and Jacobean period,[1] and we hear of the same practice in the time of Pope.[2] It is perhaps in consequence of title-pages being regarded chiefly as advertisements, and as the business of the publisher rather than the author, that custom permitted them to vaunt so shamelessly the varied delights of the book within.

We do not, of course, know the extent of this practice, nor what number of copies of a title-page would normally be used for purposes of advertisement, but if it was expected to be at all considerable, or if further copies were likely to be called for at a later date, it would be natural for a printer to keep the title-page, with whatever device it happened to bear, undistributed until the sale of the book had ceased or the type was absolutely required for something else. And we have thus quite a sufficient explanation of the variety of blocks used by some printers as devices, and of the irregularity of their use. The non-use of a particular block will simply mean that, being locked up in another title-page, it was not available.

The transfer of devices from one printer to another is a subject

up of type, *see* Dr. W. W. Greg in *The Library*, 1908, pp. 400-1. Other evidence may be found in cases where the same title-page occurs twice in a book, as in Gabriel Harvey's *Pierce's Supererogation*, 1596. Sometimes the lower part of a title-page—the imprint, with or without a device—will be found to be from the same setting-up in two different books, probably indicating that the title of the first was kept standing until the second was ready.

[1] Among allusions to it the following may be noticed: Nashe, *Terrors of the Night*, sig. A4; *Have With You*, R1 verso; Hall, *Virgidemiae*, v. ii. 45-50; Parrot, *The Mastive*, 'Ad Bibliopolam'; Davies of Hereford, *Paper's Complaint*, l. 97.

[2] *Epistle to Doctor Arbuthnot*, ll. 215-16; *Dunciad*, i. 40 and Curll's note.

full of difficulties. Some transfers indeed are simple enough, as when a whole business with all its stock and materials passes from one owner to another—for example in the case already mentioned of Vautrollier's devices passing to Field; but in a number of instances the reason and circumstances of a change of ownership are far from clear.

As a general rule devices do not pass from an owner during his business career, though even to this rule there seem to be exceptions, but it is quite common for a man's devices to be scattered at his death among a number of owners, or to pass to a different man from the one who succeeded to the business.[1]

Two reasons apart from a transfer of business seem occasionally to have led to the use of devices by other than their original owners. The first, that the new owner was using a sign represented by the device. This probably explains Charlewood's ownership of Hall's Geneva Arms block, for we can trace no connection between him and Serle, the previous owner. Charlewood may have known of the existence of the block and obtained it expressly as representing the sign which he had chosen. But this cause of transfer is no doubt very rare.

A more frequent one is the apparent wish to make a new edition of a book more or less similar to an old one. Why this should have been attempted is not at all clear, but it is difficult otherwise to explain the occasional occurrence of devices in the hands of people who seem to have no direct connection with their former owners. For example, No. 138 occurs in the 1580 edition

[1] In this connection it may be well to warn readers that certain lists of printers at different periods, such as those given in Sir John Lambe's notes printed in Arber's *Transcript*, vol. iii, are not intended, as at first sight might appear, to show the history of the *printing-houses* or businesses, but the succession of *printers*. As the number of printers allowed to carry on their trade was fixed, a new one could only start when one went out of business. The new one obtained the other's place among the recognized printers, and in this sense was his successor; but it does not necessarily follow that he took over his business, though he often did.

of *The Secrets of Alexis* by J. Kingston for J. Wight. For some fifteen years previous to this it seems to have been in the hands of Bynneman, who lived till 1583 and is unlikely to have parted with it in the ordinary way of business. The block had, however, been used in the 1566 edition of the *Third Part of Secrets* by H. Denham for J. Wight. It is just possible that some idea of making the new edition uniform with the third part of the earlier one, copies of which may have remained unsold, caused the use of the block there.

A clearer instance is, however, afforded by a large device of Peter Short's (No. 335) which appeared in the 1602 edition of the *Works of Josephus* and is afterwards used in editions of the same book issued in 1632 and 1640 with the imprint " J. L. for A. Hebb." So far as is known, Robert Young, who was at these dates in possession of the Short business, had no share in the production of the book, but it is of course possible that he had certain rights over it, and that the use of this device is an indication of them. This is a possibility which we must always bear in mind when dealing with such apparently unexplained transfers.[1]

In a small number of cases we may, I think, suppose that the change of ownership was due to simple accident or carelessness. It is thus, probably, that some of the publishers' devices came into the hands of printers. The owner of a device would send it to a printer to be used in a particular book which was being printed for him, and would presumably leave it with the printer until he wished it to appear in another book to be printed at a different press. When, however, the publisher died or went out of business, there was a considerable chance that the device would not be re-

---

[1] Other cases of devices being temporarily transferred to a new printer for use in reprints of works in which they first appeared are Nos. 391 and 392. Both these may, however, have been cut as appropriate ornaments for the books in which they were first used. A somewhat similar case is that of a compartment bearing the crest of Lord Burghley (No. 162), which was cut for a book dedicated to him and was afterwards used by another printer in a different work also dedicated to him.

claimed, and, I suppose, after a certain time the printer would feel quite justified in considering it as his own. We may thus probably explain the transfer to Bynneman of England's device No. 138, and perhaps that of No. 203 from Bynneman to Newbery.

Lastly, something must be said as to the occurrence of borders in works in which their apparent owners seem to have had no share. The borders with which the present work deals are, of course, only those which have some especial mark of ownership and which, therefore, would less naturally appear in the work of other men. But in the case of borders which have no such distinguishing mark, an apparent transference backward and forward between printers who are not known to have had business relations with one another, is exceedingly common. The simplest explanation, and the only one which seems to suit the facts, is that they were lent or hired out. A good wood-cut compartment, especially one of a large size, must have been of value, and probably was considered to add greatly to the attractiveness of a book. There is at any rate nothing improbable in the idea that printers hired such things from one another as modern publishers obtain electros of illustrations.

It results from this that we must guard ourselves against assuming that a work in which one of these more elaborate title-borders appears was necessarily printed by the probable owner of it at the time. In attempting to determine the printer of such a work we must rely chiefly for our evidence on such initial letters and smaller ornaments as it would not be worth anyone's while to borrow. Indeed, in this, as in detective work of all kinds, it is the apparently unimportant which is most valuable as evidence.

EXPLANATORY NOTE ON ARRANGEMENT, ETC.

Order of Devices: The devices and compartments have been arranged, as nearly as their sizes and shapes permitted,[1] in chronological order according to the first appearance of their designs. Thus recuttings and altered blocks are treated as of the same date as the originals, and placed with or near them.[2]

This chronological arrangement has not been adopted without careful consideration, and though at first sight it may seem a wanton departure from the obvious method of arrangement under owners, I believe that those who make use of the book will find it the most convenient one.[3] An arrangement according to owners, while satisfactory enough if we are only dealing with devices up to about 1550, becomes impossible when we reach a later date and find the majority of printers using old blocks which had belonged to others—sometimes to several others—before them. Any such system would either have meant the repetition of a very large percentage of the devices,[4] some appearing six or seven times in various parts of the book, and would have necessitated a search in a variety of places in order to discover the history of a block or its condition at a particular date; or else the later part of the book would have consisted chiefly of a complicated system of cross references, making the discovery of the devices used by any particular person, the sole purpose of an arrangement under owners, more difficult than by the use of the index which is here provided.

After all, how often does one require to discover all the devices used by a particular man? In the great majority of cases a user of the book will start with a particular device, and wish to know when and by whom it was used. No arrangement, save one according to size, will enable him to turn to it at once in the book—least of all

[1] Not by any means very nearly. The shapes are often most awkward and it has been impossible to find a place for some of the blocks within several years of where they belong.

[2] A few imitations cut at a much later date and for another printer are treated, however, as entirely separate, *e.g.*, Arbuthnet's imitations of Jugge's devices.

[3] Save one. For the purpose of ready reference the best arrangement would undoubtedly be according to size; but I am not sorry that this method was vetoed on aesthetic grounds.

[4] And not only this, but a very large and wasteful increase in the number of blocks; for evidently one would in each case be bound to reproduce the device *as used by the particular owner*, though with all save a very few blocks the resulting prints would be indistinguishable from one another.

an arrangement according to owners—for it is precisely the owner that he wants to discover; but he will be able to find it in the index either by size, or by subject, or, if it has one, by the motto.

But there is a still greater objection to the arrangement under owners, namely the large number of devices the ownership of which is either uncertain or entirely unknown. From the nature of the case, an ownerless device is an absurdity, and surely a system of arrangement that compels us to lump together a large number of blocks of every date and style in a class of *Adespota*, may safely be rejected on that ground alone.

Books Listed: It is of course to be understood that the books mentioned under each device are not by any means all those in which the device occurs. The principles on which the lists have been drawn up are as follows:

When the ownership of a device at any particular period seems to be certain, I mention as a rule only the earliest and latest book known to me in which the device appears together with an imprint bearing the owner's name.[1] A bracket connecting the two entries indicates that (in my belief) the device was in the same owner's hands during the whole of the intervening period, and that further evidence as to its history is not necessary unless it tends to indicate that this was not the case.

When the ownership is uncertain, *e.g.*, when a device occurs in a number of books with different stationers' names, but without the name of a printer or probable owner of the block, I mention all the books in which I have found it, or at least a considerable selection of them. In this case there is no bracket at the side, and further evidence as to the ownership of the device during the period is required.

When nothing to the contrary is stated, the device will, as a rule, be found on the title-page of the books named. In the case, however, of a few which I have not myself seen it may be elsewhere; as the authorities from whom I have taken these entries do not always specify where the device occurs.

Imprints: The imprints here given have been simplified from the originals. My aim has been only to preserve so much of them as throws light on the share of the persons mentioned in the production of the book, and hence on the ownership of the device. Thus all clear statements as to the person by whom a book was printed, however expressed, appear simply as 'by ——' or 'per ——'; on the other hand, such words as 'cura,' 'sumptibus,' 'impensis,' 'apud,' 'in aedibus,' etc., are retained (in abbreviated forms) in order to avoid the risk of error in interpreting them. When, for special reasons, the exact form of an imprint is given, it is within quotation marks.

When an imprint includes the name of the apparent owner of a block, this name is printed in small capitals. Small capitals have, however, only been used when the ownership is practically certain, *i.e.*, when the device includes the person's name, initials, or mark, or when it occurs in connection with several imprints to which only

---

[1] When the device has been reproduced from some other book than one of these, that book also is mentioned. In a few cases others are given for special reasons.

this one name is common, or when what is known of the history of the printing-houses leads us to expect it to be in the person's possession at the time. It must not be supposed that when no name appears in small capitals the device was necessarily not owned by any of those whose names appear in the imprints.

The names of the printers have, as a rule, been given in their generally accepted English forms, however they occur (whether in Latin or English) in the originals.

When nothing to the contrary is stated, it is to be understood that the place of printing or publication is London.

Sizes: All sizes are given in millimetres; the vertical measurement first. The measurements are those of the smallest rectangle which, placed with its sides parallel to the edges of the paper, would inclose the device.

It is well known that considerable variation in size is to be met with in different prints from the same block. This is of course due to the fact that paper was generally (? always) printed damp, and that the damping caused it to expand. Hence a print when dry is always smaller than the original block, and, with paper of the same kind, the wetter it is at the time of printing the smaller is the resulting print.

So far as I am aware little or nothing has been done to investigate the behaviour of early paper under different conditions of moisture, and I have no means of carrying out exact experiments myself. A couple of very rough tests with paper dating from about 1640 and about 1700 respectively gave the following results. A piece 100 mm. square was taken and damped so as approximately to double its weight, *i.e.*, carrying about half the amount of moisture which it would take up if simply dipped quickly into water. The pieces of paper were then found to measure respectively 100.6 and 100.7 mm. in a direction parallel to that of the widely-set water-mark lines (*i.e.*, vertically in a folio book), and 101 and 101.2 mm. in the direction of the narrow lines (horizontally in a folio).

It is, however, by no means improbable that freshly made paper would show considerably more expansion with damp than this, for the difference between the smallest and largest prints from a block is much more than 1 per cent. It seems indeed sometimes to be as high as 5 or 6 per cent., while in the case of *cracked* blocks, in which the cracks would open or close according to the conditions of the weather and the tightness with which they were locked in the chase, it might be even more.

An interesting result of the fact that paper expands more in one direction than in another is that prints in a folio or in an octavo book will tend to vary in their *proportions* from prints from the same block in a quarto book. Thus, suppose we had to deal with a block measuring 100 mm. square printed damp on a sample of the first paper mentioned above, the size of the print in a folio or octavo book might be about 99.4 mm. high by 99 wide. If it were in a quarto book, however, these dimensions would be interchanged, the greater shrinkage being now in the height of the print, and the measurements would be 99 mm. high by 99.4 wide. This probably accounts for some of the irregularities in measurement that we meet with. At first sight it is not easy to see how, for example, two prints can have the same height, but different breadth, or *vice versa*.

The sizes given are in most cases a rough average of several prints which I have measured. They are not necessarily the measurements of the particular print selected for reproduction.

Asterisk: An asterisk prefixed to an entry indicates that the facsimile has been made from the book named. When a device occurs more than once in the book, the particular example reproduced is indicated by a second asterisk. Thus in No. 18 the device has been reproduced from Lyndewode's *Provinciale*, where it occurs twice, and specifically from the second occurrence of it—in the Preliminaries of Part II.

In one or two cases of blocks taken from the *Handlists of English Printers* there is some doubt as to the book from which the reproduction was made. In these cases no asterisk will be found.

Query Marks: A query prefixed to an entry indicates that there is some doubt whether the device occurs in the book or not. It is used in the case of books which I have not seen, when the description of the device given by my authority is insufficient to distinguish it with certainty from a somewhat similar one, generally the same design in another size.

LIST OF SOME BOOKS REFERRED TO

ALDIS (H. G.). A List of Books printed in Scotland before 1700. Edinburgh Bibliographical Society, 1904. [Aldis, *with number.*]

ARBER (E.). A transcript of the Registers of the Company of Stationers of London, 1554-1640. 5 vols. London, 1875-94. [Arber.]

BIBLIOGRAPHICA. 3 vols. London, 1895-7.

BIBLIOGRAPHICAL SOCIETY. A Dictionary of Printers and Booksellers in England, Scotland, and Ireland, and of Foreign Printers of English Books, 1557-1640. London, 1910. [*Dictionary I.*]

BIBLIOGRAPHICAL SOCIETY. Hand-lists of English Printers, 1501-1556. 3 parts. London, 1895-1905. [*Hand-lists, with name of printer.*]

DARLOW (T. H.) and MOULE (H. F.). Historical Catalogue of the Printed Editions of Holy Scripture in the Library of the British and Foreign Bible Society. 2 vols. London, 1903-11. [*B. and F. B. Soc. Cat.*]

DICKSON (R.) and EDMOND (J. P.). Annals of Scottish Printing from the Introduction of the Art in 1507 to the Beginning of the Seventeenth Century. Cambridge, 1890. [Dickson and Edmond.]

Duff (E. G.). A Century of the English Book Trade, 1457-1557. Bibliographical Society, 1905. [*Century.*]

Duff (E. G.). Early English Printing. A Series of Facsimiles of all the Types used in England during the XVth Century, with some of those used in the Printing of English Books abroad. London, 1896.

Duff (E. G.). The English Provincial Printers, Stationers, and Bookbinders to 1557. Cambridge, 1912.

Duff (E. G.). The Printers, Stationers, and Bookbinders of Westminster and London from 1476 to 1535. Cambridge, 1906.

Hazlitt (W. C.). Handbook to the Popular . . . Literature of Great Britain. London, 1867. [Hazlitt, H.]

Hazlitt (W. C.). Collections and Notes, 1867-76. London, 1876. [Hazlitt, I.]

Hazlitt (W. C.). Second Series of Bibliographical Collections and Notes on Early English Literature, 1474-1700. London, 1882. [Hazlitt, II.]

Heitz (P.). Basler Büchermarken bis zum Anfang des 17. Jahrhunderts. Strassburg, 1895.

Heitz (P.). Frankfurter und Mainzer Drucker- und Verlegerzeichen bis in das 17. Jahrhundert. Strassburg, 1896.

Heitz (P.). Genfer Buchdrucker- und Verlegerzeichen in 15., 16., und 17. Jahrhundert. Strassburg, 1908.

Heitz (P.). Die Kolner Büchermarken bis Anfang des xvii. Jahrhunderts. Strassburg, 1898.

Herbert (W.). Typographical Antiquities. 3 vols. 1785-90. [Herbert.]

Plomer (H. R.). A Dictionary of the Booksellers and Printers . . . in England, Scotland, and Ireland from 1641 to 1667. Bibliographical Society, 1907.
[*Dictionary II.*]

Plomer (H. R.). Robert Wyer, Printer and Bookseller. Bibliographical Society, 1897.

Roberts (W.). Printers' Marks. A Chapter in the History of Typography. London, 1893.

Sayle (C.). Early English Printed Books in the University Library, Cambridge (1475 to 1640). 4 vols. Cambridge, 1900-7. [Sayle, *with number or page.*]

Silvestre (L. C.). Marques Typographiques . . . des libraires et imprimeurs qui ont exercé en France, depuis 1470 jusqu'à la fin du seizième siècle. 2 pt. Paris, 1853-67. [Silvestre, *with number.*]

COLLECTIONS AND LIBRARIES

AMES COLLECTION. The collection of title-pages of English Books made by Joseph Ames *c.* 1740, and now in the British Museum (463. h. 1-6). See *Bibl. Soc. Transactions*, vii. 160-2.

BAGFORD COLLECTION. The collection of title-pages and fragments of printed books made by John Bagford *c.* 1700, and now in the British Museum (C. 68). See *Bibl. Soc. Transactions*, vii. 143-59, where a summary of the contents of the volumes is given.

B.M. = British Museum.
J.R.L. = John Rylands Library.

T.C.C. = Trinity College, Cambridge.
U.L.C. = University Library, Cambridge.

PRINTERS' DEVICES

1. (130 × 106.5 mm.) Mark of William Caxton, with his initials.

Though this device first occurs, so far as is known, in a book printed for Caxton at Paris, it is generally supposed to have been cut in England. Caxton probably stamped it in, after receipt of the books from abroad (Duff, *Printers of Westminster and London*, 1906, p. 18).

Herbert, pp. 11, 237: *Hand-lists*, W. de Worde, 1.

*1487 (Dec. 4) Paris: imps. W. CAXTON arte et industria W. Maynyal. *Missale ad usum Sarum* (end).

Figure No. 1a: from Lord Newton's copy. A piece of paper is pasted over the lower left-hand corner of the print.

[1490 by W. CAXTON.] *The Book of Eneydos* (end).

The rule on the left hand is still perfect. That below is broken as in No. 1b, but traces of the broken part remain.

Passed to Wynkyn de Worde in 1491.

*1495 by W. DE WORDE. *Vitas Patrum.*

Figure No. 1b.

1516 by W. DE WORDE. *Nova Legenda Angliae* (end).

The outer rules on left and at foot are almost gone.

1531 (Feb. 23) by W. DE WORDE. *The Pilgrimage of Perfection* (end).

2. (40 × 43 mm.) William Caxton's mark and initials with floral decoration above and below.

Herbert (p. 236), 2: *Hand-lists*, W. de Worde, 2.

{ [? 1491 ? W. DE WORDE.] *Book of Courtesy.*
        Duff, *Early English Printing,* 1896, p. 35.
*1495 per W. DE WORDE. *Directorium Sacerdotum.*
1499 [W. DE WORDE.] *Liber Festivalis* (fol. 200 verso).
1499 (May 20) per W. DE WORDE. *Psalterium* (end).

3. (51 × 40 mm.) Richard Pynson's monogram in white upon a black ground.

        In general style the device somewhat resembles that of Guillaume Le Talleur, printer at Rouen, with whom Pynson had been associated (cf. Silvestre, 86). Herbert (p. 242), 2: *Hand-lists,* Pynson, 1.

(α) As figured, no white dot in cup at top of central upright.

*[? 1491] (by R. PYNSON). Chaucer (G.). *Canterbury Tales* (end).

        In the copy at the British Museum the device looks as if it had been added after the book was printed. It is neither straight nor central on the page.

[? 1492] R. PYNSON. (*Latin Grammar.*)

        Duff, *Printers of Westminster and London,* pp. 58-9.

(β) A white dot in cup at top of central upright (see No. 53, where this device is used within a border).

1492 (Nov. 13) per R. PYNSON. Alexander Grammaticus. *Doctrinale* (end).

        Mr. Duff notes that between 1522 and May 1523 a white blotch appeared between the two lower legs of the R. The distinctness of this blotch varies, however, considerably in different prints.

1528 in aed. R. PYNSON. *Natura Brevium* (end).

        Probably passed to ROBERT REDMAN in 1530.

1530 per R. REDMAN. *Parvus libellus continens formam multarum rerum.*
1537 (Dec. 8) by R. REDMAN. Whitford (R.) *A Work for Householders* (end).

(γ) With side rules cut away, reducing the breadth to 37.5 mm.

1538 per R. REDMAN. *Parvus libellus continens formam multarum rerum.*
1539 (Jan. 24) by R. REDMAN. *A good book of Medicines called the Treasure of Poor Men* (end).

        Passed to Redman's widow Elizabeth in 1540.

(δ) With top and bottom rules also cut away, reducing size to 49 × 37.5 mm.

[? 1541] by ELIZABETH, widow of R. REDMAN. *The Great Charter . . . Magna Carta* (end).

2

4. (85 × 38.5 mm.) A double cross with a circle within which is a shield charged with a saltier.

> The arms of the town and abbey of St. Albans (Duff, *Provincial Printers,* p. 39).

{ *[? 1485] Sanctus Albanus. *Chronicles of England* (end: in red).
{ [1486 at St. Albans]. Berners (Juliana). *Book of Hawking,* etc. (end).

5. (93 × 69.5 mm.) Cut of St. Nicholas restoring to life three children who had been killed and pickled, with the mark and monogram of Nicholas Lecomte and, about the cut, *In Domino confido. M. Nicolas Leconte.*

> For the story see Jameson, *Sacred and Legendary Art,* ii, 454-5, 459. Wace in his *St. Nicholas* (ed. N. Delius, 1850, ll. 216-29), often cited as an authority for the legend, tells it somewhat differently.

{ *1494 Paris: by W. Hopyl imps. N. Lecomte. Garlandia (J. de). *Synonyma* (end).
{ 1495 (Feb. 26) Paris: [by W. Hopyl] imps. N. Lecomte. *Liber Festivalis* (end).
{ 1498 [Paris:] pro N. Lecomte per J. Jehannot. *Horae (Sarum)* (end).

6. (115 × 94 mm.) Framed device of Richard Pynson's monogram surmounted by a helmet. Below, his name.

> Herbert (p. 242), 6: *Hand-lists,* Pynson, 2.

{ 1494 by R. Pynson. Boccaccio (G.). *Fall of Princes.*

> Before the end of 1496 a crack began to appear in the right-hand top corner of this device, running almost parallel to the side. By the end of 1497 (see below) the piece had split off entirely. The device is not found between 1498 and 1515 (Duff, *Early English Printing,* p. 36, and *Printers of Westminster and London,* p. 62).

{ 1497 R. Pynson iusserat imprimere. Terentius (P.) Afer. *Andria* (end).

> The right-hand outer rule gone.

{ 1498 per R. Pynson. Sulpicius (J.). *Opus Grammatices* (end of 'Carmen Sulpitii' appended).

{ 1515 R. Pynson. Whittington (R.). *Editio.*

> Duff, *Printers of Westminster and London,* p. 62.

7. (60 × 55 mm.) Marks and initials of Fredericus Egmont and Gerardus Barrevelt.

> The device 'so resembles in style and appearance the mark used by the printer John Hertzog that we may be pretty certain it was cut under his supervision at Venice' (Duff, *Printers of Westminster and London*, p. 93).

{
1494 (Sept. 1) Venice: by J. Hertzog for F. DE EGMONT and G. BARREVELT. *Missale* (*Sarum*). (fol.)
> Duff, *op. cit.*, pp. 92-3.

*1495 'FREDERICUS EGMONDT me fieri fecit.' *Breviarium* (*Sarum*): *Pars estivalis.*
}

8. (67 × 43 mm.) Mark with the monograms I.N. and I.B., and the initials I. H.

> The monograms stand for the names of Julian Notary and Jean Barbier. The owner of the initials I. H. has not been identified with certainty, but he may have been Jean Huvin, a stationer at Rouen, who was associated in the production of books for the English market (Duff, *Century*, p. 113).

(α) With I. N., I. B., and I. H.

{
*[? 1496] [J. NOTARY, J. BARBIER and I. H.] Albertus, Magnus. *Quaestiones Alberti de modis significandi* (end).

1497 [J. NOTARY, J. BARBIER and I. H.] for W. de Worde. *Horae* (*Sarum*) (end).
> Duff, *Printers of Westminster and London*, pp. 37-8.
}

(β) The initials I. H. cut out.

*1498 per J. NOTARY and J. BARBIER imps. W. de Worde. *Missale* (*Sarum*).

(γ) The monograms I.N. and I.B. also cut out and 'Iulian⁹ Notarii' inserted in type.

*1499 per J. NOTARY. **Liber Festivalis* (end) and *Quattuor Sermones* (end).

9. (112 × 93 mm.) Device of Richard Pynson's monogram on a shield upheld by a boy and girl and surmounted by a helmet. Pynson's name below.

> Generally used in a border with the Virgin and a saint in the lower corner.

> Herbert (p. 242), 3 (without border), and 4 (with border): *Hand-lists*, Pynson, 3a, 3b.

{
*[? 1496]   ?   ?
> See Duff, *Printers of Westminster and London*, p. 66.

4

1497 by R. Pynson. Alcock (J.). *Mons perfectionis* (end).

By May 1499 there is a distinct indentation in the border below the ribbon. This got deeper year by year, until the piece broke off in 1513 (Duff, *Early English Printing*, 1896, p. 37).

*1503 (June 27) by R. Pynson. *The Imitation of Christ* (end).

Figure 9b. The outer right-hand rule is much less defective in copy seen.

1516 by R. Pynson. [Fabyan (R.).] *Chronicle*.

*** Device alone, without border (73 × 60 mm.).

1506 by R. Pynson. *The Kalendar of Shepherds* (end).

1513 by R. Pynson. *The History, Siege, and Destruction of Troy* (end).

*** Border without device.

[?1508] per R. Pynson. Lugo (P. de). *Principia seu introductiones* (end).

Enclosing a cut of St. Francis.

10. (62.5 × 67.5 mm.) Device of William Caxton's mark (reversed) with W. C., and, below, a flowering bush.

Herbert (p. 236), 3: *Hand-lists*, W. de Worde, 3.

(a) No notches in outer rule.

[1498] W. de Worde. Alcock (J.). *Sermo in Luc. viii.*

*[?] by W. de Worde. *A little treatise for to learn English and French* (end).

1499 (July 10) W. de Worde. *Contemplation of Sinners.*

Duff, *Early English Printing*, p. 35, pl. xxxix (a).

(b) With notches in the outer rule.

1499 (Dec. 4) W. de Worde. Sulpicius (J.). *Grammatica.*

*[?1499] 'at Westmester by Wynkyn the Worde.' *The Life of the Three Kings of Cologne* (end).

1502 (April 22) W. de Worde. Guido de Monte Rocherii. *Manipulus Curatorum.*

One copy is known with device No. 12.

11. (32 × 47 mm.) Device of William Caxton's mark and initials. Below, *Wynkyn de worde*.

Herbert (p. 236), 4: *Hand-lists*, W. de Worde, 4. The facsimile is from a leaf prefixed to the British Museum copy of *The Life of the Three Kings of Cologne*, but presumably belonging to some other tract.

[1499] by W. de Worde. Alcock (J.). *The Abbey of the Holy Ghost.*

Duff, *Early English Printing*, p. 36, pl. xxxix (e).

1530 (June 21) per W. de Worde. Horman (W.). *Vulgaria.*

5

12. (80 × 68 mm.) Tripartite device with William Caxton's mark and initials with C reversed in central portion; the sun, two blazing stars and thirty-six small ones in the upper part, and the name Wynkyn de Worde, etc., in the lower.

> Duff, *Printers of Westminster and London*, p. 132: not in Herbert nor *Hand-lists*.

*1502 (April 22) W. DE WORDE. Guido de Monte Rocherii. *Manipulus Curatorum*.
> Bodl., Douce, G. 321. Other copies have device No. 10b.

13. (40 × 31.5 mm.) Mark and initials of Julian Notary.
{ 1503/4 (Feb. 16) by J. NOTARY. *The Golden Legend* (after Table, sig. e6 verso, and end).
{ *1505 (May 2) per J. NOTARY. *Expositio sequentiarum secundum usum Sarum* (end).

14. (107 × 55 mm.) Device of two interlaced triangles with the mottoes *Melius est modicum iusto super diuitias peccatorum multas* [*Ps.* xxxvi(-vii). 16] and *Melior est patiens viro forti et qui dominat*[*ur animo suo expugnatore urbium*] [*Prov.* xvi. 32].

> The monogram within the triangles is a separate block; see No. 15.

{ 1504 (Feb. 7) per W. FAQUES. *Psalterium* (on sig. A at beginning of the Calendar).
> Without the monogram or the word 'Guillam' and crosses.
{ *[?1504] by W. FAQUES. *Statutes*, 19 *Henry VII* (end).
> With monogram, etc., as figured.

15. (12.5 × 17.5 mm.) Monogram of G F pierced by an arrow.

> The monogram of Guillaume Faques. The meaning of the arrow has not been explained. Mr. Duff notes that it plays an important part in the device of Richard Faques, William's successor [see Nos. 31, 56] (*Printers of Westminster and London*, p. 170).

{ 1504 (Feb. 7) per W. FAQUES. *Psalterium* (end, sig. u8).
{ *[?1504] by W. FAQUES. *Statutes*, 19 *Henry VII*.
> Within No. 14.

16. (103 × 73 mm.) Device of the Trinity with the emblems of the four Evangelists.

> Compare the smaller cut, No. 33.

*1505-6 Paris: cura W. Hopylii, imps. W. Bretton. Lyndewode (W.). *Prouinciale seu Constitutiones Angliae.*
     For sale at London ' in signo sanctissime Trinitatis.'
1516 (Feb. 22) Paris: exps. et sumps. F. Byrkmam [*sic*]. *Psalterium.*
1522 (at Paris, by Prevost, ? for Birkman). *Psalterium.*
     Bibliographica, i. 100.

17. (24.5 × 72 mm.) A blank shield with the marks and initials of Henry Jacobi and Joyce Pelgrim, and *Nosce teipsum* in type on a ribband.

     The reproduction in *Bibliographica* is from a copy in the British Museum in which an owner has added his arms to the shield.

*1505-6 Paris: cura W. Hopylii, imps. W. Bretton. Lyndewode (W.). *Provinciale seu Constitutiones Angliae.*
     For sale at London ' in signo sanctissime Trinitatis.'

18. (148 × 98 mm.) The arms of William Bretton (?).

     These arms have been generally supposed to be Bretton's, and the supposition is a natural one, but I cannot find confirmatory evidence. The arms of such families of the name as I have been able to discover are quite different. Burke's *General Armory,* 1884, gives ' Ar., a fesse crenellée betw. three fleurs-de-lis sa.' and 'a fleur-de-lis per pale ar. and sa.' as the arms and crest of Lyndwood, but these arms differ entirely from those of the author of the *Provinciale* as given in W. K. R. Bedford's *Blazon of Episcopacy.* The coat of arms was afterwards copied and used as a device by the Paris printer Egidius Gourmont (Duff, *Printers of Westminster and London,* p. 196).

(α) As originally cut.

*1505-6 Paris: cura W. Hopylii, imps. W. BRETTON. Lyndewode (W.). *Provinciale, seu Constitutiones* (beginning, and *prelims. of second part).
     For sale at London ' in signo sanctissime Trinitatis.'

(β) With the shield of arms cut out and a new one inserted.

*1510 (7 Kal. Julii) Paris: opera W. Hopylii impressa . . . venundatur Londiniis sub intersignio Trinitatis. Burgo (J. de). *Pupilla Oculi* (end).

19. (103 × 89 mm.) Tripartite device with William Caxton's mark and initials in central portion; the sun, two blazing stars,

7

and twenty small ones at top; the name Wynkyn de Worde, etc., in the lower portion.

This device, as Herbert says (p. 236), appears to have been copied more than once. Mr. Gordon Duff recognizes three blocks.

Herbert (p. 236), 5: *Hand-lists, W. de Worde,* 5.

The midmost device of the three reproduced by Ames at the foot of his Wynkyn de Worde plate, and called by Herbert (p. 236) device No. 1, appears to be merely the centre portion of the upper part of this.

1504 (Dec. 19) W. DE WORDE. Sulpicius (J.). *Grammar.*

    Duff, *Printers of Westminster and London,* p. 133.

*1506 by W. DE WORDE. *The ordinary of Christian Men* (end).

1517 per W. DE WORDE. Whittington (R.). *De declinatione nominum* (end).

1518 (March 10) by W. DE WORDE. *Nicodemus' Gospel* (end).

20.   (103 × 90 mm.) Wynkyn de Worde's tripartite device recut.

The star nearest the sun to the left hand and below it has 7 points instead of 6.

Not separately described by Herbert: *Hand-lists, W. de Worde,* 10.

["1509" by W. DE WORDE. Fisher (J.). *Treatise concerning the fruitful sayings . . . in the seven Penitential Psalms* (end).

B. M., 224. h. 26. The colophon, dated 1509, is reprinted from the edition of that year, but the true date of this edition must be considerably later.]

1519 (Jan. 21) by W. DE WORDE. *The Remedy against the Troubles of Temptations* (end).

*1519 per W. DE WORDE. Whittington (R.). *De octo partibus orationis.*

1528 (April 1) per W. DE WORDE. *Ortus vocabulorum.*

21.   (103 × 85 mm.) Wynkyn de Worde's tripartite device recut for the second time.

In this there are ten small stars to the right of the sun instead of nine, and there is no star in the extreme left-hand top corner.

Not separately described by Herbert: *Hand-lists, W. de Worde,* 14.

1528 by W. DE WORDE. *Richard Cœur de Lion* (end).

*1529 (Aug. 13) by W. DE WORDE. Fisher (J.). *Treatise concerning the fruitful sayings . . . in the seven Penitential Psalms* (end).

1534 (May 16) by W. DE WORDE. Stanbridge (J.). *Accidentia.*

22. (107 × 81 mm.) Device of a windmill and the miller going up to it by a ladder, with mark and the name 'Androv myllar.' At upper corners shields with the arms of France.

Probably cut at Rouen (Duff, *Century*, p. 108). A similar design is found on bindings, with the name Jehan Moulin (Dickson and Edmond, p. 47 note).

*1506 (June 10) [at Rouen for A. MYLLAR]. *Expositio Sequentiarum* (verso of last leaf).

1508 (April 4) by W. Chepman and A. MYLLAR. *The Maying or Disport of Chaucer* (end).
Dickson and Edmond, p. 59.

1508 (April 20) by W. Chepman and A. MYLLAR. *The Porteous of Noblenes* (end).
Dickson and Edmond, p. 51.

23. (69 × 92 mm.) Tripartite device with the mark and initials of William Caxton in the central part. The sun over a crescent moon with stars in the upper portion, and 'Wynkyn de worde,' etc., below.

Three blocks are given to show gradual deterioration.
Herbert (p. 237), 6: *Hand-lists*, W. de Worde, 6.

(a) First state.

*1507 (Dec. 10) W. DE WORDE. *The Book of Good Manners* (end).

(b) Second state.

1509 by W. DE WORDE. *The vii Sheddings of the Blood of Jesu Christ.*

*1515 per W. DE WORDE. Sulpicius (J.) Verulanus. *Stans Puer ad Mensam* (end).

1516 W. DE WORDE. Sulpicius (J.). *Stans Puer ad Mensam.*

(c) Third state.

1516 W. DE WORDE. Whittington (R.). *Editio Secunda.*

*1527 by W. DE WORDE. Austin, Saint, of Abingdon. *The Mirror of the Church* (end).

1529 by W. DE WORDE. Stanbridge (J.) *Parvulorum institutio.*

24. (77.5 × 64 mm.) Tripartite device with William Caxton's mark and initials in the centre portion; the sun, two blazing stars and fourteen small ones in the upper part; and the name 'Wynkyn de worde,' etc., in the lower.

Not described by Herbert: *Hand-lists*, W. de Worde, 9.

1507 (June 21) [Paris]. *Breviarium (Sarum).*

1509 (4 Id. Feb.) by W. DE WORDE for J. Gachet and J. Ferrebouc. *Manuale (York).*
    Probably printed at Paris; see Duff, *Provincial Printers,* p. 58.

*1511 (4 Non. Apr.) Paris, ex aed. J. Barbier: venundantur Londiniis a W. DE WORDE.
    Sulpicius (J.). *Quinta recognitio.*

25. (91 × 70 mm.) Tripartite device with William Caxton's mark and initials in the central division. The sun, the moon nearly at full, a blazing star and sixteen others at top; the name 'Wynkyn de worde,' etc., below.

Herbert (p. 237), 9: *Hand-lists,* W. de Worde, 7.

(α) As figured.

*1508 per W. DE WORDE. *Incipiunt opera super Constitutiones prouinciales et Othonis* (end).

1531 (Oct. 20) per W. DE WORDE. *Stella Clericorum.*

        Probably passed to John Byddell in 1535, and to Edward Whitchurch in 1545.

(β) The upper part alone (29 × 70 mm.).

1545 (June 19) by E. WHITCHURCH. *Primer* (end).
    In evident allusion to Whitchurch's sign of the Sun.

26. (140 × 97 mm.) Compartment of birds, trees, a butterfly and two dragons, with 'I N,' the initials of Julian Notary.

For the device contained in the compartment see No. 28.

(α) As figured.

*1507 by J. NOTARY. *Statutes 7 Henry VII* etc. (end of 12 *and* 19 *Henry VII*).
    Enclosing device No. 28.

1507 by J. NOTARY. Hylton (W.). *Scala Perfectionis.*
    Enclosing cut of Virgin and Child.

1510 per J. NOTARY. Herolt (J.). *Sermones discipuli De Tempore* (end of second part).
    Enclosing device No. 28.

(β) Cut at top and sides, and now measuring 107 × 75 mm.

?   ?   *The Seeing of Urines.*
    Enclosing title. (B.M., 1189. a. 3, imperfect.)

27.   (36 × 46 mm.)   Small tripartite device, with the sun and four stars at the top; William Caxton's mark and initials below, and the name Wynkyn de Worde in type at the foot.

Herbert (p. 237), 7: Hand-lists, W. de Worde, 8.

(α) As figured.

1509 (March 23) by W. DE WORDE. *Nichodemus' Gospel.*

1514 (July 24) per W. DE WORDE. *Horae (Sarum).*

(β) The lower third cut off.

[*c.* 1523] per W. DE WORDE. *Horae (Sarum).*

Emm. Coll., Camb. (Hoskins, Horae, No. 64).

28.   (57 × 46 mm.)   Mark of Julian Notary on a shield. His name below.

Intended for insertion in his compartment, No. 26, but also used separately.

{ *1507 by J. NOTARY. *Statutes, 7 Henry VII,* etc. (end of 12 *Hen. VII*—sig. Gg 6).

{ 1518 by J. NOTARY. *The life of St. Barbara* (end).

29.   (103 × 74 mm.)   Device of a shield bearing the initials W. C., suspended to a tree and supported by a wild man and woman. Below, the name Walterus Chepman.

The figures are closely copied from a device of Philippe Pigouchet, bookseller and printer at Paris, 1486-1512; see Silvestre, 71.

{ 1508 (April 4) by W. CHEPMAN and A. Miller. *The Maying or Disport of Chaucer.*
Dickson and Edmond, p. 58.

{ *[1508 (? May)] W. CHEPMAN. Dunbar (W.). *The Ballad of Lord Barnard Stewart.*
Dickson and Edmond, p. 63.

30.   (79 × 72 mm.)   Device of William Caxton's mark upheld by a sagittary and a greyhound; the initials W. C., and the name Wynkyn de Worde.

Herbert (p. 237), 8: Hand-lists, W. de Worde, 11.

1509 (Feb. 13) per W. DE WORDE. Guido de Monte Rocherii. *Manipulus Curatorum* (end).

The rules enclosing the device are all perfect save for the small break on the left-hand side about 30 mm. from foot.

11

*1519 by W. DE WORDE. Whittington (R.). *De sillabarum quantitate.*

> Right-hand rule gone, reducing breadth to 70 mm. The block is cracked through the centre, the crack passing to left of the first colon of the name. It is much more distinct in the original than in the facsimile.

1520 (Sept.) W. DE WORDE. Erasmus (D.). *Colloquia.*

31. (100 × 71 mm.) Device of a shield supported by two unicorns and bearing a maiden's head and the initials R. F. Below, the name of Richard Faques or Fakes.

> The device is copied, with alterations, from that of Thielman Kerver the elder, printer at Paris, 1497-1522 (Silvestre, 50).

(α) The name spelt FAQUES.

*1509 by R. FAQUES. Gulielmus de Saliceto. *Salus corporis salus animae.*

(β) With QUES cut out from the name FAQUES and KES inserted in type.

*1523 by R. FAQUES. Skelton (J.). *Treatise upon a goodly Garland* (end).

1530 by R. FAQUES. *The mirror of Our Lady* (end of pt. 2).

32. (50.5 × 43 mm.) Device of Richard Pynson's initials on a shield supported by a boy and girl. Above it, a helmet and a bird. Below, his name.

> Herbert (p. 242), 1: *Hand-lists,* Pynson, 4.

(α) As figured.

1508 (3 Id. Sept.) R. PYNSON. *Magna Carta.*

*[? 1509] R. PYNSON. Savonarola (G.). *Sermo in vigilia Natiuitatis Domini* (end).

> The dedication is dated 1509; Herbert, however, considered that the book was printed later.

1514 (16 Id. March) per R. PYNSON. *Magna Carta,* etc. (end of prelims.).

> Only very slight traces of the rule below the name.

(β) The part of the rules below the ground-line cut away, but the name remaining. The device (excluding name) now measures 44.5 × 43 mm.

1519 (3 Id. Sept.) cura R. PYNSON. *Magna Carta,* etc. (end).

33. (63.5 × 46.5 mm.) Device of the Trinity with the emblems of the four Evangelists.

> Compare the larger device, No. 16. A copy of this block, with a white ground, was used by Wynkyn de Worde as a cut, cf. his *Horae*, 1523, sig. C 2 (B.M., C. 36. e. 15).

*1510 Paris: opera W. Hopylii impressa . . . : venundatur Londiniis sub intersignio Trinitatis. Burgo (J. de). *Pupilla oculi*.

34. (77 × 53 mm.) Device of the Trinity, with two figures bearing swords to left and right. Above, a crowned rose, fleur de lis and pomegranate: below, the name Henricus Jacobi and his mark on a scroll.

(α) With the name of Jacobi.

*[1513] 'Venūdantur in vniuersitate Oxonieñ. Sub intersignio sanctissime Trinitatis ab Henrico Iacobi bibliopole Londonieñ.' Sirectus (A.). *Formalitates*.

> Perhaps passed to Henry Pepwell in 1518.

(β) The name of Jacobi cut out.

{
1519 by H. PEPWELL. *Accidence.*
1520 per H. PEPWELL. *Christiani hominis institutum* (end).
> *Bibliographica*, i. 180.
*[? 1525] by H. PEPWELL. *Exoneratorium Curatorum* (end).
> Dated in *Bibliographica* 1520; in *B.M. Cat.* 1530?
}

35. (250 × 182 mm.) The arms of Richard Pynson.

> 'Gyronny of eight gu. and sa. on a fess engr. betw. three eagles displ. or as many cinquefoils pierced az. (Papworth, *Dict. of Arms*, p. 807.) *Crest*: A demi eagle displayed holding in the beak a branch of pineapples fructed or, leaved vert.' (Burke, *General Armory*, 1884). The arms described by Burke differ somewhat.

{
1509 (Dec. 14) by R. PYNSON. Brant (S.). *The Ship of Fools.*
1523 (Jan. 28) by R. PYNSON. Froissart (Sir J.). *The First Volume of the Chronicles.* (end).
*1525 (Aug. 31) by R. PYNSON. Froissart (Sir J.). *The Third and Fourth Book . . . of the Chronicles* (end).
1526 (June 4) by R. PYNSON. Chaucer (G.). *Canterbury Tales* (end).
}

36. (103 × 77 mm.) Bordered device of a shield with the mark of Robert Copland, suspended from a tree and supported by a stag and a hind. His name below, and in the border *Melius est nomen bonum* quam *diuitie multe. Prou. xxii.*

> Round the shield is a garland of roses referring to his sign, the Rose Garland in Fleet Street.

{
[*c.* 1514] by R. COPLAND. *Modus tenendi curiam Baronum.*
> Duff, *Century*, p. 31.
*1515 by R. COPLAND. *The Book of Justices of Peace.*
}

37. (103 × 72 mm.) Device of a merman and mermaid upholding the monogram I.R. Above them the Deity between two shields containing the Royal Arms and the Prince of Wales's feathers. Below him the word *Fiat.* Below the merman and mermaid a landscape with ' Johannes. Rastell.'

> After 1520 Rastell had a house with the sign of the Mermaid, but it is not known whether he used the same sign at the time when this device was cut.

{
*[Before Dec. 1516] J. RASTELL. *Liber Assisarum et Placitorum Coronae.*
> With device No. 40.
1530 by J. RASTELL. Rastell (J.). *A new Book of Purgatory* (end).
}

38. (80 × 62 mm.) Device of a shield hanging from a tree, supported by a bear and an ass. The shield bears a mill and the sun.

> The bear and the mill stand, no doubt, for the name of Ursyn Mylner, printer and stationer at York, 1513-16; the sun and the ass have not yet been explained, but it has been suggested that the sun may stand for the sign of Wynkyn de Worde and that the book in which this device occurs may have been issued in partnership with him (Duff, *Provincial Printers*, pp. 57-8).

*1516 (Dec. 20) [York:] U. MYLNER. Whittington (R.). *Editio de consinitate grammatices* (end).

39. (27 × 89 mm.) Ornament consisting of the mark of Ursyn Mylner and his name on a scroll, with a rose and pomegranate.

*1516 (Dec. 20) [York:] U. MYLNER. Whittington (R.). *Editio de consinitate grammatices* (end).

40. (41.5 × 72.5 mm.) A scroll bearing the motto *Justicia Regat*, and the monogram I.R., the initials of John Rastell.

*[Before Dec., 1516] J. RASTELL. *Liber Assisarum et Placitorum Coronae* (on title, with No. 37, and alone on sig. a 1).

41. (75 × 60 mm.) Monogram of Richard Pynson on a shield upheld by a man and a woman.

Herbert (p. 242), 8: not in *Hand-lists*.

{ *1518 per R. PYNSON. Pace (R.). *Oratio Richardi Pacei* (end).
{ 1518 per R. PYNSON. Tunstall (C.). *C. Tonstalli in laudem Matrimonii* (end).

In these the ribbon is blank.

Probably passed to Robert Redman in 1530.

{ 1532 by R. REDMAN. *The first Dialogue in English between a doctor of divinity . . . laws* (end of first dial.).
{ 1534 by R. REDMAN. *The book of Magna Carta.*

In these the name 'R. Redman' is inserted in type in the ribbon.

42. (68 × 94 mm.) William Caxton's mark with initials W. C., the sun, moon, three stars, and plants: over all, the name Wynkyn de worde.

Not mentioned by Herbert: *Hand-lists*, W. de Worde, 15.

*n.d. W. DE WORDE. *Modus tenendi unum hundredum.*

From the copy in the John Rylands Library.

43. (101.5 × 97 mm.) The arms of the University of Oxford, with two angels as supporters.

{ *[1517?] Oxford: [JOHN SCOLAR]. *Opus insolubilium.*
{ See article by A. W. Pollard in the *Library*, April 1909, pp. 212-13.
{ 1518 Oxford: per J. SCOLAR. Dedicus (J.). *Questiones super libros Ethicorum Aristotelis.*

Passed to Charles Kyrfoth in 1518-19.

1519 (Feb. 5) Oxford: per C. KYRFOTH. *Compotus manualis ad usum Oxoniensium* (end).

Duff, *Provincial Printers*, p. 70; Sayle 5222.

44. (148 × 98 mm.) Device of the monogram of Richard Pynson on a shield supported by a man and woman; above it, a helmet and an eagle displayed holding a branch with pine-cones. At foot, to left and right, the Virgin and a saint.

Herbert (p. 242), 5: *Hand-lists*, Pynson, 6.

{ 1519 per R. PYNSON. Horman (W.). *Vulgaria* (end).
*1527 (Feb. 21) by R. PYNSON. Boccaccio (G.). *The Fall of Princes* (end).

1530 by J. Haukyns. Palsgrave (J.). *Lesclaircissement de la Langue Francoyse* (end of book ii).

Apparently begun by Pynson and finished after his death by John Haukyns—perhaps his assistant—in Pynson's house.

Probably passed to Robert Redman in 1530.

1532 (March 23) by R. REDMAN. *The pipe or tun of the life of Perfection* (end).
Herbert, p. 390-1.

45. (168 × 110 mm.) Compartment with the Royal Arms at foot.

Alluding to the sign of the King's Arms borne by John Siberch's house at Cambridge. As to the history of this border, see Bradshaw's introduction to the facsimile of the *Oratio* of Henry Bullock, 1886, and Duff, *Provincial Printers*, pp. 78-80, 88.

1521 Cambridge: per J. SIBERCH. Lucian. Περὶ διψάδων.

Without the break in upper outer corner of the second quarter of the shield.

*1521 Cambridge: per J. SIBERCH. Galen (C.). *De Temperamentis*.

With break in second quarter of shield.

The block may have been taken to Antwerp by Peter Kaetz at the same time as No. 57. He is not, however, known to have used it.

1536 Antwerp: H. Piertersen van Middelburch. (*A Prognostication*) (Dutch).
Duff, *Provincial Printers*, p. 88.

*** A copy of the sill-piece of the above (not the same block) occurs in:

'1527' by L. Andrewe. Braunschweig (H.). *The Virtuous Book of Distillation*.

Below Andrewe's Device, No. 74β. The date '1527' is probably reprinted from an earlier edition. In this block no part of the shield projects above the upper enclosing rule.

16

46. (94 × 70 mm.) Device with William Caxton's mark and initials in centre on a shield upheld by two boys at sides and a winged cherub above. At the top the sun, moon, and six stars apparently on the ceiling of a building supported on four pillars. Below, the name of Wynkyn de Worde.

> Herbert (p. 237), 10: *Hand-lists*, W. de Worde, 12.

(α) With pillars, etc., in background.

1520 (March 15) in aed. W. DE WORDE. Whittington (R.). *Syntaxis.*

*1521 (Oct. 8) by W. DE WORDE. *The Flower of the Commandments* (end).

(β) Background cut away.

1523 (Decr.) in aed. W. DE WORDE. Whittington (R.). *De Octo Partibus Orationis* (end).

*1525 by W. DE WORDE. *The Image of Love* (end).

1534 (Sept. 30) by W. DE WORDE. Cicero (M. T.). *The Three Books of Offices* (end).

> Passed to John Byddell in 1535.

1535 by J. BYDDELL. Julius II, Pope. *The Dialogue between Julius the second, Genius and St. Peter* (end).

> It still has the name of Wynkyn de Worde.

47. (25 × 93 mm.) Ornament or device with H. P., the name Henry Pepwell on a ribbon and a mark in centre.

1520 per H. PEPWELL. *Christiani hominis institutum* (end).
> *Bibliographica*, i. 180.

1523-4 (Idibus Feb.) in aed. H. PEPWELL. Whittington (R.). *De Octo Partibus Orationis.*
> *Bibliographica*, i. 184.

*[? 1525] by H. PEPWELL. *Exoneratorium Curatorum* (end).
> Dated in *Bibliographica* 1520; in *B.M. Cat.* 1530?

48. (22 × 109 mm.) Border-piece (foot) with Henry Pepwell's mark in centre.

(α) With mark, as figured.

*1521 (Oct. 26) by H. PEPWELL. Pisan (Christine de). *The City of Ladies* (on recto and verso of last leaf).

> ? Passed to Peter Treveris in 1521.

(β) With mark voided and lower part of shield cut away.

[1521/2] (Id. Feb.) per P. Treveris. Whittington (R.). *Syntaxis.*

? Passed to Nicholas Bourman *c.* 1539.

[*c.* 1540] by N. 'Bowman' for J. Reynes. Duwes (G.). *An Introduction to speak French.*

49. (24 × 106 mm.) Head-piece having a shield in the centre with the mark and initials of William Caxton, and above it the sun, in reference to the sign of Wynkyn de Worde.

{ *[1521] in aed. W. DE WORDE. Whittington (R.). *Vulgaria.*
1530 (June 21) per W. DE WORDE. Horman (W.). *Vulgaria.*

50. (21 × 108 mm.) Border-piece (foot) having a shield in the centre with the mark and initials of William Caxton, and beneath it a face.

(α) With shield as figured.

{ *1521 in aed. W. DE WORDE. Whittington (R.). *Vulgaria.*
1530 (June 21) per W. DE WORDE. Horman (W.). *Vulgaria.*

Perhaps passed to John Byddell in 1535, to Edward Whitchurch in 1545, and from him to William Powell.

(β) The shield voided.

1552 by W. Powell. Borde (A.). *The Breviary of Health* (end of part i).

The block is much worn and damaged, but I think there can be little doubt that it is the same.

51. (22.5 × 108 mm.) Border-piece (foot) with the initials of John Skot.

*1521 (May 17) by J. SKOT. Pisan (Christine de). *The Body of Policy.*

52. (113 × 80 mm.) Device of the Trinity with two angels. Below, the name Henry Pepwell, and to the left, his mark.

{ *1521 (Oct. 26) by H. PEPWELL. Pisan (Christine de). *The City of Ladies* (end).

The apparent break in the right hand outer rule a little above the middle is due to a fault in the paper.

1523-4 (Idibus Februarii) in aed. H. Pepwell. Whittington (R.). *De Octo Partibus Orationis* (end).

 Bibliographica, i. 184.

53. (119 × 82 mm.) Compartment with the monogram of Richard Pynson at foot.

 Copied with alteration of the shield only from that of Johann Schoeffer at Mainz (P. Heitz, *Frankfurter und Mainzer Druckerzeichen*, No. 4) (Sayle, p. 1729). Several other printers had similar blocks. See, among others, that reproduced in *Bibl. Soc. Trans.*, xi. 204. Cf. also the sides and foot of No. 81.

 The block in the centre is No. 3. When the compartment is used on a title-page, this is of course absent.

1522 in aed. Pynsonianis. Galen (C.). *De motu musculorum* (end).

 Herbert, p. 271.

*1524 in aed. Pynsonianis. Galen (C.). *De Symptomatum Differentiis* (end).

1526 by R. Pynson. *The Pilgrimage of Perfection* (end).

1526 in aed. Pynsonianis. Henry VIII. *Literarum quibus . . . Henricus . . . respondit . . . exemplum* (title).

 Also ? in 1527 (Herbert, p. 279).

54. (? 22 × 85 mm.) Border-piece (foot) with the initials of John Skot.

*1522 by J. Skot. *The Mirror of Gold for the Sinful Soul.*

55. (31.5 × 28 mm.) Mark of John Reynes, bookseller, 1523-1544.

 Compare No. 61.

*1527 by P. Treveris at the expenses of J. Reynes. Higden (R.). *Polychronicon.*

 In red on the title-page.

56. (53 × 40 mm.) Device of the initials of Richard Faques on a shield hanging from an arrow and supported by two unicorns. His name in type below.

 Cf. No. 31.

*[1521] Paris: per J. Bignon pro R. Fakes. *Horae* (Sarum).

 Bodl., Douce BB. 53.

19

57. (77.5 × 53.5 mm.) The royal arms with a dragon and a dog as supporters, and the rose, pomegranate, fleur-de-lis, and portcullis.

Used by John Siberch at Cambridge, apparently in reference to his sign of the Royal Arms. See H. Bradshaw's introduction to the facsimile of H. Bullock's *Oratio*, 1886, p. 22; and for a reference to other similar blocks Mr. Sayle's note, *Cat.*, p. 1228.

1521 (? August) ex Cant. academia [per J. Siberch]. Baldwin (J.). *De venerabili . . . altaris sacramento* (end).

*1521 Cambridge: per J. SIBERCH. Galen (C.). *De Temperamentis* (end).

1522 (Dec. 8) Cambridge: per J. SIBERCH. Geminus (P.). *Hermathena* (end).
Duff, *Provincial Printers*, p. 82.

Passed to Peter Kaetz, who took it with him to Antwerp; see Duff, *Provincial Printers*, p. 87.

1525 Antwerp: H. van Ruremonde for sale by P. Kaetz. *Bible* (*Dutch*) (end of parts 3 and 4).

1527 Antwerp: by G. van der Haeghen. Erasmus (D.) and Lily (W.). *Grammar*.
For sale in St. Paul's Churchyard; see Duff, *Provincial Printers*, p. 87.

58. (60 × 49 mm.) Mark of John Siberch, printer at Cambridge, 1521-2.

{ *1521 Cambridge: per J. SIBERCH. Fisher (J.). *Contio* (end).
{ 1522 (Dec. 8) Cambridge: Geminus (P.). *Hermathena* (end).
Duff, *Provincial Printers*, p. 82.

59. (97 × 86.5 mm.) Device of a shield, surmounted by a helmet, suspended from a tree and supported by two fabulous beasts. On the shield is the mark (later, the monogram) of John Skot, whose name appears below. Above the shield, a helmet.

Herbert (p. 318) describes the object above the helmet as a stork's nest.

(α) With Skot's mark on the shield.

{ 1521 (May 17) by J. SKOT. Pisan (C. de). *The Body of Policy.*
{ *1522 by J. SKOT. *The Mirror of Gold for the Sinful Soul.*
{ (β) With Skot's monogram substituted for his mark.

*[c. 1530] by J. SKOT. *Modus observandi curiam cum leta.*

1531 by J. Toy. *Gradus comparationum* (end).
Probably printed by Skot (Duff, *Printers of Westminster and London*, p. 151).

[? 1537] by J. SKOT. *Nicodemus' Gospel.*

60.　(117.5 × 83 mm.)　Device of a shield bearing the initials P. T., suspended from a tree and supported by a man and woman covered with long hair and bearing bows and arrows.　Below is the name ' Petrus Treveris ' on a scroll.

　　　The man and woman are woodwoses, or woodhouses, semi-human creatures believed to inhabit the woods, and refer to Treveris' sign the ' Wodows.' They are not uncommon as heraldic supporters, and are to be found in the device of Philippe Pigouchet, printer at Paris, 1486-1512 (Silvestre, 71), and in those of Walter Chepman, Thomas Davidson, and others; see Nos. 29, 65.

{ *1525 (March 6) Southwark: by P. Treveris. Braunschweig (H.). *The noble experience of the vertuous Handy Work of Surgery* (end).
　1529 (March 17) Southwark: by P. Treveris. *The Great Herbal* (end).

61.　(211 [or, with crown, 239] × 157 mm.)　Framed cut of St. George and the Dragon.　Above, the arms of Henry VIII, a portrait of the King, and the arms of London.　In the upper corners of the frame, the mark of John Reynes, as No. 55.

　　　The cut refers to the sign of St. George, at which Reynes traded.

*1527 by P. Treveris, at the expenses of J. Reynes. Higden (R.). *Polychronicon* (end).

　　　The cut of St. George is repeated on the title-page, but without the upper part of the block.

62.　(198 × 142 mm.)　Architectural compartment with W. R., the initials of William Rastell, printer, 1530-4.

　　　The shields at the top appear to have been always blank.

{ *1531 apud W. Rastell. *Registrum omnium Brevium.*
　1533 by W. Rastell. *Fabyan's Chronicle.*

　　　Perhaps passed to Thomas Gibson in 1534-5.

1539 in aed. T. Gibson. *The Great Herbal.*

　　　Herbert, p. 490.

　　　Passed to Henry Smith, perhaps by way of John Reynes.

1542 by J. Reynes. Chaucer (G.). *Works.*
1546 excud. H. Smith. *Intrationum liber.*

　　　It still has W. R. on the pillars.

63. (64 × 48 mm.) Device of three roses on a shield suspended from a tree and supported by two lions. Below, the mark and name of Petrus Kaetz, bookseller in London, 1524-5.

*1524 Antwerp: by C. Ruremond sumps. P. KAETZ. *Psalterium cum Hymnis ad usum Sarum.*

Kaetz returned to Antwerp in 1525, and in the same year this device is found on the title-page of a Dutch *Bible* printed by Hans van Ruremond for sale by him in that town at the sign of the House of Delft.

64. (67 × 44 mm.) A cut of St. George and the Dragon.

Presumably an old block; used by Robert Redman in reference to his sign of St. George.

*?1527 (April 18) apud R. REDMAN. *Modus tenendi unum hundredrum.*

Herbert, p. 387. Only known to me from a fragment in the Bodleian Library (Douce, Add. 142), from which the facsimile is taken. Here the colophon, with the name of the book and date, is separate from the cut, and it is not certain that the two fragments are from the same work. Printing on the back of the cut shows that it comes from an edition of the *Returna breuium*, a work which seems often to have been printed with the *Modus tenendi unum hundredum.*

A print of the cut from some other book is found in the Bagford Collection, Harl. 5919, No. 110. This is within a border of type ornaments and has no printing on the back.

65. (97 × 66 mm.) A shield hanging from a tree and supported by two woodwoses or wild men. Three owls in the tree and one below.

On the shield are the initials T. D., standing for Thomas Davidson, printer in Scotland, *c.* 1530-42, 'linked with three pheons (the armorial charges of the Davidsons)' (Dickson and Edmund, *Annals*, p. 106). The 'wild men' are said to have been copied from those of Treveris, from whom Davidson seems to have obtained some of his printing material (Duff, *Century*), but they occur in many devices. To those mentioned under No. 60 may be added that of R. Chaudière I, printer at Paris, 1516-51 (Silvestre, 586). In some points Chaudière's device resembles Davidson's much more closely than does that of Treveris.

*[? *c.* 1530] apud T. DAVIDSON, Edinburgh. *Ad serenissimum . . . Jacobum Quintum . . . strena* (end).

Various dates, from 1528 to 1540, have been assigned to this book.

66. (80 × 67 mm.) Device of the mark of Richard Bankes, printer and bookseller, 1523-45, supported by two animals, of which one is a unicorn; above, St. John with an *agnus dei*; below, a snail.

1528 by R. Copland at costs and charges of R. BANKES. *The Rutter of the Sea.*
    Bagford Collection, Harl. 5919, No. 131, fragment. The rule is unbroken on the right hand side, and there is only one break of any size (3 mm.) on the left.
*n.d. by R. BANKES. *A Compendious old Treatise, showing how that we ought to have the Scripture in English.*

67. (88 × 63.5 mm.) St. John the Evangelist, with eagle. Below, the name 'Robert: Wyre.'

    Plomer, *Wyer*, device 1. Referring to Wyer's sign of St. John. Wyer spelt his name 'Wyre' in the colophon of St. Bernard's *Golden Pistle*, 1531, but not apparently afterwards.

(α) With the name, and the eagle.

    Note: No good copy of the original has been found from which a facsimile could be made, and the present one must not be regarded as accurate in details.

*[c. 1531] by R. WYER. *Compost of Ptholomeus* (end).

(β) The name, the eagle, and part of the foreground cut away, reducing the size to 75 × 63.5 mm.

    Mr. Plomer regards this as a separate block (device 3); but after careful comparison with the print in the *Compost* I can see no evidence that they are from different blocks, and much that they are from the same. As stated, however, the *Compost* print is in a bad condition, and there may perhaps be a shadow of doubt. The block as altered was perhaps intended to represent St. Bernard writing the *Golden Pistle.*

*1531 by R. 'WYRE.' Bernard, Saint. *Here beginneth . . . the Golden Pistle.*

(γ) Cut at top and foot, reducing size to 57 × 62 mm.

[before 1537] by R. WYER. Erasmus (D.). [*Paraclesis.*] *An exhortation to the . . . study of Scripture* (sig. d2 verso).

(δ) Cut at top, foot, and left hand, reducing size to 52 × 45.5 mm.

1550 'by me Rycharde Wyer.' Coke (J.). *The Debate between the Heralds of England and France* (end).

    With rules at top and foot and geometrical ornament to left (as No. 70) making the whole 55 × 58 mm. Probably printed by Robert Wyer, some of whose type and cuts appear in it.

68. (72.5 × 61 mm.) Cut of St. John the Evangelist with eagle.

> Copied from the original form of No. 67. When used by Wyer it almost always has No. 69 under it.
>
> Plomer, *Wyer*, device 2.

> *1531 by R. WYRE. Bernard, Saint. *Here beginneth . . . the Golden Pistle* (end).
> > With No. 69.
>
> 1535 by R. WYER for W. Marshal. Menandrinus (M.). *The Defence of Peace* (end).
> > With No. 69.
>
> [?1550] by R. WYER. *The Assize of Bread and Ale* (end).
> > With No. 69. B.M., C. 38. d. 3.

Probably passed to Thomas Colwell in 1560.

> [?1565] by T. COLWELL. Phillip (J.). *The Comedy of Patient and Meek Grissill* (end).
>
> [Not before 1568] by T. COLWELL. Howell (T.). *New Sonnets* (sig. A4 verso.).
>
> ?1569 by T. COLWELL. Elviden (E.). *The Closet of Counsels.*
> > Herbert, p. 931.
>
> ?1571 by T. COLWELL. *Life and Death of John Story.*
> > Herbert, p. 931.

Passed to Hugh Jackson in 1575-6.

> 1578 by H. JACKSON.   ?   ?
> > Bagford Collection, Harl. 5919, No. 100. Probably P. M. Vermigli's *Brief Exposition of the xii Articles* (cf. Herbert, p. 1133).

69. (11.5 × 60.5 mm.) The name and mark of Robert Wyer.

> Generally, but not always, used below No. 68.

> *1531 by R. WYRE. Bernard (Saint). *Here beginneth . . . the Golden Pistle* (end).
> > Below No. 68.
>
> [?1543] by R. WYER. *The Assize of Bread and Ale* (end).
> > Alone. B.M., C. 38. d. 2.
>
> [?1550] by R. WYER. *The Assize of Bread and Ale* (end).
> > Below No. 68. B.M., C. 38. d. 3.

70. (53 × 45 mm.) Cut of St. John the Evangelist.

> A rough copy of No. 67 in its altered state. Generally, if not always, with rules at top and foot and a geometrical ornament to left, making the whole *c.* 56 × *c.* 56 mm.

24

*[Not before 1541] by R. WYER for R. Bankes. *The Ordinal or Statutes concerning Artificers.*
      B.M., 1379. a. 3 (3). Plomer, No. 79.

71. (78 × 96 mm.) Device of a rose-garland containing the mark of Robert Copland, printer 1514-48; his name (apparently in type) in a scroll below; a rose and a pomegranate in the upper corners.

      R. Copland traded at the Rose Garland in Fleet Street. Afterwards used by William Copland, printer, 1548-68, with his name in place of Robert's. Cf. No. 73.

(α) As used by Robert Copland.

{ *1530 by R. COPLAND. *The Pomander of Prayer.*
{ 1535 by R. COPLAND and M. Fawkes. *The xii Fruits of the Holy Ghost* (end).

      Passed to William Copland *c.* 1548.

(β) As used by William Copland.

*[1557] by W. COPLAND. *Arthur of Britain* (*Le Morte Darthur*) (end).

72. (65 × 45 mm.) A cut of St. John the Evangelist.

      The cut appears to belong to a *Horae*, but as it is evidently used with reference to John Butler's sign of St. John the Baptist, it may be counted as a device. The book mentioned below is the only one in which it is known to occur, and no other of Butler's has a device of any kind.

*[? *c.* 1529] by J. BUTLER. *Parvulorum institutio ex Stanbrigiana collectione.*
      Bodl., Mason, H. 40.

73. (95 × 70 mm.) Device of a rose-garland with mark of Robert Copland and his name below in a scroll.
      Cf. No. 71.

*1534 by R. COPLAND. *A Devout Treatise called the Tree and Twelve Fruits of the Holy Ghost* (end of the *Tree*).

      Of this book there are only two copies now known, that at Trinity College, Cambridge, from which the facsimile is taken, and the one formerly in the Huth Collection. In both the device is in exactly the same state, the flower—presumably a pomegranate—in the right-hand upper corner being cut away.

74. (85.5 × 64.5 mm.) The mark of Lawrence Andrewe, printer 1527-1530, on a shield within a frame.

(α) The arms of the mark with plain ends.

*1527 (April 17) by L. ANDREWE. Braunschweig (H.). *The Virtuous Book of Distillation* (end).

(β) The ends of the arms pierced and indented.

*n.d. [no printer]. Braunschweig (H.). *The Virtuous Book of Distillation* (end).

> The colophon states that the book was finished in 1527, but this is presumably not meant for the date of printing. The facsimile is from a copy in the possession of Mr. E. F. Bosanquet.

75. (97 × 72 mm.) Device of a shield, bearing the monogram of J. Skot, suspended to a tree and supported by two griffins.

> Closely copied from the device of Denis Roce, or Rosse, bookseller at Paris, 1490-1518 (Silvestre, 451). The monogram of John Skot on the shield and his name below are both cut reversed.

[?1529] J. SKOT. *Enormities used by the Clergy* (end).

> T.C.C. The parliament beginning Nov. 3, 21 Hen. VIII (*i.e.*, Nov. 1529), is referred to as 'this present parliament.'

*[*c.* 1530] by J. SKOT. Stanbridge (J.). *Vulgaria.*

[*c.* 1537] by J. SKOT. *A book of the Properties of Herbs.*

> Herbert, p. 318.

76. (26 × 94 mm.) Device or sill-piece of the monogram of John Skot, with his initials at sides and his name on a ribbon.

*[*c.* 1530] by J. SKOT. Stanbridge (J.). *Vulgaria.*

77. (26 × 89 mm.) Device or sill-piece of Robert Copland's mark, with his name on a ribbon.

*1530 (Oct. 31) by R. COPLAND. *The Pomander of Prayer* (end).

78. (38 × 38 mm.) Mark and initials of John Byddell in white upon a black ground, within a circular border.

*[? 1535] by J. BYDDELL. Cicero (M. T.). *De senectute* (end).

[n.d.] by J. BYDDELL. Luther (M.). *De libertate Christiani* (end).

> Herbert, p. 489.

79. (34 × 48 mm.) Device of the initials of John Byddell with his mark, in white on a black ground. His name below, black upon white.

1538 (May 30) by J. BYDDELL. Erasmus (D.). *Enchiridion*.
       Bodleian, Douce Add. 142, No. 44a.
*1541 per J. BYDDELL. *Cura Clericalis*.
       Bagford Collection, Harl. 5963, No. 54.

80. (110 × 77 mm.) Device of Lucretia with *Lucretia Romana* and *Thomas Bertheletus*.

       Used with reference to the sign at which Berthelet traded.
*1535 by T. BERTHELET. Bartholomaeus Anglicus. *Bertholomeus de proprietatibus rerum* (end).
       In some copies only; see W. W. Greg in *Bibl. Soc. Trans.*, viii. 214.
1554 in the house of T. BERTHELET. Gwynneth (J.). *A manifest detection of the notable falshed of . . . John Frith's book* (end).

81. (119 × 79 mm.) A compartment with the Holy Dove at top and the initials I. M. and I. N. below.

       For the design of the sides and foot compare No. 53. It is uncertain to whom the initials refer, but it seems possible that the I. N. stands for Julian Notary, though the compartment has not been found in anything bearing his imprint. In the case of another compartment (No. 98) the same initials perhaps stand for the name of the Southwark printer, James Nicholson, but he is not known to have begun business before 1535.
*1534 by R. REDMAN. [Lyndewode (W.).] *Constitutions provincialles . . . in English*.
       The block is cracked to the right of the dove and initials.
[? n.d. ? by R. REDMAN.] *The Book of Justices of Peace*.
       Title only in Bodl. Douce Add. 142, under 'Robert Redman.'

82. (111.5 × 77 mm.) A device of 'Our Lady of Pity,' with the name and mark of John Byddell.

       Badly copied from the device of Jaques Sacon, printer at Lyons, 1498-1522 (Silvestre, 912). This is a copy of another device of Sacon's (Silvestre, 548), which in its turn is derived from a cut in the *Historia di Milano* of Bernardino Corio (fol. 8 verso of prelims.), printed at Milan by Alexander Minutius in 1503 (Duff, *Century*). It was used by Byddell in reference to the sign at which he traded in 1533-5.

*1534 (March 21) by W. de Worde for J. BYDDELL. Roberts (John). *A muster of schismatic bishops of Rome.*

At end of Pt. 2, *The Life of Hildebrand.*

83. (63 × 45 mm.) An emblematic device of a heart purified in a crucible. The crucible is heated by a fire which rests upon a tile bearing the word *Christus* and supported by two hands emerging from clouds. To the wrists are fastened chains attached to a sphere, on a band about which are the Zodiacal symbols. Below it, the sun in glory. On the forehead of the sun the letter G: at the sides the initials of Thomas Gibson. On a scroll the words *Horum charitas.*

> This device resembles one used by Jehan André, bookseller at Paris, 1535-1551 (Silvestre, 128), but, in view of the date at which it appears in England, it is probable that both were copied from a common source. In André's device the object suspended by the chains is a cage containing a bird: there is no sun and the legend is *Horum maior charitas.*

(α) With G on the sun's forehead, and T. G. at the sides.

*1535 by T. GIBSON. *Concordance of the New Testament.*

St. Paul's Cathedral Library.

Passed to John Day at an unknown date.

(β) The letters T. G. removed, together with the greater part of the G on the sun's forehead.

1569 by J. DAY. Gonsalvius Montanus (R.). *De Heylighe Spaensche Inquisitie* (end).
When used by John Day the device has the letters I. D. in type at the sides.

*1571 ex off. J. DAY. *Reformatio Legum Ecclesiasticarum.*

1584 by J. DAY. Latimer (H.). *Fruitful Sermons* (sig. *2 verso).

Probably passed to Robert Waldegrave *c.* 1584.

1586 by R. WALDEGRAVE to be sold by R. Jones. Day (A.). *The English Secretary* (end).
Without initials.

[? 1588] by R. WALDEGRAVE for T. Man and W. Brome. Udal (J.). *The Combat between Christ and the Devil* (end).
With R. W. at sides.

Perhaps passed into the hands of Thomas East in 1603, and from him to Thomas Snodham in 1609.

1609 by T. SNODHAM for W. Firebrand. Cooper (W.). *Three Heavenly Treatises* (end).

84. (73.5 × 75 mm.) A device with the initials R. S. and the motto, *Dominus dedit dominus abstulit sicut domino placuit ita factum est.*

> The device appears to have been used by John Hertford, printer at St. Albans 1534-9. The initials presumably stand for the name of Richard Stevenage, the last abbot of St. Albans, by whom Hertford was employed.

(α) With the initials R. S.

{ *1536 [no printer]. Gwynneth (J.). *Confutation of the first part of Frith's book* (end).

1537 [no printer]. *An introduction for to learn to reckon with the pen.*

> The last leaf, with this device, is in the Bagford Collection (Harl. 5919, No. 176); cf. Herbert, p. 1436.

> Probably passed to Nicholas Bourman in 1539.

(β) The initials R. S. cut out and N. B. inserted in type.

*1539 by N. BOURMAN. Stanbridge (J.). *Accidentia* (end).

> John Rylands Library.

85. (118 × 81 mm.) A compartment exhibiting the seven cardinal virtues. Below, the mark and name of John Byddell.

{ 1534 (March 21) by W. de Worde for J. BYDDELL. Roberts (J.). *A muster of schismatic bishops of Rome.*

> Before both parts. The date is from Pt. 2, *The Life of Hildebrand.*

*[? 1535] by J. BYDDELL. Cicero (M. T.). *Tullius de Senectute.*

1538 by J. BYDDELL. Sarcerius (E.). *Common Place of Scripture.*

> B.M., 3128. a. 33.

[?] *Whether the Blood of Christ suffice.*

> Bagford Collection, Harl. 5963, No. 58. Apparently later than Sarcerius. I cannot identify the book.

86. (130 × 82 mm.) A compartment with Thomas Petit's mark on a shield supported by cupids at the base.

{ 1538 by T. PETIT. *The Paternoster, the Creed,* etc.

> Herbert, p. 553.

*1542 by T. PETIT. *The Great Abridgement of Statutes . . . 33 Hen. VIII.*

> ? Passed to William Middleton.

29

∗ Parts of the compartment.

[Before 1547] by W. Middleton. Froissart (J.). *The First Volume of the Chronicles.*
  The top-piece and left-hand pillar on the title. Extremely bad prints, but there can, I think, be little doubt that they are the same.

    Passed to John King, ? after 1547.

1560 by J. KING. Lupset (T.). *Works.*
  Top and both side pieces on title. For the sill is substituted an ornament (22 × 81) containing a snail, also used in the Froissart title-page.

1560 by J. KING. *Interlude of Impacient Poverty* (end).
  The sill-piece alone (28 × 82 mm.) with T. Petit's mark.

    ? Passed to H. Denham at an unknown date.

1585-7 imps. J. Harrison, etc. Holinshed (R.). *Chronicle* (Vol. ii, *The Description of Scotland*, sig. A3).
  The sill-piece alone. The *Description* is dated 1585. The printer was probably H. Denham, whose device appears at the end of the volume.

    ? Passed to W. Jaggard at an unknown date.

1624 by W. Jaggard for W. Turner (Oxford). C. (G.) Ἀστρολογομανια (sig. ¶2).
  Right-hand column, placed sideways at top of page.

87. (140 × 100 mm.) Arms of William Marshall.
  From Burke's *General Armoury*, 1884, p. 662ª, it appears that the beast on the chief is meant for an antelope courant, not a tiger as Herbert calls it (p. 373). Burke gives the crest as a demi-antelope, but does not indicate to what branch of the family the arms belong.

∗1535 (July) by R. Wyer for W. MARSHALL. Menandrinus (M.). *The Defence of Peace* (end).

1567 by W. Gryffyth. Pikeryng (J.). *A new Enterlude of Horestes* (verso of title).
  I cannot explain the presence of Marshall's arms in this book unless the block is used merely as an ornament.

88. (58.5 × 40.5 mm.) A barrel or tun having a tree growing from the vent-hole; with *Fructibus eorum cognoscetis eos.*
  The rebus of Richard Grafton. Cf. Nos. 95, 104, 114.

1540 in off. R. GRAFTON. *The New Testament . . . according to the . . . Great Bible* (8vo) (end).

∗1542 in off. R. GRAFTON. Erasmus (D.). *Apophthegms* (end).

1543 in off. R. GRAFTON. Plutarch. *Precepts for Health* (end).

89. (45 × 43 mm.) A cut of Judith with the head of Holofernes.

      Alluding to the sign of Henry Tab or Dabbe, stationer 1539-48. I have been unable to trace the source of the cut.

*[? 1542] by R. Wyer for H. DABBE and R. Bankes. Guido di Cauliaco. *The Questionary of Chirurgeons.*

90. (78 × 70 mm.) A cut of the sun surrounded by concentric circles and having in the corners the four winds.

      Used in *The Mirror of the World*, printed by Lawrence Andrewe [*c.* 1527], as an illustration, and afterwards as a device by James Gaver in reference to his sign of the Sun. The facsimile is from a fragment found in a binding in the library of Viscount Clifden. The fragment is deficient on the right-hand side

*1539 by J. GAVER. Stanbridge (J.). *Accidentia* (end).

      The colophon has 'Imprynted in London in [   ] by James Gauer / dwellynge at the sygne of the Sonne.' With the exception of the colophon, this edition seems to be identical with one printed nominally by Nicholas Bourman (Duff, *Printers of Westminster and London*, p. 140).

91. (119 × 74 mm.) A compartment of four pieces, the sill having the mark of Richard Grafton.

      The pieces of which this compartment is composed were evidently separate, but they seem to have been regarded as belonging to one another and, at least in early times, to have generally been used together.

*1539 by R. Bankes. Taverner (R.). *The Second Book of the Garden of Wisdom.*

      As to the relations of Bankes with Grafton see Duff, *Century*, pp. 7-8.

? 1540 excud. R. GRAFTON. *Psalter.*

      Herbert, p. 515: apparently this border.

1542 by R. Bankes. *The Principal Laws and Statutes of England.*

      Sayle 363 and p. 1730. The name of Bankes seems only to occur in the colophon, which is wanting in this copy.

      [For the sill-piece alone see below.]

1543 in off. R. GRAFTON. Plutarch. *Precepts for Good Health.*

1552 by R. GRAFTON. Wilson (T.). *The Rule of Reason.*

      ? Passed in 1553-4 to Richard Tottell, perhaps by way of Robert Caly.

? 1554 in aed. R. Tottell. England. *The Dialogues between a Doctor of divinity and a Student in the laws.*

Herbert, p. 809: probably this compartment is meant. The B.M. copies (506. a. 4 and 39), have a different one.

*** The sill-piece alone (22 × 74 mm.).

1542 typis R. GRAFTON. Erasmus (D.). *Apopthegms*.

Nothing is known of the border between 1554 and 1607.

1607 for L. Greene, Cambridge, and to be sold by R. Bankworth. Willet (A.). *An harmony upon . . . Samuel* (sig A1).

*** A side-piece alone.

1613 Cambridge: by C. Legge. Robartes (F.). *The Revenue of the Gospel is Tithes* (sig S4).

92. (155 × 110 mm.) A compartment of four pieces; the upper one containing two semi-human figures with floral ornaments, the sill having Richard Grafton's mark on a shield upheld by *putti*.

The side-pieces are probably intended to go with the sill, but the head-piece seems to be part of a longer ornament cut at the ends.

1542 by W. Bonham. *The Epistles and Gospels of every Sunday*.

Title in Bodl., Douce Add. 142, No. 55: presumably part of Bonham's *Primer*. The four pieces are arranged as in Hardyng.

*1543 in off. R. GRAFTON. Hardyng (J.). *Chronicle* and *Continuation*.
From B.M., G. 5937 (2).

1549 (August) by R. GRAFTON. *Psalter and divers things*.
The title (in red and black) has all four pieces arranged as above.

? Passed to Robert Caly in 1553.

? 1555 per J. Kingston et H. Sutton. *Portiforium seu Breviarium: Pars Hiemalis*.
Herbert, p. 833; but cf. Sayle, 1163, the title of which is in a different compartment.

? 1556 (Jan. 4) R. Caly. Hogarde (M.). *A short treatise on the 129 Psalm*.
Herbert, p. 831, 'Grafton's compartment.'

93. (106.5 × 68.5 mm.) Device of the mark and rebus of William Middleton on a shield suspended from a tree: male and female supporters: a blank ribbon below.

*1542 by W. MIDDLETON. *The Great Abridgement*.

1544 (March 1) by W. MIDDLETON. *Institutions or principal grounds of the Laws* (end).

94. (109.5 × 69 mm.) Compartment with the sun at top and John Byddell's mark at foot.

>Byddell printed at the sign of the Sun, formerly Wynkyn de Worde's house, from 1535 to 1545.

{ ? 1539 (April 5) by J. BYDDELL. Taverner (R.). *Sum or Pith of the* 150 *Psalms.*
{ *1544 (Nov. 19) by J. BYDDELL. Erasmus (D.). *Enchiridion Militis Christiani.*

95. (68 × 49 mm.) Device of a grafted tree issuing from a tun, the rebus of Richard Grafton, with his mark and *Suscipite incitum verbum &c. Iaco. I.*

>Cf. Nos. 88, 104, 114.

{ 1543 (Jan.) ex. off. R. GRAFTON. Hardyng (J.). *Chronicle* (end).
{ >B.M., C. 30. e. 9.
{ 1545-6 ex. off. R. GRAFTON. *Orarium seu libellus Precationum* (end).
{ >Title 1546: col. Sept. 6, 1545.
{ *1547 by R. GRAFTON. Aristotle. *Ethics* (end).

96. (67 × 39 mm.) Device of boys throwing stones at a tree laden with fruit. A blank scroll in the branches.

>Compare Nos. 97, 146.

{ 1543 apud R. WOLFE. John, Chrysostom. Ὁμιλιαι δυο (end).
{ >With motto, 'Charitas non quærit que sua sunt,' etc., in Latin and Greek, in type, about it.
{ *1543 apud R. WOLFE. Leland (J.). *Genethliacon* (end).
{ >With CHARITAS in type across it.
{ 1548 per R. WOLFE. Seymour (E.), Duke of Somerset. *Epistola exhortatoria ad pacem* (end).

97. (45 × 29.5 mm.) Device of the 'Tree of Charity.' An apple tree at which children are throwing sticks. The motto, *Charitas.*

>Cf. Nos. 96, 146.

{ 1543 (August) apud R. WOLFE. John, Chrysostom, Ὁμιλιαι δυο.
{ *1553 apud R. WOLFE. *Catechismus brevis Christianae Disciplinae* (end).
{ >A large break occurred in the border on the left hand side in the years 1569-73.
{ 1573 excusum apud R. WOLFE. Nowell (A.). Κατηχισμος.

Passed to Henry Bynneman in 1574-5.

{ 1575 by H. BYNNEMAN for L. Harrison and G. Bishop. Philibert de Vienne. *The Philosopher of the Court* (end).
1580 by H. BYNNEMAN. Harvey (G.). *Two other very commendable letters.*

98. (105 × 66 mm.) A compartment with two naked boys on the jambs. On the sill the initials I. N. on a shield.

It was suggested by Herbert (p. 496) that the initials stand for the name of the Southwark printer James Nicholson, some of whose material seems to have passed (*c.* 1538) into the hands of John Mayler (Duff, *Century*, p. 111).

{ *1542 by J. Mayler for J. Gough. Basille (T.). *A Pleasant new Nosegay.*
1543 by J. Mayler for J. Gough. Basille (T.). *The right Pathway unto Prayer.*

99. (43.5 × 59 mm.) Device of the sun in glory, with *Sol oriens mundo.*

Used by Edward Whitchurch with reference to his sign of the Sun, at which he printed from *c.* 1545 to 1553.

(α) With double rule.

{ *1545 by E. WHITCHURCH. *Primer* (end).
1546 (Aug. 12) by E. WHITCHURCH. Giovio (P.). *Short Treatise of the Turks' Chronicles* (end).

Passed to Henry Bynneman, possibly by way of John Wayland.

{ 1576 by H. BYNNEMAN for J. Shepherd. *The Warfare of Christians, trans. by A. Golding* (end).

(β) Outer rule cut away, reducing size to 42.5 × 58 mm.

1579 by H. BYNNEMAN. Digges (L.). *An Arithmetical Military Treatise named Stratioticos* (sig. K4).

Bagford Collection, Harl. 5963, No. 65. Possibly a proof: the device is not in the B.M. copy of the complete book, the space being left blank.

100. (74 × 49 mm.) Compartment with the sun at top; the monogram of Edward Whitchurch and 'Anno 1545' at foot.

*[? 1545] (May 26). E. WHITCHURCH. *The Books of Solomon, etc.*
[? 1545] by E. WHITCHURCH. Phaer (T.). *The regiment of life.*
Sayle 7098.

34

101. (108 × 67 mm.) Compartment with the sun at top and the monogram (incomplete) of Edward Whitchurch below.

The cross stroke required for the H is wanting; cf. No. 100.

*1545 by E. WHITCHURCH. *Primer.*

1550 by R. Jugge. Hooper (J.). *Declaration of the Ten Commandments.*

1551 by W. Powell. *The New Great Abridgement.*

Ames Collection, i, 181-2. The sill has still Whitchurch's monogram. Possibly Whitchurch had some interest in this and the preceding work, for there seems no reason why he should have made over the compartment to other printers at this date.

102. (74 × 50 mm.) Device of the mark of William Middleton on a shield suspended from a tree with two semi-human creatures as supporters. His name on a scroll below.

*1546 (May 1) imps. W. MIDDLETON. *Intrationum liber* (? end).

See Sayle, 774. The book was originally printed *by* H. Smith, or *for* him (title and col.: the latter dated Nov. 1, 1545); but in some copies labels were pasted on the title with 'Excudebat Wilhelmus Middilton' and on the colophon with 'impensis Wilhelmi Middiltoñ.' As the facsimile in the *Hand-lists* is said to come from this book, I suppose that one of the labels also has Middleton's device.

1546-7 by W. MIDDLETON. Smith (R.). *A Defence of the Sacrifice of the Mass* (end).

The title-page is dated 1546; the colophon Feb. 1, 1547.

103. (25 × 41 mm.) A ram marked with a W and a goat marked with an L.

The initials are those of Walter Lynne, bookseller, c. 1540-1550. No explanation of the animals seems to have been suggested.

1548 for W. LYNNE. Luther (M.). *A Fruitful Exposition . . . on Jeremy* xxiii (end).

*1550 for W. LYNNE. Carion (J.). *Three Books of Chronicles* (end, sig. Pp4).

104. (147 × 104 mm.) Rebus of Richard Grafton, with *Suscipite incitum verbum &c. Iaco . I:'*

Cf. Nos. 88, 95, 114.

(α) With rule complete, as figured.

{ *1546 (Aug. 17) by R. GRAFTON. *Primer* (end).
{ 1550 (July) excud. R. GRAFTON. Marbecke (J.). *A Concordance* (in prelims. a5 verso)

(β) All upper part of rule cut away from end of shading on left to curl of scroll on right.

1569 by H. Denham for R. Tottell and H. Toy. Grafton (R.). *Chronicle* (end of vol. ii).

> The device was probably used with reference to Grafton's *authorship* of the work; it may have been in Tottell's hands at the time.

105. (102 × 63 mm.) Compartment with Royal Arms at top, and two naked boys with crown, Prince of Wales' feathers and *Ich Dien*. Below, Richard Grafton's mark supported by two half-human creatures.

{ 1546 ex off. R. GRAFTON. *Orarium seu Libellus Precationum.*
{   The colophon has Sept. 6, 1545.
{ *1547 by R. GRAFTON. *The Ethics of Aristotle.*

> Passed in 1553 to Robert Caly.

1553 by R. CALY. John, Chrysostom. *A Treatise concerning the Restitution of a Sinner.*
>   At Grafton's address.

> Probably passed in 1553-4 to Richard Tottell.

1555 (Sept. 30) by R. TOTTELL. *The Abridgement of the Book of Assizes.*
>   B.M., 1379. a. 11.

106. (104.5 × 63 mm.) Compartment with a medallion on each jamb and the mark of William Middleton on a shield supported by two cherubs below.

(α) With Middleton's mark as figured.

{ *[? 1545] by W. MIDDLETON. *The Book of Surveying.*
{ 1547 by W. MIDDLETON. *The Manner of keeping a Court Baron.*
>   Bagford Collection, Harl. 5919, No. 129.

> Passed to William Powell in 1547.

{ 1547 by W. POWELL. Fitzherbert (A.). *The New Book of Justices of Peace.*
{ 1551 (Sept. 6) by W. POWELL. Lyttleton (Sir T.). *Lytelton Tenures truly translated.*
{ ? 1556 by T. Marshe; see Herbert, p. 849.

36

(β) Middleton's mark voided.

{ 1556 by W. Seres.   Elyot (Sir T.).   *The Image of Governance.*
W. P. inserted in the shield in type.   Possibly this book and the following were printed by arrangement with William Powell.
1560 (Sept. 2) by W. Seres.   *Aggeus the Prophet declared by a large Commentary.*

107.   (110.5 × 62 mm.)   A framed cut representing the 'woman clothed with the sun' in *Revelation* xii, 1.

Presumably referring to Edward Whitchurch's sign of the Sun.   In the *Certain Psalms* the cut is surrounded by a type motto made up from *Psalm* xxvi, 5 and *Cant.* iv, 7, and alluding to the printer's name: 'Thus saith the Lorde. I haue hated the malignant congregacion. All faire and White art thou my churche, and no spot is in thee.'

{ [1547] by E. Whitchurch.   *Certain Psalms chosen out of the Bible* (end).
*1548-9 by E. Whitchurch.   Erasmus (D.).   *Paraphrase upon the New Testament* (end of each vol.).

The facsimile is from vol. ii.

108.   (143 × 89 mm.)   Compartment with the sun at the top and Edward Whitchurch's monogram below.

For the sun cf. No. 99.

(α) With Whitchurch's monogram.

{ *1547 by E. Whitchurch.   *Certain Sermons or Homilies.*
1549 by W. Baldwin, servant with E. Whitchurch.   *The Canticles or Balades of Salomon.*

1550 in off. T. Gaultier pro I. C.   *The New Testament in English.*
Sayle, 1095.   Mr. Sayle says that I. C. was probably J. Cheke.   The compartment may have been used to indicate that Whitchurch had some rights over the book.

1553 in aed. R. Tottell.   Fitzherbert (Sir A.).   *La Nouvelle Natura Brevium.*
Perhaps printed by Whitchurch for Tottell, who had been granted a patent for law-books in 1552.

Probably passed to John Wayland in 1553.

(β) With Whitchurch's monogram cut out and John Wayland's (I W joined by loops) inserted.

1554 by J. Wayland.   Hawes (S.).   *The History of Graunde Amoure and la bell Pucel.*

37

Passed to Thomas Purfoot at an unknown date.

(γ) The initials I W cut out, leaving only the loops.

[? 1581] by T. PURFOOT. Calvin (J.). *A Commentary upon the Colossians.*

> The top piece of the border, containing the sun, is upside down.

** The central piece at the top, containing the sun, is apparently used in the following:

1560 (May 7) by H. Sutton at costs of M. Lobley and J. Walley. Palfreyman (T.). *A Mirror . . . for all Estates.*

> See Bagford Collection, Harl. 5963, No. 66.

109. (231 × 145 mm.) Compartment with Royal Arms at top, and arms of Queen Catherine Parr at foot. With E. W. in the lower corners, standing for the name of Edward Whitchurch.

(α) As figured.

*1548 by E. WHITCHURCH. Erasmus (D.). *Paraphrase upon the New Testament.*

1554 (Sept. 10) in aedibus R. Tottell. Lydgate (J.). *A Treatise showing the Falls of Princes.*

> The title-page is not dated. The date occurs in the colophon of the 'Daunce of Machabree' annexed to the work, which is stated to have been 'imprinted by' R. Tottell. It seems clear that the preliminary matter, including the title-page, was executed by the same printer as the 'Daunce.' The history of the compartment is obscure.

(β) The arms of Queen Katharine Parr and the E. W. voided.

1554 in aed. J. Cawood. *Statutes,* 1 *Mary: In the Parliament begun . . . the second day of April.*

> B.M., 505. f. 7(8).

1559 by R. Jugge. *Form of making Bishops.*

> Herbert, p. 717.

1562 by J. Kingston. Bullein (W.). *Bulwark of Defence.*

110. (210 × 136 mm.) Compartment exhibiting King Edward VI in council at top and Richard Grafton's rebus on a shield upheld by two cherubs below.

? 1548 in aed. R. GRAFTON. *Statutes,* 1 *Ed. VI.*

> It is to be noted that the dates appearing in the volumes of Grafton's

Statutes are frequently not the actual date of printing, but that of the earliest edition.

*1550 excud. R. Grafton. Marbeck (J.). *A Concordance to the Bible.*

1553 (April) in aed. R. Grafton. *Statutes, 7 Ed. VI.*

Passed eventually to Richard Tottell. It is not clear who owned it between 1553 and 1565.

1557 by J. Wayland. Guevara (A. de). *The Dial of Princes.*

1559 by J. Kingston. Fabyan (R.). *The Chronicle of Fabyan* (both vols.).

1565 (Nov. 10) in aed. R. Tottell. Rastell (J.). *La table côteynant les choses en la graunde Abridgement.*

1580 in aed. R. Tottell. *Le Liver des Assises et Plees del Corone.*

111. (174 × 116 mm.) Compartment with figures at sides supporting baskets of fruit. Below, a tablet upheld by two cherubs, and bearing, at one time, the letters T R.

As used *c.* 1548 it had T on the tablet at foot of the left-hand figure, and P on that at the foot of the right-hand one. The P was later cut out. The history of this border is very puzzling. It may have been originally foreign, for no English printer with the initials T. P. is known to have used it, nor, unless we assume that the 1555 *Processionale* was printed by Thomas Raynald, which seems very doubtful, was it ever used by a printer whose initials were T. R. In any case we should expect the letters on the tablets at the foot of the figures and on the sill to be the same, and I do not feel sure that the oblique stroke of the R. in the sill tablet is not an addition. If this was the case it is possible that the border originally belonged to Thomas Petit. It may be remarked that King, who used this border in 1560, possessed another that had belonged to Petit, see No. 86.

(α) With T and P in the tablets at the foot of the side figures.

[? 1548] (Sept. 15) by W. Hill. Tyndale (W.). *The Parable of the Wicked Mammon.*
The letters in the tablet at the foot masked out.

(β) The P removed from the tablet at foot of the right-hand figure.

1555 [? by T. Raynald]. *Processionale (Sarum).*
The only reason for attributing this to Raynald seems to be the TR on the sill. Mr. Sayle places the book under Raynald, but at p. 240 also suggests Marshe. The heads on the sill are in red.

*1560 by J. King. *Interlude of Impacient Poverty.*
Also with an odd piece in place of the sill, in John King's *Proud Wife's Paternoster,* 1560 (Herbert, p. 764).

? Passed to Thomas Marshe in 1561.

1566 by T. MARSHE. Becon (T.). *A new Postil.*

Passed to Henry Middleton at an unknown date.

(γ) With T R removed from tablet on sill.

1575 by H. MIDDLETON for R. Newbery. Fenton (G.). *Golden Epistles.*
The tablet is empty.

1575 by H. MIDDLETON for J. Harrison. Veron (J.). *Dictionary.*
The tablet has I.H. in type.

112. (56.5 × 36 mm.) Device of a caduceus held by a hand emerging from a cloud; at the top a book and a dove. On a tablet the words *Love and Lyve*, and on two scrolls the words *Nosce te ipsum* and *Ne quid nimis.* Across the device the name BAL-D WIN.

Baldwin apparently used 'Love and Live' as his motto; cf. his *Treatise of Moral Philosophy* (Herbert, p. 566).

(α) As described.

*1549 by W. BALDWIN, servant with E. Whitchurch. *The Canticles or Balades of Salomon* (end).
The motto surrounding it is in type.

Passed to John Charlewood at an unknown date.

(β) 'BAL' and 'WIN' cut away.

{ 1588 by J. CHARLEWOOD and W. Brome. Tedder (W.). *The Recantations . . . by W. Tedder and A. Tyrrell.*
*1590 [? J. CHARLEWOOD]. *The First Part of Pasquil's Apology.*
1591 by J. CHARLEWOOD for the Widow Brome. Lyly (J.). *Endymion.*

Passed to James Roberts in 1593.

{ 1595 by J. R. for G. C. Southwell (R.). *St. Peter's Complaint.*
[1606] by J. R. for E. Matts. Charier (B.). *A Sermon . . . at Richmond this present year,* 1606.

Probably passed to William Jaggard in 1606; to Isaac Jaggard in 1623, and to Thomas Cotes in 1627.

{ 1634 by T. COTES for S. Waterson. Daniel (S.). *The Collection of the History of England.*
1638 by T. COTES for R. Whitaker. Λειτουργια Βρεττανικη . . . *Liber precum* (title of psalter).

(γ) Lower rule absent.

1674 for S. Mearne. Philip de Comines. *History* (folio ed.).

40

113. (82 × 62.5 mm.) An emblematic device of a hand issuing from the clouds trying a coin on a touchstone labelled *Verbum Dei*; the wind blowing.

1548 Ipswich: by A. Scoloker. Zwingli (U.). *Certain Precepts* (end).

*1548 (June 30) by A. Scoloker and W. Seres. Frith (J.). *A Book made by John Frith*.

      Under the device, in type, is: 'Proue the spirites whether they be of God. Ihon yᵉ. iiij. i. Reg. viij. d. Mat. vij.'

114. (99 × 67 mm.) Device of a grafted tree growing through a tun, the rebus of Richard Grafton, with his mark on the barrel, and *Suscipite insitum verbum &c. Iaco. I.*

      Cf. Nos. 88, 95, 104.

*1549 excud. R. Grafton. *The Form and Manner of Making Archbishops, etc.* (end).

115. (137 × 176 mm.) An ornament with the arms of Edward VI between two pillars, at the base of which are the letters I. D., the initials of the printer John Day.

      As no perfect copy of a print from the block in its original state was available for reproduction the facsimile has been made from a print in the John Rylands Library, the border on the right hand being added. It will be noticed that the upper portion of the scroll by the top of the right-hand pillar is wanting.

(α) As figured, with E. R.

*1549 J. D[ay]. Edward VI. *O Lord for thy mercyes sake, saue the Kyng*.

      A single sheet inserted in a copy of Taverner's *Bible* of 1551. (cf. Sayle, 778).

(β) The date voided and the E of E. R. replaced by M.

1557 [?] *Missale ad usum ecclesiae Sarisburiensis* (fol.).

(γ) 'Again altered.'

1563 by J. Day. Foxe (J.). *Acts and Monuments* (verso of title).

      Sayle 800. Not in either of the copies at B.M.

116. (252 × 144 mm.) Compartment with the Royal Arms at top, and, at foot, a boy waking another; the motto *Arise, for it is day*: sometimes with E. R. in type at top.

(α) With motto as figured.

*1551 by J. Day. *Bible.*

1552 ex off. W. Riddell. Huloet (R.). *Abcedarium.*
    Nothing is known of Riddell's connection with Day.

[? *c.* 1557] by J. Wayland. Bieston (R.). *The Bait and Snare of Fortune.*
    It is doubtful who owned the compartment when this and the following work were printed. The *B.M. Cat.* dates the book ? 1550.

[? *c.* 1557] by J. Wayland. Boccaccio (G.). *The Tragedie of Princes.*
    Herbert, p. 565, gives this as dated 1558.

1560 by J. Day. *Certain notes to be sung at the morning Communion.*
    Herbert, p. 633. Steele, *Earliest Music Printing*, p. 42.

1572 by H. Denham. Walther (R.). *An hundred threescore and five sermons upon the Acts.*
    Perhaps lent to Denham, who does not seem to have possessed a folio compartment at this date.

1573 by J. Day. Tyndale (W.). *The Whole Works.*

(β) The motto cut out.

1574 by J. Day. Walsingham (T.). *Ypodigma Neustriae.*
    With *Mundus transit* inserted in type in space for motto.

1583 by J. Day. *Psalms (Sternhold and Hopkins).*
    With *Arise for it is day* inserted in type (no comma after *Arise*).

? Passed to John Windet or Richard Day, *c.* 1584.

1595 by J. Windet for the ass. of R. Day. *Psalms (Sternhold and Hopkins).*
    Space for motto blank.

1604 for the Company of Stationers. *Psalms (Sternhold and Hopkins).*
    Sayle 2166.

117. (75 × 63 mm.) A cut of St. George and the Dragon.
    I insert this with much hesitation. It occurs in the Bagford Collection, Harl. 5963, No. 81, together with an imprint as follows: 'Imprinted at Lōdon in Fletestrete at the Sygne of the George . . . by Wyllyam Powell . . . M.D.L.I. the syxte daye of Septēber.' It is not certain that the two fragments were taken from the same book, but this seems at least possible; and from the way in which they are pasted into the scrap-book, it is evident that Bagford regarded them as belonging together. I have been unable to identify the book to which they belong, or to find the cut in other works from Powell's press, and it need hardly be pointed out that the character of the design is very different from that of most English cuts of the middle of the sixteenth century. Powell

is believed to have traded at the George in Fleet Street from 1547 to 1567. The foreground of the cut appears to be slightly shaved at the ends.

*? 1551 by W. POWELL.   ?   ?

       See note above.

118.   (56 × 38 mm.)   Device of the Brazen Serpent.

For the history of this device, which was used by several printers including Conrad Néobar, printer at Paris, 1538-1540 (Silvestre, 99), and by Vincentius Valgrisius at Venice from 1545 to 1587, see *Bibl. Soc. Transactions*, iv, 103 ff. As used by Reyner Wolfe it generally had NUM. XXI. across it in type, as shown. Cf. No. 119.

{ *1549 (June) by R. WOLFE. *New Testament (Coverdale)* (end, sig. Y7 verso).
{ 1573 apud R. WOLFE. Nowell (A.). Κατηχισμος (end).

      Passed to Joan Wolfe in 1573.

1574 by the Widow of R. WOLFE. Calvin (J.). *The Institution of Christian Religion.* With R. W. in type across it, and NUM. XXI. below.

      Passed to Henry Bynneman, 1574-5.

{ 1575 typis H. BYNNEMAN, imps. G. Bishop. Humphrey (L.). *Oratio ad Elizabetham.*
{ 1581 ex off. H. BYNNEMAN. Aristotle. *Ethica ad Nicomachum.*

      Probably passed to Henry Denham in 1583, and to Richard Yardley and Peter Short in 1589-90.

{ 1593 by R. YARDLEY and P. SHORT. Lodge (T.). *Life and Death of William Long-beard.*
{ 1594 by P. S. for W. Mattes. T. (I.), Gent., *An Old-fashioned Love.*
1595 for W. Ponsonby. Guicciardini (F.). *Two Discourses.*

      Passed to Henry Lownes in 1604.

{ 1604 by H. LOWNES for T. Man. Rogers (R.). *Seven Treatises.*
{ 1610 by H. L. for M. Lownes. Gardiner (E.). *The trial of Tobacco.*

119.   (89 × 55 mm.)   Device of the Brazen Serpent.

      See No. 118.

{ *1550 by R. WOLFE. Cranmer (T.). *Defence of the Sacrament.*
{ 1551 by R. WOLFE. Recorde (R.). *The Pathway to Knowledge* (end).

      Passed to Joan Wolfe in 1573, and to Henry Bynneman 1574-5.

{ 1577 ex off. typ. H. BYNNEMAN. Harvey (G.). *Ciceronianus* (end).
{ 1583 in aed. H. BYNNEMAN per ass. R. Hutton. Morelius (G.). *Verborum Latinorum . . . Commentarii.*

Probably passed to Henry Denham in 1583 and to
Richard Yardley and Peter Short in 1589-90.

{
1598 by P. SHORT for A. Wise. Rackster (J.). *W. Alablasters Seven Motives Confuted.*

1602 by P. SHORT. Josephus (F.). *The Famous Works* (on title of *The Wars of the Jews*).
}

The name of P. Short as printer appears in the colophon.

Passed to Humphrey Lownes in 1604.

1611 by H. L[OWNES] for M. Lownes. Spenser (E.). *Epithalamion.*

Passed to Robert Young in partnership with Lownes in
1625-6 and to Young alone in 1629-30.

{
1629 by R. YOUNG for N. Butter. Lake (A.). *Sundry Sermons de Tempore.*

1636 per M. Flesher and R. YOUNG. Montagu (R.). *De Originibus Ecclesiasticis.*
}

120. (121 × 77 mm.) Compartment with a fox and a wolf, the
rebus of Reyner Wolfe, and REIN WOLF below.

{
1549 R. WOLFE. *New Testament (Coverdale).*

The title-page has patches of red.

*1550 by R. WOLFE. *New Testament (Coverdale).*

From the Lenox copy in the New York Public Library.
}

121. (93 × 77 mm.) Device of a hand holding a star within an
architectural frame in which are the words *Cum priuilegio*. Below
is the monogram of Richard Tottell and his name in full.

Tottell traded at the sign of the Hand and Star.

*1556 by R. TOTTELL. *Year-Book,* 4 *Hen. VI: De Termino Michaelis Anno iiii*, etc.
(fol. xxxii).

122. (89 × 62 mm.) A cut of the Seven Sciences with Grafton's
mark.

{
*1550 excud. R. GRAFTON. Marbeck (J.). *Concordance* (end).

1552 (August) excud. R. GRAFTON. *The Form and Manner of making . . . Bishops*
(appended to *The Book of Common Prayer*), sig. C5 verso.

B.M., 468. b. 6. With R. G., in ornamental initials, at sides.
}

123. (59 × 53.5 mm.) Device of a pelican in her piety, with supporters, and below, the monogram of Richard Jugge.

Cf. No. 125, and the device used by Alexander Arbuthnet, No. 225.

1560 by J. Cawood. [Fisher (J.).] *A Godly Treatise of Prayer* (sig. A8).

John Cawood was at this time in partnership with Jugge.

{ 1561 by R. Jugge. Joseph ben Gorion. *History of the Jews' Commonweal* (sig. ‡8).

*1565 by R. Jugge. Rainalde (T.). *The Birth of Mankind* (end).

1577 by R. Jugge. *Bible* (end).

B. and F. B. Soc. Cat., No. 112.

Passed to Jugge's widow Joan in 1577.

1579 by Joan Jugge.   ?   ?

Bagford Collection, Harl. 5963, No. 12. Apparently belonging to an edition of *A Treatise of the Nobility of Womankind*, translated from H. C. Agrippa, but I have met with no edition of 1579.

1579 by J. Walley. Joseph ben Gorion. *History of the Jews' Commonweal* (end).

R. Jugge's 1575 edition with new col. (Kk7), with Walley's name, the date 1579, and this device.

124. (31 × 43.5 mm.) A cut of the Resurrection.

Alluding to the sign of John Day.

*1553 by J. Day. Christian Discipline. *A Short Catechism* (end).

125. (111 × 85 mm.) Device of a pelican in her piety, with the monogram of Richard Jugge.

Compare No. 123 and the device used by Alexander Arbuthnet, No. 228.

(α) In frame with figures of Prudentia and Justitia.

{ *1552 by R. Jugge. *New Testament* (before Epistles of St. Paul, and at end).

1577 by R. Jugge. *Bible* (at end).

B.M., 339. a. 15. B. and F. B. Soc. Cat., No. 113.

Apparently passed to Andrew Maunsell, date unknown.

(β) The centre oval alone (66 × 51 mm.).

{ 1588 by J. Windet, sold at the Brazen Serpent. Martin (A.). *An Exhortation to stir up . . . her Majesty's Faithfull Subjects.*

The Brazen Serpent was Andrew Maunsell's sign from 1584 to 1590

45

{ 1589 by T. Orwin for A. MAUNSELL. Martin (A.), *A second Sound or Warning of the Trumpet unto Judgement.*

*1592 by J. Windet. Turnbull (R.). *An Exposition upon Saint Jude.*
There is no mention of Maunsell's name or sign.

{ 1595 by J. Windet for A. MAUNSELL. Maunsell (A.). *First (Second) Part of the Catalogue of English Printed Books.*

126. (11 × 6.5 mm.) Mark of John Cawood.

There are apparently at least two blocks of this, but as they are not easy to distinguish in reproductions (or in the original prints) only one is here given. It is most frequently used for insertion in the sill of one of Cawood's compartments. Cf. No. 129, where the mark is apparently part of the block.

{ *1554 in aed. J. CAWOOD. *Statutes*, 1 *Mary.*
{ 1563 by R. Jugge and J. CAWOOD. England, Church of. *Certain Sermons or Homilies.*
Herbert, p. 720-1.

127. (14.5 × 14 mm.) A shield with mark and rebus of Hugh Singleton.

Cf. Nos. 198, 250.

*1553 'Rome before the castell of S. Angell.' Bale (J.). *The Vocation of John Bale* (end).
Probably printed by Singleton; see article by H. R. Plomer in *The Library*, Jan. 1910, pp. 54-72.
1579 by H. SINGLETON. Bèze (T. de). *A little Catechism* (end).

128. (107 × 78 mm.) Emblematic cut of an old man displaying a skeleton to a younger one with the words *Etsi mors, indies accelerat.* From the skeleton issues a tree with the motto on a ribbon *Vivet tamen post funera virtus.* In the lower left-hand corner the initials I. D.

{ *1559 by J. DAY. Cunningham (W.). *The Cosmographical Glass* (end).
{ 1578 ex off. J. DAY. *Tractatus contra Missae Sacrificium* (end).
Annexed to Baro (P.)., *In Jonam Prophetam Praelectiones* 39, 1579.

46

129. (58 × 145 mm.) Sill-piece of a compartment of naked boys, one astride a barrel, on the end of which is the mark of John Cawood.

The four pieces of which the compartment was composed were separate, and the side-pieces are sometimes used with cuts of the four Evangelists as head- and foot-pieces.

{ *1555 in aed. J. CAWOOD. Statutes, 2 and 3 P. and M., *Acts in the Parliament* . . . 21 *Oct.*

B.M., 505. g. 14 (8).

{ 1563 by R. Jugge and J. CAWOOD. Statutes, 5 Eliz. *Acts in the Parliament*

B.M., 505. g. 14 (11).

1563 by T. Marshe. Shute (J.). *The First and Chief Grounds of Architecture.*

1569 by R. Tottell. Grafton (R.). *Chronicle.*

As Cawood lived until 1572 it seems probable that the appearance of the sill-piece with his mark in these two books indicates that he had some share in them.

130. (124 × 83.5 mm.) Compartment with, at foot, a shield or scroll supported by two boys and bearing the mark of Sibertus Roedius.

The mark and portions of the lettering have been painted over in the copy at the Bodleian from which the facsimile is taken, the only complete copy of the book which I have been able to hear of. There is a title-page in the Bagford Collection, Harl. 5919, No. 175, and in this the upper part of the mark is different, having only a cross stroke instead of the '4.' The mark has, however, been altered with the pen, apparently in order to make it into the initials of some owner, and part may have been erased. I have found no third copy with which to compare these, and it should therefore be noted that the facsimile may be inaccurate so far as this mark is concerned.

*1556 excud. S. ROEDIUS. Erasmus (D.). *De Copia Verborum et Rerum.*

131. (120 × 77 mm.) Compartment with the letters O. R. on the sill.

The initials stand for the name of Owen Rogers, printer, 1555-1566.

*1559 (May 4) by O. ROGERS. Lydgate (J.). *The Serpent of Division.*

Camb. Univ. Lib.

132. (107 × 76 mm.) Compartment with the monogram of Richard Jugge at top; termini at sides; blank tablet below.

Qy. did this ever have the pelican at foot, cf. No. 137?

*1560 by J. Cawood. [Fisher (J.).] *A Godlie Treatise . . . of Prayer.*

133. (125 × 80 mm.) Compartment with a medallion of Lucretia at foot.

The medallion presumably refers to the sign of Thomas Powell, who succeeded T. Berthelet at the Lucretia in 1556.

{ 1556 by T. POWELL. Heywood (J.). *A Dialogue containing . . . all the Proverbs.*
Sayle 1243.
*1562 by T. POWELL. Jewel (J.). *An Apology of Private Mass . . . with an Answer* (title to the *Answer, on D8).

? Passed to William Jaggard at an unknown date.

1614 by W. Jaggard. Dering (E.). *A short Catechism for Householders.*
Sayle 2781.

134. (149 × 102 mm.) Compartment with Richard Jugge's monogram at top, termini at sides, and two lions couchant at foot.

The oval at foot was perhaps intended for the date, but in all examples that I have met with it is empty.

1561 by W. Seres. Castiglione (B.). *The Courtier.*
{ *1563 by R. JUGGE and J. Cawood. *The second Tome of Homilies.*
1571 by R. JUGGE and J. Cawood. *Articles agreed by the Archbishops and Bishops in 1562.*
1572 by H. 'Benneyman' for R. Watkins. Lavater (L.). *Of Ghosts and Spirits walking by night.*

The colophon has 'Imprinted by Richard Watkins.' The block still has Jugge's monogram at top. He lived until 1577, and this book was perhaps printed under some arrangement with him by Watkins, who was his son-in-law.

135. (48 × 37 mm.) Device of a half rose and half pomegranate with I. R. and a shield containing three tiaras.

The half rose and half pomegranate represents the sign of James Rowbotham,

48

bookseller (and printer ?) 1559-80. The three tiaras are the arms of the Drapers' Company, to which Rowbotham probably belonged.

{
*[? 1562] by J. Rowbotham. *The most excellent . . . book of . . . Arcandam, trans. by W. Ward.*
    Camb. Univ. Lib.
1563 by R. Hall for J. Rowbotham. Lever (R.). *The Philosopher's Game* (end).
}

136.   (43.5 × 43.5 mm.) The arms of the city of Geneva.
    Rowland Hall worked at Geneva from 1559 to 1560, and used the arms as his sign in 1562 and 1563. See the *Library*, 1908, pp. 119-20.
*1562 by R. Hall. *The Laws and Statutes of Geneva.*
    Probably passed to Richard Serle in 1563.
[? 1565] R. Serle. Bèze (T. de). *A brief sum of the Christian Faith.*
    Passed to John Charlewood at an unknown date.

{
1582 by J. Charlewood. Northbrook (J.). *A brief Sum of the Christian Faith* (end).
1584 by J. Charlewood. Wimbledon (R.). *A godly Sermon preached in* 1388.
}

    ? Passed to Richard Jones c. 1586.

{
1591 by R. Jones. Regius (U.). *The Solace of Sion* (end).
    Sayle 7261.
1594 by R. Jones. Regius (U.). *The Solace of Sion* (end).
}

    ? Passed to James Roberts c. 1598.
1599 by J. Roberts. Wimbledon (R.). *A Sermon preached in* 1388 (end).
    The title-page has Roberts's imprint with the date 1593. The date 1599 appears in the colophon, which also has Roberts's name, on the same page as the device.
1605 [? by T. Purfoot]. Dent (A.). *The Plain Man's Pathway* (end of Table, sig. Cc7 verso).
    This has No. 344 on the title.
    ? Passed to William Jaggard in 1606.
1607 for N. Butter.   ?   ?
    Fragment in a collection of title-pages at the British Museum (618. k. 17), fol. 51.
1617 by W. Jaggard to be sold by D. Speed. Wimbledon (R.). *A godly Sermon preached in* 1388 (end).
    Passed to Thomas Cotes in 1627.

{
1630 T. Cotes. (Sayle, p. 999).
1637 by T. Cotes for A. Crook and W. Cook. Shirley (J.). *Hyde park.*
}

137. (72 × 52.5 mm.) Compartment with Richard Jugge's monogram at the top and a pelican in her piety below.

> I have been unable to find any instance of the use of this compartment by Jugge, who printed very few small books. It was, however, presumably cut at the same time as No. 132, which it closely resembles.

[? *c.* 1560. See above.]

*1629 by M.F. to be sold by F. Grove. *Pasquil's Jests* (placed sideways on verso of title).

138. (66 × 53.5 mm.) Framed device of a woman with two horses. The motto *Armipotenti Angliae*.

> It has always been assumed that the motto refers to the name of Nicholas England, and this seems probably correct, but the history of the device is not quite clear.

1560 by J. Kingston for N. ENGLAND. Macchiavelli (N.). *The Art of War* (end).

1562 by R. Hall for N. ENGLAND. Virgilius Maro (P.). *The nine first books of the Eneidos . . . by T. Phaer.*

*1566 by H. Denham for J. Wight. Alessio, Piemontese, *The Third Part of Secrets.*

> The 1560-1562 edition of the *Secrets* had been printed for N. England, and he may have retained an interest in the book. Otherwise it is difficult to account for the presence of this device.

1567 by H. Bynneman for N. ENGLAND. Painter (W.). *The second Tome of the Palace of Pleasure* (end).

Nicholas England died or went out of business in 1568-9. The device apparently remained in the hands of Henry Bynneman.

1568 by H. Bynneman for J. Wight. Alessio, Piemontese. *The Secrets of Alexis* (part 1).

1572 by H. Bynneman. Dionysius, Periegetes. *Survey of the World* (verso of title).

1573 in aed. H. Bynneman imps. H. Toy. Price (J.). *Historiae Britanniae defensio.*

1580 by J. Kingston for J. Wight. Alessio, Piemontese. *The Secrets of Alexis* (parts 1 and 2).

> Perhaps used in this work on account of its appearance in earlier editions.

139. (110 × 71 mm.) Compartment with the Royal Arms at top and the Stationers' below. The monogram of William Seres at the sides.

*1562 by W. SERES. *Aggeus and Abdias.*

50

1562 by H. Sutton for T. Hacket. Veron (J.). *A strong Battery against the . . .
invocation of . . . saints.*
Presumably by Seres' assignment.
1576 by W. SERES. Cheke (Sir J.). *The Hurt of Sedition.*
1581 by the assign of W. SERES. Oldwanton (O.). *A little Treatise called the Image of
Idleness.*

140. (111 × 72.5 mm.) Compartment with the Royal Arms at top and the Stationers' at foot. At the sides the mark of Thomas Purfoot.

*[? 1563] by L. Askell for T. PURFOOT. *How and whither a Christian man should fly
the Pestilence.*

141. (34 × 50 mm.) A cut of two naked boys seated on the ground.

Mr. Gordon Duff regards this as Henry Sutton's device (*Century*, p. 154), and I have therefore included it, though with some hesitation. It seems to be of rare occurrence in Sutton's books—I have only found it once—and his sign was one black boy, not two white ones.

*1561 by H. SUTTON. Seneca (L. A.). *Tragedia prima quae inscribitur Hercules furens*
(end).

142. (44 × 54 mm.) A boy with wings upon his right arm and with his left hand holding, or fastened to, a weight.

An emblem signifying talent kept from rising by the burden of poverty (Alciat, ed. 1567, emblem 64, and in earlier editions). The emblem was used as a device by Barthélemy Berton, printer at Rochelle, 1564-71; see Silvestre, 864. Cf. No. 393.

*1563 by R. HALL for T. Gale. Gale (T.). *An Excellent Treatise of Gunshot Wounds.*
Passed to William Howe, perhaps by way of Richard Serle.
[1570] by W. HOWE. Davie (S.). *Confession of T. & C. Norton.*
Bibl. Soc. Transactions, iv. 86.
1571 by W. HOWE for J. Allde and W. Pickering. Knel (T.). *A Declaration of
Tempestious Floods.*
Bibl. Soc. Transactions, iv. 89.

{ 1597 by V. Simmes for A. Wise. *The Tragedy of King Richard the Second.*
{ 1604 by V. S[immes] for T. Bushell. Marlowe (C.). *Doctor Faustus.*

1604 for T. Thorpe. W. (T.). *A Succint . . . Declaration of . . . Clymacterial Years.*
   Issued with T. W.'s *Passions of the Mind*, printed by Valentine Simmes for W. Burre.

143. (101 × 56 mm.) Rebus of Richard Harrison, printer 1561 and 1562; a hare, a sheaf of rye, and the sun.

   Cf. nos. 169, 171, 275, 319. Referred to by Camden in his *Remains*, sect. 'Rebus': 'an Hare by a sheaf of rye in the sun for Harrison.'

*1562 by R. Harrison. Calvin (J.). *The Institution of Christian Religion.*

144. (43 × 49 mm.) A griffin holding a spray of sweet-william in its beak and between its claws a shield bearing the mark of William Gryffyth.

   In 1552-3 Gryffyth used the griffin as his sign, but by 1556 he had moved to 'the Falcon against St. Dunstan's Church.' It is doubtful whether his use of the griffin as a device refers to his early sign or to his name. Cf. Nos. 157, 158.

(*α*) With rule border.

{ *1565 (Sept. 22) by W. Gryffyth. Norton (T.) and Sackville (T.). *The Tragedy of Gorboduc.*
{
{ (*β*) Without the rule (38.5 × 47).
{
{ *1566 by W. Gryffyth. Erasmus (D.). *One Dialogue entitled Diuersoria.*
   John Rylands Library.

144*. (38 × 35 mm.) Device of a griffin segreant within an oval border.

   I have been unable to obtain a photograph of this.

1565 (Sept. 22) by W. Gryffyth. Norton (T.) and Sackville (T.). *The Tragedy of Gorboduc* (verso of title).

   With ornamental initials W.G. at sides.

145. (178 × 132 mm.) Portrait of John Day, the printer, dated 1562.

1563 (March 30) by J. DAY. Fox (J.). *Acts and Monuments* (end).
*1563-4 by J. DAY. Becon (T.). *Works* (end of the *First and Third Parts).
1571 by J. DAY. Alley (W.). *The Poor Man's Library* (end).
    The block is cracked through the nose and beard.

146. (114 × 79 mm.) Device of boys throwing sticks at a tree.
    Cf. Nos. 96, 97.

*1563 by R. WOLFE. Musculus (W.). *Common places of Christian Religion.*
    In red and black. Within rules (127 × 95 mm.), enclosing type motto, as shown. The rules do not appear to be part of the block, but the device must have been intended to be framed in some way, as the foreground is otherwise incomplete.
1570 excusum apud R. WOLFE. Paris (M.). *Historia Maior* (col. on sig. 5Y8).
    Without rules round it or motto. The block is cracked vertically. The title-page is dated 1571.

147. (300 × 180 mm.) Compartment with figures with folded arms at sides, and fawns. Below, R. T., the initials of Richard Tottell.
    Compare the reduced copy, No. 196.

(α) With R. T. as figured.
*1565 in aed. R. TOTTELL. Fitzherbert (A.). *La Graunde Abridgement.*
1578 in aed. R. TOTTELL. Plowden (E.). *Les Commentaries.*
    ? Passed to Henry Denham at an unknown date.

(β) With R. T. voided.
1586 by H. Denham. Holinshed (R.). *Chronicle* (title to vol. ii).
    Also title to the *History of England* in vol. i, and to vol iii.

148. (164 × 107 mm.) Compartment with the Royal Arms at top and the Stationers' below. At the sides, the monogram of William Seres and four boys playing musical instruments.
    Cf. No. 139.

*1565-6 by W. SERES. Blundeville (T.). *The four chiefest Offices belonging to Horsemanship* (title of third part).
[1570] by W. SERES. Blundeville (T.). *The four chiefest Offices, etc.*

53

Probably passed to Henry Denham as Seres' assign in 1574.

1580 by H. Denham. Tusser (T.). *Five Hundred Points.*
 The colophon adds 'being the assigne of William Seres.'

1584 by H. Bynneman. Lupton (T.). *Siuqila.*
 One of Bynneman's copyrights, but probably finished by Denham after Bynneman's death.

1585 by H. Denham. Tusser (T.). *Five Hundred Points.*

Probably passed to Richard Yardley and Peter Short in 1589-90.

1593 by R. Yardley and P. Short. Blundeville (T.). *The four chiefest Offices belonging to Horsemanship.*
 Sayle 2323.

Passed to Humphrey Lownes in 1604.

1604 by H. Lownes for C. Burby. Hayward (Sir J.). *The Sanctuary of a troubled Soul.*
 Sayle 2473.

1609 by H. Lownes for the Comp. of Stationers. Blundeville (T.). *The four chiefest Offices belonging to Horsemanship.*

1615 for the Comp. of Stationers. *The Psalter after the translation of the Great Bible . . . With the Morning and Evening Prayer* (general title, and that of the *Psalter*).
 It still has Seres' monogram. The book was presumably printed by H. Lownes. On the title of the *Psalter* is the device of a shield with two keys (No. 373), and on sig. A 2 of the same an ornament with *Cor unum via una* (31 × 81 mm.) used by Lownes from 1611 to 1630.

149. (71.5 × 53.5 mm.) Framed device of a mermaid, with the Stationers' arms, the legend *Omnia Tempus Habent*, and the monogram of Henry Bynneman.
 Bynneman traded at the sign of the Mermaid from 1567 to 1580. Cf. No. 155.

1567 by H. Bynneman for L. Maylard. Epictetus. *Manual, trans. by J. Sanford.*

*1568 per H. Bynneman. Londinensis. *De Antiquitate Cantabrigiensis Academiae* (end).

1579 by H. Bynneman. Digges (L.). *An Arithmetical Military Treatise named Stratioticos* (end).

54

Probably passed to Henry Denham in 1583, and from him to Richard Yardley and Peter Short in 1589-90, and to Humphrey Lownes in 1604 (with Robert Young from *c.* 1625).

{ 1611 by H. L[ownes] for M. Lownes. Spenser (E.). *The Shepherd's Calendar.*

{ 1628 by H. L[ownes] and R. Y[oung]. B. (R.). *A Sixth Book to the Countess of Pembroke's Arcadia* (appended to the 1627 edition of the *Arcadia*).

It still has Bynneman's monogram.

*** A coarsely cut copy of the frame of this device is found on the title-page of the following:

[? *c.* 1592] for T. N. and I. W. *A Pleasant Comedy of Fair Em.*

It has the engraver's initials W. D., which are found on some inferior ornaments and borders used about 1590.

150. (36 × 36 mm.) Device of a star with *Os homini sublime dedit.*

The star was the sign of Henry Denham, 1560-89; cf. Nos. 211, 214.

The purport of the motto (from Ovid, *Met.* i. 85) is clear if the quotation is completed.

'Os homini sublime dedit, caelumque videre
Iussit, et erectos ad sidera tollere vultus.'

1566 H. Denham.   ?   ?
See *Bibl. Soc. Transactions,* iv. 117.

{ 1569 by H. Denham. Crowley (R.). *A Setting-open of the Sophistry of T. Watson* (end).

{ *1569 by H. Denham. Alessio, Piemontese. *The Fourth Book of Secrets* (end).

{ 1579 by H. Denham.   ?   ?
Bagford Collection, Harl. 5927, No. 260, a book by Abraham Fleming, ? *The Conduit of Comfort*: not *A Paradox . . . on Baldness.*

Probably passed to Richard Yardley and Peter Short in 1589-90, to Humphrey Lownes in 1604, and to Robert Young in 1625-30.

[? 1636] by R. Young. *The Way to True Happiness . . . by Questions and Answers.*

151. (111 × 80.5 mm.) Device of Lucretia with the name of Thomas Purfoot.

Cf. Nos. 161, 173. Thomas Purfoot senior and junior traded at the sign of Lucretia throughout the whole of their business careers.

{ *1566 by T. Purfoot and W. Pickering. Lindsay (Sir D.). *A Dialogue between Experience and a Courtier* (verso of title).
1573 by T. Purfoot. Fulke (W.). *Praelections upon the Revelation of St. John* (end).

152. (29 × 145 mm.) Ornament (? head-piece of a compartment), with a mask in centre and two fat boys holding pens, or palms, at sides: below them the letters I. D., presumably standing for the name of John Day. At the top E. B., perhaps the engraver.

{ 1563 by J. Day. Fox (J.). *Acts and Monuments* (sig. B2 verso).
*1564 by J. Day. Vermigli (P. M.). *Most Fruitful ... Commentaries* [*on Judges*] (end of prelims., sig. B4).
1573 by J. Day. Tyndale (W.). *The Whole Works of W. Tyndale, J. Frith, etc.* (sig. O4 verso and at end of Tyndale).

153. (91 × 91 mm.) Framed device of Christ with the lost sheep. The motto: *Periit et inventa est.*

Cf. Nos. 202, 207. The elephant below this device in its first state refers to Henry Wykes' sign of the Oliphaunt or Black Elephant in Fleet Street.

(α) With three faces in the border; a lion rampant and an elephant below.

{ 1567 by H. Wykes. Jewel (J.). *A Defence of the Apology of the Church of England.*
1571 by H. Wykes. Jewel (J.). *A Defence of the Apology of the Church of England.*

Probably passed to Ralph Newbery *c.* 1571.

{ ?1574 by H. Middleton for R. Newbery. Guevara (A. de). *Familiar Epistles* (end). Herbert, p. 902.
1577 by R. Newbery. Bullinger (H.). *Fifty Godly Sermons.*

Herbert, p. 904, says that this is without the elephant, but it has it in the B. M. copy. Qy. whether some copies may have the smaller device, No. 202.

Probably passed to Henry Middleton in 1577-8.

{ 1578 by H. Middleton for J. Harrison and G. Bishop. Calvin (J.). *Commentary on Genesis* (end).
*1579 for G. Bishop and T. Woodcock. Calvin (J.). *Sermons . . . on . . . Timothy and Titus.*

{ (β) The faces in border and rampant lion and elephant removed, and new pieces inserted (92.5 × 91 mm.).

1583 by H. MIDDLETON for G. Bishop. Calvin (J.). *Sermons upon . . . Deuteronomy.*
*1584 by H. MIDDLETON. Bullinger (H.). *Fifty Godly Sermons.*
1585 by H. MIDDLETON for T. Chard. Sandys (E.). *Sermons.*

154. (172 × 113 mm.) Compartment with the arms of the Stationers' Company at top and T. M. joined at foot, the initials of Thomas Marshe.

> *Note*: The imperfections towards the right end of the upper rule are due to a fault in the paper of the copy from which the facsimile was made.

(α) With T. M. as figured.

*1567 by T. MARSHE. Fenton (G.). *Certain Tragical Discourses.*
1567 by T. MARSHE. *Horace his Art of Poetry, etc., Englished by T. Drant.*
1584 by T. MARSHE. *The Famous History of Herodotus, translated by B. R.*
1584 by G. Dewes. Chaloner (T.). *A Short Discourse of . . . Nitre.*
> Probably printed by arrangement with Marshe.
1587 by H. Marshe, ass. of T. MARSHE. Higgins (J.). *The Mirror for Magistrates.*

Probably passed to Thomas Orwin in 1591.

(β) The T. M. voided.

1591 by T. ORWIN. Ripley (G.). *The Compound of Alchemy.*
> With 1591 in the oval below.

155. (55 × 43 mm.) Device of a mermaid with monogram of Henry Bynneman.

> Compare No. 149. It looks as if there had at one time been a legend around the figure, but I have only been able to find this device in a single work, and there it has none.

*1568 by H. BYNNEMAN for J. Wight. Alessio, Piemontese. *The Secrets of Alexis.* (First part) (end).

156. (39 × 29 mm.) A cut of a plant with R. I. in type at sides.

> Apparently from some herbal; but I have not succeeded in tracing it. Jones' intention in using it is obscure, and it is doubtful whether we are to regard it as a device or not.

*1572 by R. JONES. Heidelberg Catechism. *The Catechism or manner to teach . . . the Christian Faith* (end).

157. (38 × 46 mm.) Device of a griffin with '*Geve . God the Glorye Nowe . and : Ever . more.*'

 The Griffin was one of the signs used by William Gryffyth. See Nos. 144, 158.

*1570 by W. GRYFFYTH. Edwardes (R.). *A Book of very godly Psalms.*

158. (82 × 62 mm.) A cut of a griffin in a ruled border.

 Used with reference either to the name of William Gryffyth or to the sign at which he worked in the early days of his business; see Nos. 144, 157.

*1570 by W. GRYFFYTH. Bodonius. *The Fortress of Faith Defended* (end).

 John Rylands Library.

159. (67 × 58 mm.) Framed device of the sun with the letters M. S. W. and I. round about it.

 It is not clear whose device this was or what the letters mean.

*1571 by J. Kingston for W. Williamson. Northbrook (J.). *A brief and pithy sum of the Christian Faith* (end).

160. (116 × 76 mm.) Compartment with the Royal Arms at top, the Stationers' below, and at sides the initials I. A.

[? 1563] by J. ALLDE. *A treatise containing certain Meditations of Consolation.*
　　　　Sayle, 1291.

*1571 by W. Howe for J. ALLDE and W. Pickering. Knel (T.), junior. *A Declaration of Tempestious . . . Floods*, 1570.
　　　　G. J. Gray in *Bibl. Soc. Trans.* iv. 87, 88.

1584 by J. ALLDE. W. (A.). *A Book of Cookery.*
　　　　Bagford Collection, Harl. 5910, iv, No. 2.

161. (97 × 64 mm.) Device of Lucretia with *Lucretia Romana* in tablet below.

 Referring to the sign of Thomas Purfoot. Cf. Nos. 151, 173.

*1570 by T. PURFOOT. Evans (L.). *The Hateful Hypocrisy of the Romish Prelacy* (end).

1612 by T. PURFOOT. Baker (H.). *The Well Spring of Sciences* (end).

58

162. (263 × 182 mm.) Compartment with the Royal Arms above; the crest of Lord Burghley and a beehive below. At foot the initials H. D., and in the centre a star, Denham's sign.

> Note: In consequence of this compartment being considerably larger than the type-page of the *Alveary*, it has almost always been shaved by the binder, while the rule on the left-hand side is generally too far into the back of the book to photograph. In the present reproduction parts of the two side rules have been drawn in.

{ *[1573] by H. DENHAM. Baret (J.). *An Alveary*.
> Dedicated to William Cecil, Lord Burleigh.
[1580] excud. H. DENHAM. Baret (J.). *An Alveary*.

1596 by A. Hatfield for J. Norton. Comines (P.). *History*.
> The translation is dedicated to Lord Burghley, and it is no doubt for this reason that the compartment is used.

1601 by A. Hatfield for J. Norton. Comines (P.). *History*.

1614 for J. Bill. Comines (P.). *History*.
> It still has the initials H. D.

163. (72 × 51.5 mm.) A hooded hawk on a perch, with *Tenebras lux forte sequetur*, and a monogram apparently to be read as R. W. I.

> It seems possible that these letters may stand for 'Reginaldus Wolfius Impressor'—a designation which Wolfe used at least once, instead of the usual 'Typographus.' The block was perhaps an old one in 1571, as it appears to be worn.

{ 1571 by R. WOLFE. N. (A.). *Catechismus* (p. '190,' *i.e.* 160).
*1572 by R. WOLFE. N. (A.). *Catechismus* (p. 160).

164. (42.5 × 34.5 mm.) Device of an anchor with *Anchora Spei*.
> See No. 170.

{ *1574 by T. VAUTROLLIER. *Novum Testamentum* (T. Beza).
1587 by T. VAUTROLLIER. *Novum Testamentum* (T. Beza).

Passed to Richard Field in 1588-9.

{ 1593 by R. FIELD for T. Cooke. Burton (W.). *A Caveat for Sureties*.
1624 de l'imprimerie de R. FIELD. Camden (W.). *Annales . . . traduites . . . par P. de Bellegent*.

Passed to George Miller in 1624.

1625 by G. MILLER to be sold by R. Thrale. Desainliens (C.). *The French Littleton.*
    Bagford Collection, Harl. 5990, No. 70.
1644 apud G. M. pro A. Kembe. Cicero (M. T.). *Orationes.*
    Bagford Collection, Harl. 5990, No. 69.

Passed to Abraham Miller in 1646.

1647 by A. MILLER. G.D.L.M.N. [*i.e.*, G. Delamothe]. *The Treasure of the French Tongue.*

165. (36.5 × 30 mm.) Device of a pelican in her piety, on a shield of irregular outline.

    Cf. Nos. 123, 125.

1575 by R. JUGGE. Joseph ben Gorion. *A Compendious . . . History of the . . . Jews' common weal.*

    The upper scroll on the right hand side of the shield ends square, as that on the left.

Passed to William White, possibly by way of R. Watkins.

*1599 by W. WHITE. Peele (G.). *The Famous Chronicle of . . . Edward I.*
1604 by W. W. for T. Man. Hopkins (J.). *A Sermon before the King's Majesty.*
    Sayle, 2301.

166. (70 × 60 mm.) Framed device of a boy seated on a dolphin, encircled by a snake swallowing its tail. The motto *Immortality is gotten by the study of letters.* Below, an oval containing the monogram of WILLIAM and the sun, standing for the name of William Williamson, printer 1571-4. Within the oval is also the date 1573.

    The device is based on an emblem of Alciat (*Emblemata*, ed. 1574, p. 133, and in earlier editions), entitled ' *Ex literarum studiis immortalitatem acquiri,*' but the central figure is there a Triton, not a boy. This was used as a device by the printer Jean Waesberghe of Antwerp and Rotterdam, 1557-1588 (Silvestre, 1223).

(α) With monogram as figured.

*1573 by W. WILLIAMSON. Northbrook (J.). *The Poor Man's Garden* (end of prelims and *colophon).

60

(β) With monogram, but legend and date voided.

[? 1574] by W. WILLIAMSON. *Certain news of the whole description . . . of the Christian Princes . . . in the Low Countries.*

Sayle, 1796.

Passed to John Legate (I or II) at an unknown date.

1617 for T. Adams. Wirsung (C.). *The General Practise of Physic.*

Attributed to J. Legate by Mr. Sayle (No. 3765).

(γ) Sun alone in oval, no legend nor monogram.

1632 by J. L. for A. Hebb. Josephus (F.). *The Famous . . . Works* (title of *The Wars of the Jews,* facing p. 554).

1637-8 by J. LEGATE. Sandys (G.). *A Paraphrase upon Divine Poems.*

The colophon, dated 1637, gives the printer's name. The title, dated 1638, has 'At the Bell in St. Pauls Churchyard'—Andrew Hebb's address.

---

167. (60.5 × 56 mm.) Emblematic device of Fortune with a palm (?) in the right hand and a sword in the left, standing upon the globe; with *Fortuna* and T. M.

Probably copied from an emblem-book; but though somewhat similar designs are frequent I have not met with exactly this.

(α) With T. M.

*1574 apud T. MARSHE. Châteillon (S.). *Dialogorum Sacrorum libri quatuor.*

1577 apud T. MARSHE. Seton (J.). *Dialectica.*

Herbert, p. 866.

1584 by G. Dewes. Chaloner (Sir T.). *A Short Discourse of Nitre* (end of prelims.).

Perhaps printed by arrangement with Marsh.

Probably passed to Thomas Orwin in 1591 and to Felix Kingston in 1597.

(β) The T. M. voided.

1598 for M. Lownes. [Carew (R.).] *A Herring's Tail.*

1599 by F. KINGSTON for W. Aspley. Fenton (R.) *An Answer to W. Alablaster.*

---

168. (254 × 158 mm.) Compartment with cherub's head at top; flowers and fruit in the corners; a mermaid representing Bynneman's sign below.

(α) With the mermaid, as figured.

{ 1574 for H. Toy by H. BYNNEMAN. Whitgift (J.). *The Defence of the Answer to the Admonition.*

*1574 apud H. BYNNEMAN. Walsingham (T.). *Historia.*

1577 for G. Bishop. Holinshed (R.). *The First (Last) volume of the Chronicles.* Other copies are for Lucas Harrison.

Probably passed to Henry Denham in 1583.

(β) With the mermaid cut away.

1585 [? by H. Denham] Holinshed (R.). *Description of Scotland* (in vol. ii of the Chronicles, the general title of which is dated 1586).

The colophon of the volume, dated Jan. 1587, states that it was printed at the Star (H. Denham's sign) at the expenses of J. Harrison and others.

? Passed to Charles Yetsweirt, 1594.

1594 in aed. C. Yetsweirt. Plowden (E.). *La Second Part de les Reports* (fol. 402). The first title is dated 1599.

? Passed to Jane Yetsweirt in 1595.

{ 1595 in aed. Jane Yetsweirt. *Registrum Omnium Brevium.*

1596 in aed. Jane Yetsweirt. *Year-books,* 1-10 Ed. III.

? Passed to Thomas Wight or Bonham Norton in 1599.

{ 1599 in aed. T. Wight and B. Norton. Plowden (E.). *Les Commentaries ou reports.*

1605 in aed. T. Wight. *Year-books, Henry IV and Henry V* (sig. 3I6).

The later history of this compartment is obscure.

1609 for the Comp. of Stationers. *Le Premier Part des Ans del Roy Henri le 6.*

1622 by A. Islip. Malynes (G. de). *Consuetudo vel lex mercatoria.*

1623 for the Comp. of Stationers. Dalton (M.). *Officium Vicecomitum.*

1628 by G. M. for E. Brewster. Hildersham (A.). *Lectures upon the Fourth of John.* Also with date 1629.

1629 by A. Islip, to be sold by N. Bourne. Malynes (G. de). *Consuetudo vel lex mercatoria.*

1634 by J. Beale. Hall (J.). *Contemplations upon Holy History (Works,* vol. i, p. 929).

1634 by N. Okes for C. Bee. Polybius. *History.*

The preliminary leaves perhaps by Beale; see Sayle, 3696.

169. (120 × 78 mm.) Compartment having the Royal Arms at top and the Stationers' below, and the devices or rebuses of six printers at the sides.

The devices or rebuses are those of C. Barker (cf. No. 190), W. Norton (cf. Nos. 174, 175), Gerrard or Garrat Dewes (two men dicing in a garret

62

and casting a 'deuce,' or two; cf. Camden, *Remains*, ed. 1870, p. 181), J. Wight (see No. 205), J. Harrison (see No. 143), and R. Watkins (alluding presumably to the name 'Wat' applied to a hare, as in Shakespeare's *Venus and Adonis*, l. 697). These men were the assigns of Francis Flower, patentee for books in Latin, Greek, and Hebrew, and for grammars. For a larger size of the same design see No. 171.

{ *1574 excud. T. Vautrollier, per assignationem Francisci Florae. *Liber precum publicarum.*

1574 by THE ASSIGNS OF F. FLOWER. Lily (W.). *A Short Introduction of Grammar.*

170. (108 × 75 mm.) An anchor held from the clouds, with *Anchora Spei.*

The anchor as a symbol of Hope is of course derived from *Hebrews* vi, 19. It is one of the commonest and most obvious of emblems, but I have not found any particular source from which Vautrollier may have taken it. Cf. Nos. 164, 192, 195, 210, 222, 232, 233. It is pointed out by Mr. Roberts, *Printers' Marks*, p. 73, that the border of this device is a close copy of one used at Basle by T. Guarin in 1564 (see Heitz, *Basler Büchermarken*, No. 204).

{ *1574 excudebat T. VAUTROLLIER. Marlorat (A.). *Propheticae . . . Scripturae Thesaurus.*

1585 by T. VAUTROLLIER. Eusebius Pamphili. *The Ancient Ecclesiastical Histories.*

Passed to Richard Field in 1588-9.

{ 1590 by R. FIELD. Digges (L.). *An Arithmetical Warlike Treatise named Stratioticos* (sig. Q1 verso).

1619 by R. FIELD. Eusebius Pamphili. *The Ancient Ecclesiastical Histories.*

Passed to George Miller and Richard Badger in 1624.

{ 1629 by G. MILLER for R. Badger. Andrewes (L.). *XCVI Sermons.*

1633 by G. MILLER. Harington (Sir J.). *Most Elegant Epigrams*, at end of *Orlando Furioso*, 1634.

171. (163 × 107 mm.) Compartment with the Royal Arms at top, the Stationers' below, and the devices or rebuses of six printers at the sides.

Cf. No. 169. It has unfortunately been impossible to find a satisfactory copy of this print for reproduction. It probably dates from the same time as the smaller one, and was originally just as good a block.

63

1577 by THE ASSIGNS OF F. FLOWER. Lily (W.). *A Short Introduction of Grammar.*

*1588 by THE ASSIGNS OF F. FLOWER. Lily (W.). *A Short Introduction of Grammar . . . *Brevissima Institutio.*

172. (62.5 × 53 mm.) An angel crowned, holding in his right hand a blazing heart and in his left a cross.

The heart is labelled *Charitas*, the cross *Fides*, and elsewhere we read: *Victoria, Premiũ spes, Lumen Æternum, Dum tempus abemus offeremur donum, Diabolus*. By the feet of the angel is the monogram of Henrie Disle, and round the design the motto *Ego sum via et Veritas*. The device is perhaps intended to represent Religion treading the devil underfoot.

[? 1574] [? by H. DISLE] Rich (B.). *A right Excellent Dialogue between Mercury and an English Soldier . . . written in 1574.*

At Disle's address: The South-west Door of Paul's.

*1576 by H. DISLE. Edwards (R.). *The Paradise of Dainty Devices.*

1577 by H. DISLE. Edwards (R.). *The Paradise of Dainty Devices.*

Herbert, p. 685.

173. (67 × 51.5 mm.) Oval device of Lucretia, with the Stationers' arms above, and the initials T. P., standing for Thomas Purfoot, at the sides.

Cf. Nos. 151, 161.

*1574 excud. prelum T. Purfeetij. Corranus (A.). *Dialogus Theologus . . . quo Epistola Pauli ad Romanos explanatur* (end).

1608 by T. Purfoot. Desainliens (C.). *The Italian Schoolmaster* (end).

174. (69 × 53 mm.) Device of a cask or tun with a sweet-william growing through it. On the tun the word 'nor,' and on the root of the plant the letter W.

A rebus of the name William Norton; cf. Nos. 169, 171. Distinguished from the re-cutting, No. 175, by the S on the central flower.

1574 apud W. NORTON. Horatius Flaccus (Q.). *Poemata.*

Title in Bodleian, Douce Add. 142, under 'Norton.' No break on the right hand upper edge of cask.

64

{ *1587 by H. Middleton for W. Norton. Calvin (J.). *Institution of Christian Religion*.

1593 in aed. R. Field, imps. W. Norton. Kis (S.) Szegedinus. *Tabulae Analyticae*.
Some copies, 'imps. J. Oxenbridge,' have device No. 289.

Passed to Bonham Norton in 1594.

1596 by R. Field for B. Norton. Cogan (T.). *The Haven of Health*.
It still has W on the root.

175. (74 × 57.5 mm.) A tun with 'nor' and a sweet-william.

A re-cutting of No. 174, from which it is distinguished by the central flower of the sweet-william being without the letter S.

*1579 by T. Vautrollier for W. Norton. Guicciardini (F.). *History*.

The block apparently had a heavy rule all round, but part is masked out. Some copies of this book have the 'Anchora Spei' device, No. 170.

176. (99 × 70 mm.) Device of an anchor and brazen serpent upheld by hands emerging from clouds.

Copied from a device of Jean Crespin, printer at Geneva 1551-1571 (see Heitz, *Genfer Buchdruckerzeichen*, 47), with the initials of Thomas Bassandyne added. Compare Bassandyne's smaller device, No. 178.

*1574 Edinburgh: by T. Bassandyne. Lindsay (Sir D.). *The Warkis* (sig. P3 verso).

Britwell Court.

177. (27.5 × 36.5 mm.) A cut of Mars (?) in a car.

The zodiacal signs of the bull and the scorpion on the wheels of the car suggest that the cut originally belonged to some almanac, but I have been unable to trace any earlier occurrence of it. As used by East it is perhaps hardly to be considered a device, but as the sign at which he was trading in the years 1575-6 is unknown, it seemed better to include it.

{ *1575 by T. East. Borde (A.). *The Breviary of Health*.
{ 1576 by T. East. Rowlands (R.). *The Post of the World*.

178. (33 × 31 mm.) Device of an anchor and brazen serpent upheld by hands emerging from clouds.

Copied from a device of Jean Crespin, printer at Geneva 1550-1571 (see Heitz, *Genfer Buchdruckerzeichen*, 50; Silvestre, 891; and Dickson and

Edmond, *Annals*, p. 291), the initials T. B. being substituted for I. C. Compare the larger device, No. 176.

{ 1574 Edinburgh: by T. Bassandyne. Lindsay (Sir D.). *The Warkis* (title).
*1575 Edinburgh: by T. Bassandyne. *The CL. Psalms of David* (general title and title of *Catechism*).

179. (49 × 50 mm.) Ornament of a woman's head with cornucopias and the initials T. V.

The initials are perhaps type inserted in the block. There are a large number of blocks of this ornament which can only be distinguished by careful comparison; some may be metal, but the present at any rate was apparently a wood-cut, for later prints show horizontal cracks. Vautrollier had at least two blocks, one with initials and the other without (see below under 1585). Compare Andrew Hart's ornament, No. 378.

(α) With T. V. as figured.

{ *1575 by T. Vautrollier. Luther (M.). *Commentary upon Galatians* (verso of title).
1585 by T. Vautrollier. Eusebius Pamphili. *The Ancient Ecclesiastical Histories* (sigs. *3 verso and Yy3 verso).

On sig. Kk 5 verso is another block without T. V.

Passed to Richard Field in 1588-9.

(β) Without T. V.

{ 1602 by R. Field. North (Sir T.). *Lives of Epaminondas*, etc. (end).
1619 by R. Field. Eusebius Pamphili. *The Ancient Ecclesiastical Histories* (sigs. Ll2 verso, Yy1 verso).

Passed to George Miller (and Richard Badger) in 1624.

1637 by G. M. for the Comp. of Stationers. *The Whole Book of Psalms* (Sternhold and Hopkins; 12mo) (sig. E10 verso).

The block is here much worn; the lower part of the nose is gone.

180. (48 × 48 mm.) Framed device of Mars with sword and shield; with monogram T.M.

Probably used as a pun on the name Marshe.

(α) With monogram as figured.

{ *1574 apud T. Marshe. Palingenius (M.). *Zodiacus Vitae*.
1580 T. Marshe. Cicero (M. T.). *Sententiae Ciceronis*, &c.

Herbert, p. 868.

66

Probably passed to Thomas Orwin in 1591.

(β) Monogram voided.

1592 by T. ORWIN for I. B.   Warner (W.).   *Albions England.*

1592 excud. T. ORWIN.   Rhys (J. D.).   *Cambrobrytannicae Cymraecaeve Linguae Institutiones.*

Passed to Felix Kingston in 1597.

1598 by F. KINGSTON for H. Lownes.   R. (F.).   *Thule, Or Vertues History.*

181.   (162 × 104 mm.)   Compartment with the Royal Arms at top; a pelican in her piety at foot with, to left, Cupid (?) holding the letter R, and, to right, a nightingale in a (? thorn) bush, with the word 'Iugge.'

> The pelican was a device of Richard Jugge, cf. No. 125; and the nightingale is an allusion to his name, the word 'jug' being commonly used as an imitative representation of one of the notes of the bird's song.

*1575 [by R. JUGGE].   [Patten (W.)?]   *The Calendar of Scripture.*

Probably passed to Richard Watkins in 1579.

{ 1579 by R. WATKINS.   Petrarch (F.).   *Physic against Fortune.*
{ 1591 by R. WATKINS and J. Roberts.   D[ade] (J.).   *A triple Almanac,* and *A Prognostication for . . . MDXCI.*

> The printers are named in the imprint of the *Prognostication.*

? Passed to Thomas Dawson or William White c. 1598.

1610 imps. T. Adams.   Calvin (J.).   *A Harmony upon . . . Matthew, Mark and Luke.*

> The colophon of the second part—the *Commentary on St. John*—has 'by Thomas Dawson for Thomas Adams.'

> The Royal Arms are unaltered.

182.   (158 × 106.5 mm.)   Compartment with masks at top and sides, and, at foot, a nightingale in a thornbush.   The motto *Omne . bonū . supernæ.*

> The nightingale alludes to the name Jugge; cf. No. 181.

(α) With motto as figured.

{ *1575 by R. JUGGE.   *Bible* (title to the second part).
{ 1577 by R. JUGGE.   *Bible.*

Probably passed to Richard Watkins in 1579.

1591 for G. Simson and W. White.   Broughton (H.).   *Treatise of Melchisedek.*

67

1594 by R. WATKINS. Lewkenor (L.). *The Resolved Gentleman.*
Herbert, p. 1028.

? Passed to Thomas Dawson or W. White, *c.* 1598.

(β) With legend voided.

1605 for G. Bishop and T. Adams. Stow (J.). *Annals.*
Mr. Sayle (No. 1754) suggests T. Dawson as the printer.

1612 by N. Okes. Heywood (T.). *An Apology for Actors.*
I cannot explain the presence of the compartment in this book.

1612 by W. White. Broughton (H). *A Letter . . . touching Mardochai.*

1613 for T. Adams. Roesslin (E.). *The Birth of Mankind.*
Mr. Sayle (No. 3651) thinks it was probably printed by T. Dawson.

1627 for J. Parker and to be sold by G. Vincent. Sclater (W.). *An Exposition upon 1 and 2 Thessalonians.*
Mr. Sayle places this under M. Flesher (No. 4244).

---

183. (9 × 59 mm.) Ornament with mark of John Walley, printer, *c.* 1546-86.

The mark resembles that of Robert Wyer, No. 69.

1576 by J. WALLEY. *A brief Treatise containing many proper Tables* (sig. A4, and elsewhere).

*1579 by J. WALLEY. *A brief Treatise*, etc. (sig. A4).
Most of the rule at the left-hand end broke away in 1579-82.

1582 by J. WALLEY. *A brief Treatise*, etc. (sig. A4).

? Passed to John Charlewood in 1582-3.

1583 by J. Charlewood, ass. of R. Tottell. *A Book of Precedents* (on title).
Ames Collection, ii. 408.

---

184. (29 × 31 mm.) Ornament or device of a tiger's head, the crest of Sir Francis Walsingham, over a shield bearing the date 1576.

Alluding to Christopher Barker's sign, the Tiger's Head.

(α) With date as figured.

*1577 by C. BARKER. Frederic III, Elector Palatine. *A Christian Confession.*

1579 by C. BARKER. *Bible* (*New Testament*, sig. *2 verso).
B.M., 346. a. 4.

(β) With date voided.

1580 by C. BARKER. *The Third Part of the Bible.*

1583 by C. BARKER. Statutes. *Magna Charta to 23 Eliz.* (after table).

68

185. (121 × 73 mm.) Compartment with the Royal Arms at top, Sir F. Walsingham's crest of a tiger's head to left, and his arms to right. At the lower corners, to left, three tiaras, the arms of the Drapers' Company, with C. B.; to right the arms of the Stationers' Company.

> Christopher Barker was at one time a member of the Drapers' Company.

(α) With arms in lower corners as figured.

*1575 by C. BARKER. *The New Testament.*

(β) With the shields in the lower corners blank.

1579 by C. BARKER. Mornay (P. de). *A Treatise of the Church.*
1581 by C. BARKER. Charke (W.). *An Answer to a Seditious Pamphlet.*

> Probably lent to Ralph Newbery in 1581, and remained in his hands.

1581 by R. Newbery and H. Bynneman, ass. of Ri. Tot. and CHR. BAR. Lambard (W.). *Eirenarcha.*
1589 imps. G. Bishop. Ramus (P.). *Dialecticae libri duo.*
> Sayle, 1720.
1589 typis G. Bishop. Bèze (T. de). *Jobus.*
1591 excud. G. Bishop and R. Newbery. Lambard (W.). *Eirenarcha.*
1594 by R. Newbery. Lambard (W.). *Eirenarcha.*

186. (56 × 50 mm.) Device of time bringing truth to light, with *Tempore patet occulta veritas* and R. S.

> This was the device of C. Badius, printer, used at Geneva in 1554 (Heitz, *Genfer Buchdruckerzeichen*, No. 7). It is also said to have been the badge or impresa of Queen Mary, with the motto *Veritas temporis filia* (Camden, *Remains*, under 'Impreses'). Cf. Nos. 312, 331.

[1575] for R. SMITH. Gascoigne (G.). *Posies ... corrected ... by the Author* 1575.
*[1576] for R. SMITH. Gascoigne (G.). *The Steel Glass.*

> No date nor printer's name, but Gascoigne's *Phylomene*, the signatures of which are continuous with those of the *Steel Glass*, was printed by H. Bynneman in 1576.

187. (50 × 42 mm.) Framed device of woman with book labelled *Verbum Dei*, and candle. The motto *Vincet tandem Veritas*.

> Used by John Ross with the letters I. R. at the sides, apparently in type, but perhaps inserted in the block. Compare Ross's larger device, No. 189.

(α) With 'Verbum Dei' on the book, as figured.

{ *1575 by J. Ross. Scotland. *Statutes, James VI: In the Parliament at Striviling* 28 *Aug.* 1571.

1579 by J. Ross for H. Charteris. Smeton (T.). *Ad virulentum A. Hamiltonii dialogum responsio.*

Probably passed to Robert Waldegrave in 1590.

1590 excud. R. WALDEGRAVE. Damman (H.). *Schediasmata* (sig. A4).

{ (β) The words *Verbum Dei* removed from the book.

1590 excud. R. WALDEGRAVE. Rollock (R.). *In Epistolam Pauli . . . ad Ephesios . . . Commentarius.*

Probably passed to Thomas Finlason in 1604.

1612 excud. T. FINLASON. Hume (A.). *Prima elementa grammaticae.*

Probably passed to Robert Young, and from him to George Anderson in 1637.

1638 by G. ANDERSON. Abernethie (T.). *Abjuration of Popery.*

1638 by G. ANDERSON. Adamson (H.). *The Muses' Threnody.*

Used by A. Anderson in 1670 and by his Heirs and Successors in 1699 (H. G. Aldis).

188. (42 × 36 mm.) Framed device of a chariot drawn by dragons, the driver presumably being either Triptolemus or Demeter.

(α) With shading.

{ 1575 by R. W. Daneau (Lambert). *A Dialogue of Witches.*
    R. W. is presumably Richard Watkins.

*n.d. by R. W. Pettie (G.). *A Petite Palace.*
    B.M., G. 10442.

n.d. by R. W. Pettie (G.). *A Petite Palace.*
    B.M., C. 27. b. 16.

(β) With shading cut away.

*n.d. by R. W. Pettie (G.). *A Petite Palace.*
    B.M., C. 40. d. 5.

Probably passed to William White c. 1598.

{ 1600 by W. WHITE for W. F. Rowlands (S.). *Letting of Humours Blood.*

1614 by W. WHITE. *A Brief Discourse of the Scriptures: Declaring the . . . Lives . . . of the Fathers.*

Probably passed to John White *c.* 1617, and from him
to Augustine Mathewes in 1622-3.

{ 1623 by A. M. for J. Grismand.   Webster (J.).   *The Devil's Law-Case.*
Sayle, 4521.
1630 by A. M. for R. Hawkins.   Shakespeare (W.).   *Othello.*

189.   (96 × 72 mm.)   Framed device of woman with book labelled
Verbum Dei and candle.   The motto *Vincet tandem Veritas.*

When used by Ross it has I. R. at the sides, apparently in type, but perhaps
inserted into the block.   Compare the smaller device, No. 187.

(α) With 'Verbum Dei' on the book as figured.

{ 1575 by J. Ross.   Rolland (J.).   *The Court of Venus* (title and end).
{ *1579 by J. Ross.   Scotland.   *Statutes, James VI: In the Parliament at Striviling*
25 July, 1578.
1580 by J. Ross.   H. (P.).   *The Promine.*
Dickson and Edmond, No. 149.

? 1582 by H. Charteris.   Lyndsay (Sir D.).   *The Warkis.*
Possibly printed by Ross for Charteris in 1580; see Dickson and Edmond,
pp. 363-4.   Apparently the device has here I. R.

Probably passed to Robert Waldegrave in 1590.

1590 excud. R. WALDEGRAVE.   Damman (H.).   *Schediasmata* (sig. F2 verso).

{ (β) The words 'Verbum Dei' removed from the book.   The
bracket below remaining.
1592 excud. R. WALDEGRAVE.   Jacchaeus (T.).   *Onomasticon Poeticum.*
1594 excud. R. WALDEGRAVE.   Melville (A.).   *Principis Scoti-Britannorum Natalia.*

Probably passed to Thomas Finlason in 1604.

1620 by T. FINLASON.   Parisiis (———A).   *Consilia medicinalia* (verso of title).

Probably passed to Robert Young and from him to
George Anderson in 1637.

1638 [G. Anderson].   Scotland, Church of.   *Confessio Fidei Ecclesiae Scoticanae.*
No printer's name.   The legend *Vincet tandem Veritas* and the bracket on the
book remain as in 1592.

190.   (41.5 × 32.5 mm.)   A cut of a man barking logs, with motto
A Barker If ye will =
In name, but not in skill.

Alluding to the name of Christopher Barker; cf. Nos. 169, 171.

71

*1575 by H. Middleton for C. BARKER. Gascoigne (G.). *The Glass of Government* (at end of prelims., sig. A4 verso, facing A).

191. (61 × 53 mm.) Barker's smaller 'tiger's' head and lamb device.

    See No. 194.

*1576 by C. BARKER. *New Testament* (p. 813).

    The title is dated 1575, the colophon 1576.

192. (57.5 × 48.5 mm.) Framed device of an anchor suspended by a hand from the clouds, with *Anchora Spei.*

    See No. 170. Compare the recutting, No. 195.

*1576 by T. VAUTROLLIER. Calvin (J.). *Institutio Christianae Religionis.*

    The point before 'Anchora' disappeared in 1578-9.

1585 by T. VAUTROLLIER. Eusebius Pamphili. *The Ancient Ecclesiastical Histories* (sigs. R5 and Ll1).

    The device passed to Jacquelin Vautrollier in 1587.

1588 by J. VAUTROLLIER for R. Field. *The Copy of a Letter . . . to Don Bernardin Mendoza.*

    Passed to Richard Field in 1588-9.

1589 by R. FIELD. *The Restorer of the French Estate.*

1606 excud. J. Norton. Horatius Flaccus (Q.). *Poemata.*

    Title-page in Ames Collection, ii. 107; but this imprint seems to occur on books printed *for* Norton, not by him; see *Dictionary I*, p. 204.

1623 by R. FIELD for N. Newbery. Du Moulin (P.). *The Buckler of Faith.*

    Passed to George Miller (and Richard Badger) in 1624.

1642 by G. M[ILLER] for W. Lee. Warde (H.). *The True Protestant Soldier.*

193. (35 × 35 mm.) Ornament of a woman's head between two cornucopias: below it the letters C. B.

    The initials are perhaps type inserted in the block.

(α) With C. B. as figured.

1577 by C. BARKER. Frederic III, Elector Palatine. *A Christian Confession* (end).

1579 by C. BARKER. *Bible* (*New Testament*, sig. *4).

    B.M., 394. a. 4.

(β) Without C. B. or the lower tassel; reduced in size to 31 × 35 mm.

1581 by C. Barker. *Bible* (8vo).
    B. and F. Bible Soc. Cat.
1582 by C. Barker. *Bible* (fol.) (sig. ¶3).
    B.M., 348. b. 2 (1).

      Probably passed to Robert Barker in 1599.

1617 apud J. Bill. England, Church of. *Doctrina et Politia Ecclesiae Anglicanae* (p. 271).
1637 by R. Barker and the ass. of J. Bill. *The Book of Common Prayer* (4to) (sig. C3 verso).

194.   (82.5 × 70 mm.) Framed device of a 'tiger's' head with a ducal coronet about his neck, erased out of a mural crown, with a crescent for difference, being the crest of Sir Francis Walsingham. Below the tiger's head is a lamb, and on a scroll joining the two the motto: '*Tigre: reo. animale del. Adam. vecchio. figliuolo ∼ merce. l' euangelio ∼ fatto. n'estat. agnolo.*'

    The word 'agnolo' was found to be an error, and the part of the scroll bearing it (all behind the lamb) was cut out and replaced by a new one with 'agnello.'

    Cf. No. 191, the same device in a smaller size.

(α) With 'AGNOLO.'

*1576 by C. Barker. *Bible* (at end of *New Testament*).
    B.M., 3052. e. 10.

(β) With 'AGNELLO.'

1576 by C. Barker. *Bible* (at end of *New Testament*).
    B.M., 1214. k. 6.
1583 by C. Barker. *Bible* (at end of *Prayer Book* and of *Old Testament*).
    B.M., 675. e. 18.

195.   (55.5 × 47 mm.) Framed device of an anchor with *Anchora Spei*.

    A recutting of No. 192. In this the foreheads of the two figures at the sides are much less bulgy, and the o of ANCHORA does not touch the cloud.

*1628 for R. Badger and are to be sold by J. Stempe. Davenant (J.) *One of the Sermons preached at Westminster.*

Probably passed to George Miller *c*. 1630.

1634 by G. MILLER. Borrough (P.). *Method of Physic*.

1679 sumps. J. Dunmore, etc. Suarez (F.). *Traĉtatus de Legibus*.

196. (225 × 142 mm.) Compartment with figures with folded arms at sides, and fawns. Below, R. T., the initials of Richard Tottell.

A roughly cut copy in a reduced size of No. 147 (reversed).

{

1576 (Oĉt. 12) in aed. R. TOTTELL. Brook (Sir R.). *La Graunde Abridgement* (both parts).

*1579 [in aed. R. TOTTELL]. Plowden (E.). *Cy ensuont certeyne Cases*.

Forming the second part of Plowden's *Commentaries*, 1578.

1587 by R. TOTTELL. *Le Longe Report de Anno Quinto Edwardi quarti*.

197. (86 × 68 mm.) The burning bush in frame with date 1576.

It is doubtful whether this is to be considered as a printer's device, or as an ornament or emblem especially cut for the *Loci Communes*. It does not seem to have been used elsewhere.

*1576 ex typ. J. KINGSTON. Vermigli (P. M.). *Loci Communes*.

198. (44 × 30.5 mm.) Rebus and mark of Hugh Singleton with *God is my Helper*.

Cf. his earlier device, No. 127; also No. 250. In 1579 he was trading at the sign of the Golden Tun.

{

*1578 by H. SINGLETON. Robinson (R.). *A Dial of Daily Contemplation* (end).

1579 by H. SINGLETON. Spenser (E.). *The Shepherds' Calendar* (end).

199. (49 × 45 mm.) Crest of George Clifford, Earl of Cumberland: Out of a ducal coronet or, a wyvern rising gules.

Nothing seems to be known of the circumstances under which Aggas made use of the Earl of Cumberland's crest as his device.

{

1578 for E. AGGAS. Ratcliffe (Æ.). *Politique Discourses*.

*1588 by T. Orwin for T. Cadman and E. AGGAS. La Noue (F. de). *Politic Discourses* (end).

The title is dated 1587, the colophon 1588.

[? 1590] for E. AGGAS. C. (E. D. L. J.). *A Catholic Apology*.

200. (74 × 61.5 mm.) Arms: ermine, on a chief indented two eaglets; crest, out of a ducal coronet an eagle rising ermine; motto: *Mihi Vita Christus*.

> Presumably the arms of John Day; see Berry, *Encyclopedia Heraldica*, under the name of Day (London).
>
> Cf. No. 245; the arms (presumably) of his son Richard.

{ 1577 by J. DAY. *A Catechism or Institution of Christian Religion* (end).
> Herbert, p. 662.

*1578 by J. DAY. Nowell (A.). Χριστιανισμου στοιχειωσις (end).

201. (51 × 47 mm.) Rebus of Thomas Dawson and Thomas Gardiner.

> Apparently cut for use as a factotum initial rather than as a device.

*1577 by T. DAWSON and T. GARDINER. S. (C.). *The Testimony of a True Faith* (sig. B9).
> With T. D. T. G. in the square.

1577 for J. Harrison and G. Bishop. Calvin (J.). *Commentary upon . . . the Corinthians* (as a factotum initial on sigs. A1 and Cc8).

Gardiner died or retired from the partnership in 1577 or 1578.

{ 1579 by T. DAWSON for R. Sergier. Knewstub (I.). *An Answer unto certain Assertions* (end).
> With T. D. alone in the square.

1592 by T. DAWSON for R. Watkins. Bravonius (F.). *Chronicon ex Chronicis* (as a factotum initial on sig. A1).

202. (64 × 55 mm.) Framed device of Christ with the lost sheep. The motto: *Periit et inventa est*.

> Cf. Nos. 153, 207.

(α) With a face at top of frame.

*1578 typis H. MIDDLETON, imps. G. Norton. ?   ?
> Book unknown. Bagford Collection, Harl. 5963, No. 183. The print is torn at corners.

(β) The face at top cut out and an ornament with leaves inserted.

*1579 excud. H. MIDDLETON, imps. C. B. *Testamenti Veteris Biblia Sacra* (parts 2, *3, 4).
> The general title is dated 1580.

(γ) The leaves at top cut away, reducing size to 62 × 55 mm.

*1580 excud. H. MIDDLETON, imps. C. B. *Testamenti Veteris Biblia Sacra* (general title).

Also title of the *Novum Testamentum* belonging, which has 'Excudebat T.V. Typographus impensis C. B.'

1582 by R. Newbery and H. Bynneman. Jewel (J.). *View of a Seditious Bull.*

1583 by R. Newbery and H. Bynneman. Jewel (J.). *Exposition upon . . . Thessalonians.*

1583 excud. H. MIDDLETON, imps. T. Man. Bright (T.). *Medicinae therapeuticae pars: de Dyscrasia.*

1584 by R. Newbery. Jewel (J.). *Exposition upon . . . Thessalonians.*

1585 excud. H. MIDDLETON, imps. J. Harrison. Ovidius Naso (P.). *Opera.*

1587 by R. Newbery and H. MIDDLETON. Lambard (W.). *The Duties of Constables.*

Passed to Robert Robinson in 1588.

1591 excud. R. ROBINSON. Cicero (M. T.). *Epistolae ad Familiares.*

1592 by R. ROBINSON for T. Man and J. Porter. Perkins (W.). *A Case of Conscience.*

Probably passed to Richard Bradock in 1597-8.

1607 by R. B. for T. Pavier. Smith (H.). *God's Arrow against Atheists.*

? Passed to J. Legate II at an unknown date.

(δ) The inserted piece at top fallen out.

1635 for J. L[egate] and R. Mab. Austin (W.). *Devotionis Augustinianae Flamma.*

203.   (73 × 62 mm.)   A phoenix looking at the sun.

Copied, with the omission of a winged globe and motto, from a device used by Gabriele Giolito de' Ferrari, of Venice, in Castiglione's *Cortegiano*, 1544, the *Dialoghi di M. Lodovico Domenichi*, 1562, etc. (different from that reproduced in *Bibl. Soc. Trans.*, x. 91). In the *Emblemata* of J. Sambucus, ed. 1569, p. 28, under the heading *Nimium Sapere*, the phoenix looking at the sun appears as an emblem with the lines:

Cominus adversum qui spectat lumine Phoebum
Nititur et radiis vincere, caecus abit.

But the first edition of Sambucus was not till 1564.

*1578 by H. BYNNEMAN. Harvey (G.). *Gratulationes Valdinenses* (end).

1579 by H. BYNNEMAN. Digges (L.). *An Arithmetical Military Treatise named Stratioticos* (end).

1581 by R. Newbery by ass. of H. BYNNEMAN. Bateman (S.). *The Doom Warning all Men to the Judgement*, p. 25 (as an illustration).

76

1581 by R. Newbery. Anderson (A.). *A Sermon preached at Pauls Cross the 23 of April* (end).

Herbert, p. 908.

204. (301 × 190 mm.) Compartment with the Royal Arms at top between Justice and Mercy (?). A lion and a dragon at foot, and C. B., the initials of Christopher Barker.

Compare the quarto comp., No. 220.

(α) With arms of Elizabeth at top, etc., as figured.

1578 by C. BARKER. *Bible* (gen. title, and before *New Testament*).

*1583 by C. BARKER. *Bible* (before the *Apocrypha*).

1591 by the deputies of C. BARKER. *Bible* (before the *New Testament*).

Passed to Robert Barker in 1599.

1602 by R. BARKER. *Bible* (before *Apocrypha*).

(β) With arms of James I replacing those of Elizabeth at top, and the dragon at foot replaced by a unicorn. The initials C. B. remain.

1616 by R. BARKER. *Bible* (A.V.) (gen. title and before *New Testament*).

1618 by B. Norton and J. Bill. *The Statutes at Large.*

(γ) With a new lower block, having a lion and a unicorn, both facing outwards, instead of the lion and the dragon. No initials.

1632 by R. BARKER and the ass. of J. Bill. *Bible* (before *New Testament*).

205. (81.5 × 68.5 mm.) A man in a gown carrying a book lettered 'Scientia'; beside him the letters I. W. with the motto *Welcom the wight: that bringeth such light.*

The figure is regarded as a portrait of the printer John Wight, 1551-1589. Cf. Nos. 169, 171. The small rose at the foot of the border represents the sign at which he worked.

*1578 by T. Dawson for J. WIGHT. Alessio, Piemontese. *Third Part of the Secrets.*

1586 for J. WIGHT. Heresbach (C.). *Four Books of Husbandry* (end).

∗ This device is sometimes found set in a compartment (168 × 117 mm.) with figures of Grammatica and Rhetorica at the sides; a tablet with date above, and one with the imprint below.

{ 1584 by T. East for J. WIGHT. Bourne (W.). *A Regiment for the Sea* (end).
  Herbert, p. 783.
{ 1587 by T. East for J. WIGHT. Bourne (W.). *A Regiment for the Sea* (end).
  In this, part of the compartment above and to the left of the device is broken away or fails to print.

206.   (57 × 48 mm.) Device of a black horse upon a wreath with *Mieux vault mourir ē vertu que vivre en honēte.*

The crest of Thomas East, printer, 1567–1609. See the arms of John East in *The Visitation of London*, 1633-4, i. 245 (Harleian Soc., vol. xv).

{ *1579 by T. EAST. Guido de Cauliaco. *Guido's Questions.*
{ 1581 by T. EAST for G. Cawood. Lyly (J.). *Euphues* (end of Part 1).

207.   (30.5 × 26.5 mm.)   Framed device of the lost sheep.

Cf. Nos. 153, 202.

{ 1579 ex. off. H. MIDDLETON for J. Harrison. Ravisius (J.), Textor. *Epithetorum Epitome.*
{ *1582 by H. MIDDLETON, imps. G. Bishop. Humphreys (L.). *Jesuitismi pars prima.*

Probably passed to Robert Robinson in 1588.

{ 1589 by R. ROBINSON and T. Newman. White (T.). *A Sermon . . . 17 Nov.* 1589.
{ 1591 by R. ROBINSON. Manuzio (P.). *Epistolae.*

Probably passed to Richard Bradock in 1597-8.

{ 1598 by R. BRADOCK. Bell (T.). *The Hunting of the Romish Fox.* Sayle, 1993.
{ 1600 by R. B. for G. Seaton. Westerman (W.). *Two Sermons of Assise.* Sayle, 2570. Mr. Sayle assigns this book to R. Barker.

1607 for W. Cotton. Powel (G.). *The resolved Christian.* Sayle, 7521.

1612 for N. Butter. Sheldon (R.). *The Motives of R. Sheldon.* 'Probably printed by Stansby.' Sayle, 3088; but Bradock was still in business at this date.

208.   (85 × 71 mm.) Framed device of Christ rising from the tomb, a palm branch in his hand, and treading upon a skeleton signifying death, and a dragon signifying the devil. About it,

78

*Confidite vici mūdū . Ioa . 16 : Vbi tua mors victoria? 1 . Cor : 15 :
Conteret caput tuū . Gen . 3 : Ero morsus inferni tuus . Oze . 13.*
Above and below, *Jesus Christus.*

> The cut corresponds so well with the subject of J. Foxe's *Christ Jesus Triumphant*, J. and R. Day, 1579, on the verso of the title of which it occurs (Herbert, 667-8), that it seems by no means improbable that it was designed especially for this work. It appears, however, to have been first used in the preceding year.

1578 ex. off. J. DAY. *Doctissimi cuiusdam viri Tractatus contra Missae Sacrificium* (appended to P. Baro's *Praelectiones in Ionam,* 1579. The *Tractatus* is dated 1578 on the title-page and 1579 at end).

1584 by J. DAY. Latimer (H.). *Fruitful Sermons* (end).

Probably passed to John Windet in 1584.

1588 by J. WINDET. B. (S.). *The Razing of the Foundations of Brownism.*

*[1594] by J. WINDET. Hooker (R.). *Of the Laws of Ecclesiastical Polity.*

1595 by J. WINDET for ass. of R. Day. *Psalms (Sternhold and Hopkins).*

1605 for the Co. of Stationers. *Psalms (Sternhold and Hopkins).*

Probably passed to William Stansby in 1611.

1626 for the Co. of Stationers. *Psalms (Sternhold and Hopkins).*

1634 by W. S. for the Co. of Stationers. *Psalms (Sternhold and Hopkins).*

> Sayle, 3196.

209. (79 × 63 mm.) The arms of Thomas East: A chevron between three horses' heads erased, a crescent for difference.

> For the arms see those of John East in *The Visitation of London,* 1633-4, i. 245 (Harleian Soc., vol. xv).

*1579 by T. EAST. Viret (P.). *The Christian Discipline* (end).

1596 by T. EAST for T. Wight. Hood (T.). *The Mariner's Guide* (end).

210. (34.5 × 29.5 mm.) Device of an anchor with two sprays of foliage in a border with horn-like projections. The motto, *Anchora Spei.*

> Compare No. 170.

(α) With T. V. as figured.

*1579 excud. T. VAUTROLLIER. Cicero (M. T.). *Rhetoricorum ad C. Herennium libri quatuor.*

> The upper horn on the left hand disappeared in 1583-4.

1587 excud. T. VAUTROLLIER imps. W. Norton. Cicero (M. T.). *Orationes.*

Passed to Richard Field in 1588-9.

(β) Without T. V.

1589 excud. R. FIELD imps. J. Harrison. Osorius (H.). *De Gloria.*
1616 excud. R. FIELD. Cicero (M. T.). *Orationes.*
1619 for R. Milbourne. Dyke (Jer.). *A Counterpoison against Covetousness.*

Probably passed to George Miller and Richard Badger in 1624.

1625 for P. Stephens and C. Meredith. Horn (R.). *The Shield of the Righteous.*

211. (81 × 61 mm.) Framed device of a star in an oval, with the motto *Os homini sublime dedit*; the arms of the City of London above, the Stationers' arms below, and H. D. at sides.

See No. 150.

1579 by H. DENHAM, being the assign of W. Seres. *The Psalter* (8vo) (col. on Q4 verso).
The depression in the upper rule is as in the facsimile.

*1580 by H. DENHAM. Salvianus, Massiliensis. *A Second and Third Blast of Retrait from Plays* (end).
The device cracked vertically (cf. *Bibl. Soc. Trans.*, iv. 126) in or before 1584 (Caradoc, *Hist. of Cambria*).

1587 imps. H. DENHAM (and others). Holinshed (R.). *Chronicles* (Colophon of vol. ii).
Printed at the sign of the Star.

Probably passed to Richard Yardley and Peter Short in 1589-90.

1594 by P. SHORT for assigns of R. Day. Becon (T.). *The Sick Man's Salve* (end).
1602 by P. SHORT. Marbury (F.). *A Fruitful Sermon . . . preached at the Spittle* (end).

Probably passed to Humphry Lownes in 1604.

1609 by H. L[OWNES] for M. Lownes. Spenser (E.). *The Faery Queen* (end).
1611-12 by H. L[OWNES] for M. Lownes. Spenser (E.). *The Faery Queen,* etc. (p. 364).

212. (19 × 68 mm.) Ornament of foliage with, in the centre, Sir Francis Walsingham's crest: out of a mural coronet a tiger's head ducally gorged.

Cf. Nos. 296, 323, and for Christopher Barker's use of this crest, Nos. 183, 185, 191, 194.

80

*1582 by C. BARKER. *Bible* (Sig. ¶3 verso).

    B.M., 348. b. 2(1).

1612 excud. W. I. H. (Fr.). *Poemata Miscellanea* (Sigs. A3, B6 verso).

    Qy. for R. Barker? The book contains another ornament, No. 248, which was apparently his.

1627 for T. Jones and J. Marriott. Lucan. *Pharsalia* (trans. *T. May*) (Sigs. a2 and A1).

213. (67 × 48 mm.) The arms of Christopher Barker.

    See the arms of his grandson Matthew in *The Visitation of London*, 1633-5 (Harleian Soc., xv, 1880), i. 47, and those on his funeral monument as described by Lipscomb, *Buckinghamshire*, iv. 440.

*1580 by C. BARKER. *The third part of the Bible* (end).

214. (69 × 52 mm.) Framed device of a star in an oval, with the motto *Os homini sublime dedit.*

    Compare Nos. 150 and 211.

*1581 by H. DENHAM. 'Augustine, Saint.' *A precious book of Meditations. Saint Augustine's Prayers. *St. Augustine's Manual.* (At the end of each.)

1586 by H. DENHAM.   ?   ?

    Bagford Collection, Harl. 5927, No. 249: book not identified.

        Probably passed to Richard Yardley and Peter Short in 1589-90.

1590 by R. YARDLEY and P. SHORT for ass. of W. Seres. *Psalms of David* (Beza and Tremellius) (end).

1602   ?   ?

    Bagford Collection, Harl. 5993, No. 86: on yellow paper; book not identified. The block is cracked.

215. (37 × 37 mm.) Ornament of a lion's face over a shield, two owls, and the initials H. M.

(α) With H. M.

1580 by H. MIDDLETON imps. I. H. Osorius (H.). *De Gloria* (end).

1580 excud. H. Denham, ass. of W. Seres. *Psalmi Davidis . . . illustrati ab I. Tremellio et F. Junio* (end).

    Middleton's name does not appear, but one must suppose him to have been somehow connected with the Book.

*1583 excud. H. Middleton imps. T. Man.   Bright (T.).   *Medicinae Therapeuticae Pars* (p. 13).

1587 by H. Middleton for W. Norton.   Calvin (J.).   *The Institution of Christian Religion.*

? Passed to Nicholas Okes.

(β) Without H. M.

1609 by N. Okes for C. Knight.   Tichborne (J.).   *A Triple Antidote.*

1612 by for [sic] W. Barrenger.   Daborn (R.).   *A Christian turn'd Turk.*

1622 [no printer or publisher].   *An Answer to the Hollanders' Declaration.*

1648 for R. Best.   *His Majesty's Final Answer concerning Episcopacy, delivered 1 Nov. 1648.*

216.   (42 × 32 mm.)   A fleur-de-lis seeding.

Copied from one of the devices of the Giunta family (cf. No. 298).   It appears most to resemble the central part of a device of Jacques de Junte, printer at Lyons, 1533-46; see Silvestre, 449 (cf. also Silvestre, 707); but there may be others which it approaches still more closely.   In 1581-2 it is used with VBIQVE FLORESCIT, and in 1583 with VBIQVE FLORET, up and down the sides in type; later generally without a motto.

1581 appresso G. Wolfio [*i.e.*, J. Wolfe].   Ubaldini (P.).   *La Vita di Carlo Magno.*

*1582 by J. Wolfe.   Strigelius (V.).   *Part of the Harmony of King David's Harp.*

1600 by J. Wolfe.   Clapham (H.).   *Antidoton . . . against Schism.*

Sayle, 1986.

Perhaps passed to Ralph Blower in 1601.

n.d. by R. B. for T. Man.   Arthington (H.).   *The Seduction of Arthington by Hacket.*

The B.M. Catalogue dates this book 1592, that being perhaps the date of the first appearance of the work, but it seems probable that it is a good deal later.   The R. B. is presumably Ralph Blower, who was using another of Wolfe's fleur-de-lis devices in 1609 (see No. 298).

217.   (37 × 35 mm.)   Device of three lilies on one stalk, thorns growing about the base; with *Sicut lilium inter spinas Cant.* 2.

It is stated by Herbert (p. 680) that Richard Day used this device of three lilies on one stalk as his sign, but this appears to be an inference from the device.   I have seen no book in which his address is so given.

*1580 apud R. Day.   Baro (P.).   *De Fide.*

82

218. (119 × 75 mm.) Compartment with the Royal Arms and supporters at top between two female figures with cornucopias. In lower corners, two other females with agricultural implements. At the sides, the monogram and mark of Henry Denham; and below, the arms of the Stationers' Company.

*1579 by H. Denham, the assign of W. Seres. *The Psalter.*

From a copy in the possession of Mr. E. F. Bosanquet. A title-page probably from the same setting of type, save for the imprint, which runs 'Imprinted at London by E. S. for the assigne of Wylliam Seres,' is in a collection of title-pages at the British Museum (618. k. 17), fol. 38. I do not know for what name the initials E. S. can stand.

219. (47 × 34.5 mm.) Ornament of a cherub's head on a bracket.

It is doubtful whether this should be regarded as a device or not, but it may have been so used by William Kearney, whose sign is unknown. It is perhaps a cast block. It is impossible to be sure that the blocks used by Vautrollier and Kearney are identical; but, if not, they must have been cast from the same matrix.

1581 by T. Vautrollier. Mulcaster (R.). *Positions* (sig. **1 verso).

{ *1591 by W. Kearney. Smith (H.). *The Magistrate's Scripture.*

{ 1592 by W. Kearney. Broughton (H.). *An apology . . . defending that our Lord died in the time properly foretold.*

Kearney probably took the block with him to Ireland in 1593.

1602 Dublin: by J. Franckton. *New Testament.*

Cf. *Bibl. Soc. Trans.,* viii. 226.

220. (170 × 120 mm.) Compartment with Royal Arms at top between Justice and Mercy (?). Lion and dragon in lower corners. At foot the initials C. B., standing for the name of Christopher Barker.

Compare Barker's folio compartment, No. 204, and Bynneman's, No. 230.

*1579 by C. Barker. *Bible* (4to) (general title and before *New Testament*).

During, or before, the printing of the 1583 *Bible* the block cracked vertically (2 mm. to r. of centre at top, and 7 mm. to l. of centre at foot). Several other cracks appeared later.

1595 by the deputies of C. Barker. *Bible* (4to).

1600 by R. BARKER.   *The Book of Common Prayer with the Psalter* (4to).
  Sayle, 7414.

1626 by B. Norton and J. Bill.   *The Book of Common Prayer with the Psalter* (4to).
  The C. B. and the arms remain as in 1579.

221.   (157 × 106 mm.)   Compartment with the Queen's arms at top, Fides and Humilitas at sides; the ensigns of the four evangelists at the corners, and a tiger's head, the crest of Sir F. Walsingham, below.

(α) With tiger's head as figured.

{ *1579 by C. BARKER.   *Bible* (4to) (*Psalter*, at end of *Book of Common Prayer*).
  B.M., 347. a. 3 (1).
{ 1583 by C. BARKER.   *Articles to be enquired* . . .

{ 1588 by the deputies of C. BARKER.   *A Form of Prayer* . . . *for the present time.*
  Sayle, 7294.
{ 1597 by the deputies of C. BARKER.   *Certain Prayers for her Majesty's Forces and Navy.*

  Probably passed to Robert Barker in 1599.

(β) With the arms of James I replacing those of Elizabeth at top. The tiger's head voided.

[? 1603-4] by R. BARKER.   *A form of Prayer with Thanksgiving to be used* . . . *the 24 of March.*
  Sayle, 2579.

1616 par J. Bill.   *La Liturgie Anglaise.*

1618 by B. Norton and J. Bill.   *A form of Prayer with Thanksgiving* . . . *for the fift of August.*

1620 by R. BARKER and J. Bill.   *Prayers and Thanksgiving* . . . *for* . . . *the 5 of November, 1605.*

1631 by R. BARKER and the ass. of J. Bill.   *New Testament.*
  Ames Collection, ii. 975.

1639 by R. BARKER and the ass. of J. Bill.   *Book of Common Prayer.*

222.   (71 × 59 mm.)   An anchor held by a hand from the clouds, with *Anchora Spei.*
  Cf. No. 170.

{ 1581 by T. VAUTROLLIER.   Mulcaster (R.).   *Positions.*
{ 1585 by T. VAUTROLLIER.   *The Ancient Ecclesiastical Histories* (sigs. Vv2 and Zz1).

{ 1589 by R. FIELD. *The Art of English Poesie.*
*1594 for A. Wise. Nashe (T.). *Christ's Tears over Jerusalem.*
1619 by R. FIELD. Eusebius Pamphili. *The Ancient Ecclesiastical Histories* (sigs. R4, Kk5, etc.).

Passed to George Miller and Richard Badger in 1624.

{ 1629 by G. MILLER for R. BADGER. Buckeridge (J.). *A Sermon at the Funeral of Lancelot Andrewes* (appended to the 1629 ed. of Andrewes' *Xcvi Sermons*).
1630 by G. MILLER. Slatyer (W.). *Genethliacon.*

Probably passed to Richard Badger alone in 1630.

{ 1631 by R. BADGER. Buckeridge (J.). *A Sermon ... Andrewes* (appended to the 1631 ed. of Andrewes' *Xcvi Sermons*).
1635 by R. BADGER. Andrewes (L.). *Xcvi Sermons.*

223. (74 × 48 mm.) Device of a sheep at the base of a plant in which is entwined a scroll bearing the legend *Virgula divina.* At the base a tablet with: *Sub hac patienter vivit ovis. I. B.*

> For the *virgula divina* compare Silvestre, 1063. I cannot say whether this is a device of the publisher F. Bouvier, or of John Jewel, in whose book it appears; nor can I interpret the initials I. B.

*1584 apud F. Bouvier. [Jewel (J.).] *Apologia Ecclesiae Anglicanae.*

224. (77 × 101 mm.) Device (?) of the sun with radiant beams, a rose, a sunflower, and the initials H. K., standing for Henry Kirkham, bookseller 1570-93.

> Kirkham's sign was The Black Boy, and I do not know what, if anything, is signified by the sun, etc. The corner of the leaf on which this device appears is wanting in the only print of it which I have been able to find.

*[? *c.* 1580] for H. KIRKHAM. Ryce (R.). *An Invective against Vices taken for Virtue* (end).

225. (67 × 55 mm.) Framed device of a pelican in her piety.
See the larger device, No. 228; cf. Jugge's device, No. 123.

(α) As figured.

{ 1579 Edinburgh: by A. Arbuthnet.   *Bible* (end of prelims.).
  *1582 Edinburgh: apud A. Arbuthnet.   Buchanan (G.).   *Rerum Scoticarum Historia* (*end of prelims. and end).
  1584 Edinburgh: by A. Arbuthnet.   Statutes.   *In the Parliament haldin at Edinburgh, May 22, 1584* (title and end).

   Passed to Thomas Finlason at an unknown date.

(β) With name, one initial, engraver's mark, and shield voided.

{ 1604 Edinburgh: T. Finlason.   *Miraculous . . . union of England and Scotland.*
      Aldis, 383.
  1609 Edinburgh: by T. Finlason.   Skene (Sir J.).   *Regiam majestatem Scotiae Veteres Leges* (end, ' *Commissa et Omissa* ').

226.   (78 × 57 mm.) Framed emblematic device of serpents and toads (representing calumny and envy) about the roots of a palm tree with *Il vostro malignare non giova nulla.*

   See Whitney, *Emblems*, p. 118, 'Invidia integritatis assecla,' from Adrianus Junius, *Emblemata*, ed. 1569, No. 9.   The device seems to have been originally cut, like Nos. 249 and 252, for use in John Wolfe's Italian books with fictitious imprints.

1584 Palermo, Appresso gli heredi d' Antoniello degli Antonielli.   Macchiavelli (N.). *Discorsi*, and *Il Principe.*

   Printed, as the book which follows, in England, probably by John Wolfe.

1587 Palermo, Appresso Antonello degli Antonelli.   Macchiavelli (N.).   *Dell' Arte della Guerra* (cancel title on T4).

{ *1593 by J. Wolfe.   Harvey (R.).   *Philadelphus.*
  1593 by J. Wolfe.   Harvey (G.).   *Pierce's Supererogation.*

   Passed to Adam Islip.

{ 1594 by A. Islip.   Clerke (W.).   *Trial of Bastardy.*
  1616 by A. Islip for T. Adams.   Huarte (J.).   *Examen de Ingenios.*
  1681 for J. W. and sold by Langley Curtis.   *Reasons for his Majesty's passing the Bill of Exclusion.*

   U. L. C.   The device is cracked.

227.   (41 × 35 mm.)   Device of a swan standing on a wreath, within a border of intertwined snakes: a man's head below.   The motto: *God is my Helper.*

   It may be suggested—but merely as an unsupported guess—that there is

86

possibly some connection between this device and a mysterious incident alluded to in Martin Marprelate's *Hay any Work for Cooper* (ed. Petheram, p. 68). Martin is giving a list of the occasions when Waldegrave has been imprisoned by the ecclesiastical authorities. Among them he mentions 'that time when he was straungely released by one of the Lorde of good Londons [*i.e.*, the Bishop of London's] Swans.' Nothing further is known about the matter, but so far as can be made out the imprisonment alluded to must have taken place at about the date when Waldegrave adopted the swan as his device. As used by Waldegrave the device sometimes has *God is my Defender* in type at the sides.

Note: A device almost exactly similar to this, save that the head below is that of an old man, is found in editions of Sternhold and Hopkins' paraphrase of the *Psalms* appended to certain Geneva bibles having Barker's imprint and the date 1599, but supposed to have been printed later at Dort. See *B. and F. Bible Soc. Cat.*, p. 117, No. 194.

1583 by R. WALDEGRAVE. Gerardus (A.), Hyperius. *The Foundation of Christian Religion.*

> Sayle, 1895.

1587 by R. WALDEGRAVE for T. Man. W. (T.). *A Christian Exposition upon certain verses of Romans viii.*

Probably passed to Thomas East in 1603.

{ 1603 T. EAST.   ?   ?

> Sayle, p. 317.

1606 by T. E. for T. Man. Dod (J.) and Cleaver (R.). *A Plain ... Exposition of Proverbs IX and X.*

> Sayle, 1616.

Probably passed to Thomas Snodham in 1609.

*1612 for W. Welby. Greenham (R.). *Works* (general title).

> Mr. Sayle attributes this to T. Snodham (p. 708). Parts ii–iv (dated 1611) are printed by T. Creed, and the text of Part i seems to be by the same printer. The preliminaries may, however, be Snodham's work.

{ 1613 by T. SNODHAM. S. (W.). *True History of Thomas Lord Cromwell.*

1624 excud. T. SNODHAM. Seneca (L. and M. A.). *Tragediae.*

Passed to Thomas Harper ? 1629.

{ 1629 by T. HARPER for R. Allot. Sclater (W.). *Three Sermons.*

1634 excud. T. HARPER. Lucian. *Dialogorum Selectorum Liber Primus.*

> Bagford Collection, Harl. 5990, No. 147.

1638 imps. E. Blackmore. Mason (F.). *Vindiciae Ecclesiae Anglicanae.*

> Apparently only a cancel title for Kingston's edition of 1625.

1639 by T. HARPER and R. Hodgkinson. Du Bosc (J.). *The Complete Woman.*

1641 'at London.' Jonson (B.). *The Devil is an Ass.*

> In vol. ii of his *Works.*

228. (111 × 85 mm.) Framed device of a pelican in her piety.

Closely copied from Jugge's device, No. 125. At top the name of Alexander Arbuthnet, and at foot his initials and arms. The block is signed A. VL., which is thought to stand for the name of Assuerus vol Londersel, a Flemish artist who executed woodcuts for Nicolas de Nicolay's Travels printed at Antwerp in 1576 (Dickson and Edmond, *Annals*, p. 317).

Compare Arbuthnet's smaller block, No. 225.

[? 1580 Edinburgh: by A. ARBUTHNET. *The Buik of Alexander the grit*] (sigs. G5 verso, Ff6 verso).

See Dickson and Edmond, p. 326.

*1582 Edinburgh: apud A. ARBUTHNET. Buchanan (G.). *Rerum Scoticarum Historia.*

229. (34 × 34 mm.) Framed device of a hind on a wreath with *Cerva charissima et gratissimus hinnulus. Pro. 3.*

The crest of Sir Christopher Hatton.

*1582 ex off. H. BYNNEMAN. Neville (A.). *Kettus, sive de furoribus Norfolciensium.*
1582 apud R. Newbery, ex ass. H. BYNNEMAN. Ockland (C.). *Anglorum Praelia.*
1583 by H. BYNNEMAN. Stanyhurst (R.). *First Four Books of Vergil.*

230. (169 × 114 mm.) Compartment with the Royal Arms between Fame and Victory at the top; the Stationers' arms, a lion, and a dragon below. The initials H. B.

Various dates are inserted in type in the tablet at foot.

Compare the very similar compartment owned by Christopher Barker, No. 220.

(α) With H. B. as figured.

1581 by H. BYNNEMAN and R. Newbery. John, Chrysostom. *Exposition upon the Epistle to the Ephesians.*
*1582 by R. Newbery. Fenton (G.). *Golden Epistles.*

Ralph Newbery and Henry Denham were working at this date as Bynneman's deputies.

Probably passed to Henry Denham in 1583.

(β) With B cut out and D inserted in type.

1584 by R. Newbery and H. DENHAM. Caradoc. *The History of Cambria.*

88

Probably passed to Peter Short and Richard Yardley in 1589-90.

1595 by E. Allde. *Certain Sermons or Homilies* (title to each volume).

    There seems to be no indication of Denham or Short having any connection with this book.

(γ) The space at first occupied by B left blank.

  1595 by P. SHORT for S. Waterson. Daniel (S.). *First four books of the Civil Wars.*
    T. C. C. Apparently a re-issue with new title, cf. Corser, *Collectanea Anglo-Poetica*, iii (part 5), 28-9.
  1599 by P. S. for S. Waterson. Daniel (S.). *Cleopatra.*

    The later history of the compartment is obscure.

(δ) A hand inserted in the space formerly occupied by the B.

1614 for the Co. of Stationers. *The Whole Book of Psalms* (Sternhold and Hopkins).

1615 by E. Allde for C. Knight. Maxwell (J.). *Admirable and notable Prophecies.*

(ε) The space again left blank.

1637 for the Co. of Stationers. *The Whole Book of Psalms* (Sternhold and Hopkins).
    B.M., 472. a. 10(2).

231. (177 × 107 mm.) Compartment with the Royal Arms at top; four biblical scenes at sides, and, half way up, the letters H. D., standing for Henry Denham. Below, the Church(?) as a female figure with a seven-branched candlestick and a book; to left and right the arms of London and of the Stationers' Company.

*1582 by H. DENHAM. Bentley (T.). *The Monument of Matrons.*

    Probably passed in 1589-90 to Richard Yardley and Peter Short and, in 1604, from Short to Humphrey Lownes.

*** The head- and foot-pieces of the compartment used separately.

  1609 for M. Lownes. Edmondes (C.). *Observations upon Caesar's Commentaries.*
    Head-piece on sig. A2.
  1624 by H. LOWNES for N. Newbery. *A True Relation of the Unjust Proceedings . . . at Amboyna.*
    Head-piece on sig. B1; foot-piece on A1.

    Passed to Robert Young in 1625-30.

1632 in aed. R. YOUNG imps. J. Davies. Davies (J.). *Antiquae Linguae Britannicae . . . Dictionarium.*
    Head-piece on sig. *2; foot-piece on sig. *3.

1636 by the assigns of J. More. Coke (Sir E.). *La Size Part des Reports.*
    Head-piece on sig. O4 verso.

232. (58.5 × 44.5 mm.) Device of an anchor upheld by a hand from the clouds, with *Anchora Spei*.

> Cf. No. 170.

*1584 Edinburgh: by T. VAUTROLLIER. James VI. *The Essays of a Prentice*.

233. (35.5 × 26.5 mm.) Device of an anchor held by a hand from the clouds, with *Anchora Spei*.

> The roughest of Vautrollier's anchor devices. Cf. No. 170.

*1584 Edinburgh: by T. VAUTROLLIER. Musculus (W.). *The Temporisor*.

> Probably passed to Richard Field in 1588-9, and from him to George Miller in 1624.

1637 by G. MILLER. Bolton (R.). *A Short . . . Discourse . . . concerning Usury*.

> Passed from George Miller to Abraham Miller in 1646.

1649 excud. A. MILLER. Macropedius (G.). *Methodus de Conscribendis Epistolis*.

234. (48 × 36 mm.) Arms of the University of Cambridge in an oval.

> This block looks somewhat like a binding stamp—or a cast from one; but I cannot learn of any binding on which it appears.

*1584 Cambridge: ex off. T. THOMAS. Bright (T.). *In Physicam G. A. Scribonii Animadversiones*.

235. (16 × 15.5 mm.) A small fleur-de-lis with rule border.

> Probably used by Wolfe as a device. Cf. No. 251.

*1584 by J. WOLFE for T. Cooke. Gifford (G.). *A Sermon on the Sower*.

236. (23 × 23 mm.) Device of three cranes and a vine.

> The sign of Thomas Dawson, printer, 1568-1620. Compare the larger one, No. 241.

1587 imps. G. Bishop. Foxe (J.). *Eicasmi seu Meditationes in . . . Apocalypsin*.

*1588 excud. T. DAWSON ex ass. C. Barker. I. (S. A.). *Carminum Proverbialium . Loci Communes*.

237. (33 × 27 mm.) A shield charged with a pair of wings and the word *Sursum* in pale.

1586 by J. WINDET. Norden (J.). *A Mirror for the Multitude.*
      With *Non vi, sed veritate* up and down the sides in type.

*1590 for T. Cooke. Hood (T.). *The Use of the Celestial Globe in plano.*
      No motto at sides.

Probably passed to William Stansby in 1611.

1621 apud W. STANSBY. [Butler (C.).] *Rhetoricae libri duo.*
      Ames Collection, ii. 597.

1627 excud. W. STANSBY. Smith (S.). *Aditus ad Logicam.*

238. (51 × 51 mm.) Framed device of a pheasant upon a wreath within an ornamental frame, at the sides of which are the initials R. W., standing for the name of Robert Ward.

(α) With initials R. W.

[? 1585 by R. WARD. Lambard (W.). *The Duties of Constables, Borsholders, etc., Collected . . . 1582.*

1589 by R. WARD for T. Cadman. Blundeville (T.). *A brief description of Universal Maps.*

*1590 by R. WARD for J. Sheldrake. Du Chesne (J.). *The Sclopotary of J. Quercetanus.*

Probably passed to Abel Jeffes c. 1595.

(β) Initials voided.

1596 by A. JEFFES. *The Pleasant History of Lazarillo de Tormes, trans. by D. Rowland.*

Perhaps passed by way of William and John White to Augustine Mathewes in 1622.

1622 by A. Mathewes for J. Marriott, J. Grismand, and T. Dewe. Drayton (M.). *The Second Part . . . of Poly-olbion.*

1626 by I. N. to be sold by H. Perry. *Englishmen for my Money.*
      Perhaps printed by Mathewes for John Norton, junior. The two men seem to have been working in partnership at about this date.

239. (55.5 × 60 mm.) Framed device of Abraham and Isaac with *Deus providebit. Gene. Cha.* 22.
      This is apparently one of the devices used in common by the printers at the Eliot's Court Press; see note on this press.

91

*1585 apud J. Jackson pro G. Bishop. Rebuffus (P.). *Tractatus de decimis* (apx. to
Duarenus (F.), *De Sacris Ecclesiae Ministeriis*, imps. G. Bishop).

1585 apud E. Bollifant, imps. H. Denham and R. Newbery. Ponticus (L.). *Britanniae Historiae libri sex* and *Itinerarium Cambriae* (parts of same work).

1589 per E. Bollifant. Livius (T.). *Titi Livii . . . libri omnes quotquot ad nostram
aetatem peruenerunt*.

    The colophon has in some copies 'impensis G. Bishop,' in others 'impensis
R. Watkins.'

1590 imps. G. Bishop. Camden (W.). *Britannia* (before 'Hibernia ').

1590 imps. J. Harrison. Verro (S.). *Physicorum . . . libri x.*

    Bagford Collection, Harl. 5993, No. 89. Qy. also imps. G. Bishop; see
Harl. 5936, No. 259.

240. (63 × 51 mm.) Framed device of a lion passant crowned
and collared, a mullet for difference, on an anchor; with *Desir n'a
repos*, and the date 1586.

    I have been unable to ascertain whose arms or crest this device repre-
sents.

(α) As figured.

*1586 per R. NEWBERY. Camden (W.). *Britannia* (on title and also before
'Hibernia ').

1587 by R. NEWBERY. Bullinger (H.). *Fifty Godly Sermons.*

(β) Date and legend cut out, leaving blanks.

1634 Cambridge: apud T. Buck and R. Daniel. Davenant (J.). *Determinationes
Quaestionum Quarundam.*

    Bagford Collection, Harl. 5929, No. 403. Other copies have device
No. 327.

241. (47.5 × 49 mm.) Device of three cranes and a vine.

    Representing the Three Cranes in the Vintry, the address of Thomas
Dawson, printer, 1568-1620. Compare the smaller one, No. 236.

*1587 by T. DAWSON. Laudonnière (R. de). *A Notable History containing Four
Voyages.*

1607 by T. D[AWSON] for C. Burby. Smith (H.). *Two Sermons of Jonah's Punish-
ment.*

242. (82 × 61.5 mm.) Device of a fleur-de-lis with cherubs at top, and a satyr and a human figure at foot. The motto: *Ubique floret*. The block is signed G. B.

> Presumably copied, like Nos. 216, 294, and 298, from one of the Giunta devices, but I have found none which exactly resembles it.

{
*1586 by J. WOLFE for the assigns of R. Day. *Psalms (Sternhold and Hopkins)* (8vo) (recto of last leaf).

1588 'Anversa Il di primo di Gennaio.' Ubaldini (P.). *Descrittione del Regno di Scotia.*
> One of Wolfe's books with a fictitious imprint.

1591 by J. WOLFE. Loque (B. de). *Discourse of Warre and Single Combat, trans. by J. E.*
}

243. (80.5 × 62 mm.) Framed device of Time with a wheatsheaf and bible. *Verbum Dei manet in æternum* [1 Peter i. 25], I.W., and *Non solo pane vivet homo : Luke* 4. In the frame the Royal Arms and those of London and the Stationers' Company. Below, a white bear.

> The bear represents the sign at which John Windet, printer, 1584-1611, worked until about 1589.

(α) With I. W.

{
*1585 by J. WINDET for A. Maunsell. Rogers (T.). *The English Creed.*

1585 by J. WINDET. Augustine, Saint. *The Glass of Vain Glory* (end).

1591 by J. WINDET. Turnbull (R.). *An Exposition upon . . . St. Jude* (end).
}

> Probably passed to William Stansby in 1611.

(β) I. W. voided.

1628 W. STANSBY for N. Butter. Hall (J.). *Works* (end of 'First Tome' [Contemplations, lib. xxi] facing general Alphabetical Table).

244. (68 × 54 mm.) A wreath enclosing armorial bearings—fretty with a martlet for difference.

> I have been unable to identify the arms.

{
*1587 by R. ROBINSON. [Broke (A.).] *The Tragical History of Romeus and Juliet.*

1588 by R. ROBINSON. Bellot (J.). *The French Method.*
}

93

245. (50 × 38 mm.) A framed shield with armorial bearings.

> Presumably the arms of Richard Day, but I have been unable to verify this. Compare the arms of his father, John Day, No. 200.

*1585 by the assigns of R. Day. Becon (T.). *The Sick Man's Salve* (end).

245*. (67 × 66 mm.) A framed shield with armorial bearings.

> Presumably the arms of Richard Day, but differing from No. 245 in the third coat.

{ 1586 by J. Wolfe for the assigns of R. Day. *Psalms (Sternhold and Hopkins)* (8vo) (end).

1591 by J. Wolfe for the assigns of R. Day. *Psalms (Sternhold and Hopkins)* (end).
> Sayle, 7329.

246. (31.5 × 29 mm.) A griffin seated on a stone (or a book ?) under which is a ball with wings.

> Copied from a device of Sebastian Gryphius, printer at Lyons 1529-1550 (Silvestre, 486). Compare the larger device, No. 339.

1587 excud. T. Vautrollier. 'H KAINH ΔIAΘHKH (fols. 48, 130, 282, 309 verso).

> Probably passed to Richard Field in 1588-9.

1602 [no place or printer]. [Watson (W.).] *A Decacordon.*
> B.M. queries Douay; Sayle (6848) suggests R. Field.

1604 for G. Bishop. Sutcliffe (M.). *A full and round answer to N.D.*

1605 by R. Field. G. D. L. M. N. [*i.e.*, G. Delamothe]. *The French Alphabet.*
> Bagford Collection, Harl. 5990, No. 59.

> Passed to George Miller and Richard Badger in 1624.

*1627 apud G. Miller. Echlin (D.). *Periurium Officiosum.*

1633 by G. Miller for E. Brewster. Hildersam (A.). *A Sermon at Ashby Church,* Oct. 4, 1629.
> Appended to his *Doctrine of Fasting.*

> Passed to Abraham Miller in 1646.

1647 by A. Miller, to be sold by T. Underhill. G. D. L. M. N. [*i.e.*, G. Delamothe]. *The French Alphabet.*

247. (71 × 67 mm.) A cock on a wood-pile, with *Cantabo Iehovæ qui benefecit mihi.*

> A rebus on the name Woodcock.

{ *1587 by T. Dawson for T. Woodcock. Bourne (W.). *The Art of Shooting in great Ordnance.*

1589 by T. O[rwin] for T. Woodcock. Virgilius Maro (P.). *Bucolics . . . together with his Georgics, trans. by A. F.*

248. (36.5 × 36 mm.) Ornament of a two-tailed mermaid blowing two horns. A fringe of tassels below.

To be distinguished from No. 259, a much simpler form of the same idea. So far as I have observed, there is only one block of this; but its apparent use by William Jones in 1612 is puzzling.

1586 by C. Barker. C. (R.). *The Copy of a Letter to the Earl of Leicester.*

*1587 typis G. Bishop. Lively (E.). *Annotationes in quinque priores ex minoribus prophetis.*

1589 excud. G. Bishop and R. Newbery. *Antimartinus.*

[1593] by the deputies of C. Barker. *An Apology for Sundry Proceedings by Jurisdiction Ecclesiastical* (Part ii).

The first part is dated 1593.

Probably passed to Robert Barker in 1599.

1612 excud. W. I. H. (Fr.). *Poemata Miscellanea.*

T. C. C. Perhaps *for* Barker, but it was licensed to W. Jones, as well as presumably printed by him. It contains another ornament, No. 212, which may have been Barker's.

1616 by R. Barker. *Constitutions and Canons Ecclesiastical . . . by the Bp. of London.*

1617 apud J. Bill. England, Church of. *Doctrina et Politia Ecclesiae Anglicanae* (pp. 77, 123 and end).

1618 by B. Norton and J. Bill. *A Declaration of the Demeanor of Sir W. Ralegh.*

1619 by B. Norton and J. Bill. *A Declaration of his Majesty's Pleasure . . . in matter of Bounty.*

1640 by R. Barker and the ass. of J. Bill. *A Grant of the Benevolence . . . to his Majesty by the Clergy of Canterbury.*

249. (36 × 53.5 mm.) Device of two 'sea-goats' or *capricorni*, supporting a vase with their tails. The motto *Sic semper ero.*

A copy of the lower part of the device of Domenico Giglio used at Venice in 1552, which is itself modelled on one of the Giolito devices (*Bibl. Soc. Trans.,* x. 98). Apparently first used in John Wolfe's Italian books.

(α) With D. G. F. on the vase.

*1588 'In Roma.' Macchiavelli (N.). *L'Asino d'Oro* and *Clitia*.

Probably printed by J. Wolfe in London.

? Passed to Robert Waldegrave, or to Ralph Blower.

(β) Initials D. G. F. voided.

1603 Edinburgh: by R. WALDEGRAVE. Alexander (W.). *The Tragedy of Darius*.

On verso of title the Scoto-Danish arms 118 × 86 mm. I cannot explain the occurrence of this device here if the book was really printed in Edinburgh, nor that of the arms if it was printed in London. It may be noticed that two other devices of Wolfe's (Nos. 216 and 298) apparently came into the hands of Ralph Blower, who perhaps owned this one in 1606.

1606 by R. B. for W. Ferbrand. Dekker (T.). *News from Hell*.

' R. B.' was perhaps Ralph Blower. See note above.

Passed to Augustine Mathewes at an unknown date.

{ 1622 by A. MATHEWES for T. Dewe. 'Shakespeare (W.).' *First and Second Part of the Troublesome Reign of King John.*

*1633 typis A. MATHEWES. Wotton (Sir H.). *Ad regem è Scotia reducem.*

1636 for J. Grismond. Ward (S.). *A Collection of such Sermons . . .* (facing p. 34).

250. (24 × 24 mm.) Framed device of a tun with the monogram H. S.

The rebus of Hugh Singleton. Cf. Nos. 127, 198.

{ *[? c. 1583] by H. SINGLETON. Lemnius (L.). *The Sanctuary of Salvation.*
Bagford Collection, Harl. 5995, No. 25.

{ 1588 by J. Windet for H. SINGLETON. Oldcastle (H.). *A Brief Instruction . . . how to keep books of Accompts* (end).

? 1591 by R. Robinson. Nordon (J.). *A Pensive Man's Practice.*

Herbert, p. 1234. 'Singleton's rebus.' I have not seen the book, and cannot say which of Singleton's three devices is meant.

251. (27 × 26 mm.) Ornament of a fleur-de-lis.

This was presumably cast, and there seem to be two or more blocks, which are exceedingly difficult to distinguish, as they only differ in details of shading. It must, however, count as a device, as it was used by John Wolfe and N. Okes, both of whom used other forms of the fleur-de-lis on their productions.

In the following notes I have differentiated those prints in which the shading

96

of the central stem slopes downwards from right to left (as in the facsimile) from those in which it slopes from left to right. But there may well have been more than one block of each type.

*** From right to left.

*1591 per J. WOLFE, a spesi di G. Casteluetri. Guarini (B.). *Il Pastor Fido.*

Passed to Adam Islip ? *c.* 1593-4.

1598 by A. ISLIP for E. Blount. Marlowe (C.). *Hero and Leander.*

Passed to Richard Hearne in 1639.

1640 by R. HEARNE. *The Expert Gardener* (Part iii of *The Countryman's Recreation*).

*** From left to right, somewhat smaller, 25.5 × 24 mm., and more roughly cut.

1586 by J. WOLFE. Lloyd (L.). *The Pilgrimage of Princes.*
1589 by J. WOLFE. *The Contre-League* (trans. by E. A.).

1592 by R. Bourne and J. Porter. Perkins (W.). *An Exposition on the Lord's Prayer.*

1609 by N. OKES for W. Welby. Bell (T.). *A Christian Dialogue.*
1634 by N. OKES. *Albumazar, a Comedy.*

1629 by J. Norton to be sold by M. Law. Shakespeare (W.). *Richard III.*
    John Norton was in partnership with Nicholas Okes from some time before 1634, and later with his son John. *Cf.* No. 381.
1638 by J. Norton for A. Crooke. Killigrew (H.). *The Conspiracy, a Tragedy.*

252.   (39 × 27 mm.) Device of a phoenix rising from flames which issue from the mouth of an urn supported on the shoulders of two satyrs. The mottoes: *Dela mia morte eterna vita i vivo: Semper eadem.* On the vase the initials G. G. F.

This is closely copied from a device used by Gabriel Giolito de' Ferrari, printer at Venice, 1539-78, in *La Vlyxea de Homero,* 1553 (facsimile in *Bibl. Soc. Trans.,* x. 105), the *Dialoghi de M. Lodovico Domenichi,* 1562, and elsewhere. It is undoubtedly a different block. In the original the left wing of the bird touches the scroll; the shading of the urn differs, and that below the ground-line is much less prominent. It seems to have been originally cut, as were Nos. 226 and 249, for use in Wolfe's Italian books.

1587 'In Piacenza appresso gli heredi de Gabriel Giolito de Ferrari.' Macchiavelli (N.). *Historie.*

Probably printed at London by J. Wolfe.

1600 'B. Sermartelli, Florence.' C[hambers] (R.). *Palestina.*

Probably secretly printed in England.

*1611 At Britain's Burse for J. Budge. *A True Transcript . . . of his Majesty's Letters Pattent for . . . the . . . Register for . . . Commerce.*

1612 [no place or printer]. Vives (J. L.). *De Disciplinis.*

1613 by W. Stansby, imps. J. Budge. Aretius (J.). *Primula Veris* (title on B4).

1619 Cambridge ex off. C. Legge. Angelus (C.). Ἐγχειριδιον (*Enchiridion de Institutis Græcorum*). In Greek and Latin. (Title-page to each part.)

[? 1621] Th[orius] (R.). *In obitum Jo. Barclaii Elegia.* No printer. In the B.M. copy, the only one I have seen, the date is cut off.

253. (86 × 61 mm.) Device of a bell with *Praise the Lorde with Harpe and Songe.* In the upper corners the arms of London and those of the Stationers' Company: in the lower, the initials A. I.

The bell alludes to the Christian name of Abel Jeffes. Cf. No. 279.

{ 1587 by A. JEFFES to be sold by T. Woodcock. Boccaccio (G.). *Thirteen most pleasant . . . questions . . . Philocopo* (end).

*1589 by A. JEFFES. Ascham (R.). *The Schoolmaster* (end).

254. (42 × 37.5 mm.) A phoenix in flames emerging from a vase which is supported on the shoulders of two satyrs holding roses (?). *Della mia morte eterna vita vivo,* and *Semper eadem. T.O.*

A rough copy of one of the devices of Gabriele Giolito de' Ferrari, printer at Venice—or perhaps rather combined from two of his devices (cf. *Bibl. Soc. Trans.,* x. 105 and 95), with the initials of Thomas Orwin in place of G. G. F. Cf. No. 252.

*1589 by T. ORWIN for T. Man and T. Cooke. Ive (P.). *The Practice of Fortification.*

1589 apud T. ORWIN. Leland (J.). *Principium ac illustrium Virorum Encomia,* (sig. P 1).

1589 ex aed. T. ORWIN imps. T. Man and R. Gubbin. La Ramée (P. de). *Grammatica.*

Herbert, p. 1243.

255. (123 × 74.5 mm.) Compartment with the Royal Arms above; at the sides, Moses and David; below, the Stationers' Arms with the initials H. D. and a star.

The compartment was obviously made for Henry Denham, who traded at the sign of the Star and must date from before 1589, when he went out of business.

Note: The only print of the block which I was able to find is in bad condition. In reproducing it, it has been necessary slightly to touch up David's face, the surface of the paper being there worn away.

[Before 1589: see above.]

> Probably passed to Peter Short and Richard Yardley in 1589-90.

*1594 by P. SHORT for the assigns of R. Day. Beacon (T.). *The Sick Man's Salve.*

256.   (111 × 62 mm.)   Compartment with the Royal Arms at top; David and Goliath below; four small pictures and the initials H. D. at the sides.

In general character the compartment resembles those used by Denham in the *Monument of Matrons*, 1582 (see No. 231), and it was probably cut at about the same date. In any case it must date from before 1589, when Denham went out of business.

[Before 1589: see above.]

*1598 [?   ]. P[arsons], (R.).   *A Book of Christian Exercise* (general title).

The first part has merely 'Imprinted at London,' as shown; the second 'Printed by I. Roberts for Simon Waterson.'

257.   (61 × 56.5 mm.)   Framed device of a right hand pointing to a star, with *Deus Imperat Astris* and R. D.

The right hand obviously alludes to the name of Richard Dexter, but the meaning of the star has not been explained: Dexter's sign was the Brazen Serpent. Is it fanciful to suggest that it may be an allusion to the blazing star which was seen from 10 to 21 October 1580? Dexter was apprenticed from Michaelmas of that year and he may have taken it as an omen of good fortune.

1590 for T. Cooke and R. DEXTER.   Hood (T.).   *The Use of the Jacob's Staff.*

*1596 by R. Field for R. DEXTER.   Hood (T.).   *The Use of two Mathematical Instruments* (sig. B4).

1597 by the Widow of T. Orwin, imps. R. Jackson and R. DEXTER.   Foord (J.). *Apocalypsis Jesu Christi.*

99

258. (38 × 24 mm.) A fleur-de-lis roughly cut, with two marigolds (?).

At its first appearance this was perhaps merely an ornament, but as it was afterwards used by John Wolfe, whose numerous devices were all forms of the fleur-de-lis, it seems proper to include it. In the *Heroical Devices of C. Paradin*, 1591, p. 331, a similar fleur-de-lis with marigolds, crowned, is given as the impresa of Magaret of Navarre and Margaret of France. The block is different from that used on the title-page.

1591 by W. Kearney. Paradin (C.). *The Heroical Devices, trans. by P. S.*

Perhaps passed to John Wolfe *c.* 1593, when Kearney went to Ireland.

*1597 by J. WOLFE. Lopes (D.). *A Report of the Kingdom of Congo* (second title, after prelims.).

259. (37.5 × 37.5 mm.) A two-tailed mermaid blowing two horns.

This is called a device by Mr. Sayle (pp. 805, 910, and 1018, but not at p. 1235), but seems rather to be an ornament. It is included here on account of the frequency with which it appears on title-pages and because of its liability to be confused with No. 248. It was probably metal, and there seem to have been at least two very similar blocks.

⎧ 1590 Cambridge: ex off. J. LEGATE. Willet (A.). *De Iudaeorum vocatione.*

⎨ *1592 Cambridge: ex off. J. LEGATE. Lipsius (J.). *Tractatus ad Hist. Rom. Cognoscendam.*

⎩ 1598 Cambridge: ex off. J. LEGATE. Perkins (W.). *De Praedestinationis modo.*

1601 [Cambridge:] for J. Porter. Perkins (W.). *The Foundation of Christian Religion.*

Sayle, 5605.

Legate moved to London in 1610, probably taking the block with him.

1615 for T. A. Rich (B.). *The Honesty of this Age.*

1616 for T. Adams. Rich (B.). *My Lady's Looking-glass.*

Probably passed to John Legate II in 1620.

1632 by J. L. for R. Allot. Xenophon. *Cyropædia, trans. by P. Holland.*

*** Another block of the same, distinguished by details of shading, etc.

The piece of shadow above the chest is broader and slopes somewhat upward to the right. The knot of the head-band above the figure's left ear has two points, instead of being round like the one over the right ear. The figure's left breast has no indication of a nipple.

1624 for N. Butter. Webbe (J.). *Catalogus Protestantium.*

{ 1626 by M. FLESHER for R. Mylbourne. *A joint attestation . . . that the Church of England was not impeached by the Synod of Dort.*

1633 excud. M. FLESHER. Ames (W.). *Technometria.*

1636 for R. Dawlman. *The Art of Contentment.*

      Ames Collection, ii. 1356.

260. (34.5 × 28 mm.) Device of a hand pointing to a star, with the motto *Deus Imperat Astris* and R. D.

      See No. 257.

{ *1592 for R. DEXTER. Cupper (W.). *Certain Sermons concerning God's late visitation.*

1603 apud R. DEXTER. Manutius (P.). *Epistolae.*

261. (72 × 58 mm.) Device of a tun floating on the sea; the rebus of Gregory Seton, bookseller, 1577-1608. In a lily growing from the vent-hole of the tun is entwined a snake, and about the device is the motto *Sibi et aliis venenum invidia.* Below is a coat of arms.

      The arms appear to be those of Gregory Seton; cf. Burke, *General Armoury,* 1884, p. 913[b].

*1589 by J. Wolfe. Bland (T.). *A Bait for Momus.*

1589 by J. Windet for G. SETON. Smith (Sir T.). *The Commonwealth of England.*

1590 'in Broad-streete at the signe of the Pack-staffe.' *Plain Perceval the Peacemaker of England.*

1645 by T. Forcet. *The True Character of Mercurius Aulicus.*

      Bagford Collection, Harl. 5921, No. 136.

262. (43.5 × 43.5 mm.) A griffin in rule border.

      Probably representing the sign of Thomas Gubbin, bookseller, 1587-1629, who was trading at the Griffin in 1588 [Hazlitt, II. 194]. It was presumably taken from one of the griffin devices of Sébastien Gryphe or Gryphius, printer at Lyons 1529-1550. See Silvestre, 214, 869.

(α) With background of short lines.

{ *1589 by R. R. imps. T. Man and T. Gubbin. Seneca (L. A.). *Tragœdiæ.*

{ (β) Background cleared away; the upper rule rather broken.

{ 1591 by T. Orwin for J. Porter and T. Gubbin. Perkins (W.). *A Treatise . . .*
    whether a man be in the estate of damnation.

263. (28 × 24 mm.) Framed device of a fleur-de-lis, with I. W. at the sides of the frame. Dotted background.

    The device is distinguished from all similar ones by the initials (not very clear in the facsimile). Traces remain of a motto—almost certainly *In Domino Confido*—round the frame. It seems probable that it originally belonged to John Wolfe and dates from about 1593, when he was using another fleur-de-lis with this motto (No. 298).

(α) With motto.

    [I have been unable to find an example of the device in this state.]

(β) Motto voided.

*1602 by A. Islip. Blundeville (T.). *The Theoric of the Seven Planets.*

       Probably passed to Richard Hearne in 1639 and to Susan Islip in 1646.

1647 excud. S. I. sumps. Soc. Stat. Aesop. *Fabulae.*
       Ames Collection, ii. 1930.

1672 for W. Lee. *New Additions unto Youths Behaviour* 1650.

1685 for H. Herringman, E. Brewster, etc. Shakespeare (W.). *Comedies, Histories, &c.*

264. (28.5 × 25 mm.) Framed device of a fleur-de-lis with *In Domino confido.* Dotted background.

    This block is distinguished from the others by an imperfection at the right hand of the notch at foot of the border, where a piece of shading is wanting.

{ *1609 Cambridge: by C. Legge. Playfere (T.). *A Sermon . . . 6 Aug.,* 1605;
{   **A Sermon . . . 27 Aug.,* 1605.

{ 1619 Cambridge: by C. Legge. Gurnay (E.). *Corpus Christi.*

       Probably passed to John and Thomas Buck, c. 1626.

{ 1633 Cambridge: ex Academiae typographeo. Châteillon (S.). *Dialogorum sacrorum libri IIII* (end).

{ [1638] Cambridge. Norwich, Diocese of. *Articles of Enquiry . . .*

       Probably passed to Roger Daniel alone in 1640.

1640 Cambridge: by R. Daniel. Ovidius Naso (P.). *Ovid's Festivals.*

265.   (29 × 27.5 mm.)   Framed device of a fleur-de-lis with *In Domino confido*.   Dotted background.

In this block there is a small notch at the right hand (not clear in the facsimile), but none at the foot.

{ *1630 by R. B. for R. Allot.   [Earle (J.).]   *Microcosmography.*
  'R. B.' is apparently Richard Badger.
  1635 by R. Badger.   Hereford, Diocese of.   *Articles to be enquired of.*
  1641 by R. B. for R. Badger and J. Williams.   Davenant (J.).   *An Exhortation to Brotherly Love.*

266.   (29.5 × 26.5 mm.)   Framed device of a fleur-de-lis with *In Domino confido*.   Dotted background.

Notch to left very slight, or absent.   Possibly to be regarded as James Boler's.   He at one time used the flower-de-lis as his sign.

*1635 by R. Y. for J. Boler.   *The Burthen of a Loaden Conscience.*
   Ames Collection, ii. 1297.   'R. Y.' must be Robert Young.

267.   (29.5 × 25.5 mm.)   Framed device of a fleur-de-lis with *In Domino confido*.   Dotted background.

Notch at foot, but none to right.   Note direction of shading of lower right-hand projection.

*1639 excud. J. Norton pro R. Thralo.   Dawson (J.).   *Summa Moralis Theologiae.*
1639 by J. Norton for R. Bostock.   Reynolds (E.).   *Meditations on the Last Supper.*
    ? Passed to T. W. [? Thomas Warren] in 1645.
1648 excud. T. W. pro C. Meredith.   Farnaby (T.).   *Phrases oratoriae elegantiores.*
1648 typis T. W. imps. S. Thomson.   Calvin (J.).   *Catecheses Religionis Christianae.*

268.   (29 × 25 mm.)   Framed device of a fleur-de-lis with *In Domino Confido*.   Plain background.

In this block the curl on the left hand of the centre at the top of the frame comes close down on to the oval without a part of the inside of the curl being visible, as in all the other blocks.   The fault at the outer edge of the bottom left-hand projection of the frame occurs in all prints seen.   The blotch on the right-hand side of the bud seems only to occur in copies of the book from which the device was reproduced.

103

1596 by A. ISLIP. Busche (A. vanden), called le Sylvain. *The Orator.*

*1597 ex typographica A. ISLIP. Stockwood (J.). *Progymnasma Scholasticum.*

      A break began to appear in the top right-hand scroll in 1611-14.

1614 for the Comp. of Stationers. *Vn abridgement de touts les ans del Roy Henrie le sept.*

1628 for the Comp. of Stationers. Dalton (M.). *The Office and Authority of Sheriffs.*

1629 by A. I. for S. Waterson. Camden (W.). *Remains.*

1630 ex typ. Stationariorum. Ovidius Naso (P.). *Metamorphoses.*

      Probably printed by Islip, who lived until 1639.

269. (29.5 × 26 mm.) Framed device of a fleur-de-lis with *In Domino confido.* Plain background.

      In this the bud is so broad that there is no space between it and the leaf of the flower on the left hand.

*1597 by J. WOLFE. Lopez (D.). *A Report of the Kingdom of Congo.*

      It is not known into whose hands the device passed on Wolfe's death in 1601.

1621 for T. Walkley. Theodoric II, King of Austrasia. *The Tragedy of Thierry and Theodoret.*

270. (29 × 25 mm.) Framed device of a fleur-de-lis with *In Domino confido.* Plain background.

      Note the unequal length of the two points projecting from the lower side of the frame.

*1603 by R. Waldegrave. *Certain Psalms of David reduced into English Metre by H. D.*

      Bagford Collection, Harl. 5990, No. 90. No place of printing appears on the title.

      Passed to Edward Allde in 1603-4.

1605 by E. A. for N. Fosbroke. White (T.). *A Discovery of Brownism.*

1624 by E. ALLDE for J. Harrison. Massinger (P.). *The Bondman.*

1633 by E. A. for R. Allot. Earle (J.). *Microcosmography.*

      Probably the same block; not certain.

271. (29 × 25 mm.) Framed device of a fleur-de-lis with *In Domino confido.* Plain background.

      This is very similar to No. 269, but differs in several details. At the top of the bud the pieces turning outwards are shorter, especially on the left; and the leaf projecting to the left from below the ring is double. There is a small break in the left-hand curl at top.

1606 by I. W. for M. Law. Barlow (W.). *One of the four Sermons . . . the Antiquity of Bishops.*

*1607 by I. W. for M. Law. Barlow (W.). *The First of the four Sermons . . . at Hampton Court in September last.*

1610 by J. WINDET for J. Browne. Cornwallis (Sir. W.). *Essays. Newly enlarged.*

272. (29.5 × 25.5 mm.) Framed device of a fleur-de-lis with *In Domino confido*. Plain background.

Note shape of the top of the bud.

*1619 by E. G. for T. Walkley. Wither (G.). *Fidelia.*

Presumably printed by Edward Griffin.

273. (43 × 39 mm.) Framed device of clasped hands emerging from clouds, holding a caduceus and two cornucopias, with T. O. below the hands. The motto, *By wisdom peace. By peace plenty.*

A device of clasped hands emerging from clouds with a caduceus, but without cornucopias or motto, was used by T. Richard, bookseller at Paris, 1547-1568; see Silvestre, 224, 580, 783. Compare also the Wechel devices, Nos. 315-17.

(α) With T. O.

1590 by R. Jones. Smythe (Sir J.). *Certain Discourses . . . concerning . . . Weapons.*

*1590 by T. ORWIN. Williams (Sir R.). *A Brief Discourse of War.*

1593 by T. ORWIN for T. Woodcock. Southerne (E.). *A Treatise concerning Bees.*

Passed to Thomas Orwin's widow Joan in 1593.

1594 by the WIDOW ORWIN for T. Woodcock. Marlowe (C.) and Nashe (T.). *Dido.*

(β) The T. O. voided.

1595 by the WIDOW ORWIN, to be sold by M. Lownes. Elyot (Sir T.). *The Castle of Health.*

Herbert, p. 1251.

1597 by the WIDOW ORWIN for I. B. Warner (W.). *Albion's England.*

Passed to Felix Kingston in 1597.

1597 by F. KINGSTON for T. Man. Gifford (G.). *Two Sermons upon 1 Peter.*

Sayle, 2904.

The device began to crack through the Y of PLENTY in 1600-1.

1607 by F. KINGSTON to be sold by J. Flasket. Heyward (Sir J.). *A Report of a Discourse concerning Supreme Power.*

Bagford Collection, Harl. 5927, No. 98.

The device was replaced by No. 274 in 1607-9.

274. (44 × 39 mm.) Framed device of clasped hands emerging from clouds, holding a caduceus and two cornucopias. The motto, *By wisdom peace. By peace plenty.*

A re-cutting of No. 273, from which it may be distinguished by its having a cross in the centre at the top instead of a rivet-head.

1609 by F. KINGSTON. Linton (A.). *News of the Complement of the Art of Navigation.*

*1610 by F. KINGSTON for T. Man. Rogers (R.). *Seven Treatises.*

The centre cross broke on the right-hand side of the top in 1612.

1612 typis J. Norton. Clenard (N.). *Graecae Linguae Institutiones.*

Probably printed *for* Norton.

1620 by F. KINGSTON for R. Moore. *Pentelogia or the Quintessence of Meditation.*

Bagford Collection, Harl. 5927, No. 218.

275. (44 × 41 mm.) Framed device of St. John the Evangelist, a hare holding a stalk of rye in its mouth, and the sun. Below, the initials I. H., and about it, *Dum spero fero.*

A rebus of John Harrison, cf. No. 143.

1590 excud. T. Dawson pro J. HARRISON. ?   ?

Bagford Collection, Harl. 5995, No. 33; book not identified.

Used by two or more John Harrisons in succession.

*1603 by J. HARRISON for R. Bankworth. Bell (T.). *The Anatomy of Popish Tyranny.*

1636 by A. Griffin for J. HARRISON. Markham (G.). *The Inrichment of the Weald of Kent.*

276. (27.5 × 39 mm.) Device of a crowned shield bearing the letters S. P. Q. R. Beside the shield St. Peter and St. Paul.

A similar device occurs in a fragment dated 1577 in the Bagford Collection, Harl. 5991, No. 136: (J. Wild, *In Euangelium secundum Joannem ac in eius epistolam primam Commentaria*). The imprint is 'Romae, In Ædibus Populi Romani.' Mr. Sayle (p. 1235) refers to a device used by one of the Vincents at Lyons (Silvestre, 267), but beyond the fact that this also depicts St. Peter and St. Paul, there seems to be little resemblance.

{ *1592 Cambridge: by J. LEGATE. Perkins (W.). *A Golden Chain.*
{ 1596 Cambridge: by J. LEGATE. Du Jon (F.). *The Apocalyps . . . newly translated.*

277. (31.5 × 29 mm.) Framed device of an eagle carrying one of its young in its talons, with the motto, *Sic crede.*

        See No. 280.

*1591 by T. SCARLET. Smith (H.). *The Pride of King Nebuchadnezzar.*
1596 for J. Drawater. [Lewkenor (Sir L.).] *The Estate of English Fugitives.*
        Some copies are dated 1595.

278. (40.5 × 35 mm.) Framed device of an open book surrounded by beams of light; with *Et vsqve ad nubes veritas tua* [Ps. lvi. 11]. Below, the initials P. S. for Peter Short.

{ *1592 by P. SHORT. Timme (T.). *Plain Discovery of English Lepers.*
{ 1602 by P. SHORT. Marbury (F.). *A Sermon at Paul's Cross,* 13 *June,* 1602.

        Probably passed to Humphrey Lownes in 1604.

{ 1604 by H. LOWNES for C. Knight. Digges (T.). *Four Paradoxes.*
{ 1618 by H. LOWNES for M. Lownes. Williams (Sir R.). *The Actions of the Low Countries.*
1623 for Thomas Lownes. Crakanthorpe (R.). *A Sermon of Predestination.*
1623 apud Antonium Stephanum, Lutetiae Parisiorum. *Cardinalium, Archiepiscoporum . . . de anonymis quibusdam libellis sententia.*
1626 for R. Milbourne. Fawkenor (A.). *Comfort to the Afflicted.*

        Sayle, 4966; under R. Young, who about this time entered into partnership with Humphrey Lownes.

279. (60.5 × 60.5 mm.) A frame containing the arms of London, those of the Stationers' Company, a bell with the letters A. I., and 'God saue the Queene.'

        The bell is the device of Abel Jeffes; cf. No. 253.

{ *1591 by A. Jeffes. Smith (H.). *The Benefit of Contentation.*
　　　　Not in the edition of 1590.
{ 1592 by A. Jeffes. Curtius Rufus (Q.). *The History of Quintus Curtius.*

280.　(54 × 53 mm.)　Framed device representing an eagle carrying in its talons a newly hatched eaglet, which it must be supposed to be forcing to gaze at the sun as a test whether it is worthy to be reared.　The motto: *Sic crede.*

> See the *Symbolorum et Emblematorum Centuriae Tres* of J. Camerarius, ed. 1595-6, ' Ex volatilibus,' No. 9.　Camerarius gives ' Sic crede ' as one of the appropriate mottoes.　Part of this work of Camerarius seems to have been published in 1590, but I have seen no edition earlier than the one named. Compare No. 277.

{ *1592 by T. Scarlet for C. Burby. Smith (H.).　*Mary's Choice.*
{ 1596 for I. B.　Norden (J.).　*A Christian Familiar Comfort.*

Apparently passed to Robert Robinson in 1596

? 1597 per R. R. imps. S. Waterson.　*Institutio Graecae Grammatices . . . in usum Regię Scholę Westmonasteriensis.*

> Bagford Collection, Harl. 5993; the date cut off.

Probably passed to Richard Bradock in 1597-8.

{ 1598 by R. Bradock.　Grimaldus Goslicius (L.).　*The Counsellor.*
{ 1608 by R. Bradock for T. Pavier.　*The History of Hamblet.*
1609 for R. Jackson.　W. (W.).　*A Second Memento for Magistrates.*

> Probably printed by Bradock, who continued in business until 1615.

281.　(39.5 × 34 mm.)　Framed device representing Opportunity standing on a wheel which floats in the sea; with the motto, *Aut nunc aut nunquam.*

> Occasio, whose principal characteristic was that the hair on her forehead was long, but that the back of her head was bald, so that she could be easily seized when approaching, but not at all when once past, was one of the very commonest emblems from classical times (among other references, see Ausonius, *Epig.*, 12).　References to its occurrence in the emblem-books will be found in H. Green's *Shakespeare and the Emblem-writers*, pp. 259-65, and in his edition of Whitney (notes, pp. 238-9).　As a device it was used by Nicholas Basse and

his heirs, printers at Frankfurt, in the second half of the sixteenth century; see Heitz, *Frankfurter Druckerzeichen*, plates lxvii-lxix. They did not, however, use the motto, 'Aut nunc aut nunquam,' nor do any of the forms of their device resemble Danter's closely in the details.

1592 excud. J. DANTER, imps. T. Man. Smith (H.). *Jurisprudentiae . . . Dialogus.*
*1594 by J. DANTER for W. Jones. Nashe (T.). *The Terrors of the Night.*
1597 by J. DANTER. [Shakespeare (W.).] *Romeo and Juliet.*

Probably passed to Simon Stafford in 1599.

1599 by S. STAFFORD for C. Burby. *A Pleasant Conceited Comedy of George a Greene.*
1609 by S. STAFFORD. *Six Demands from an unlearned Protestant.*

Probably passed to George Purslowe c. 1614.

1617 by G. PURSLOWE. Mornay (P. de). *A Work concerning the Trueness of the Christian Religion.*
1630 by G. PURSLOWE to be sold by F. Grove. Goodfellow (R.). *Tarlton's News out of Purgatory.*

282.   (39 × 39 mm.)   Framed device of an old man receiving gifts from the clouds; two doves at his feet, bearing scrolls with the words, 'Peace' and 'Plentie.'   Motto: *Thou shalt labor for* or *For thou shalt labor.*
Cf. No. 292.

1592 by J. WINDET. Turnbull (R.). *An Exposition upon the Epistle of St. James . . . St. Jude* (General title).
See Herbert, p. 1229, Sayle, 2133; but the B.M. copy has the Resurrection device No. 208.
*1599 by J. WINDET. Blundeville (T.). *The Art of Logic.*
1609 by J. WINDET for M. Lownes. Boethius (A. M. T. S.). *Five Books of Philosophical Comfort.*

Probably passed to William Stansby in 1611.

1611 by W. STANSBY for H. Featherstone. Meriton (G.). *A Sermon at Glasgow, 10 June 1610.*
1634 by W. STANSBY. Bridgeman (John), Bp. ot Chester. *Articles of which the Churchwardens are to take notice.*

Passed to Richard Bishop in 1634-38.

1638 by R. Bɪͫ [*sic*] for J. Blome and R. Bishop. Herbert (T.). *Some years Travel into Asia and Africa.*

283.   (41 × 35 mm.) Framed device of a rose, a gillyflower and another flower on one stalk; with *Heb Ddieu heb ddim* and the initials R. I.

> The motto, part of a Welsh proverb, means *Without God, without anything*; the initials are those of Richard Jones.

{ *1592 by R. Jones. Nashe (T.). *Pierce Penilesse.*
{ 1595 by R. Jones. Sabie (F.). *The Fisherman's Tale.*

> Passed to William Jaggard in or before 1615. The intermediate history of the block is obscure.

[1600 by J. Roberts. Shakespeare (W.). *The Merchant of Venice.*]

> As to this and the Shakespearian quartos dated 1608 and bearing this device, see A. W. Pollard, *Shakespeare Quartos and Folios*, and the article of W. J. Neidig in *Modern Philology*, October 1910.

1606 for J. Hardie. *The Popes Bull gelded or an edict published by the Duke . . . of Venice.*

> No printer, but J. Wolfe's device No. 294 on A4.

1610 for the Comp. of Stationers. Elyot (T.). *The Castle of Health.*

1610 for T. Adams. Rich (B.). *A New Description of Ireland.*

{ 1615 by W. Jaggard for N. Bourne. H. (J.) *This World's Folly.*
{ 1621 by W. I. for W. Burre. [Culpeper (Sir T.).] *A Tract against Usury.*

> Passed from William to Isaac Jaggard in 1623, and from Isaac to Thomas and Richard Cotes in 1627.

1628 for M. Sparke. Cooper (T.). *The Church's Deliverance.*

{ 1629 by T. C[otes] for R. Meighen. Fletcher (J.). *The Faithful Shepherdess.*
{ 1640 by T. Cotes, to be sold by J. Benson. Shakespeare (W.). *Poems.*

> Passed to Richard Cotes alone in 1641.

{ 1643 by R. Cotes. F. (E.), Esq. *The Scripture's Harmony.*
{ 1648 typis R. C., sumpts. A. Crooke. *Cancer, Comoedia.*

> The device still has the initials I. R.

284.   (51 × 42 mm.) Framed device of a griffin segreant.

> Probably used in reference to the sign of the Griffin in Paternoster Row at which Thomas Gubbin, or Gubbins, bookseller 1587-1629, was trading in 1588 (Hazlitt, II. 194). Cf. No. 262.

{ 1592 by T. Orwin for J. Porter and T. Gubbin. Perkins (W.). *A Treatise . . . whether a Man be in the Estate of Damnation.*
{ *1596 for T. Gubbins. Misodiaboles. *Ulysses upon Ajax.*

Probably passed to Edward Allde in 1598-1600.

1600 for W. Ferbrand. *A pleasant Comedy called Look About You.*
     With No. 310 at end.

1602 for W. Ferbrand. *A Larum for London.*
     An ornament commonly used by Allde on verso of title.

{ 1603 by E. ALLDE for E. W[hite] and others. *His Majesty's Instructions to . . . Henry the Prince.*

{ 1613 by E. ALLDE for J. Tapp. [Breton (N.).] *Wit's Private Wealth.*

1626   ?   ?
     Sayle, p. 417, book not stated.

1642   ?   ?
     Bagford Collection, Harl. 5963, No. 396, ' *London*, Printed in the yeere 1642.' Book not identified.

285. (94 × 73.5 mm.) Framed device of the arms of the University of Oxford, with *Sapientiae et Felicitatis*, and *Academia Oxoniensis.*

{ 1588 Oxford: by J. BARNES. Sparke (T.). *A Catechism or short kind of Instruction.*
       Sayle, 5232.

{ *1591 Oxford: ex off. J. BARNES. Trigg (F.). *Analysis Cap. 24 Evangelii sec. Matthaeum.*

{ 1613 Oxford: excud. J. BARNES. Oxford Univ., Merton Coll. *Bodleiomnema.*

Probably passed to John Lichfield and William Wrench in 1617.

{ 1622 Oxford: excud. J. LICHFIELD and J. Short. Oxford, Univ. of. *Ultima Linea Savilii.*

{ 1623 Oxford: excud. J. LICHFIELD and J. Short. Oxford, Univ. of. *Carolus Redux.*

Passed to Leonard Lichfield in 1635.

1635 Oxford: excud. L. LICHFIELD. Montagu (R.). *Apparatus ad origines ecclesiasticas.*

1635 Oxford: by W. Turner. Field (R.). *Of the Church.*
     William Turner was printer to the University at the same time as the Lichfields, father and son. He does not seem, however, to have worked in partnership with Leonard Lichfield, and it is not clear how he came to use this block.

286. (52 × 46 mm.) Device of a vase of flowers, with a hare, sheaf of rye, and the sun, also the arms of the Stationers' Company and two cornucopias.

> The rebus of Harrison, cf. No. 143. I cannot interpret the two oval objects at the top of the design. Cf. No. 343.

*1592 excud. R. Field, imps. J. HARRISON. Verepaeus (S.). *De Epistolis Latine Conscribendis.*

1592 by R. Field for J. HARRISON. Figueiro (V.). *The Spaniard's Monarchy, Englished by H. O.*

287. (61 × 46 mm.) Framed device of an anchor suspended by a hand from the clouds with two cornucopias (?), in the ends of which are a skull and a child's head.

> I cannot explain the meaning of the device, which was probably borrowed from some book of emblems.

{ *1592 by A. JEFFES for J. Busby. Lodge (T.). *Euphues Shadow.*
{ 1592 by A. JEFFES for I. B. Nashe (T.). *Pierce Penilesse* (ed. 2).
{ 1593 by A. JEFFES, to be sold by W. Barley. Peele (G.). *Edward I.*

288. (? c. 65 × 54 mm.) Device of an ox upon a bridge with *Labore et Constantia.*

> Compare No. 289. The only print of this that I have been able to find is the incomplete one mentioned below.

*[?] [? for J. OXENBRIDGE.] ? ?

> Fragment in the Bagford Collection, Harl. 5963, No. 400. From the printing on the back it appears to be taken from some religious treatise in English.

289. (45 × 39 mm.) Device of an ox on a bridge, with the letter N, and *Labore et Constantia.*

> The rebus of John Oxenbridge, stationer 1589-1600. Cf. No. 288.

*1593 in aed. R. Field, imps. J. OXENBRIDGE. Kis (S.). Szegedinus. *Tabulæ analyticæ.*

> Some copies have 'impensis G. Nortoni' and device No. 174.

1598 for J. OXENBRIDGE. Rich (B.). *A Martial Conference.*

290. (36 × 28 mm.) Device of a flower vase above which is the sun, and below, the arms of the City of London. Two empty ovals at sides.

> A comparison of this device with No. 286 suggests that it may at one time have been Harrison's, and had a hare and sheaf of rye—or initials—in the ovals, but in all examples that I have seen they are empty.

1592 by E. ALLDE for E. Aggas. Fisher (W.). *Godly Sermon.*
*1616 for E. ALLDE. W. (W.), Gent. *Moral Observations.*
> Bagford Collection, Harl. 5910, iv, No. 24.

1626 by E. ALLDE for T. Walkley. E., R.A. *Lessus in Funere R. Thorii.*

Passed to Elizabeth Allde in 1628.

1633 by ELIZ. ALLDE. *Treasury of Hidden Secrets.*
> Sayle, 2042.

Probably passed to Richard Oulton in 1635-6.

1637 by R. OULTON. *Treasury of Hidden Secrets.*
> Sayle, 5131.

291. (52 × 52 mm.) Circular device of a landscape above which is a coronet: about it the motto, *Marcantia Reale.*

> I have been unable to obtain any information whatever about this device, which seems only to be used in a single book.

*1593 [no printer or publisher]. R. (B.). *Greene's News both from Heaven and Hell.*
> The book was entered to T. Adams and J. Oxenbridge, Feb. 3, 1592/3. The imprint is 'At London,' and the workmanship appears certainly to be English.

292. (61 × 49 mm.) Framed device of a man standing with hands upraised and receiving an indistinguishable object (Herbert, p. 1229, calls it a book) and a wheatsheaf from the clouds. At his feet two birds labelled Peace, Plentie. Motto, *Thou shalt labor for,* or, *For thou shalt labor.*

> Cf. No. 282.

1592 by J. WINDET. Turnbull (R.). *An Exposition upon the XV Psalm.*
*1597 by J. WINDET. Hooker (R.). *Laws of Ecclesiastical Polity, Fifth Book.*
1605 excud. J. WINDET, imps. T. Man. Powel (G.). *Disputationum Theologicarum libri ii.*

Probably passed to William Stansby in 1611.

{ **1611** by W. STANSBY for E. Blunt and W. Barret. Florio (J.). *Necessary Rules upon
the Italian Tongue* (suppl. to *Queen Anna's World of Words*) (end).

1626 by W. STANSBY. Ovidius Naso (P.). *Ovid's Metamorphosis Englished by G.
S[andys]*.

Probably passed to Richard Bishop in 1634-8.

1640 by R. BISHOP for A. Crooke. Jonson (B.). *Works, Part ii.*

293. (59.5 × 54 mm.) Mercury's hat and caduceus with two
cornucopias and sea-scape.

The design is taken from an emblem signifying that those who possess
intelligence and a ready tongue will be blessed with abundance (Alciat, ed.
1567, emblem 65, and in earlier editions; P. Giovio, *Dialogo dell' imprese
militare*, ed. 1574, p. 155). The background of the sea, hills, etc., does not
occur in such of the emblem-books as I have seen.

The device was considered by Herbert to be Arnold Hatfield's (p. 1211),
but though he used it at least twice I see no reason to connect it especially
with him. It may at first have been either G. Bishop's or R. Barker's, but by
1594 it seems to have got to the Eliot's Court printing house (see note on this).
While there it was used by the partners indiscriminately.

*1592 by G. B[ishop], R. N[ewbery] and R. B[arker]. *Biblia Sacra* (before pts.
*v and vi).

Some copies have ' Impensis W. Norton,' and do not give the printers.

Passed to the Eliot's Court Printing House about 1594.

1594 imps. G. Bishop. Camden (W.). *Britannia* (title of ' Hibernia ').

1594 excud. J. Jackson. *Liber precum publicarum* (fol. 188).

Sayle, 2101.

1600 excud. E. Bollifant. Sutcliffe (M.). *De Vera Christi Ecclesia.*

1600 by A. Hatfield for E. Blount. *The Uniting of Portugal to Castille.*

1606 for J. Bill. Sarpi (P.). *Full . . . answer to the . . . Bull.*

Apparently taken to Eton by Melchisedec Bradwood,
c. 1609.

1610 Etonae in Collegio Regali excud. J. Norton. John, Archbishop of Euchaita.
Versus Iambici, cura Matthaei Busti.

1613 Etonae in Collegio Regali. Xenophon, Κυρου παιδεια, *De Cyri Institutione.*

Probably passed to Edward Griffin, 1615-16.

1616 by E. GRIFFIN for H. Fetherstone. Sclater (W.). *A Sermon at the last Assize
at Taunton.*

114

Probably passed to John Haviland in 1621.

1623 by J. HAVILAND for W. Aspley. Minsheu (J.). *Dictionary in Spanish and English.*

294. (60 × 48 mm.) Framed device of a fleur-de-lis with two cherubs and I. W.

Apparently modelled on a device of the Giunti of Florence (see *Il Decamerone*, Firenze, 1587), but it varies considerably in details from this, and there may be another Giunta device which it more closely resembles.

{ *1593 by J. WOLFE. *A Survey of the pretended Holy Discipline.*

1599 by J. WOLFE. Hayward (Sir J.). *The first part of the Life of Henry IV.*

In one edition only of this year.

The later ownership of the device is uncertain. It is possible that it passed from Wolfe to James Roberts and later to John Wright or John Windet.

1606 for J. Hardie. *The Pope's Bull gelded or an edict . . . of Venice against the late Bull of Pope Paul V.* (sig. A4).

This has device 283 on the title-page.

1607 by I. W. for G. Chorlton. Turner (R.). *Nosce Te.*

1609 for N. Butter. Greville (F.) *The Tragedy of Mustapha.*

295. (21 × 67 mm.) Ornament of two men blowing horns. The initials I. D. in the centre, standing for the name of John Danter.

It is not absolutely certain that the initials are part of the block; possibly it may be a cast factotum with type inserted, but I have not found it with other initials.

(α) With I. D.

{ *1592 excud. J. DANTER imps. T. Man. Smith (H.). *Jurisprudentiae . . . Dialogus* (sig. A2).

1594 by J. DANTER for C. Burby. [Greene (R.).] *Orlando Furioso.*

? Passed to Richard Jones.

(β) Without initials; the oval left blank.

[? 1597 by R. Jones.] Breton (N.). *The Arbour of Amorous Devices* (sig. A2).

T. C. C. (Capell), imperf., no title. No other copy being now known, the date and printer must be regarded as doubtful. We should have expected the block to pass directly into the hands of Stafford, as No. 281 seems to have done.

> ? Passed to Simon Stafford in 1599.

1609 by S. STAFFORD. Papists. *Six Demands from an Unlearned Protestant* (sig. B4).

296. (19 × 49 mm.) Ornament having in the centre a tiger's head, with the motto *Auspicante Deo.*

It is not clear to whom this belonged, and it is doubtful whether it has any claim to be regarded as a device. Neither Peter Short nor Ponsonby seems to have been under the patronage of Walsingham, whose crest the tiger's head was. Cf. Nos. 212, 323.

*1595 by P. S. for W. Ponsonby. Platt (H.). *A discovery of Certain English Wants.*

> Probably passed to Humphrey Lownes in 1604.

1627 for R. Dawlman. Senhouse (R.). *Four Sermons.*

> Probably passed to Robert Young in 1630.

1637 by R. Young for R. Norton. Danes (J.). *A Light to Lilie.*

297. (48.5 × 47 mm.) Device of a phoenix in flames with *Semper eadem* and the initials C. B.

Compare the Giolito device, Nos. 252, 254; but the phoenix with this motto seems to have been a common emblem. The initials stand for the name of Cuthbert Burby.

{ *1594 by T. Scarlet for C. BURBY. Nashe (T.). *The Unfortunate Traveller.*
{ 1594 by J. Danter for C. BURBY. [Greene (R.).] *Orlando Furioso.*
{ 1596 by R. Jones for C. BURBY. Schilander (C.). *Cornelius Shilander his Chirurgery.*

298. (60 × 67 mm.) A fleur-de-lis with two cherubs. *In Domino Confido* and I. W.

Copied from one of the devices of the Giunti: see that of Jacques de Junte, bookseller at Lyons, 1533-1546 (Silvestre, 449).

(α) With I. W.

{ *1593 by J. WOLFE. [Bancroft (R.).] *Dangerous Positions.*
{ 1599 by J. WOLFE. H[arsnet] (S.). *A Discovery of the Fraudulent Practices of J. Darrel.*

The device passed to Ralph Blower between 1599 and 1609.

(β) I. W. voided.

1609 by R. BLOWER. Lichfield and Coventry, Diocese of. *Articles to be enquired of* (verso of title).

The device probably passed to William Jones in 1616-17.

1617 by W. JONES. [Cooke (A.).] *Work for a Mass-priest.*

299.　(50 × 40.5 mm.) Framed device of Truth being scourged by a hand from the clouds. Between her feet the initials T. C. The motto *Viressit vulnere veritas.*

> According to Corser's *Collectanea Anglo-Poetica*, vol. iii, p. 242-4, *The French History* of Anne Dowriche, printed by T. Orwin for T. Man, 1589, has on the title 'the printer's singular device, viz.: a figure of Truth crowned, standing naked, with a scourge at her back, and around it the motto, "Virescit vulnere Veritas."' The cut appears again on the last page, where it is inscribed 'Veritie purtraied by the French Pilgrime.' It would seem likely that Creede's device is copied from this, but I have been unable to see a copy of the book, and therefore cannot say if the resemblance is close.

{ *1594 by T. CREEDE for T. Woodcock. Abbot (R.). *Mirror of Popish Subtleties.*
{ 1614 by T. CREEDE. Quintus Curtius. *The History.*

300.　(54 × 48 mm.) Framed device of an open book with light shining from the clouds. The motto, *Dat esse manus, superesse Minerva.*

> Mr. Sayle (p. 343) regards this device as George Bishop's. It seems equally possible that it may have been originally Christopher Barker's and have been used by Bishop and R. Barker as his deputies.

1595 by the Deputies of C. BARKER. Sutcliffe (M.). *An Answer unto a certain calumnious Letter.*

*1596 excud. G. Bishop, R. Newbery, and R. Barker. Savile (Sir H.). *Rerum Anglicarum Scriptores.*

1597 excud. G. Bishop. Piscator (J.). *Analysis Logica Septem Epistolarum Apostolicarum.*

Probably passed to Robert Barker in 1599.

1603 excud. R. BARKER. Abbot (R.). *Antichristi Demonstratio.*

1616 apud J. Bill. Dominis (M. A. de). *Suæ profectionis Consilium.*
1616 by J. Bill. Dominis (M. A. de). *A Manifestation of the Motives,* etc.
1616 ex off. Nortoniana apud J. Bill. James I. *Declaratio pro Jure Regio.*
1624 by J. Bill. Hayward (Sir J.). *Of Supremacy in affairs of Religion.*
1624 by T. Harper. Texeda (F.). *Scrutamini Scripturas.*
> Sayle, 3978. I cannot account for the presence of the device in this book.

301. (60 × 54 mm.) Device of a ling and honeysuckle, with N. L.

> The ling is manifestly a rebus on the name of Nicholas Ling, but the honeysuckle does not appear to have been explained.

{ *1595 by T. C. for N. LING. Nashe (T.). *Pierce Penilesse.*
{ 1607 by F. K. for N. LING. Smith (H.). *Three Sermons.*

302. (39 × 37 mm.) Framed device of a tree broken by the wind, with the initials T. M.

> From an emblem given by Whitney, *Choice of Emblems,* 1586, p. 220: see Adrianus Junius, *Emblemata,* ed. 1569, No. 43. The emblem signifies that Envy, hatred, and contempt, which are the storms and tempests of this life, if endured patiently and not resisted, will pass over us without doing harm.

{ 1595 by P. S. for T. MILLINGTON. *The True Tragedy of Richard Duke of York.*
{ 1597 by J. Roberts for T. MILLINGTON. Maulette (G. P.). *Devoreux, Vertues teares for the loss of . . . Henry III . . . of France,* etc.
> Bagford Collection, Harl. 5921, No. 52.

303. (11.5 × 12 mm.) A swan.

> Probably alluding to the sign of the White Swan used by Valentine Simmes, printer, from *c.* 1595 to *c.* 1605.

{ 1596 reprinted by V. SIMMES. Latimer (H.). *Fruitful Sermons.*
{ *1597 ex off. V. SIMMES imps. T. Gellibrand. Sturtevant (S.). *Anglo-Latinus Nomenclator.*

304. (53 × 53.5 mm.) Framed device of a death's head, hourglass, scythe, etc., with *Non plus.* Above it a circle containing an indistinguishable object (? a skull). Below, W. B. in an oval.

(α) As figured, with W. B.

*1595 by A. I[effes] to be sold by W. BARLEY. Hawkins (J.). *A Salad for the Simple
. . . out of Proverbs.*
> Bagford Collection, Harl. 5993, No. 103.

1595 for W. BARLEY. I. (T.). *A World of Wonders.*

(β) Solid black disk at top. Initials below voided.

1601 by W. BARLEY. *Articles . . . in the diocese of London.*

> The history of the device is obscure between this date
> and 1633.

1618 for T. Thorpe. Oldenbarneveld (J. van). *Barnevel's Apology.*

1632 by W. J. for N. Bourne. Capell (M.). *God's Valuation of Man's Soul.*

> Passed to Augustine Mathewes, 1632-3.

(γ) With A. M. roughly cut or scratched on the black disk at
top. No initials below.

1633 by A. MATHEWES for R. Milbourne. Stafford (T.). *Pacata Hibernia.*

> Passed to Marmaduke Parsons *c.* 1635.

1637 for A. Crooke. Saluste du Bartas (G. de). *A learned summary upon the famous
poem of . . . Bartas.*
> Sayle, 4592.

1639 by M. P. for R. Meighen. *The Lady's Cabinet Opened.*

305. (59 × 50 mm.) A rake, hay-fork, and scythe, with *Sed adhuc
mea messis in herba est* [Ovid, *Heroid.* xvii. 263].

> It is probable that this is really an emblem of the composer's, rather than a
> printer's device, but I have been unable to find any certain evidence on the
> point.

1595 by T. East. Morley (T.). *The first Book of Ballets to Five Voices.*

*1600 by T. East, ass. of T. Morley. Morley (T.). *The first Book of Ballets to Five
Voices.*

306. (60.5 × 54 mm.) Framed device of Truth attacked by
Calumny and upheld by Time, with the motto, *Veritas Filia
Temporis.*

> Mr. Sayle (No. 3376 and p. 869) calls this Bollifant's device. It perhaps
> was one of those used in common by the printers at the Eliot's Court Press.

1596 by E. Bollifant for T. Dawson. Clowes (W.). *Brief Treatise touching* . . . *Lues Venerea.*

Bodl., Douce Adds. 142, No. 57a.

1596 by A. Hatfield for J. Norton. Comines (P. de). *History* (on pp. 44, 81, 152, etc., at the end of the several books).

1600 excud. A. Hatfield. James (T.). *Ecloga Oxonio Cantabrigiensis, Liber Secundus.*
The first part, printed impensis G. Bishop and J. Norton, has no device.

1601 by A. Hatfield for J. Norton. Comines (P. de). *History* (on pp. 38, 71, 104, etc.).

*1605 imps. G. Bishop. Morton (T.). *Apologia Catholica.*

1614 for J. Bill. Comines (P. de). *History* (pp. 104, 186, 224, 348).

1615 for G. Purslowe.   ?   ?

Bagford Collection, Harl. 5963, No. 405; book not identified.

Probably passed to Edward Griffin in 1615-16 and to John Haviland in 1621.

{ 1624 by J. HAVILAND. Wilcox (T.). *Works.*
{ 1635 by J. HAVILAND. Martin (R.). *Catalogus Librorum.*

Passed to Anne Griffin, *c.* 1636.

1637 by A. GRIFFIN for E. Brewster. Gataker (T.). *Noah his Obedience* (*An Anniversary Memorial, A Marriage Prayer*, etc.).
Some parts of the book were printed for F. Clifton.

Passed to Edward Griffin II, *c.* 1638.

1639 typis E. GRIFFIN, sumps. R. Whitaker. Du Boys (J.). *Pharmacopoei Parisiensis Observationes.*

307. (63 × 52 mm.) Device of two women labelled *Justitia* and *Religio*, the latter standing on a skull; with mottoes, *Suum cuique* and *Deum cole*, and below, *His suffulta durant* and the initials of Henry Charteris.

(α) With H. C.

{ 1596 Edinburgh, by H. CHARTERIS. *The Order of the General Fasting* . . . and *The Order of Excommunication* (Parts 4 and 5 of *The Book of Common Order*).
Dickson and Edmond, No. 167.
{ 1597 Edinburgh: by H. CHARTERIS. Lyndsay (Sir D.). *The Warkis* (end).

Passed to his son Robert Charteris in 1599.

{ 1606 excud. R. CHARTERIS. *Descriptio Horrendi Parricidii* . . . *in Iacobum,* 5 *Nov.* 1605.
{ *1609 excud. R. CHARTERIS. *Nobilissimi Domini, Domini Kethi* . . . *Epithalamium.*
{ 1610 excud. R. CHARTERIS. Julius (A.). *Paraphrasis Prophetiae Chabakkuki Poetica.*

120

Passed to Andro Hart ? *c.* 1610, and to his heirs in 1621.

(β) With H. C. excised.

1633 apud Heredes A. Hart. Ramsay (A.). *Poemata sacra* (verso of title).

308. (57 × 52.5 mm.) Framed device of a reverent old man pray-ing, and an angel appearing to him.

> Perhaps designed with special reference to the subject of Broughton's work, in which it seems first to be used.

1597 by G. Simson. Broughton (H.). *Daniel his Chaldee Visions.*

> With sentences paraphrased from Daniel ix. 16, and 23 in type about it.

> Probably passed to George Eld in 1604.

*1606 by G. Eld. Meredith (R.). *Two Sermons.*

1620 apud G. Eld. Buchanan (G.). *Ecphrasis paraphraseos . . . in Psalmos Davidis.*

> Probably passed to Miles Fletcher or Flesher in 1624.

1626 ? ?

> Sayle, p. 910.

1633 excud. B. Norton. *Novum Testamentum* (T. Beza).

> Probably *for* Norton.

1637 by M. Flesher. Babington (G.). *Works.*

> (Sigs. 3 P and (a).)

1649 by J. Flesher for M. F., J. Marriot, and R. Royston. Donne (J.). *Fifty Sermons.*

> Miles Flesher lived until 1664, being assisted in his business from about 1649 by his son James.

309. (74 × 70 mm.) Framed emblematic device with bird-headed pillar, scales, cat, snake, etc.; with the legend, *Quibus respublica conservetur.*

> Copied with slight simplification of detail from the *Emblemata* of J. Sam-bucus, ed. 1566, p. 97. The verses accompanying it do not explain the symbolism of the picture. Sometimes used within a compartment; see No. 324.

*1598 by A. Islip. Aristotle. *Aristotle's Politics.*

> Some copies appear to be dated 1597; see Herbert, p. 1287.

1613 by A. Islip. Maurice, Prince of Orange. *The Triumphs of Nassau.*

310. (29.5 × 48.5 mm.) Device of an old man standing beside an olive tree; above him, on a scroll, the motto, *Noli altum sapere.*

> Copied from a device of the Etienne family (cf. Nos. 348-51). It appears most to resemble that used by Henri Etienne II in his *Apophthegmata Graeca,* 1568; cf. also Heitz, *Genfer Buchdruckerzeichen,* No. 96.

1599 by J. Wolfe. Netherlands. *A Copy of the Proclamation made by . . . Isabella . . . touching the defence . . . of all communication* (end).

> **? Passed to Edward Allde in 1599.**

1599 for J. Hunt and W. Ferbrand. *The Pleasant History of the two Angry Women of Abington* (end).
> With E. Allde's ornaments.

1600 for W. Ferbrand. *A Pleasant Comedy called Look About You* (end).
> With No. 284 on title. Probably printed by E. Allde.

1611 for M. Lownes. Gardiner (Edmund). *Physical and approved Medicines.*
> Sayle, 2508. A cancel title.

> **? Passed to Elizabeth Allde in 1628.**

*1632 by Eliz. Allde for R. Allot. Smith (Miles). *Sermons* (title and before the **Sermon at the Funeral of the Bishop of Gloucester*).

311. (29 × 50 mm.) Device of an old man standing by an olive tree; above him, on a scroll, the motto, *Noli altum sapere.*

> A re-cutting of No. 310, from which it may most easily be distinguished by the finish of the ground at the right hand.

1618 by G. P. for R. Mylbourne. Dyke (D.). *Two Treatises.*
*1621 for W. Lee. Ossolinski (J.). *A True Copy of the Latin Oration.*
1629 by G. Purslowe for J. Bartlet. Harris (R.). *Peter's Enlargement.*

> **Passed to Elizabeth Purslowe in 1632-3.**

1633 by E. P. for H. Seile. Donne (J.). *Juvenilia.*
1638 by E. P. for H. Seile. Norwich, Diocese of. *Articles of Enquiry.*
1638 apud J. Raworth pro R. Whitaker. Brerewood (E.). *Elementa Logicae.*
> Apparently the same block.

1639 by E. P. for N. Bourne. Woodall (J.). *The Surgeon's Mate* (title to 'Viaticum').

312. (58.5 × 58 mm.) Framed device of Time bringing Truth to light, with the motto, *Tempore patet occulta Veritas,* and the initials R. S.

> This is closely copied from a device used by C. Badius, printer at Geneva, in

1554; see Heitz, *Genfer Buchdruckerzeichen*, No. 7. The initials are those of Richard Smith, bookseller 1567-95. Cf. Nos. 186, 331.

1595 by I. R. for R. SMITH. Chapman (G.). *Ovid's Banquet of Sense* (end).

Probably passed to William Wood *c.* 1598.

1599 by T. Creede for W. WOOD. Buttes (H.). *Diet's Dry Dinner* (sig. B1).
'To be sold . . . at the signe of Tyme.' It is, however, perhaps used rather as an illustration to some verses headed 'Grace before *Diet's dry Dinner* served in by Time,' than with reference to the publisher's sign.

Passed to Augustine Mathewes at an unknown date.

1624 by A. MATHEWES and J. Norton. [Turner (R.).] *Youth Know thy Self.*

1628 [?] Bacon (F.). *The New Atlantis.*
Appended to *Sylva Sylvarum*, by J. H. for W. Lee, but the signatures are not continuous. Perhaps printed by Mathewes.

*1633 typis A. MATHEWES. Martin (R.). *Catalogus Librorum quos . . . ex Italia selegit R. M.*

Passed to Marmaduke Parsons *c.* 1635.

1639 by M. PARSONS for J. Bellamy. Ainsworth (H.). *Annotations upon . . . books of Moses.*

313. (36.5 × 37 mm.) Framed device of Justice striking a bushel of corn; with *Such as I make. Such will I take.*

*1600 by V. S[immes] for T. BUSHELL. Gardiner (S.). *A Pearl of Price.*

1604 by V. Simmes for T. BUSHELL. Marlowe (C.). *Faustus* (end).

314. (92 × 78 mm.) Framed device of a mailed hand upholding a burning sword, with the motto *Contrahit avaritia bellum* on a scroll entwined about it. All within a frame bearing the monogram of Thomas Creede.
Cf. No. 359.

*1598 by T. CREEDE. *An Historical Collection of the most memorable Accidents . . . of France.*

1602 by T. C.   ?   ?
Bagford Collection, Harl. 5919, No. 593; book not identified.

Probably passed to Bernard Alsop in 1617.

1623 excud. B. ALSOP. Leech (J.). *Epigrammatum libri quatuor.*
It still has Creede's monogram.

315. (51 × 45 mm.) Framed device apparently representing a flower open in the beams of the sun, and another, on the same stalk, closed at night. The motto, *Non licet exiguis.*

{ *1598 by F. KINGSTON for P. Linley. Marlowe (C.) and Chapman (G.). *Hero and Leander.*

1606 ex typ. KINGSTON, imps. C. Burby and E. Weaver. Parry (H.). *De Regno Dei et Victoria Christiana.*

316. (42 × 26 mm.) Device of a Pegasus above a caduceus and cornucopia upheld by hands emerging from clouds.

Copied from a device used by Chréstien Wechel, printer at Paris 1522-53 (Silvestre, 923, 922), and by Andreas Wechel at Frankfurt 1577-1601 (Heitz, *Frankfurter Druckerzeichen*, tafel lxi, No. 94).

There were at least three blocks of this device in use before 1640; see Nos. 317, 318. I have not attempted to follow them later, as, when worn or badly printed, the blocks are hardly to be distinguished. The design continued in use for many years; it will be found, for example, on the title-page of editions of Abraham Cowley's *Works*, published in 1681 and 1684.

1600 by J. Harrison for T. Man. *Treatise of Christian Beneficence.*
Ames Collection, ii. 7.

? Passed to George Snowdon *c.* 1605.

1606 for M. Lownes. Suetonius. *The Twelve Caesars.*
1606 by G. S[nowdon] for C. Knight. Covell (W.). *Brief Answer unto Certain Reasons.*

Passed to N. Okes *c.* 1607.

{ *1608 for N. Butter (Pide Bull). Shakespeare (W.). *King Lear.*
1622 by N. O. for T. Walkley. Shakespeare (W.). *Othello.*

317. (42 × 26 mm.) Device of a Pegasus above a caduceus and cornucopias upheld by hands emerging from clouds.

Cf. Nos. 316, 318, from which it is most easily distinguished by the arrangement of the shading on the horse's flank and belly.

*1605 for S. Waterson. [Sandys (Sir E.).] *A Relation of the state of Religion.*
Not in the edition of this date printed by Simmes.

318. (42 × 27 mm.) Device of a Pegasus above a caduceus and cornucopias upheld by hands emerging from clouds.

Cf. Nos. 316, 317, from which it may be distinguished by the horse's tail not being bent outwards at end, and by differences in the clouds, especially that on the left side.

*1607 for N. Butter. Coke (Sir E.). *The Lord Coke his speech and charge (at the Norwich Assizes).*

319. (48 × 40 mm.) Framed device of a hare, rye, and the sun, the rebus of Harrison, with a dove, and the motto, *Dum spero fero.* In the lower left-hand corner I. H.

Cf. Nos. 275, 143. Probably owned by John Harrison II.

1595 for J. HARRISON. Dent (A.). *A Sermon of Repentance.*
  Bodl., Douce Add. 142.

*1600 by I. H. for J. HARRISON. [Shakespeare (W.).] *Lucrece.*
  Probably by John Harrison III for John Harrison II.

1607 by N. O. for J. HARRISON. [Shakespeare (W.).] *Lucrece.*

320. (35.5 × 33 mm.) A gilly-flower with initials G. S.

[1592 for G. SIMSON and W. White. Cotton (R.). *A Direction to the Waters of Life* (T. C. C.).

The device, *without* G. S., is on the last page immediately above the colophon, which is dated 1592. The title-page is not dated. It is not quite certain that the block is the same. If it is, the date is perhaps reprinted from an earlier edition, as it seems somewhat unlikely that the initials would be inserted *in wood-cut* into the block after it had been in use for many years.]

(α) With G. S.

*1600 by G. SIMSON. Hylles (T.). *The Art of Vulgar Arithmetic.*

? Passed to Richard Read in 1601.

(β) Without initials.

1601 for E. Matts. Cornwallis (Sir W.). *A Second part of Essays.*

Passed to George Eld *c.* 1604.

1607 by G. ELD. S. (W.). *The Puritan.*

1608 for W. Barrett. Malelief (C.). *An Historical Discourse of a voyage in May 1605.*

Passed to Miles Fletcher or Flesher in 1624.

(γ) Border all cut away save piece below flower (33 × 27 mm.).

1639 typis M. F., sumptibus L. Fawne and S. Gellibrand. Comenius (J. A.). *Pansophiae Prodromus* (sig. A6 verso).

321. (49.5 × 65.5 mm.) Framed device of a kingfisher catching a fish, with the motto, *Motos soleo componere fluctus*, and below, *Alcione*.

> The device puns on the name of the owner Thomas Fisher, bookseller 1600-1602. The kingfisher (Alcyone) is, of course, an emblem of fair weather, cf. Green, *Shakespeare and the Emblem-Writers*, pp. 390-2. The motto, apparently based on *Aen.* i. 135, perhaps comes from one of the emblem-books, but I have not traced it.

{ 1600 for T. FISHER. Shakespeare (W.). *A Midsummer Night's Dream.*
  *1602 for M. Lownes and T. FISHER. Marston (J.). *The History of Antonio ana Mellida. The First Part.*

322. (56 × 46 mm.) A frame enclosing a shield with five fusils conjoined in fess, and in chief three mullets; the motto, *Deus in æternum.*

> The arms are perhaps those of the author of the *Works of Armory*, 1597; see Burke's *General Armory*, under Bosvile of Wormsworth, co. York. If so, however, it is not easy to see how the block came to be used in Holborne's *Pavans.*

1597 by H. Ballard. Bossewell (J.). *Works of Armory.*
*1599 by W. Barley, assign of T. Morley. Holborne (A.). *Pavans, Galliards, etc.*

323. (24 × 112.5 mm.) Ornament having in the centre the crest of Sir Francis Walsingham; out of a mural coronet a tiger's head ducally gorged.

> Possibly belonging originally to Christopher Barker; cf. Nos. 212, 296.

*1595 by J. WINDET for A. Maunsell. Maunsell (A.). *Catalogue of English Books, Part I* (head of fol. 4 of prelims.).

> Probably passed to William Stansby in 1611.

{ 1621 by W. STANSBY for R. Meighen. Slatyer (W.). *History of Great Britain* (sigs. Cc4 verso, Cc6).
  [1636] by W. STANSBY, to be sold by G. Latham. Hooker (R.). *Ecclesiastical Polity* (sig. E6).

324. (127 × 126 mm.) Compartment emblematic of the history of Rome; at top, ROMA; at foot, the initials A. I., standing for Adam Islip.

> Used to contain the device No. 309.

*1600 by A. ISLIP. Livius (T.). *The Roman History . . . trans. by P. Holland.*

325. (63.5 × 48 mm.) Oval device of a woman with the sun in one hand and in the other a cup, into which drops of liquid are falling from the clouds; with *Alma mater Cantabrigia* and the motto, *Hinc lucem et pocula sacra*.

Compare Nos. 326, 327, 329, 416.

*1601 Cambridge: by J. LEGATE. Hill (R.). *Life Everlasting*.
1606 Cambridge: ex off. J. LEGATE. Thomas (T.). *Dictionarium . . . Septima Editio*.

Sayle, 5639.

Probably taken by John Legate the elder to London in 1610, but apparently not used by him there. Passed to John Legate II in 1620.

1620 by J. LEGATE. Hieron (S.). *The Sermons*.

Sayle, 4692.

1631 by J. LEGATE, and sold by S. Waterson. Perkins (W.). *An Exposition of the Symbole or Creed*.

1637 for R. Meighen and J. LEGATE. Austin (W.). *A Meditation for Holy Thursday* (in *Devotionis Augustinianae flamma*).

326. (44.5 × 26 mm.) Oval device of a woman with the sun in one hand and a cup in the other, etc., as No. 325.

Cf. No. 327. In this form of the device the cup does not touch the enclosing rule.

1601 Cambridge: by J. LEGATE. Perkins (W.). *A Warning against the Idolatry of the last times*.

The break in the outer rule a little to the left of the foot occurred in 1606-7.

*1607 Cambridge: ex off. J. LEGATE. Lipsius (J.). *Tractatus ad Hist. Rom. Cognoscendam*.

Probably taken by John Legate the elder to London in 1610.

1611 by J. LEGATE. Perkins (W.). *A Reformed Catholike*.

? Passed to John Legate II in 1620.

1635 by the Printers to the Univ. of Camb., for sale by R. Allot. Kellet (E.). *Miscellanies of Divinity*.

327. (44.5 × 34.5 mm.) Oval device of a woman with the sun in one hand and a cup in the other, etc., as No. 325.

Cf. No. 326. In this form of the device the cup touches the enclosing rule.

*1629 Cambridge: by T. and J. Buck. *Psalms (Sternhold and Hopkins)* (fol.).

1631 Cambridge: ex Academiae Typographeo. Ovidius Naso (P.). *Metamorphoses . . . G. Bersmani aliorumque . . . notationibus illustratae* (end).

1636 Cambridge: ex Academiae Typographeo. Benlowes (E.). *Sphinx Theologica* (verso of title and sig. B3).

1637 Cambridge: by T. Buck and R. Daniel. *Bible.*
    Sayle, 5818.

1638 Cambridge: by the Printers to the University. *The Book of Common Prayer.*
    B.M., 3408. g. 2.

Probably passed to Roger Daniel alone in 1640.

1640 apud R. Daniel. *Voces votivae ab Academicis Cantabrigiensibus pro novissimo Caroli et Mariae principe filio enissae.*
    Sayle, 5836.

1642 by R. Daniel for J. Williams. Fuller (T.). *The Holy State.*

328. (72 × 58 mm.) Oval device of the two summits of Parnassus with *Parnasso et Apolline digna.*

If the device is not found earlier than 1600, we may suppose that it has special reference to Bodenham's *Belvedere,* a collection of quotations from contemporary poets.

1600 by F. K. for H. Astley. Bodenham (J.). *Belvedere.*

*1620 by F. Kingston. Elton (E.). *Exposition of the Epistle . . . to the Colossians.*

329. (97 × 71 mm.) Oval device of a woman with the sun in one hand and a cup in the other, etc., as No. 325.

*1603 Cambridge: by J. Legate. Perkins (W.). *Works* (general title, * sig. L3, and before the other several treatises).

1609 Cambridge: by J. Legate, and sold by S. Waterson. Perkins (W.). *Works,* vol. ii.

Probably taken to London by John Legate the elder in 1610.

1612 by J. Legate. Perkins (W.). *Works,* vol. i.
    Sayle, 3751.

1617 by J. Legate. Perkins (W.). *Works,* vol. ii.

1635 by J. Legate. Perkins (W.). *Works.*
    Sayle, 4727.

330.   (125 × 96 mm.) Emblematic device referring to Pliny's *Historia Naturalis*, inscribed ΜΑΚΡΟΚΟΣΜΟΣ, ΜΙΚΡΟΚΟΣΜΟΣ. *Pingit utrumque tibi Plinius*; at the base the monogram of Adam Islip.

{ *1601 by A. Islip. Plinius Secundus (C.). *The History of the World* (vols. i and *ii).
{ 1634 by A Islip. Plinius Secundus (C.). *The History of the World.*

331.   (38 × 37 mm.) Framed device of Time bringing Truth to light with *Tempore patet occulta veritas*, and R. S.

A smaller form of No. 312, and presumably cut for Richard Smith, though I have not found it used by him. It was probably employed by William Wood in allusion to his sign of Time.

*1601 by V. S. for W. Wood. Weever (J.). *Mirror of Martyrs.*

332.   (11 × 10.5 mm.) A crowned rose.

It is doubtful whether this is to be regarded as a device or merely as an ornament. As, however, Valentine Simmes apparently possessed it in two sizes (see No. 333), it seemed better to include it. The only printer known to have used the Rose and Crown as a sign at this date was Richard Jones.

{ [*c.* 1598] by V. Simmes. Romei (Annibale). *The Courtier's Academy.*
{ [? 1603] by V. S. for J. Harrison the younger. James I. *A Fruitful Meditation.*
    Sayle, 2854.

Perhaps passed to Felix Kingston *c.* 1608.

{ *1609 by F. Kingston for E. Weaver. Parsons (R.). *A Book of Christian Exercise.*
{ 1609 excud. J. Norton. [James I.] *Triplici nodo triplex cuneus, Editio altera.*
    Probably printed *for* Norton.
{ 1612 by F. Kingston for T. Man. Dent (A.). *A Pastime for Parents.*
{ 1615 by F. Kingston for E. Weaver. Parsons (R.). *A Book of Christian Exercise.*
    Sayle, 2993.

333.   (23 × 13.5 mm.) A crowned rose.
        Cf. No. 332.

{ 1601 by V. Simmes for W. Burre. Wright (T.). *The Passions of the Mind.*
    Fragment in Collection of Title-pages at B.M. (618. k. 17), fol. 39.
{ *1602 by V. Simmes. Mason (R.). *Reason's Monarchy.*

129

S

334. (44 × 39 mm.) Device of a pair of compasses, with *Labore et Constantia.*

Copied from one of the devices of the firm of Plantin. Cf. No. 411.

*1601 apud R. Dexter. Sallustius Crispus (C.). *Omnia Opera.*

{ 1601 by J. HARRISON. Chamber (J.). *A Treatise against Judicial Astrology.*
{ 1603 by J. HARRISON for T. Man. C. (R.). *The Bright Star which leadeth . . . to . . . Jesus Christ.*

Perhaps passed to Nicholas Okes *c.* 1607 by way of George Snowdon.

{ 1607 ex off. N. OKES imps. E. Blount. Gwinne (M.). *Vertumnus.*
{ 1608 excud. N. OKES imps. R. Banckworth. Ravisius (J.), Textor. *Epithetorum Epitome.*

335. (120 × 110.5 mm.) Combination device containing in the border reproductions of two devices used by Peter Short (*cf.* Nos. 278, 150), the arms of the Stationers' Company, and a monogram of ' Shorte.'

Within the frame is the device of an anchor and snake supported by two hands emerging from clouds, also used separately, see No. 366.

1602 imps. G. Bishop, S. Waterson, P. SHORT, and T. Adams. Josephus (F.). *The Famous . . . Works.*

The colophon gives Short's name as the printer's.

? Passed to Humphrey Lownes in 1604.

{ 1609 by H. L. for M. Lownes. Spenser (E.). *The Faery Queen.*
{ *1613 by H. L. for M. Lownes. Spenser (E.). *The Faery Queen,* etc. (p. 187: title to Second Part).

The title of Part I is dated 1611; the colophon of Part II ' 16012.'

? Passed to John Legate II.

{ 1632 by J. L. for A. Hebb. Josephus (F.). *The Famous . . . Works.*
{ Presumably used here and in the following for the sake of uniformity with the earlier edition.
{ 1640 by J. L. for A. Hebb. Josephus (F.). *The Famous . . . Works.*

336. (31.5 × 26 mm.) The arms of the University of Oxford, with AC : OX.

Cf. No. 338.

1603 Oxford: excud. J. BARNES. *Academiae Oxoniensis Pietas.*
*1606 Oxford: by J. BARNES. King (J.). *The Fourth Sermon at Hampton Court.*
1616 Oxford: excud. J. BARNES. Godwin (T.). *Synopsis Antiquitatum Hebraicum.*

Passed to John Lichfield in 1617.

1617 Oxford: by J. LICHFIELD and W. Wrench. Angelos (C.). *Christopher Angel Grecian, who tasted of Stripes, etc.*
1618 Oxford: excud. J. LICHFIELD and J. Short. Sanderson (R.). *Logicae Artis Compendium.*
    Sayle, 5333.
1625 Oxford: excud. J. LICHFIELD and W. Turner. Butler (C.). Συγγένεια. *De Propinquitate Matrimonium impediente.*
1635 excud. J. LICHFIELD. James (T.) *Catalogus Interpretorum Scripturae . . . in Bibl. Bodleiana.*

Passed to Leonard Lichfield in 1635.

1636 L. LICHFIELD.   ?   ?
    Sayle, p. 1220.
1639 by L. LICHFIELD for J. Godwin. N. (C.). *The Unfortunate Politique.*

337. (46 × 44.5 mm.) Device of a reverend old man holding up a mirror, in which his young companion sees not his own image, but that of Death, who stands at his shoulder. The legend, *Behoulde your glory.*

Presumably an emblem, but I have not met with it elsewhere in precisely this form.

[? 1603 A Plague-bill.]

A fragment in the Bagford Collection, Harl. 5919, No. 71: the total deaths are 35,254, whereof those who died of the plague were 29,301. This does not seem to correspond exactly with any figures given elsewhere, but is nearer to those of the 1603 plague than to those of any other. Windet entered the bills on 1 August 1603 (Arber, iii. 243).

*1606 by J. WINDET. Turnbull (R.). *Exposition upon the Epistles of James and Jude* (title to *Jude*).

The Jude title has only Windet's name, that to James adds that the books are to be sold by R. Bankworth.

338. (33 × 27 mm.) The arms of the University of Oxford on a shield, with AC : OX at sides.

An imitation of No. 336, from which it can be distinguished by the shape

131

of the central ornament at the top of the shield, and by the absence of a break at the left-hand top corner. It is also somewhat larger.

*1616 'by Ioseph Barnes for Iohn Barnes.' A. (N.). *The Dignity of Man.*

The imprint is false, and the book was not printed at Oxford; see Madan, *Oxford Books*, p. 106.

1624 [no printer]. A. (R.). *In Obitum Thomae Rhaedi.*

Not printed at Oxford; see Madan, *Oxford Books*, p. 120.

339. (35 × 29.5 mm.) Device of a griffin seated on a stone (or a book?), under which is a ball with wings.

See the smaller device, No. 246.

1602 by T. Creede. Vigor (S.). *Acts of the Dispute and Conference . . . at Paris . . . 1566, translated by J. Golburne.*

Probably passed to Bernard Alsop in 1617.

{ *1627 by B. A. and T. Fawcet for John Parker. Sydenham (H.). *The Athenian Babbler* (in his *Five Sermons*, 1626).

1638 by B. A. for H. Seile. J. (W.). *Dictionarium Quadruplex.*

1640 for R. Meighen. Jonson (B.). *Works. The second volume.*

340. (60 × 50 mm.) Device of a winged serpent on a rod upheld by two hands emerging from the clouds, with motto, *Salus Vitæ*

(α) With motto as figured.

*1604 by A. Islip for T. Man. Downham (G.). *The Christian's Sanctuary.*

(β) Without motto.

1607 for C. Burby. Perkins (W.). *A Grain of Mustard Seed.*

Bagford Collection, Harl. 5927, No. 433.

341. (45 × 44.5 mm.) Device of a winged skull resting on a globe; above the skull an hour-glass and a book with the motto, *I liue to dy. I dy to liue.*

A close copy of an emblem of Johannes Sambucus (*Emblemata*, ed. 1566 p. 99). The motto is there *In morte vita*, and the meaning is that if a man gives up his life to the pursuit of knowledge his fame may fly all over the world when he himself is dead. The device seems to have no particular connection with William Leake, bookseller, 1592-1633, who at the time at which it is found in books printed for him was trading at the sign of the Holy Ghost, and from its condition it seems probable that it is a good deal older than 1602, the earliest date at which I have found it.

{ *1602 for W. LEAKE. Shakespeare (W.). *Venus and Adonis.*

1609 by T. Snodham for W. LEAKE. Southwell (R.). *Mary Magdalen's Funeral Tears.*

342. (54 × 45 mm.) Device of a clock affixed to a wall, with the motto *Ponderibus Sonitum*, and the name *Iacobus Rimeus*.

A device of a clock was in use by Jacomo Vidali at Naples in 1574, but Rime's is not particularly like it, and may have been derived from an emblem.

*1605 excud. J. RIME. Zanchius (H.). *In D. Pauli Apostoli Epistolas*, and *De Religione Christiana Fides*.

343. (67 × 55 mm.) Very roughly cut device, having the sun at top, a hare and sheaf of rye (?) at sides, a vase of flowers in centre, and the Stationers' arms below.

Cf. No. 286, which was owned in 1592 by J. Harrison.

*1604 for E. White. N. (B.). *Grimello's Fortunes.*

[The device occurs also in the Bagford Collection, Harl. 5963, No. 310, with No. 290 on verso, but I have not been able to identify the book from which the fragment was taken. It seems likely to be one printed by E. Allde for J. Harrison, but is not Massinger's *Bondman*.

344. (45 × 34 mm.) Two figures, apparently representing Peace and Plenty, under a canopy, with the initials T. P.

The initials are probably those of Thomas Purfoot, junior.

1605 [? T. Purfoot] for the Comp. of Stationers. Dent (A.). *The Plain Mans Pathway to Heaven.*

Sayle, 1384. There is some doubt as to the printer of this book. It contains the half-eagle and key device (No. 136), which is not otherwise known to have been used by Purfoot.

*1607 by T. PURFOOT. Lloyd (L.). *The Jubilee of Britain.*

345.   (55 × 45 mm.)   Framed device of a pavior paving.   The motto, *Thou shalt labor till thou returne to duste*.   Above the frame the initials T. P.   At the upper corners two paving-beetles; at the lower, a spade, picks, etc.

{ 1605 for T. PAVIER.   Thynne (F.).   *The Case is altered.*
*1607 for T. PAVIER.   A[rthington] (H.).   *Principal Points of Holy Profession.*
1618 by W. I. for T. P.   Rogers (   ).   *The Glory and Happiness of a True Christian.*
     Sayle, 3326.

346.   (85 × 59 mm.)   Floral border with crowned roses, and below a mark containing the initials R. B.

1604 by R. BRADOCK.   *A Godly Garden.*

      Probably passed to Thomas Haviland and William Hall in 1609, and from them to John Beale *c.* 1612.

{ 1619 by J. BEALE for T. Pavier.   *A Godly Garden.*
*1640 by J. BEALE for R. Bird.   *A Godly Garden.*

347.   (31 × 87 mm.)   Device or ornament of an open book upon which is laid a sword and a sceptre: the motto, *Doctrina parit virtutem.*

      I cannot discover that this represents the arms of any person or society, though it seems probable that it does, nor is the ownership of the block at all clear.   From 1607 to 1629, save for a single appearance at Eton in 1613, its use seems almost to have been confined to official publications by the King's Printers and law-books issued by the Stationers' Company.   If the Eton imprint is authentic, the block must, presumably, at that time have been in the possession of M. Bradwood (cf. Nos. 293, 380), in which case we might suppose it to have formerly belonged to the Eliot's Court Press; but the earlier imprints seem rather to indicate that it was owned by the Barker, Bill, and Norton partnership.

*1607 for the Soc. of Stationers.   Coke (Sir E.).   *La Size Part des Reports.*
1607 ex Typog. Soc. Stationariorum.   Stanford (Sir W.).   *Les Plees del Corone.*
1609 excud. J. Norton.   James I.   *Apologia pro Juramento Fidelitatis* (sig. B1).
1612 by R. Barker.   James I.   *His Majesty's Declaration . . . in the cause of D. C. Vorstius.*

134

1615 Eton: in Collegio Regali.   Gregory of Nazianzus.   Λογος εις τα θεοφάνια.
1623 for the Comp. of Stationers.   Pulton (F.).   *De Pace Regis.*
1629 for the Comp. of Stationers.   Coke (Sir E.).   *La Sept Part des Reports.*
1635 by A. Islip.   Heywood (T.).   *The Hierarchy of the blessed Angels* (sig. ¶3).

348.   (53 × 41 mm.)   Device of an old man standing by an olive-tree, with the motto *Noli altum sapere* on a scroll entwined in the branches.

   Copied from the device of Charles Estienne, printer at Paris, 1551-1561 (Silvestre, 959).

   It is stated by T. B. Reed in his *Old English Letter Foundries*, p. 140, on the authority of the *Histoire de l'Imprimerie* of Paul Dupont, 1854, i. 488, that permission to use the Estienne device was granted to John Norton by Paul Estienne, while on a visit to England in 1594, as a mark of admiration for his printing.   I have, however, been unable to trace the story back beyond Dupont, or to find an example of the use of the device in England earlier than 1605.   This device was re-cut at least twice; see Nos. 349, 350.

   *1605 excud. J. NORTON.   Morton (T.).   *Apologia Catholica.*
   1605 'excudi curavit' J. BILL.   Lydiat (T.).   *De Natura Coeli.*
   1607 ex off. J. NORTON.   Keckermannus (B.).   *Systema Ethica.*
   1626 Londini imps. R. Rounthwaite.   *Phrases Elegantiores ex optimis autoribus.*
      Ames Collection, ii. 573.

349.   (52.5 × 43 mm.)   Device of an old man standing by an olive-tree, etc.

   No. 348 re-cut.   The two blocks may be most easily distinguished by the form of the man's right hand.   There are also differences in the foliage on the left hand side of the tree.

   1616 apud J. BILL.   Draxe (T.).   *Bibliotheca Scholastica.*
   *1619 apud J. BILL.   Brerewood (E.).   *Elementa Logica.*
   1622 apud J. BILL.   Της Καινης Διαθηκης απαντα . . . *cum notis Stephani, Scaligeri, Casauboni.*
   1624 apud B. NORTON and J. BILL.   Casaubon (M.).   *Vindicatio Patris.*

350.   (53 × 42 mm.)   Device of an old man standing by an olive-tree, etc.

   No. 348 re-cut for the second time.   Most easily distinguished from the other

135

blocks of this device by the shape of the clump of herbage behind the man. The execution of the block is also somewhat coarser than that of the others.

*1631 ex typographia Soc. Stationariorum. Ravisius (J.), Textor, *Epistolae*.

351. (53 × 39 mm.) Device of an old man standing by an olive-tree, with the motto *Noli altum sapere* on a scroll entwined in the branches.

> The device is probably one of those belonging to the Estienne family (see Silvestre, 1134; cf. 163, 958), and not English at all. I have, however, included it, as I have been unable definitely to identify the block with any of those used abroad.

*1615 apud heredes J. Norton and J. Bill. Ἰσοκρατους λογοι και ἐπιστολαι.

> The book may have been printed abroad; see Sayle, 2377.

352. (53 × 47 mm.) Device of two men, one planting and the other watering, under a sky in which is set the sacred name in Hebrew characters.

> This is closely copied from a device of Thomas Courteau, printer at Geneva, 1557-1567 (Silvestre, 851; Heitz, *Genfer Buchdruckerzeichen*, No. 10). Courteau used it with the motto: 'Celuy qui plante n'est rien, ne celuy qui arrouse: mais Dieu qui donne accroissement. 1. Corinth. 3.' The ownership of the device is not clear. Mr. Sayle (p. 428) regards it as Hatfield's, but the evidence seems rather to connect it with Norton and Bill.

1600 by E. Bollifant for B. Norton. Estienne (C.) and Liébault (J.). *Maison Rustique, or the Country Farm, trans. by R. Surflet.*

1603 for S. Waterson and C. Burby. Hayward (J.). *An answer to the first part of a certain Conference . . . of R. Dolman.*

1606 for J. Bill. Forset (E.). *A comparative discourse of the Bodies Natural and Politic.*

1606 by A. Islip. Rider (J.) *Dictionary.*

*1607 for J. Norton. Mason (F.). *The Authority of the Church.*

1614 excud. B. Norton and J. Bill. *Novum Testamentum.*

353. (73 × 56 mm.) The arms of the Stationers' Company in an oval frame with figures representing Grammar and Geometry at foot.

1607 ex typographia Soc. Stationariorum. Cicero (M. T.). *Epistolae ad Familiares.*
> Ames Collection, ii. 143.

A horizontal crack appeared through the dove in clouds in 1607-11. The defect at foot also appeared during the same period.

{ *1611 by H. L. for M. Lownes. Spenser (E.). *The Faery Queen, &c.* (title to *Tears of the Muses*).

1617 by H. L. for M. Lownes. Spenser (E.). *The Faery Queen, &c.* (title to *Tears of the Muses*).

354. (49 × 37 mm.) Prince of Wales's feathers, with crown and *Ich Dien.*

(α) Within rule, as figured.

*1608 by A. Hatfield for E. Edgar and S. Macham. Hall (J.). *Epistles* (vol. i, p. 103).

1608 by M. Bradwood for W. Aspley. Abbot (G.). *A Sermon . . . at Westminster, May 26, 1608.*

Probably belonged to the Eliot's Court Press, and passed to Edward Griffin *c.* 1613.

(β) Rule cut away, reducing size to 38.5 × 32 mm.

1614 for J. Bill. King (J.). *Vitis Palatina, a Sermon . . . at Whitehall.*

1615 excud. E. GRIFFIN. Barclay (J.). *Poemata.*

355. (68 × 59 mm.) Device of a hand emerging from the clouds, with a snake entwined about the wrist, holding a staff surmounted by a portcullis, and sprays of foliage. The motto, *Prudentia.*

Save for the portcullis (the arms of the City of Westminster) at the top, and for the substitution of 'Prudentia' for the printer's name 'Vincenti,' the device seems to have been copied from that of Barthélemy Vincent, bookseller at Lyons, 1571-1626; see Silvestre, 1263. Compare also the devices of Antoine Vincent, Silvestre, 934-8, 618.

{ 1606 by W. JAGGARD. Trogus Pompeius. *The History of Justin,* trans. by *G. W.*

1609 in a combination device; see No. 370.

*1619 by W. JAGGARD. *The Treasury of Ancient and Modern Times* (Part ii).

356. (65 × 45 mm.) A garb, or wheatsheaf, on a wreath. Possibly the crest of the printer's patron, but it was used by several families, and I have been unable to identify the person intended.

Mr. Sayle (No. 7439) notes that the sermon by R. Wilkinson preached at the marriage of Sir James Hay and Honora Denny in 1607 and published as *The Merchant Royal*, by F. Kingston for J. Flasket, has a smaller garb. This sermon has on the title a ship (63 × 86 mm.), and above it to left and right the garb referred to and a crest of a cubit arm holding five wheat ears. The latter is the crest of the Denny family, and perhaps the garb was that of Sir James. Hay, but I have been unable to find evidence of this.

*1607 for J. Flasket. Wilkinson (R.). *A Sermon at Northampton* 21 *June* (1607).

1626 for R. Milborne. *Pelagius Redivivus.*

1633 excud. M. F., imps. R. Whitaker. Draxe (T.). *Bibliotheca scholastica.*

357. (33.5 × 30 mm.) Device or (?) crest of a closed fist, with *Ex Avaritia Bellum.*

   Cf. Nos. 314, 359.

1610 for T. Pavier. Wilkinson (R.). *A Jewel for the Ear.*

*1616 for W. Butler. Richardson (C.). *A Sermon concerning the punishing of Male-factors.*

358. (39 × 39 mm.) Ornament with mark of Thomas Finlason, printer at Edinburgh, 1604-27.

(α) With monogram as figured.

{ *1609 Edinburgh: excud. T. FINLASON. Skene (Sir J.). *Regiam Majestatem: Scotiæ veteres leges* (sig. *A*10 verso).

1623 Edinburgh: excud. T. FINLASON. Simson (A.). *Hieroglyphica Natatilium* (Part. iii of *Hier. Animalium*) (end of prelims.).

   Passed *c.* 1632 to Robert Young, and later, by way of George Anderson, to Robert Bryson.

(β) Monogram altered to R.B.

{ 1640 Edinburgh: [R. BRYSON]. *The intentions of the Army of Scotland.*
   Aldis, 971.

1642 Edinburgh: [R. BRYSON]. *Another declaration from . . . Parliament . . . to His Majesty March* 23, 1641.
   Aldis, 1027.

359. (33.5 × 30 mm.) Device or (?) crest of a closed fist with *Contrahit avaritia bellum.*

   Compare No. 357, and for the motto No. 314.

*1613 typis W. Stansby, imps. J. Budge. Aretius (J.). *Primula Veris.*

360.   (123 × 75.5 mm.) Compartment with four armillary spheres, cherubs, foliage, and the initials E.A., standing for the name of Edward Allde, printer, 1584-1628.

*1609 by E. A. for J. Busby. M[ELTON] (J.). *A Six-fold Politician.*

*** The lower part alone as a head ornament.

n.d. per E. ALLDE. *Litera Cuiusdam Pistoris Bononiensis ad Papam.*
    Bodl., Douce Add. 142, No. 36.

361.   (41 × 36 mm.)   A two-headed eagle.

This is evidently intended for the arms of William Barlow, Bishop of Lincoln, the author of the book in which it appears. The arms are described as 'Sable, an eagle displayed double-headed, holding a staff raguly barwise argent, beaked and membered and a fleurdelys in chief or' (Bedford, *Blazon of Episcopacy*, p. 74). The fleur-de-lis should be between and above the heads.

It is very doubtful whether this is to be considered as a printer's device, for neither Haviland nor Law are known to have been otherwise connected with Barlow or under his patronage. It seemed, however, useful to include it, as an imitation of it was undoubtedly used as a device by another printer; see No. 362.

*1609 by T. Haviland for M. Law. Barlow (W.). *An answer to a Catholic Englishman* (verso of title).

362.   (44 × 38.5 mm.)   Device of a two-headed eagle.

A rough copy of No. 361, which see.

{ 1611 by W. W. for T. Man. Gardiner (S.). *The Scourge of Sacrilege.*
{ *1612 by W. WHITE. Broughton (H.). *Observations upon first ten Fathers.*
{ 1617 by W. WHITE. Greene (R.). *Greene's Farewell to Folly.*

363.   (77 × 104 mm.)   Ornament with mark of Thomas Finlason, printer in Edinburgh, 1602-28.

*1609 by T. FINLASON. Skene (Sir J.). *Regiam majestatem. The auld lawes* (end), and *Scotiae Veteres Leges* (sig. *A*6, B1, etc., *VI verso).

1621 by T. FINLASON. Statutes. *The xxiii Parliament of James . . . at Edinburgh, the 4 day of August 1621* (end of prelims.).

Passed to Robert Young *c.* 1632.

1633 by R. YOUNG. *The Acts made in the first Parliament of Charles . . . 28 day of June* 1633 (sig. I1 verso).

 Probably passed later to George Anderson and Robert Bryson.

364. (7 × 12 mm.) Monogram of Francis Burton, stationer, 1603-17.

{ *1613 by G. Eld for F. BURTON. Wither (G.). *Abuses Stript and Whipt.*
  B.M., 1076. c. 2.
1615 by H. Lownes for F. BURTON. Wither (G.). *Abuses Stript and Whipt.*

365. (17 × 18 mm.) Device or emblem of two heads joined at the back.

 As used in 1610 it seems probable that this was meant to refer to the title of the book in which it appeared. As, however, it may have been suggested by the devices used by P. Brubach at Frankfurt, 1543-4 (Heitz, *Frankf. Druckerzeichen*, xxxi. 17, 18, 20), and as it was later used in other works, it seemed best to include it.

{ *1610 typis T. S. procur. J. Helme. Selden (J.). *Jani Anglorum Facies altera.*
1623 typis T. SNODHAM. Aristotle. *De Poetica.*
1624 by T. S. for N. Newbery. Du Moulin (P.). *The Jesuits Shifts.*
1624 excud. J. Bill. Dominis (M. A. de). *Alter Ecebolius.*

366. (71.5 × 53.5 mm.) Oval device of an anchor and snake upheld by two hands emerging from clouds.

 The device was that of Jean Crespin, printer at Geneva, 1551-72; see Heitz, *Genfer Buchdruckerzeichen*, 43-53, and cf. the devices of Thomas Bassandyne, Nos. 176, 178. Short may have adopted it on account of its being in some degree similar to his brazen serpent (No. 119). This design was afterwards closely copied in a device used by Griffin and Haviland, see No. 390.

1602 [As the centre of a combination device, see No. 335.]

Passed from Peter Short to Humphry Lownes in 1604.

{ 1609 by H. L[OWNES] for R. Moore. Benson (G.). *A Sermon at Paul's Cross*
  7 May 1609.
  *1614 by H. LOWNES for A. Johnson, etc. Hall (J.). *Meditations and Vows.*
  1632 [In the combination device as above.]
  1640 [In the combination device as above.]

367. (64 × 54 mm.) Oval device of Jove with eagle and thunder-bolt, and two oak-trees; the initials N. O., for Nicholas Okes, printer, 1606-39, and the sign of Jupiter. The legend *Tam Robur .*
Tam Robor . Ni-colis arbor Iovis. 1610.

> Beyond the obvious pun on the oak, sacred to Jupiter, and the name Okes,
> I cannot interpret this motto.

{ 1610 by N. OKES for H. Rocket. Web (R.). *Christ's Kingdom.*
  *1611 by N. OKES for H. Rocket. Web (R.). *Christ's Kingdom.*
  1616 for the Comp. of Stationers. Hopton (A.). *A Concordancy of years* (end).
  1616 by N. OKES.   ?   ?

> Bagford Collection, Harl. 5927, No. 211: book not identified.

368. (40 × 39 mm.) Framed device of a bird, probably a smew, with the word 'wick' in its bill. The motto, *Non altum peto.* I. S.
> See No. 376.

{ *1609 for J. SMETHWICK. Smith (Sir T.). *The Commonwealth of England.*
  1640 by R. Young for J. SMETHWICK. Smith (Sir T.). *The Commonwealth of England*
  (end).

> The block, which was presumably a metal one, shows no sign of wear.

369. (46.5 × 46.5 mm.) Device or emblem of a circle within a triangle, with *Non cercami fuori.*

> It is possible that this is the device of the author of the book in which it
> is found, not of the printer.

*1610 by G. E. for J. Helme. S[elden], J. *The Duello.*

141

370. (122 × 116 mm.) Compartment containing a copy of the Geneva arms device used first by Rowland Hall (see No. 136), and the mark of William Jaggard with the motto, *Be Thankfull to God.* Below, the arms of the Stationers' Company.

For the device within the compartment see No. 355.
*1609 by W. JAGGARD. Heywood (T.). *Troia Britannica.*

371. (35 × 39 mm.) Cut or device of a lamb, with *Sacrifizio Agnello Salvazione Mundo.*

It is doubtful whether this is to be regarded as a device, and to whom it belonged. Clement Knight, bookseller, traded at the sign of the Holy Lamb in St. Paul's Churchyard, 1595-1624 (H. B. Wheatley in *Bibl. Soc Trans.* ix. 94).
*1611 imps. Soc. Stationariorum. Aphthonius. *Progymnasmata.*
1619 ex typ. Soc. Stationariorum. Châteillon (S.). *Dialogorum Sacrorum libri quatuor.* Sayle, 7408.

372. (34 × 32 mm.) Ornament or device of clasped hands, rope and flames.

It is doubtful to whom this ornament belonged. It is sometimes one way up and sometimes the other. George Vincent used the sign of the Hand in Hand, but I have not found him connected with the books in which this block appears.
*1615 by G. Purslowe. Wright (L.). *A Summons for Sleepers.*
1620 ex. off. Soc. Stationariorum. Lubinus (E.). *Clavis Graecae linguae.*

373. (25 × 42 mm.) Device of a shield bearing two keys, with crest a wyvern's head.

I have not been able to identify the arms.
*1611 by H. L. for M. Lownes. Croce (G.). *Musica Sacra.*
1615 for the Comp. of Stationers. *The Psalter . . . with the Morning and Evening Prayer.*

Probably used by Humphrey Lownes and Robert Young in partnership *c.* 1625-30.
[? *c.* 1625] by R. Young for T. Downes and E. Dawson. Ussher (J.). *A Brief Declaration of the Universality of the Church.*

1627 by H. L. for J. Bartlet. Harris (R.). *Peter's Enlargement.*
1629 for T. Downes. *Articles of religion agreed upon by the Archbishops . . . at Dublin,* 1615.
1630 'Imprinted at London.' Downham (J.). *A brief concordance to the Bible.*

    Apparently N. Bourne had the printing of this (see *Dictionary I,* under Clement Cotton); but he may have let it out to Lownes and Young, to whom Mr. Sayle attributes the book (Sayle, 2563).

374. (41 × 36 mm.) Device with a griffin's head erased in the centre, and the arms of the Stationers' Company and those of John Beale in the upper corners.

    For Beale's arms see *Visitation of London in* 1634 (Harl. Soc. xv), p. 58. The crest should be a unicorn's head *semée d'estoiles.*

{ *1613 by J. BEALE for W. Welby. Downame (J.). *Consolations for the Afflicted.*
{ 1613 by J. BEALE. Spelman (Sir H.). *A Tract of the Rights due unto Churches.*
{ 1634 by J. BEALE. Hall (J.). *Works* (vol. i, p. 931—*Contemplations, The Ninth Book*).

375. (96 × 87 mm.) Device of the sun emerging from clouds, in a border with flowers in vases and two birds. The motto *Sic Augustinus dissipabit.*

    The motto appears to be part of the block, which, therefore, was presumably cut for the work in which it is first met with. Later, this motto was removed, and the device is used either with other mottoes inserted in type, or with none. The inner part was then entirely separate from the frame, as is clear from the different position which it occupies in different books.

(α) With motto, *Sic Augustinus dissipabit,* as figured.
*1610 by G. ELD. Augustine, Saint. *Of the City of God.*

(β) Without motto, or with a motto inserted in type.
1620 by G. ELD and M. Flesher. Augustine, Saint. *Of the City of God.*

    In this there is the same motto as in the edition of 1610, but it is inserted in type (italic caps.).

        Passed to Miles Fletcher or Flesher in 1624.

1628 for N. Butter. Hall (J.). *Works* (sig 5T6).
{ 1632 by M. FLESHER for N. Butter. Hall (J.). *A Paraphrase upon Hard Texts of the New Testament.*
{ 1634 for N. Butter. Hall (J.). *Works* (vol. i, p. 659, etc., vol. ii, p. 293).
{ 1637 by M. FLESHER. Babington (G.). *Works* (pp. 163, 345, etc.).

376. (61 × 48 mm.) Framed device of a bird bearing the word 'wick' in its bill, with *Non altum peto.* *I. S.*

The bird is presumably a smew, and a pun is intended on the name John Smethwick, the owner of the device. It may be noted, however, that the bird's name occurs in a great variety of forms, among others 'smee' and 'smeath,' so we can infer nothing as to the contemporary pronunciation of 'Smethwick.' The frame appears to be copied from that of No. 292. As the condition of the block had not noticeably deteriorated after twenty-five years of use, we may suppose it to have been a metal one.

Cf. the smaller size, No. 368.

{ 1612 for J. SMETHWICK. L. (T.) Gent. *Euphues Golden Legacy.*
{ 1637 by R. Young for J. SMETHWICK. Shakespeare (W.). *Romeo and Juliet.*
{ *1637 for J. SMETHWICK. Smith (Henry). *Three Sermons.*

377. (20 × 89 mm.) Ornamental head-piece with A and a heart.

{ 1611 Edinburgh: by A. HART. Julius (A.). *Paraphrasis Prophetiae Maleaci poetica* (sig. A2).
{ *1619 Edinburgh: excud. A. HART. Scot (J.). *In Jacobi Sexti . . . e Scotia sua decessum Hodoeporicon* (sigs. *A2, C2).

Passed to Andro Hart's heirs in 1621.

{ 1622 Edinburgh: excud. HEREDES A. HART. *Theses Philosophicae* (sig. A).
{ 1633 Edinburgh: by the HEIRS of A. HART. Ἐισόδια *Musarum Edinensium.*

378. (49.5 × 50.5 mm.) Device or ornament of a woman's head with cornucopias and the initials of Andro Hart.

Cf. Vautrollier's device, No. 179.

{ 1611 Edinburgh: by A. HART. Julius (A.). *Paraphrasis Prophetiae Maleaci poetica* (title and sig. B3 verso).
{ *1619 Edinburgh: excud. A. HART. Scot (J.). *In Jacobi Sexti . . . e Scotia sua decessum Hodoeporicon* (sig. B4 verso).
{ 1621 Edinburgh: A. HART. Despauter (J.). *Grammatica.*

Aldis, 571.

379. (33 × 30 mm.) A mask with rings: the letters A. H. below.

This is perhaps a cast ornament with the letters inserted.

144

{ *1613 Edinburgh: by A. HART. Symson (P.). *A Short Compend of Persecutions* (end of Preface).

{ 1619 Edinburgh: excud. A. HART. Scot (J.). *In Jacobi Sexti . . . decessum Hodoeporicon.*

380. (33.5 × 36.5 mm.) Device of an owl, two snakes, and a rod, with initials M. B.

The initials stand for the name of Melchisedec Bradwood.

(α) With M. B. as figured.

*1615 Eton: in Collegio Regali. Gregory of Nazianzus. Λογος εἰς τα θεοφάνια.

Probably passed to Edward Griffin in 1615-16.

{ 1616 by E. GRIFFIN for T. Barlow. Barlow (W.). *Magnetical Advertisements.*

{ 1618 for R. Milborne. Dyke (D.). *Two Treatises* (p. 325, title to *The School of Affliction*).

The rest of the book was printed by 'G. P.,' and there is nothing to indicate that he did not execute the whole.

(β) The 'M. B.' voided.

1619 ex typ. Soc. Stationariorum. Cicero (M. T.). *Sententiae.*

Ames Collection, ii. 408.

1619 excud. E. GRIFFIN. Campion (T.). *Epigrammatum libri ii.*

381. (15 × 14 mm.) A fleur-de-lis, without border.

I cannot be certain whether there was more than one block of this. The measurements of different prints seem to vary perplexingly between 16 × 15 and 14 × 13.5 mm., but most of the difference is perhaps caused by the wear of the projecting points.

{ 1609 excud. N. O. sumptibus R. Boyle. Paul III. *Consilium Delectorum Cardinalium.*

{ *1618 ex off. N. de Quercubus sumpt. S. Waterson. Owen (J.). *Epigrammata.*

{ 1624 by N. OKES. Westerne (T.). *The Flaming Bush.*

1634 by J. Norton. Shakespeare (W.). *Richard II.*

John Norton was in partnership with Okes from some time before 1634; cf. No. 251.

Passed to John Okes, c. 1636.

1640 by J. OKES for S. Browne. Rutter (J.). *The Second part of the Cid.*

Probably passed to William Wilson c. 1644.

{ 1648 by W. WILSON for T. Jackson. Ravius (C.). *Sesquidecuria epistolarum.*

{ 1650 by W. WILSON for H. Mosely. Rutter (J.). *The Cid.*

382. (52 × 47 mm.) Mercury standing upon the globe.

This appears to have been copied from the device of Jean Gueffier, bookseller at Paris, 1585 (Silvestre, 617), or that of J. and G. von Kempen, used at Cologne in 1592 (Heitz, *Kölner Buchermarken*, No. 147). The device may have been owned by J. Bill, but Mr. Sayle, in his index, queries whether the *Terra Australis* and the *Argenis* were printed at Frankfurt.

1617 for J. Hodgets. Fernandes di Queiros (P.). *Terra Australis incognita.*
1619 appresso Giov. Bill. Gatti (A.). *La Caccia.*
*1622 pro Soc. Bibliopolarum. Barclay (J.). *Argenis.*

383. (34 × 31 mm.) The so-called ' Protestant Angel.'

See Sayle, p. 953, note 1. The device is said to have been used by the French Protestants at Rochelle in 1621 as representing 'Religion' trampling on the Church of Rome (see C. Chalons, *History of France*, 1752, ii. 403); but is much older than this, and may have originally stood simply for Faith triumphing over Death. It was used by several French printers, see Silvestre, Nos. 607, 894, 956, and Heitz, *Genfer Buchdruckerzeichen*, 25, 70, 160. It also appears as the centre of an ornament on the title-page of Plutarch's *Morals*, printed by Arnold Hatfield in 1603.

1619 for the Co. of Stationers. *Psalms (Sternhold and Hopkins)*, 32mo.
*1639 by G. M. for N. Bourne and R. Harford. Sibbes (R.). *Beames of Divine Light* (sig. F8—' *Gods Inquisition* ').

384. (49 × 42 mm.) The ' Protestant Angel.'
Cf. No. 383.

{ *1616 Edinburgh: excud. A. Hart. Spottiswood (J.). *Concio . . . ad Clerum Andreanopoli.*
1621 Edinburgh: by A. Hart. Hunnis (W.). *A Handful of Honeysuckles* (verso of title).

385. (35 × 32 mm.) The ' Protestant Angel.'

A re-cutting of No. 383, most easily distinguished from it by the size and shape of the angel's head. There is no break in the upright of the cross.

*1626 for the Co. of Stationers. *Psalms (Sternhold and Hopkins)*.
B.M., 3436. a. 19.
1635 for the Co. of Stationers. *Psalms (Sternhold and Hopkins)*.
B.M., C. 65. h. 2.

386. (48 × 41 mm.) Rebus of Henry Bell—a hen, rye, and bell, with the monogram of Henry Bell.

> Cf. No. 388.

{ *1616 for H. BELL. Greenwood (H.). *Works* (title to *The Race Celestial*, sig. I2).
{ 1621 by N. O. for H. BELL. Greene (R.). *Greene's Groatsworth of Wit.*

387. (30 × 25 mm.) Monogram of Thomas Langley, stationer, 1615-35.

*1616 by G. E. for T. LANGLEY. ? ?

> Bagford Collection, Harl. 5963, No. 160: I have been unable to identify the book from which the fragment is taken.

388. (39 × 33 mm.) A hen, rye, and bell; with the monogram of Henry Bell.

> Cf. No. 386.

{ *1618 by G. P[urslowe] for H. BELL. Greenwood (H.). *Works.*
{ 1620 by G. Purslowe for H. BELL. Greenwood (H.). *The Jailer's Jail-delivery.*

389. (67 × 89.5 mm.) Device of a printing-press with men at work. The men have lighted candles fixed on their heads. Motto, *Aliis serviemus, nosmetipsos conterimus.*

{ *1619 per W. JONES. Pontanus (R.). *De Sabbaticorum Annorum Periodis.*
{ 1622 by W. JONES. Cooke (A.). *Yet more work for a Mass Priest.*

390. (73.5 × 57 mm.) Device of an anchor and snake upheld by two hands from the clouds; with motto, *Anchora Fidei ∴ Sic elevabitur filius hominis. Io.3 ∴*

> Save for the motto, this device is closely copied from No. 366.

*1617 by E. GRIFFIN for H. Featherstone. Hall (J.). *A recollection of such treatises.*
> (*Sig. C5 and on other separate titles.)

Probably passed to John Haviland in 1621.

1628 [? by J. Haviland]. Hall (J.). *Works*, Part I.
> The title has, 'Printed by M. Flesher for N. Butter,' but the book was the work of a number of printers; see Sayle, 4248, and p. 1043.

147

{ 1629 by J. HAVILAND for R. Allot. Guicciardini (F.). *A Brief Inference upon Guicciardini's digression*.
{ 1639 by J. HAVILAND for W. Lee. Bacon (F.). *Sylva Sylvarum* (title to *New Atlantis*).

391. (74.5 × 63.5 mm.) A cut of the Pope, a cardinal, a bishop, two monks, and the devil blowing at the world [or England], which remains unmoved in the midst of them: the word *Immota* round the central object.

It is doubtful whether this is to be considered as a device or not. The sign of Thomas Snodham, who appears to have owned it, is unknown.

1618 by T. S. for R. Jackson and W. Bladen. Ward (S.). *Balm from Gilead*.

*1622 by I. H. for R. Jackson and W. Bladen. Ward (S.). *Balm from Gilead*.

1623 excud. T. S. pro R. Milbourne. Texeda (F. de). *Hispanus Conversus*.

392. (36.5 × 37 mm.) Device or ornament of a burning heart within a wreath.

Possibly cut as an appropriate ornament for Ward's *Coal from the Altar*, but used by Haviland and his successors as a regular device.

1618 by E. G[riffin] for J. Macham. Ward (S.). *A Coal from the Altar*.

Probably passed to John Haviland (and Anne Griffin) in 1621.

1622 by A. M. for J. Marriott and J. Grismand. Ward (S.). *A Coal from the Altar*.

The device may have been lent to Augustine Mathewes for the purpose of this particular reprint. He does not seem to have used it otherwise.

{ *1622 by J. HAVILAND for N. Butter. Hannay (P.). *Sheretine and Mariana*.
{ 1631 by I. H. and are to be sold by J. Boler. Lyly (J.). *Euphues* (both parts).

Probably passed to Anne Griffin alone in 1634.

{ 1634 by A. GRIFFIN. King (H.). *Exposition upon the Lord's Prayer*.
{ 1637 by A. GRIFFIN for E. Brewster. Gataker (T.). *Noah his Obedience*, etc.

Passed to Edward Griffin II *c.* 1638.

1638 typis E. GRIFFIN prostant ven. apud R. Whitaker. Bacon (F.). *Opera Moralia et Civilia*.

1650 [no printer]. La Fountain (   ), Dentist. *A Brief Collection of many Rare Secrets*.

Edward Griffin was still in business at this date.

393. (34 × 34 mm.) Emblematic device of a boy with wings on one wrist, and in the other hand a weight; the motto, *Mollia cum duris.*

For the emblem see No. 142.

[?] 'Genevæ apud Jacobum Stoer.'

The device, apparently from the same block as that used by Stansby, occurs in a fragment with the above imprint in the Bagford Collection (Harl. 5963, No. 407). There is no indication of the book from which the fragment was taken, and I have been unable to identify it. As, however, the device is not known to have been used by Stoer, who printed at Geneva from *c.* 1580 to 1625, and as the type of the imprint appears to be the same as one possessed by Stansby, it seems not improbable that the imprint is false and that the book was printed in England.

*1619 imps. W. STANSBY pro H. Fetherstone. Rainolds (J.). *Orationes duodecim.*

1621 ex off. Bibliopolarum. Casaubon (M.). *Pietas.*

1624 ap. J. Bill. Caninius (A.). Ἑλληνισμος.

1625 ex off. G. S. Korudaleus (T.). Περι ἐπιστολικων τυπων.

G. S. is presumably William Stansby.

Probably passed to Richard Bishop in 1634-8.

1640 by R. BISHOP for J. Emery. Holmes (N.). '*Usury is injury*' . . . *answered.*

394. (67 × 70 mm.) **The arms of Aberdeen.**

Edward Raban printed at Aberdeen at the sign of The Town's Arms from 1622 to 1650.

1622 Aberdeen: excud. E. RABAN. Tilenus (D.). *De disciplina ecclesiastica.* Sayle, 5998.

*1624 Aberdeen: by E. RABAN. Logie (A.). *Rain from the Clouds.*

1625 Aberdeen: excud. E. RABAN. Wedderburne (D.). *Abredonia atrata.*

395. (26 × 26 mm.) **Device of the sun in glory.**

Referring to the sign of John Partridge, bookseller, 1623-1649. Mr. Plomer (*Dictionary II*, p. 145) says that this is not a device but an ornament, and is 'a portion of an old wooden block.'

*1624 in off. J. Haviland sumptibus J. PARTRIDGE. Buchler (J.). *Phrasium Poeticarum Thesaurus.*

1628 by J. Haviland to be sold by J. PARTRIDGE. King (H.). *An Exposition upon the Lord's Prayer.*

Partridge's address is given as 'at the sign of the Sunne.'

149

| 1629 typis J. Haviland imps. J. PARTRIDGE. Martinius (M.). *Graecae Linguae Fundamenta.*

1642 for J. Wright. *Replication of the Lords and Commons.*

      Bagford Collection, Harl. 5921, No. 302.

396. (39 × 20 mm.) A crowned rose.

This is a cast ornament belonging to a set which included the crowned harp (No. 398), a crowned thistle, and a crowned fleur-de-lis. These are frequently used together, as in J. Longland's *Great Britain's Salomon*, J. Bill, 1625 (sig. A2), and Bacon's *Sylva Sylvarum*, J. H. for W. Lee, 1628 (prelims.), and then, of course, are merely ornaments. The rose, however, is fairly often used alone, and as it then may be taken for a device, it seems useful to give it. It is to be distinguished from the rose used at Oxford (No. 400).

1625 by J. Bill. *Orders thought Meet by His Majesty . . . Towns . . . infected with the Plague.*

*1626 ex off. Soc. Stationariorum. Ravisius (J.), Textor. *Epithetorum Epitome.*

1632 apud J. Norton and R. Whitaker. Pelegromius (S.). *Synonymorum Sylva.*

397. (36 × 34 mm.) Device of clasped hands, cornucopias, and F. K.; with *Sapientia Pacem. Pax Opulentiam.*

      See No. 402.

*1621 by F. KINGSTON for J. Budge. Prideaux (J.). *Eight Sermons.*

1626 by F. KINGSTON for R. Milburne. Bernard (R.). *Rhemes against Rome.*

1627 ex typ. Soc. Stationariorum. *Plutarchi . . . de Liberorum Institutione . . . item Isocratis Orationes Tres.*

      Presumably printed by Kingston.

·398. (39.5 × 20 mm.) A crowned harp.

This is merely a cast ornament, belonging to the same set as the crowned rose (No. 396), which see. As used by the Dublin Stationers, however, it may be regarded more or less as a device, and it therefore seemed best to include it.

*1624 Dublin: by the Soc. of Stationers. Usher (J.). *An answer to a challenge made by a Jesuit.*

399.   (29 × 25.5 mm.) A shield with the arms of the University of Cambridge.

1625 Cambridge: excud. C. LEGGE. Cambridge, Univ. of. *Epithalamium Caroli Regis et H. Mariae.*

Passed to Thomas and John Buck *c.* 1626.

{ 1627 Cambridge: apud T. & J. BUCK. Davenant (J.). *Expositio Epistolae ad Colossenses* (third leaf of prelims.).

{ *1630 Cambridge: apud T. & J. BUCK. Davenant (J.). *Expositio Epistolae ad Colossenses* (title).

400.   (33.5 × 19 mm.) Ornament of a crowned rose.
      Cf. No. 396.

*1629 Oxford: by W. T. for W. Turner and T. Huggins. Heylyn (P.). *Mikrocosmus.*

401.   (36 × 34.5 mm.) Crowned falcon with sceptre.
      Perhaps to be regarded as merely an ornament. It was the badge of Queen Elizabeth (Holinshed, *Chronicles*, ed. 1807-8, iv. 382). Sheffard's sign is not known.

*1626 by R. Young for W. Sheffard. Cary (W.). *The Present State of England.*
      Some copies are dated 1627.

402.   (73 × 60 mm.)   Device of clasped hands, caduceus, and cornucopias, with *Sapientia Pacem. Pax Opulentiam,* and F. K.
      The design is evidently modelled on the device of Thomas Orwin, which passed to Felix Kingston in 1597, see No. 273, and the motto is merely a Latinized form of Orwin's.
      Cf. the smaller sizes, Nos. 397, 403.

1622 for B. Downes, and to be sold by him and W. Sheffard. *Relation of the Death of Sultan Osman.*

1622 for the Comp. of Stationers. *Psalms.*
      Sayle, 3020.

{ *1625 per F. KINGSTON. Mason (F.). *Vindiciae Ecclesiae Anglicanae.*

{ 1629 by F. KINGSTON for R. B. and A. Hebb. Casaubon (I.). *Stricturae: or a brief answer to Cardinal Perron's reply to King James' answer.*

403. (57 × 48 mm.) Device of clasped hands, cornucopias, and F. K.; with *Sapientia Pacem. Pax Opulentiam.*

See No. 402.

{ 1627 by F. KINGSTON. Downame (G.). *An Abstract of the Duties . . . in the Law of God.*

*1629 excud. F. KINGSTON pro R. B. and A. Hebb. Andrews (L.). *Concio coram Regiam Maiestatem 5 Aug.* 1606.

404. (39 × 35 mm.) Device of an altar with *Deus Providebit, Fide Justus Vivet,* and R. Y.

Cf. No. 405. The device must of course have been from the beginning owned by Robert Young, though the first work in which it appears has Lownes' imprint.

{ 1627 H. L. for J. Boler. Leslie (H.). *A Sermon at Woking,* 28 *Aug.* 1627.
Robert Young worked in partnership with Henry Lownes *c.* 1625-30.

*1628 for J. Bartlet. Harris (R.). *David's Comfort at Ziklag.*

{ 1633 R. YOUNG for sale by R. More. Ursinus (Z.). *The Sum of Christian Religion.*

1635 per assignationem J. More. Coke (E.). *Le Quart Part des Reports.*

1640 typis M. Flesher and R. YOUNG, prost. ven. apud J. Kirton and T. Warren Montague (R.). Θεανθρωπικον, *seu De Vita Jesu Christi.*

1641 by ass. of J. More to be sold by M. Walbancke and W. Coke. Bacon (Sir F.). *Cases of Treason.*

405. (58.5 × 46.5 mm.) Device of an altar with *Deus Providebit, Fide Justus Vivet,* and R. Y.

Cf. No. 404. The device must of course have been owned from the beginning by Robert Young.

1628 for J. Bartlet. Harris (R.). *St. Paul's Confidence.*

1639 by his Majesty's Printer for Scotland [*i.e.* YOUNG]. *An Explanation of the Oath and Covenant published by the . . . High Commissioner* [*i.e.* James Duke of Hamilton].

1640 by the assigns of J. Moore. Britton (J.). *Britton. The Second Edition.*

1640 typis R. Olton and E. Purslow, prost. ven. apud J. Kirton and T. Warren. Montagu (R.). Θεανθρωπικον, *seu De Vita Jesu Christi . . . pars posterior.*

The general title before part i has the small device (No. 404) and the imprint of M. Flesher and R. Young. The *title* of the second part appears to have

152

been printed by them also—though the text was not—which would account for the appearance of Young's device.

*1641 by R. Young for sale by M. Walbancke and W. Coke. Spelman (Sir H.). *De Sepultura.*

406. (27 × 19 mm.) Mark of Michael Sparke.
*1628 for M. Spark. S. (M.). *The Crumbs of Comfort* (end, sig. C 11).

407. (56 × 48 mm.) Device with the arms of the University of Oxford on a shield within a rectangular frame. With the motto, SAPIENTIA FELICITATIS, and ACADEMIA. OXONIENSIS.

{ *1628 Oxford: excud. W. Turner. Brerewood (G.). *Tractatus quidam Logici.*
1639 Oxford: excud. W. Turner, imps. H. Cripps. Fromondus (L.). *Meteorologicorum Libri Sex.*

Passed to Henry Hall in 1644.
1644 Oxford: by H. Hall. *Of Scandal.*

408. (49 × 43 mm.) Device of the arms of the University of Oxford, with four female figures, and the mottoes, SA PI et FE : *Christus Lucrum : Suum Cuiœ* (?) : *Vita breuis : Veritas in Profundo :* and ACADEMIA . OXONIENSIS .

{ 1627 Oxford: by J. Lichfield and W. Turner. H. (G.), D.D. *An Apology of the Power . . . of God.*
*1628 Oxford: by J. Lichfield for H. Cripps. Democritus junior. *The Anatomy of Melancholy* (end).
1633 Oxford: excud. J. L[ichfield and] W. T[urner]. *Musarum Oxoniensium pro Rege suo Soteria.*
    With device No. 407 at end.
1635 Oxford: excud. J. Lichfield. Rouse (J.). *Appendix ad Catalogum librorum in bibl. Bodleiana.*

Passed to Leonard Lichfield in 1635.
{ 1640 Oxford: excud. L. Lichfield. *Horti Carolini Rosa Altera.*
1654 Oxford: by L. Lichfield. [Ward (S.).] *Vindiciae Academiarum . . . animadversions upon Mr. Webster's Book.*

153   X

409. (49 × 45 mm.) Device of a crowned eagle displayed on a shield.

>Several printers and stationers used at different times the sign of the spread or splayed eagle, but it is doubtful whether this should not be regarded as merely an ornament.

1630 by J. Haviland for R. Meighen. Holiday (B.). ΤΕΧΝΟΓΑΜΙΑ.

1631 for J. Wright. *A Pleasant Comedy of Fair Em.*

>Passed to Anne Griffin *c.* 1636.

*1636 by A. Griffin for A. Bouler. Baker (Sir R.). *Meditations.*

>Passed to Edward Griffin II in 1638.

1639 typis E. G. sumps. G. Emerson. Theognis. *Sententiae cum versione Latina . . . a P. Melanchthone.*

410. (61.5 × 53 mm.) Device of a shield suspended to a tree, beside which are two female figures (Athena and ? Fame). On the shield, a battle-axe. The motto, *Sic omni tempore verno,* on a scroll entwined in the branches.

>I have been unable to discover an owner for the arms and motto. The device may have belonged to Richard Badger.

1628 apud J. Bill. *Catalogus Universalis pro nundinis Francofurtensibus.*

>Sayle, 4341.

*1631 by R. Badger. Andrewes (L.). *XCVI Sermons.*

1632 for R. Allot. H. (G.), D.D. *A Sermon at Barnstaple.*

>Sayle, 7594.

411. (36 × 45 mm.) Framed device of a hand emerging from a cloud, and holding a pair of compasses, with the motto, *Labore et Constantia.*

>Copied from one of the Plantin devices, probably from that which appears in G. Whitney's *Choice of Emblems,* Leyden, in the house of Christopher Plantin, by Francis Raphelengius, 1586.

*1630 by T. P., imps. I. S. Ruggle (G.). *Ignoramus.*

>Sayle (p. 1124) queries whether T. P. is T. Paine or T. Purfoot II. The I. S. is presumably J. Spencer, to whom the rights of *Ignoramus* were assigned on July 3, 1630, by the widow of W. Burre.

>** A close copy of this device, but certainly not the same block, was used in T. Whitfeld's *Discourse of Liberty of Conscience,* for J. Wright, 1649, and in books printed by Jane Bell in 1653 and 1658.

412.   (45 × 40 mm.)   Device of a candle burning, with *Prælucendo Pereo.*

Cf. the larger form of the same, No. 413.   It is not clear to whom these devices belonged.   Mr. Sayle, p. 503, treats this as Islip's.

1629 by A. I. for G. Edwardes.   Smith (J.).   *Essex Dove.*

*1633 by G. Miller for G. Edwardes.   Smith (J.).   *Essex Dove.*

413.   (71 × 61 mm.)   Framed device of a candle burning, with *Prælucendo Pereo.*

Cf. the smaller size of the same, No. 412.   It is not clear to whom these devices belonged.   This one *may* have been Robert Dawlman's, but the other, which must surely have belonged to the same person, seems to have no connection with him.

*1629 by M. Flesher for R. Dolman [*i.e.,* Dawlman].   *The Art of Contentment.*

Ames Collection, ii. 859.   The block cracked vertically to right of centre in or before 1637.

1637 for R. Dawlman.   *Salvation Applied.*

Ames Collection, ii. 1360.

414.   (74 × 59.5 mm.)   Framed device of a dolphin and anchor, with motto, *Princeps subditorum incolumitatem procurans,* and I. D., the initials of John Dawson.

See the *Emblemata* of Alciat, ed. 1574, p. 167, where the design occurs with the same motto as here.   The emblem is explained as signifying that a king should be an anchor to his people.

*1632 by J. Dawson for G. Humble.   Speed (J.).   *The History of Great Britain.*

Passed to Mary Dawson *c.* 1634 and to John Dawson II *c.* 1637.

1641 by J. Dawson for T. Walkley.   [Desmarets de Saint Sorlin (J.).]   *Ariana in two Parts.*

415.   (54.5 × 49 mm.)   Device of a fleur-de-lis within a border of leaves and berries.

Presumably the device of George Gibbs, bookseller 1613-33, who traded at the Flower de Luce in St. Paul's Churchyard.

*1631 by T. Cotes for G. Gibbs.   Done (J.).   *Polydoron.*

155

416. (32 × 25 mm.) Oval device of a woman with the sun in one hand and a cup in the other: *Alma Mater* and *Hinc lucem et pocula sacra*.

Cf. Nos. 325-7, 329. Mr. Sayle, on pp. 1269 and 1286, notes a device of this type measuring 33 mm., and on p. 1284 one measuring 31.5 mm., apparently considering that these differ. There is, indeed, an extraordinary variation in the size of prints of the device: I have found it of all heights from 31 to 33.5 mm., but after careful examination of a number of prints, I have failed to discover any evidence that there was more than one block. The differences in size, great as they are, might, I think, be accounted for by the use of different kinds of paper, and varying degrees of dampness at the time of the impression.

(α) With *Alma Mater* in capitals arranged .AL.|MAM|ATER.

*1630 'Excusum Cantabrigiae.' Paolo, Servita. *Quaestio Quodlibetica.*

(β) With ' ALMA MATER ' cut out, and ' Alma Mater ' inserted in type in two lines.

*1631 Cambridge: ex Academiae typographeo. Aphthonius. *Progymnasmata.*

1632 Cambridge: apud T. Buck. Ἡ Καινὴ Διαθήκη (end).

1635 Cambridge: apud T. Buck and R. Daniel . . . Acad. Typographos. *Poetae minores Graeci.*

1636 Cambridge: ex Academiae typographeo. Benlowes (E.). *Sphinx Theologica* (sig. F3 verso).

1639 Cambridge: apud T. Buck, unum ex Academiae typographis. Davenant (J.). *Determinationes quaestionum.*

417. (60 × 48.5 mm.) A phoenix in flames, with the mark of Richard Badger; his arms to right, and those of the Stationers' Company to left: the motto, *Ex igne resurgit virtus*.

The arms of the Badger families of Cambridgeshire, Gloucestershire, and Leicester are described by Berry, *Encyclopaedia Heraldica*, as ' erm. on a bend gu. three eagles or.'

*1632 by R. Badger for the Comp. of Stationers. *The Whole Book of Psalms* (*Sternhold and Hopkins*).

1638 by R. Badger for W. Aspley. Boys (J.). *An Exposition of the Dominical Epistles and Gospels.*

Perhaps passed to Thomas Badger *c.* 1642.

1644 for R. Bostock. ? ?

Bagford Collection, Harl. 5963, No. 158; book not identified.

418. (34 × 60.5 mm.) Ornament of a crowned thistle and two cornucopias with E. R.

> The initials are those of Edward Raban, printer at Edinburgh, St. Andrews, and Aberdeen, 1620-50.

{ 1631 Aberdeen: excud. E. RABAN. Forbes (J.). *Gemitus Ecclesiae Scoticanae.*
{ *1632 Aberdeen : excud. E. RABAN. Johnston (A.). *Epigrammata.*

419. (167 × 115 mm.) Compartment with the initials G. M. in a circle at foot.

{ *1632 by G. MILLER. Bolton (R.). *Mr. Bolton's last and learned Work.*
{ 1632 by G. MILLER for E. Brewster. Rogers (N.). *The true Convert.*
{ 1639 by G. MILLER. Bolton (R.). *Mr. Bolton's last and learned Work.*

       Sayle, 4473.

420. (32.5 × 32.5 mm.) Factotum of a lily, used with a rose, a burning heart, or a fleur-de-lis, as an ornament or device.

(A) With rose.

*1637 by J. HAVILAND for E. Brewster. Gataker (T.). *Certain Sermons.*
     No. 420 a. Other copies 'for Fulke Clifton.'

⁂ The rose (11 × 11 mm.) is sometimes used alone, as in :

1638 by I. H. for J. Parker. Usher (J.). *Immanuel.*

(B) With burning heart.

*1639 by J. HAVILAND for W. Lee. Bacon (F.). *Sylva Sylvarum.*
     No. 420 b.

       Passed to Edward Griffin II in 1639.

{ *1640 apud E. GRIFFIN. Buchanan (G.). *Psalmorum Davidis paraphrasis poetica.*
{   No. 420 c. The block is here another way up.
{ 1648 apud E. GRIFFIN. Buchanan (G.). *Psalmorum Davidis paraphrasis poetica.*

(c) With fleur-de-lis.

1638 typis J. HAVILAND. Gataker (T.). *Antithesis, de sorte thesibus reposita.*

421. (27 × 27 mm.) Factotum block representing (?) flames, used, with a burning heart or a fleur-de-lis inserted, as an ornament or device.

       Cf. No. 420.

(A) With burning heart.

*1635 by J. HAVILAND for F. Constable and E. B. Read (A.). *Chirurgical Lectures of Tumors.*

(B) With fleur-de-lis.

1637 by J. HAVILAND for G. Edwards. Smith (H.). *Twelve Sermons.*

422. (42 × 42 mm.) Factotum block of a rose, used with a burning heart or a fleur-de-lis inserted as an ornament or device.

Cf. No. 420.

(A) With burning heart.

*1637 by J. H. for E. Brewster and R. Bird. Smith (H.). *God's Arrow against Atheists.*

1637 by J. HAVILAND. Gataker (T.). *David's Instructor.*

Passed to Edward Griffin II in 1639.

1639 by E. GRIFFIN for W. Leak. Beaumont (F.) and Fletcher (J.). *Philaster.*

(B) With fleur-de-lis.

1640 by E. GRIFFIN. Yorke (J.). *The Union of Honour.*

423. (87 × 66 mm.) An anchor with foliage twined about it: the motto, *Floreat in æternum.*

It is not clear whether this is to be regarded as a printer's device or not.

*1635 typis W. Jones. Thorndike (H.). *Epitome Lexici Hebraici, Syriaci, etc.*

424. (63 × 53 mm.) Time, Death, Hour-glass, and Book.

Perhaps referring to Michael Sparke's sign of the Blue Bible.

1637 A. G. for M. SPARKE. *The English, Latin, Dutch, Schoolmaster* (facing title). Sayle, 3965.

*1639 by T. Cotes for M. SPARKE. Ovidius Naso (P.). *Ovid de Ponto* (verso of title).

1640 by T. Cotes for M. SPARKE. Ovidius Naso (P.). *Ovid de Ponto* (verso of title).

425. (40.5 × 36 mm.) Device of Time mowing; with *Hanc aciem sola retundit virtus.*

Several printers used a similar figure as a device, most of them with the same motto. Compare the devices of Simon de Colines, Paris, 1520-46 (Silvestre, 80), and Guillaume Chaudière, Paris, 1564-98 (Silvestre, 286); see also Silvestre, 329, 432, 434, 504, 1142.

*1635 imps. N. Butter. Hall (J.). Ἀυτοσχεδιασματα.

{ 1635 by M. FLESHER for E. Forrest, and sold by R. Royston. Pemble (W.). *A Brief Introduction to Geography* (part of *Works*).

1640 by M. FLESHER, to be sold by N. Butter. Hall (J.). *Christian Moderation.*

426.   (28 × 26 mm.)   Framed device of an angel bearing a shield on which is a crowned rose; the letters E. R. at sides.   About the angel, *Granted by her Mᵃ Prohibited to be counterfeted.*

> Though not found, so far as I can learn, before 1652, this block is evidently Elizabethan. It may originally not have been a printer's device, but some kind of stamp used for marking goods manufactured under a special licence, as, for example, music-paper or playing cards.

*1652 for R. Lownes. *A Tragicomical History of . . . Lisander and Calista.*

1659 for R. Pollard and T. Dring. Day (J.). *The Blind Beggar of Bednal-Green.*

1659 'Cambridge.' *University Queries, In a gentle Touch by the By.*
Bowes, *Catalogue of Cambridge Books*, 1894, No. 110 (c).

427.   (35.5 × 35.5 mm.)   The Arms of the University of Oxford, with *Academia Oxoniensis* and *Sapienctia et Felicitatis.*

> This is presumably Mr. Madan's device K (*Oxford Books*, i. 290). Mr. Madan gives the last line of the motto on the recto page of the book as ATE, and states that this was altered in or after 1634 to ATIS, but all examples that I have seen, from 1630 onwards, have ATIS.

{ 1630 Oxford: by W. TURNER. Thornborough (J.). *The Last Will and Testament of Jesus Christ.*

*1631 Oxford: excud. W. TURNER. Strada (F.). *Prolusiones Academicae.*

1636 Oxford: excud. W. TURNER, imps. W. Webb. Barclay (J.). *Poematum libri duo.*

Passed to Henry Hall in 1644.

1644 Oxford: by H. Hall for E. Forrest junior. G. (I.), M.A. *Notes and Observations upon . . . Scripture.*

1651 for R. Davis. *Of Receiving the Communion.*
Probably printed by Hall, who worked till 1679.

159

428. (41 × 45 mm.) Device of a palm-tree, with *Depressa resurgo*.

Mr. Sayle (p. 1290) compares J. Bebel's device at Basle (P. Heitz, *Basler Büchermarken*, pp. 72-3), but it has no marked resemblance with Daniel's, nor has it the same motto. Other Basle printers used a palm-tree, *e.g.*, M. Isengrin in 1539-1567, and T. Guarin in 1564-1578 (see Heitz, *op. cit.*, pp. 84-7, 102-5). The device alludes to the notion that the palm-tree has an especial power of straightening itself when held down by weights.

> *1640 Cambridge: ex off. R. DANIEL. Heinsius (D.). *Sacræ Exercitationes ad Novum Testamentum.*
>
> 1648 Cambridge: ex off. R. DANIEL. Calvin (J.). Κατήχησις τῆς χριστιανικῆς πίστεως.

APPENDIX OF UNTRACED DEVICES, MISDESCRIPTIONS, AND GHOSTS

1. The devices of Hugo Goes, printer at York, 1509.

Two devices of Goes are mentioned, one by Ames, who describes a broadside '" Emprynted at Beverlay in the Hyegate, by me Hewe Goes," with his mark or rebus of a great 𝕳 and a goose' (Herbert, p. 1439), and another in a note of Bagford's (Harl. MS. 5974. 95), 'Donatus cum Remigio impressus Londoniis per me Hugonem Goes and Henery Watson, with the printer's device H.G.' (Duff, *Century*, p. 57). Neither of these books can be traced at present, and I am consequently unable to give the devices.

It is, however, probable that the device of Goes exists, though, we must suppose, hardly in the same form as in the productions mentioned above, in some wall-paper fragments found in May 1911 in the course of restoration at the Lodge of Christ's College, Cambridge (see Mr. Sayle's paper on *Cambridge Fragments*, with facsimile of the wall-paper pattern, in the *Library*, October 1911, pp. 339 ff., and his 'Postscript' in July 1912, pp. 336-339). On one side of the pattern is an 𝕳, and on the other a bird which at least resembles a goose as much as anything else.

2. The supposed device of Thomas Godfray.

In the engraved plate of devices given by Ames (in Herbert, facing p. 238—but often elsewhere) is a plain monogram within a shield, under which is the name Thomas Godfray. The monogram appears however to consist of the letters F G, and occurs, not in a book, but on a panel binding in renaissance style with heads in medallions (Duff, *Century*, p. 56).

3. A forgery of one of John Day's devices.

In 1581 or 1582 Roger Ward printed a surreptitious edition of the *A B C and little Catechism*, which belonged to John Day. At the end of this was Day's mark, which Ward had had imitated by a Frenchman dwelling within the Blackfriars (Arber, ii. 760). I have not been able to find a copy of this pirated edition, and do not know which of Day's marks was copied. In one of the documents concerning the matter it is called Day's 'marke or Armes,' in another his 'marke or stampe' (Arber, ii. 762, 768). It seems not unlikely that it was a form of No. 200, which Day used at the end of certain books of a similar class.

4. The devices of John Hester.

Two devices having the monogram of John Hester within a frame are found in *A Brief Answer to Joseph Quercetanus* [*i.e.*, J. Du Chesne] 'At London, Printed Anno. Dom. 1591.' The first of these, occurring on the general title-page, measures 50 × 42 mm.: the second, on a title-page to the second part of the book entitled *The True and Perfect Spagerike preparation of Minerals*, and also at the end of the same part, measures 64 × 50 mm. This has I. H. in the frame. The dedication of the book is signed by John Hester. There is no printer's name. At the end of the text of part two is a notice: 'These are to bee solde by Iohn Hester, dwelling at Poole's wharfe at the sign of the Stillitorie, 1591.' This evidently refers, not to the books, but to certain medicines which Hester has been describing. There is no evidence that he had anything to do with the book trade, and I have therefore not included his devices. The larger of these devices is reproduced in Mr. Roberts's *Printers' Marks*, p. 70, as that of Andrew Hester, bookseller, 1538-57.

5. A device of an angel with trumpet, etc.

In the Ames Collection, ii. 217, is a title-page of a 12mo *New Testament* in Latin (Beza's version, 1610), with the imprint 'Excudebat' J. Norton. On the title is a device (41 × 32 mm.) representing Fame with a trumpet and two serpents. About it, *Perpetuaque gloria comparatur virtute*: below, a monogram containing the letter S. The condition of the print is too bad to permit of reproduction, and I have been unable to find another copy of the book, or to trace the device elsewhere. From the general appearance of the page it seems not improbable that the book was printed abroad.

6. Device or emblem of a gnomon rising from the sea (74 × 77 mm.), with motto, *Sibi conscia reƈti*.

> This occurs on the title-page of G. Chapman's *Ovid's Banquet of Sense*, by I. R. for R. Smith, 1595. It is probable that it is an emblem of the author's and has nothing to do with the printer or publisher.

7. Device of a horse's head in a lozenge (21 × 28 mm).

> This is regarded by Mr. Sayle (p. 1147) as the device of John Raworth, printer 1638-1645. It seems, however, to occur in but few of his publications, and as his sign is unknown, its claim to be considered as a device is very questionable. In the prints known to me the block is so badly worn and broken that I think it can hardly have been originally cut for Raworth, and is more probably an old ornament. I have therefore not included it.

NOTES

NOTES ON THE TRANSFER OF DEVICES FROM ONE PRINTING-HOUSE TO ANOTHER

THE purpose of the notes which follow is twofold. In the first place they are intended to explain and, so far as is possible, to justify the statements made in the preceding part of the book as to the transference of devices and compartments from one printer to another. In the second place they are intended to bring together in a convenient form all the information as to the relation between the various printing and publishing houses which is to be derived from the study of these transferences.

It should be clearly understood that many of the statements made in these notes, especially as to the *dates* of transfer, are conjectural. Only rarely do we get precise information on the subject from external sources, and even when we seem to do so, as in the notes of Sir John Lambe printed in vol. iii of Arber's *Transcript*, it often proves misleading. Certainty can only be arrived at by tracing the type, ornaments, and initial letters from one printer to another, and to do this for the whole of the English printing trade from its beginnings up to 1640 would be the work of years. In the meantime it is often useful to know that *some* of such and such a printer's material passed or is *likely* to have passed to such and such another, and I have therefore not been sparing in suggesting possible connections between the various printing-houses, even when the evidence of the devices is very far short of proof.

It is sometimes convenient to be able to trace material backwards as well as forwards. I have therefore added an alphabetical list of the transfers in the reverse order. It seemed less confusing to give this list separately than to insert it among the notes in the form of cross references.

ALLDE (E.) to ALLDE (ELIZ.).   1628
Edward Allde, printer 1584-1628, apparently died in the latter year. His business was carried on by his widow, Elizabeth, until about 1635-6. She used his device No. 310 in 1632 and No. 290 in 1633.

ALLDE (ELIZ.) to OULTON (R.).   1635-6
Elizabeth Allde seems to have retired from business in 1635-6. She was succeeded by her son-in-law (*Dictionary I*, p. 6) or son (*Dictionary II*, p. 142; Arber, iii. 704), Richard Oulton, to whom in 1640 she transferred all her copyrights. In 1637 he used her device No. 290, formerly Edward Allde's.

ANDERSON (G.) to BRYSON (R.).   1638
George Anderson, who had begun print-

ing in Edinburgh in 1637 and had then bought from Robert Young certain material formerly Finlason's, removed from Edinburgh to Glasgow in 1638. Before leaving he appears to have sold part of his material to Robert Bryson, whom we find using Finlason's ornament No. 358 in 1640. The rest of his material seems eventually to have passed to Andrew Anderson (cf. No. 187).

ARBUTHNET (A.) to FINLASON (T.).
1585-1604
Alexander Arbuthnet died in 1585. One of his devices, No. 225, was used by Thomas Finlason in 1604. Nothing is known of how it came into his hands, but it is possible that he obtained it from Waldegrave, whose material he bought in or about that year.

BADGER (R.) to BADGER (T.). ? 1642
Richard Badger seems not to be heard of after 1642. A Thomas Badger who printed from 1639 to 1646 was his son, and may have inherited his devices, etc. Richard Badger's device No. 417 was used in 1644, but I have not discovered by whom. As it included the Badger arms it seems more likely to have been used by his son than by a stranger.

BADGER (R.) to MILLER (G.).
See Field (R.) to Miller (G.) and Badger (R.).

BALDWIN (W.) to CHARLEWOOD (J.).
1549-88
William Baldwin was for some time an assistant to Edward Whitchurch, but seems only to have printed a single work on his own account, *The Canticles of Solomon*, 1549. The device used in this (No. 112) eventu-ally came into the hands of John Charlewood, and is found in books printed by him in 1588 and later, but nothing is known of any connection between the two men, nor is the device known to occur during the intervening thirty-eight years.

BARKER (C.) to DEPUTIES, to BARKER (R.)
1588, 1599
In 1588 Christopher Barker nominated as his deputies George Bishop and Ralph Newbery, and after this date we find most of Barker's compartments and ornaments in books stated to have been printed by these men, either in their own names (as No. 185) or as Barker's deputies (as Nos. 221, 204, 248, 220, 300). In 1589, or soon after, he took his son Robert into partnership at the royal printing-house, and in 1596 and later we find Robert printing with his father's deputies (No. 300). In 1599 Christopher Barker died and Robert succeeded him. The above-mentioned compartments and ornaments came into his hands, and also No. 193, which I have not found in use by the Deputies (cf. also No. 212).

BARKER (C.) to BISHOP (G.) and NEWBERY (R.). See Barker (C.) to Barker (R.).

BARKER (R.) to BILL (J.), and NORTON (B.). *c.* 1617
Robert Barker succeeded his father, Christopher, at the royal printing house in 1599. About 1611 Bonham Norton and John Bill acquired an interest in the business; but their names do not appear on books issued from the printing-house until 1616, when we find Bill's name in conjunction with Barker's compartment and device, Nos. 221, 300. From 1617 to May 1619, and from 1621 to 1629, Barker's

name disappears from the imprints, which bear the names of Bill or Norton, or both. For an account of the quarrel which occasioned these changes, and a list of the various imprints, see *Dictionary I*, p. 32. The devices, etc., properly belonging to Barker which appear in the possession of Bill and Norton are Nos. 193, 204, 220, 221, 248, 300. I have not attempted to give examples of their occurrence in conjunction with all the varieties of imprint between 1616 and 1629.

BARLEY (W.) [? to JONES (W.)] to MATHEWES (A.).   1614-33

William Barley died in 1613-14, and in the latter year his widow assigned all her rights to John Beale. It is not known what became of his printing material, but his device No. 304 is found in 1633 in the possession of Augustine Mathewes. In 1632 it had been used by 'W. J.,' who may perhaps have been William Jones, the printer, of Redcross Street.

BARNES (J.) to LICHFIELD (J.).   1617

Joseph Barnes was printer to the University of Oxford from 1584 to the beginning of 1617, when he retired from business. John Lichfield was appointed to succeed him in Feb. 1617, together with William Wrench. Wrench soon left the partnership, his place being taken by James Short, who was associated with Lichfield from 1618 to 1624. Barnes's device No. 336 was used by Lichfield in 1617, and his No. 285 in 1622.

BLOWER (R.) to JONES (W.).   ? 1617

Ralph Blower printed from 1595 until at least 1615, and entered a book in the Registers as late as March 1617/18. It is

possible, however, that before this last date his business had been taken over by William Jones of Redcross Street, who in 1617 used a device, No. 298, which had passed through Blower's hands. In 1626 Blower's copyrights were transferred by his widow to Jones.

BLOWER (R.) to MATHEWES (A.).   ? 1615-22

Ralph Blower's business seems to have passed about 1617 or earlier to William Jones of Redcross Street; but one device apparently used by him, No. 249, is found in the hands of Augustine Mathewes in 1622.

BRADOCK (R.) [to HAVILAND (T.) and HALL (W.)] to BEALE (J.).   1609-14

Richard Bradock continued to print until 1609, when the business was bought by Thomas Haviland and William Hall. They sold it about 1614 to John Beale, who for a time took in as partner Thomas Brudenell. (Arber, iii. 544; *Dictionary II*, p. 17.) Bradock seems to have been still alive in 1615, but there is no evidence that he was in business. Compartment No. 346 passes from Bradock to Beale in 1604-19.

BRADOCK (R.) to LEGATE (J.) II.   1609-35

The last heard of Richard Bradock is in July 1615. A device, No. 202, used in 1607 by an R. B. who is presumably Bradock, was used in 1635 by John Legate II. It is not clear how it came into his hands.

BRADWOOD (M.) to GRIFFIN (E.).   1615-16

Melchisedec Bradwood, who in 1602 had succeeded to the place of Bollifant in the Eliot's Court Printing House (*q.v.*), went down to Eton *c.* 1609 to manage a press established there by John Norton. He seems to have kept on his London business until at least 1613, and Mr. Sayle attributes to him a book printed in 1622. According, however, to Mr. Plomer (*Dictionary I*, p. 48) he died in 1618 at Eton. He printed at Eton 1610-15, and it seems probable that in the latter year, or early in 1616, his materials were returned to London and handed over to Edward Griffin, who had succeeded—or then succeeded—to his business there. We find Griffin using in 1616 in London two devices, Nos. 293 and 380, which had been used by Bradwood at Eton in 1613 and 1615. See also under Eliot's Court Press.

BUCK (J. and T.) to DANIEL (R.). 1640
John and Thomas Buck, who were appointed printers to the University of Cambridge in 1625, were joined by Roger Daniel in 1632. After 1635 John Buck's name disappears from the imprints and from 1640 to 1650 that of Thomas Buck also. During these ten years the business seems to have been managed by Daniel alone, though the Bucks retained an interest in it until 1668-70. The Bucks' devices, Nos. 264, 327, were used by Daniel alone in 1640.

BYDDELL (J.) to POWELL (W.).
See Whitchurch (E.) to Powell (W.).

BYDDELL (J.) to WHITCHURCH (E). 1545
John Byddell appears to have died in 1545, his partner, or at least joint-occupier of Wynkyn de Worde's house, The Sun in Fleet Street, James Gaver, dying in the same year. After their death the house and business came into the hands of Edward Whitchurch, who probably took over such of Wynkyn de Worde's devices as still remained. He used in 1545 part of one of these (No. 25).

BYNNEMAN (H.) to DENHAM (H.). 1583
Towards the end of Henry Bynneman's life he worked in partnership with Henry Denham, and to a certain extent with Ralph Newbery. We find one of his devices in Newbery's hands in 1581, No. 203. On Bynneman's death in 1583 all his other devices and compartments seem to have passed to Denham, whom, with Newbery, he had appointed his executor. His business was taken over by the Eliot's Court printers, but they seem never to have had any of his devices. Denham used one of his compartments, No. 230, in 1584, and another, No. 168, in 1585. Device No. 118, afterwards used by Yardley and Short, and No. 149, used by Henry Lownes, probably also passed through Denham's hands.

BYNNEMAN (H.) to NEWBERY (R.).
See Bynneman (H.) to Denham (H.).

CALY (R.) to TOTTELL (R.).
See Grafton (R.) to Caly (R.).

CAXTON (W.) to DE WORDE (W.). 1491
William Caxton died in 1491, probably towards the end of the year. The only device which he is known to have used (No. 1) passed, with the rest of his printing material, to Wynkyn de Worde. As device No. 2 is used in books which probably appeared within a short time of Caxton's death, it is possible that this also was cut for him, though it has not been found in any work certainly printed in his lifetime.

CHARLEWOOD (J.) to JONES (R.). 1586-91

The relations between these printers present some difficulty. John Charlewood, who worked from 1578 to 1586 at the Half-Eagle and Key in Barbican, continued to print until his death in 1593; but, so far as I can discover, he does not mention the sign in his imprints after 1586, nor does Roberts, who succeeded to the business soon after Charlewood's death. In 1587 Charlewood is believed to have had a press in the Charterhouse (Marprelate, *Epistle*, ed. Arber, p. 23), but whether this was in addition to his older establishment is not clear. It is therefore possible that he ceased to use the sign in 1586 or leased the house to some one else. Be this as it may, in 1591 and 1594 we find his Half-Eagle and Key device, No. 136, used by Richard Jones, whose sign it certainly was not. Why or how the device came into his hands is a mystery. It has been suggested by Mr. Pollard (*Shakespeare Folios and Quartos*, p. 106) that the books in question may have been printed by Charlewood and Jones in partnership, as they had printed others. This is quite possible, but it must be remembered that the block would not be particularly distinctive of Charlewood, especially if he had ceased to use the sign, and would hardly by itself indicate his share in the book.

CHARLEWOOD (J.) to ROBERTS (J.). 1593

John Charlewood died in 1593 and his widow Alice in the same year married James Roberts, who had been printing since 1569. Charlewood's material probably all passed to Roberts, who is found using his device No. 112, which had been originally Baldwin's, in 1595. A large number of Charlewood's copyrights were transferred to Roberts on May 31, 1594.

CHARTERIS (H.) to CHARTERIS (R.). 1599

Henry Charteris, printer at Edinburgh, died in August 1599 and his business passed to his son Robert who used his device No. 307 in 1606.

CHARTERIS (R.) to HART (A.) and HIS HEIRS.   ? 1610, 1621

Robert Charteris, printer at Edinburgh, seems to have got into difficulties of some sort and to have fled from Scotland in or soon after 1610. Andro Hart, who had previously been a bookseller, began to print in that year and took over some of Charteris' printing material. His heirs used Charteris' device No. 307 in 1633.

COLWELL (T.) to JACKSON (H.). 1575-6

Thomas Colwell died in or about 1575, and was succeeded, at the sign of St. John the Evangelist in Fleet Street, by Hugh Jackson, who married Colwell's widow. Colwell's device No. 68 was used by him in 1578.

COPLAND (R.) to COPLAND (W.). *c.* 1548

Robert Copland died *c.* 1548 and was succeeded, at the Rose Garland in Fleet Street, by his son (?) William, who used one of his devices, No. 71, in a book printed about 1557.

COTES (T.) to COTES (R.).   1641

Thomas and Richard Cotes, who were brothers, worked in partnership under the style of Robert Cotes from about 1627 to 1641, when Thomas died and Richard succeeded alone to the business. He used device No. 283 in 1643.

CREEDE (T.) to ALSOP (B.).   1617

Thomas Creede took Bernard Alsop into partnership in 1616, and in the following year on Creede's death or retirement from the business, Alsop succeeded to it. He used Creede's device No. 314 in 1623 and No. 339 in 1627. His principal device, No. 299, is apparently not found after his death.

DANTER (J.) to JONES (R.).
  See Danter (J.) to Stafford (S.).

DANTER (J.) to STAFFORD (S.).   1598-9
  John Danter died in 1598 or 1599. He seems to have been succeeded by Simon Stafford, who was admitted a freeman of the Stationers' Company in May 1599, but had engaged in more or less illicit printing for two years previously. Stafford used Danter's device No. 281 in 1599. It may be noted that No. 295 was used by Danter until 1594 and by Stafford in 1609. It appears in a book believed to have been printed by R. Jones in 1597, but there is a good deal of doubt. If it had not been for this book, it would have been natural to suppose that No. 295 also passed direct to Stafford.

DAWSON (J.) I to DAWSON (MARY), to
  DAWSON (J.) II.   c. 1634, 1637.
  John Dawson the elder is last heard of in 1634, and probably died in the course of that year. His widow Mary carried on the business for a time, her name appearing in imprints from 1635 to 1637. In the latter year she seems to have married again and transferred the business to her son, John Dawson II. See No. 414.

DAY (J.) to DAY (R.).
  See Day (J.) to Windet (J.).

DAY (J.) to WALDEGRAVE (R.).   c. 1584
  John Day died in 1584. His materials seem not to have passed to his son Richard who, at the time of his father's death, was on bad terms with his stepmother, and was refused any portion of his father's goods; and they were perhaps dispersed. We find one device used by him, No. 83, in the possession of Robert Waldegrave in 1586.

DAY (J.) to WAYLAND (J.).   ? 1553
  On the accession of Mary, John Day, who was throughout his life a strong anti-Romanist, appears to have fled from London. In October 1554 he was, however, captured in Norfolk and sent to the Tower (*Century*, p. 38). It appears from Foxe's *Acts and Monuments* (ed. Townsend, vi. 610) that he was afterwards imprisoned in Newgate for religion, but it is not known how long he remained there. In any case there seems to be no evidence that he resumed printing before 1557. A compartment of his, No. 116, was used in two undated books stated to be printed by John Wayland. These cannot be later than 1557, as Wayland seems to have died or gone out of business in that year. An ornament with the initials I. D., No. 115, appears in a *Sarum Missal* dated 1557, without printer's name. It seems a most unlikely book for Day to have printed, and as Wayland had a patent for service books it is possible that he printed this also. Both Nos. 115 and 116 were later again in the possession of Day.

DAY (J.) to WINDET (J.).   c. 1584
  As stated above (Day to Waldegrave) on John Day's death, in 1584, his printing materials may have been dispersed; at any rate they did not immediately pass

169   z

to his son Richard. One of his devices, No. 208, was used in 1588 by John Windet, who also used his compartment No. 116 in 1595. It is, however, to be remarked that most (but not all) of the books in which Windet used this device and compartment were printed for the assigns of Richard Day. They may, therefore, perhaps have been his property, and only lent to Windet; but one at least passed to Windet's successor.

Denham (H.) to Jaggard (W.).
1585-1624

A sill-piece of a border, No. 86, originally Petit's, seems to have been used by Henry Denham in 1585, and another part of the same border is used by William Jaggard in 1624. I have been unable to trace the connection.

Denham (H.) to Yardley (R.) and Short (P.).   1589-90

Henry Denham is last heard of in 1589, and in this year or the following his devices and compartments, including some formerly Bynneman's, passed to Richard Yardley and Peter Short, who were at the time in partnership. They used Denham's device No. 214 in 1590, his compartment No. 148 in 1593, and a device, formerly Bynneman's, No. 118, in the same year. Yardley now disappeared from the partnership, and the devices and compartment continued to be used by Short alone. In 1594 he used Denham's device No. 211, and his compartment No. 255, and again Bynneman's No. 118. He later used Bynneman's device No. 119 and his compartment No. 230. Devices Nos. 149, 150, and compartment No. 231 also probably passed through the hands of Yardley and Short, but are not known to have been used by them. After Short's death in 1603 his materials passed to Henry Lownes.

Denham (H.) to Yetsweirt (C.). ? 1594

In 1594 Charles Yetsweirt, clerk of the Signet, was granted a patent for law books. He died in 1595, and his widow, Jane, held the patent until 1597. In 1599 it was granted to Thomas Wight and Bonham Norton for thirty years. Several books issued by C. Yetsweirt are distinctly stated to have been printed *by* him, but it seems very doubtful whether he was ever a printer. Denham's compartment No. 168 appears in law books issued by the Yetsweirts in 1594-6, and later in those by Wight and Norton.

East (T.) to Snodham (T.).   1609

Thomas East, printer, 1567-1609, probably died shortly before June 17 of the latter year, when Mistress East transferred his copyrights to Thomas Snodham, formerly his apprentice. East's printing materials probably passed to Snodham at the same time, for in 1609 we find him using device No. 83, which seems likely to have passed through East's hands, and in 1613 another, No. 227, which had been used by East in 1606.

Eld (G.) to Fletcher or Flesher (M.).
1624

Miles Fletcher or Flesher was in partnership with George Eld from 1617 until Eld's death of the plague in 1624, when Fletcher succeeded to his business. He used Eld's devices, Nos. 308, 320, and 375.

Eliot's Court Press.

The use of devices by the printers

forming the Eliot's Court Press group is somewhat puzzling, and suggests that our information on the subject of this press is still incomplete. So far as I have been able to make out, its history is somewhat as follows: In 1584 Arnold Hatfield and Ninian Newton were printing in partnership at an address which does not seem to be known. In 1585 John Jackson and Edmund Bollifant were printing in partnership, probably at Eliot's Court, Little Old Bailey, which was Bollifant's address at this date (Hazlitt, I. 4). In or before 1586 all four men were in partnership (Herbert, p. 1218). After this date, save for one book printed by Hatfield and Newton jointly in 1587, the imprints generally (? always) bear the name of Hatfield, Bollifant, or Jackson alone. Newton seems to have printed nothing more, and is not heard of after 1587. Jackson was still one of the group in October 1593, when a book was entered to him and his partners, and he continued to print until 1596, after which date he disappears. In 1602 Edmund Bollifant died, and his place was taken by Melchisedec Bradwood, the firm now consisting only of Hatfield and Bradwood. Bradwood presumably worked at Eliot's Court until he went down to Eton c. 1609 (see Bradwood to Griffin), but he seldom or never gives an address in his imprints. Hatfield is thought to have died in 1612, and it is possible that his place was at once taken by Edward Griffin, to whom the business eventually passed. Bradwood remained at Eton, where he died in 1618, but he apparently sent his printing materials to London in 1615 (Bradwood to Griffin). The devices belonging to the partners were perhaps used by them indifferently. We find one, No. 239, used by Bollifant and Jackson; another, No. 306, used by Bollifant and Hatfield, later passing to Haviland, probably by way of Edward Griffin; a third, No. 293, by Jackson, Bollifant, Hatfield, and at Eton, later passing to Griffin; a fourth, No. 354, by Hatfield and Bradwood, also passing eventually to Griffin.

ENGLAND (N.) to BYNNEMAN (H.).
1568-9

Nicholas England published from 1558 to 1568, but was never a printer. Device No. 138 is supposed to have been his, but it occurs in at least one book printed during his lifetime in which his name does not appear. Towards the end of his career it is found in a book printed for him by H. Bynneman, who seems to have retained it after his death.

FIELD (R.) to MILLER (G.) and BADGER (R.). 1624

Richard Field died in the autumn of 1624, and his business passed into the hands of one of his apprentices, George Miller, who at the time was in partnership with Richard Badger. All the devices which Field had inherited from Vautrollier seem to have passed to them. Nos. 164, 170, 179, 192, 222, 233, 246, and perhaps 210, were used by Miller, and a re-cutting of one of them, No. 195, was used by Badger. About 1630 the partnership was dissolved, when all these devices (including No. 195) passed to Miller alone, except No. 222, which was used by Badger in 1631-5, and No. 210, which does not seem to occur after 1625.

FINLASON (T.) to YOUNG (R.). 1630-2

Thomas Finlason, printer in Edinburgh, died in 1628, and his heirs printed for two years. His materials, or part of them, passed to Robert Young, who was appointed King's Printer in Scotland in 1632. He used Finlason's ornament No. 363 in 1633. Nos. 187, 189, and 358 probably also passed through Young's hands.

GIBSON (T.) to DAY (J.).   1539-69
Thomas Gibson ceased to print in 1539, and his device, No. 83, eventually came into the possession of John Day, who used it from 1569, but it seems impossible to trace the course by which it came into his hands.

GIBSON (T.) [? to REYNES (J.)] to SMITH (H.).   1539-46
Thomas Gibson appears only to have printed in the years 1535-9. A border used by him, No. 62, is found in the *Works of Chaucer*, 1542, which is stated to be printed by John Reynes. As, however, Reynes is only known to have been a stationer, it is probable that the book was printed *for* him, though the occurrence of his initials in some of the ornamental letters shows that he had an important share in its production. Reynes died in 1544, and the border is next found in the possession of Henry Smith (1546).

GRAFTON (R.) to CALY (R.) to TOTTELL (R.).   1553, 1554
In 1553, on the accession of Queen Mary, Richard Grafton was deprived of his office of Royal Printer and excluded from the general pardon. It seems probable that he was at the same time dispossessed of his house, for we find Robert Caly, a printer of Catholic books, printing in 1553 at Grafton's address. In that year

Caly made use of Grafton's compartment, No. 105, and in 1556 probably of his compartment, No. 92. In or before 1555, however, No. 105 seems to have been transferred to Tottell, Grafton's son-in-law, who also apparently used his compartment No. 91 in 1554. It therefore seems likely that in 1553 Caly had been put in possession of all Grafton's printing materials and that he shortly afterwards disposed of part of it to Tottell. Later Tottell had Grafton's King in Council compartment, No. 110, and perhaps his device No. 104.

GRAFTON (R.) to WAYLAND (J.).   ? 1553
As stated above (Grafton to Caly and Tottell), Grafton seems to have been dispossessed of his house in 1553. One of his compartments, that of the King in Council, No. 110, seems somehow to have come into the hands of John Wayland, who had succeeded Whitchurch at the Sun, and who used this compartment in 1557. The compartment is, however, important enough to have been lent by one printer to another, and it is quite possible that it was really Tottell's at this date, as it certainly was later.

GRIFFIN (A.) to GRIFFIN (E.) II. *c.* 1638
Anne Griffin, widow of Edward Griffin I, after carrying on business by herself (see Haviland to Griffin) for about two years, made it over to her son Edward Griffin junior in 1637 or 1638. Devices Nos. 306 and 392 passed from Anne Griffin to him in 1637-8.

GRIFFIN (E.) I to HAVILAND (J.).   1621
Edward Griffin died before June 1621. His business at Eliot's Court was carried

172

on by John Haviland, Griffin's widow being a partner. Haviland used Griffin's devices Nos. 293, 306, 390, and 392.

GUBBIN or GUBBINS (T.) to ALLDE (E.).
?1600

Thomas Gubbins traded in London as a bookseller from 1587 to 1629. In the year 1603, however, he was admitted a freeman of York, and in the same year a device which seems to have represented one of his signs, No. 284, is found in the hands of Edward Allde, who had probably used it also in 1600 and 1602. Gubbins published a number of books up to 1598, but after that there is a gap of some sixteen years. We may therefore conjecture that in 1599 or 1600 he sold his business to Allde and went to York. He was back in London in 1614 and apparently continued to carry on business until his death in 1629, but published very little.

HALL (R.) to HOWE (W.).   1563-70
Rowland Hall died in September 1563. One of his devices, No. 142, is found in use by William Howe in 1570-1. It is possible that it passed through the hands of Richard Serle, who had his device No. 136 in or about 1565, but there is no evidence on the point.

HALL (R.) to SERLE (R.).   1563-5
On Rowland Hall's death in September 1563 his sign and business seem to have been taken over by Richard Serle. Serle, however, dwelt in Fleet Lane, not in Gutter Lane as Hall had done. He used Hall's device No. 136.

HARRISON (J.), senior and junior.
There is so much difficulty in distin-
guishing the various John Harrisons that I have not attempted to note the transfers of devices from one to another.

HARRISON (J.) III to OKES (N.).
See Harrison to Snowdon *and* Snowdon to Okes.

HARRISON (J.) III to SNOWDON (G.).
1604-6

John Harrison III is said to have succeeded to Thomas Judson's printing business in 1600. He was dead by February 1604, and in 1606 the business had apparently been taken over by George and Lionel Snowdon. Device No. 316 (? Harrison's) was used by George Snowdon in 1606. No. 334, which is found in 1607 in the possession of Nicholas Okes, probably also passed through the hands of the Snowdons.

HART (A.) to HIS HEIRS.   1621
Andro Hart died in 1621, and his printing materials passed to his heirs. They used his device No. 377 in 1622. Cf. No. 307.

HAVILAND (J.) to GRIFFIN (A.). ? 1634-6
John Haviland took over Edward Griffin's business in 1621, apparently in partnership with his widow Anne. From 1634 her name is found in imprints, and about 1636 Haviland seems to have retired from the partnership and Anne Griffin to have taken over the whole business. Device No. 306 passed from Haviland to Anne Griffin in 1635-7, while No. 392 appears to have been in her hands by 1634. No. 409 passed to her by 1636.

HAVILAND (J.) to GRIFFIN (E.) II.
See above and Griffin (A.) to Griffin (E.)

173

II. Nos. 420 and 422 seem to have passed direct to Edward Griffin II in 1639.

HEARNE (R.) to ISLIP (S.).   1646.

Richard Hearne to whom Adam Islip had left his printing materials in 1639, died or retired from business about 1646, and was succeeded by Adam Islip's widow, Susan. Device No. 263, used by her in 1647, probably had passed through his hands.

HERTFORD (J.) to BOURMAN (N.).   1639

John Hertford, printer at St. Albans 1534-9, got into trouble concerning the printing of 'a little book of detestable heresies' in 1539, and was sent to London with (? in charge of) Henry Pepwell and another stationer. The name of the last abbot of St. Albans was Richard Stevenage or Boreman, and his initials R. S. appear in Hertford's device, No. 84. This device is found in the same year 1539 in the hands of Nicholas Bourman in London. As Mr. Duff has suggested (*Provincial Printers*, p. 103), it is quite likely that this Nicholas was a relative of the abbot's, to whom the printing material had been entrusted during Hertford's absence, and by whom it was brought to London on the suppression of the monastery in December 1539.

HOWE (W.) to SIMMES (V.).   ? 1596

William Howe, who was admitted a freeman of the Stationers' Company in 1556, continued to print until about 1596 (Hazlitt, II. 141). A device used by him in 1570-1, No. 142, is found in 1597 in possession of Valentine Simmes, who had then been printing for about three years. The precise date of change of ownership is not known.

ISLIP (A.) to HEARNE (R.).   1639

Adam Islip died in 1639, leaving all his presses and printing material to Richard Hearne, who is found using his device or ornament No. 251 in 1640. No. 263, used by Susan Islip in 1647, probably also passed through his hands.

JACOBI (H.) to PEPWELL (H.).   *c.* 1518

Henry Jacobi, stationer, traded in London at the sign of the Trinity from 1506 to 1512, when he moved to Oxford and opened a shop there with the same sign. He died at Oxford in 1514, administration of his estate being granted to Joyce Pelgrin, who had been his partner. In 1518 Henry Pepwell began to print at the London house which had formerly been Jacobi's, and by 1519 the device used at Oxford by Jacobi in 1513, No 34, had come into his hands. The exact relation of the two men is not clear. It is complicated by the fact that the real owner of the Jacobi-Pelgrim business in London may have been the wealthy merchant William Bretton, who financed several of their publications in 1506 and 1510, and had also an interest in the Oxford business (*Century*, p. 118).

JAGGARD (W.) [to JAGGARD (I.)] to COTES (T. and R.)   1623-7

William Jaggard died in 1623 and his business passed to his son Isaac, who only survived him for some three years. Soon after Isaac's death in February or March 1627, his widow transferred the business to Thomas and Richard Cotes, who used William Jaggard's devices Nos. 136 and 283; and also No. 112, which had probably passed through his hands, but is not known to have been used by him.

JEFFES (A.) [? to WHITE (W.) to WHITE (J.)] to MATHEWES (A.).

? 1599-1622

Abel Jeffes printed little after 1595, and in 1599 made over certain copyrights to William White. He perhaps transferred his printing materials at the same time, for one of his devices, No. 238, originally Ward's, is found later in the hands of Augustine Mathewes, who used another device obtained from W. White, No. 188.

JONES (R.) to JAGGARD (W.). 1595-1615

There seems to be no trace of any direct connection between Richard Jones and William Jaggard, but a connection is of course possible through Roberts. Jaggard is found in 1615 using Jones's *Heb Ddieu heb ddim* device, No. 283, which Jones had used in 1592-5. It is found in 1606 in a book which bears also device No. 294, the ownership of which at the time is obscure (see Wolfe to Roberts).

JONES (R.) to ROBERTS (J.). 1594-9

A single device, No. 136, seems to have passed from Richard Jones to James Roberts. It had, however, formerly been the property of Charlewood, to whose business Roberts succeeded in 1593, and its use by Jones may have been a temporary arrangement (see Charlewood to Jones). Jones apparently continued to print until 1602, though it has been stated that he sold his business in 1597 or 1598 (*Dictionary I*, pp. 159, 289).

JONES (R.) to STAFFORD (S.).
See Danter (J.) to Stafford (S.).

JONES (W.) to MATHEWES (A.).
See Barley (W.) to Mathewes (A.).

JUGGE (R.) to JUGGE (JOAN) to WATKINS (R.). 1577, 1579

Richard Jugge died in 1577, his business being carried on until at least 1579 by his widow Joan in partnership with his son John (see No. 123). She died in 1588, but long before this date most of her husband's printing material seems to have been dispersed. Two of Jugge's borders, Nos. 181 and 182, passed to Richard Watkins, his son-in-law, by whom they were used in 1579 and 1594 respectively. It is possible that No. 165, which is found in the hands of William White in 1599, also passed through Watkins's hands (see Watkins to White).

JUGGE (R.) to JUGGE (JOAN) to MAUNSELL (A.). 1577, ? 1588

The central part of Richard Jugge's larger pelican device, No. 125, appears to have passed to Andrew Maunsell by 1588, the year of Joan Jugge's death. I have found no other indication of a connection between the two men.

JUGGE (R.) to WHITE (W.).
See Jugge (R.) to Jugge (Joan) to Watkins (R.).

KEARNEY (W.) to FRANCKTON (J.).

1597-1600

William Kearney, who went to Dublin *c.* 1593 and printed there until 1597, was succeeded in 1600 by John Franckton, who had perhaps been his pupil. An ornament, No. 218, used by Kearney in England in 1591-2 was used at Dublin by Franckton in 1602.

KEARNEY (W.) to WOLFE (J.). *c.* 1593

Device No. 258 apparently passed from William Kearney to John Wolfe *c.* 1593;

175

or possibly, as it represented a fleur-de-lis, Wolfe's usual device, the book in which it appeared in 1591 may have been undertaken by Kearney in partnership with Wolfe.

KING (J.) to DENHAM (H.).   1560-85
We find the sill-piece of compartment No. 86, originally Petit's, which had been in the hands of John King in 1560, apparently in those of Henry Denham in 1585. No other connection seems to be traceable between the two men. We should rather have expected the compartment to pass to Marshe.

KING (J.) to MARSHE (T.).   1560-6
John King printed from 1555 to 1561, when he is supposed to have died. He may possibly have been for a time in partnership with Thomas Marshe, for *Certain Books by Master Skelton* was printed by them in Creed Lane. As this work is, however, not dated it is impossible to say whether this association had anything to do with the appearance in Marshe's hands of King's compartment No. 111 in 1566. It may be remarked that Marshe in 1561-2 had licence to print the *Chronicle* in octavo which he had bought of John King's wife (Arber, i. 178).

LEGATE (J.) I to LEGATE (J.) II.   1620
John Legate the elder appears to have removed from Cambridge to London in 1610. The date is sometimes given as 1609 but an edition of Thomas's *Dictionarium* has the imprint 'Cantabrigiae Ex officina Iohannis Legati . . . 1610' (Sayle, 5647). He brought his devices to London with him, and on his death in 1620 they passed to his son. See Nos. 166, 259, 325, 326, 329.

LEGGE (C.) to BUCK (J. and T.).   *c.* 1626
Cantrell Legge, who was appointed printer to the University of Cambridge in 1606, is believed to have died in 1626. His printing materials apparently were taken over by John and Thomas Buck, who used his device No. 399 in 1627 and No. 264 in 1633.

LICHFIELD (J.) to LICHFIELD (L.).   1635
John Lichfield, printer to the University of Oxford, retired in 1635 and was succeeded by his son Leonard, who used his devices, Nos. 285, 336, and 408.

LOWNES (H.) to LEGATE (J.) II.
See Young (R.) to Legate (J.) II.

LOWNES (H.) to YOUNG (R.).   1625-30
In 1625 or 1626 Humphrey Lownes was joined by Robert Young, and one of Lownes's devices, No. 373, appears in a book printed about this date with Young's imprint (cf. also No. 278). On the other hand one that certainly belonged to Young, as it bears his initials, was used by Lownes in 1627 (No. 404). It is therefore probable that during the partnership the devices of both were used indifferently. Lownes died in or before June 1630, and most of his devices and signed compartments, some of which were formerly Denham's (see Nos. 119, 231), are afterwards found in the possession of Young. Nos. 150 and 296, which had probably passed through the hands of Lownes but are not known to have been used by him, are also found in Young's possession.

MARSHE (T.) to MIDDLETON (H.).
                                       1566-75
Compartment No. 111, which had apparently belonged in turn to John King

176

and Thomas Marshe, seems to have been owned by Henry Middleton in 1575, but there is no evidence as to the date of transfer. Marshe printed until 1587.

MARSHE (T.) to ORWIN (T.).   1591

Thomas Marshe printed a large number of books up to 1584, and at least one appeared with his name as printer in 1587. In the last few years of his life, however, most of his business was carried on by his son Henry as his assign. Henry Marshe seems only to have printed until 1587, and is last heard of in 1589. Towards the end of 1591 the representatives of Thomas Marshe transferred a large number of his copyrights to Thomas Orwin (Arber, ii. 586-7), and part or all of his printing material was probably transferred at the same time, for we find Orwin using Marshe's compartment No. 154 in 1591, and a device of his, No. 180, in 1592. No. 167, which was used by Orwin's successor Felix Kingston in 1599, probably also passed through Orwin's hands, but is not known to have been used by him.

MATHEWES (A.) to PARSONS (M.). c. 1635

About 1635 the printing-house of Augustine Mathewes passed into the hands of Marmaduke Parsons. He is found using Mathewes's devices Nos. 304 and 312, in 1639.

MIDDLETON (H.) to NEWBERY (R.).
See Newbery (R.) to Middleton (H.).

MIDDLETON (H.) to OKES (N.). 1587-1609

On Henry Middleton's death in 1587-8 his material passed to Robert Robinson and from him to Richard Bradock, who printed until 1615. One device or ornament of his, however, No. 215, seems to have passed to Nicholas Okes by 1609. How it came into his hands is not clear. It may be noted that in 1612 Okes used a compartment, No. 182, which also does not seem to have belonged to him. It is possible that, like Norton, he had a habit of putting his name as printer on books really printed *for* him.

MIDDLETON (H.) to ROBINSON (R.). 1588

Henry Middleton died between July 1587 and July 1588. In 1588 his widow sold his printing materials to Robert Robinson, who is found using his device No. 207 in 1589, and No. 202 in 1591.

? MIDDLETON (W.) to KING (J.).
See Petit (T.) to King (J.).

MIDDLETON (W.) to POWELL (W.). 1547

William Middleton died in June 1547, leaving his property to his wife Elizabeth, who, as Mr. Duff says, 'testified her sorrow by marrying, within two months, another printer, William Powell.' We find Powell using Middleton's compartment, No. 106, in 1547.

MILLER (G.) to BADGER (R.).
See Field (R.) to Miller (G.) and Badger (R.).

MILLER (G.) to MILLER (A.).   1646

George Miller, printer 1601-46, died in the latter year and was succeeded by his son Abraham, who used several of his devices, originally Vautrollier's. See Nos. 164, 233, 246.

NEWBERY (R.) to BUCK (T.) and DANIEL (R.).   1587-1634

A device, No. 240, used by Ralph Newbery in 1586-7 is found in 1634 in a book with the imprint 'apud' T. Buck and R. Daniel, Cambridge. It is not definitely stated that it was printed at Cambridge, and we therefore cannot be certain in whose possession the block was at the time.

NEWBERY (R.) to MIDDLETON (H.).

                                    1577-8

The relations between Ralph Newbery and Henry Middleton are somewhat puzzling. In 1577-8 Middleton seems to have taken over from Newbery the Lost Sheep device, No. 153, which had formerly belonged to Wykes, and about the same time to have obtained two smaller blocks of the same design, Nos. 202, 207, which I have not yet found in earlier use. The largest and smallest of these continued in Middleton's possession, but the middle-sized one, No. 202, appears to pass backward and forward between Newbery and Middleton in a most perplexing manner. I cannot offer any satisfactory explanation of this.

NORTON (J.) to W. (T.).   ? 1645

This John Norton printed from 1621 to 1645. Nothing seems to be known as to what became of his printing material on his death in 1645, but one of his devices, No. 267, is later found in the hands of 'T. W.' (? Thomas Warren, who printed in Foster Lane ? 1638-? 1661).

NORTON (W.) to NORTON (B.).   1594

William Norton died at the end of 1593, and his son Bonham was admitted as a free-

man of the Stationers' Company, and succeeded to his business, in 1594. He used his father's device, No. 174, in 1596.

OKES (J.) to WILSON (W.).   c. 1644

John Okes died about 1643, and his widow seems to have carried on the business for a year or two. Later she perhaps sold the printing materials to William Wilson, who is found in 1648 using an ornament, No. 381, that had originally belonged to John Okes's father Nicholas.

OKES (N.) to OKES (J.).   c. 1636

Nicholas Okes is last heard of in 1636, and at about that date his business passed to his son John, who had been associated with him for some years previously. His ornament, No. 381, was used by John Okes in 1640.

ORWIN (T.) to ORWIN (JOAN) to KINGSTON (F.).   1597

Thomas Orwin died before 25th June 1593, and was succeeded by his widow Joan. She used his device No. 273, with his initials in 1594, and without them in 1595-7. In that year she made over the business to her son by an earlier marriage, Felix Kingston. He continued to use device No. 273, and also made use of two which had formerly belonged to Thomas Marshe, one of which, No. 180, had been used by Orwin, while the other, No. 167, had perhaps passed through Orwin's hands, though it does not seem to be used in any book of his.

PEPWELL (H.) to TREVERIS (P.).   c. 1521

Henry Pepwell printed at the sign of the Trinity in St. Paul's Churchyard from 1518 to 1521, after which date he seems to have traded principally as a stationer, though a grammar of 1523 is stated to have been printed by him. Possibly he disposed of part of his printing material in 1521, for we find a border of his, No. 48, used by Peter Treveris in 1522.

PETIT (T.) [? to MIDDLETON (W.)] to KING (J.).   1547-60

Thomas Petit printed from 1536 to 1554. Parts of one of his compartments, No. 86, are found in an undated edition of Froissart, which purports to have been printed by William Middleton, and must therefore date from before June 1547, when Middleton died. It seems unlikely that Petit should have disposed of this compartment, which included his mark, and it may be questioned whether the volume was not partly printed by Petit, or finished by him after Middleton's death. The compartment later (1560) came into the hands of John King, but, as nothing is known of his connection with either Petit or Middleton, it is impossible to say when or how the change of ownership occurred.

POWELL (T.) to JAGGARD (W.). 1563-1614.

Thomas Powell, who succeeded his uncle, Thomas Berthelet, at the Lucrece in Fleet Street in 1555, only printed until 1563, when the house seems to have passed into the hands of Ralph Newbery, who gives 'the late shop of Tho. Barthelet' as his address in that year. The sign of Lucrece was, however, abandoned, and there seems no evidence that Powell's printing material passed with the house, though it may well have done so. A border, No. 133, used by Powell in 1556-62, is found in the possession of William Jaggard

in 1614, but I have been unable to trace it between these dates.

PURSLOWE (G.) to PURSLOWE (ELIZ.).
                                c. 1632

George Purslowe died about 1632, and was succeeded by his widow Elizabeth, who used his device No. 311 in 1633. She was apparently succeeded by Haviland, Young, and Fletcher in partnership (Arber, iii. 701).

PYNSON (R.) to REDMAN (R.).   1530

Richard Pynson died early in 1530, and was succeeded in the same year at the sign of St. George, in Fleet Street, by Robert Redman, who used his device No. 3 in 1530, and Nos. 41 and 44 in 1532.

RASTELL (W.) to GIBSON (T.). ? 1534-5

William Rastell only printed in the years 1530-4, after which date he may have dispersed his printing material. One of his compartments, No. 62, is used by Thomas Gibson in 1539. There seems no other sign of any connection between the two men, but as Gibson's first book appeared in 1535, it seems not impossible that he succeeded to Rastell's business.

READ (R.) to ELD (G.).

See Simson (G.) to Read (R.).

REDMAN (R.) to PICKERING or REDMAN (ELIZ.).   1540

Robert Redman died between 21st Oct. and 4th Nov. 1540, and was succeeded by his widow, Elizabeth Pickering. She carried on the business for a short time until her marriage to Ralph Cholmondeley, when the printing office passed to William Middleton. She used Robert Redman's device No. 3 about 1541.

179

REYNES (J.) to SMITH (H.).
See Gibson (T.) to Reynes (J.).

ROBERTS (J.) to JAGGARD (W.). ? 1606
In the year 1606 William Jaggard seems to have taken over the printing business of James Roberts, in Barbican, though Roberts perhaps retained some interest in it till 1615, when he transferred certain copies to Jaggard (Arber, iii. 575). Roberts's device No. 136 (originally Hall's) was used by Jaggard in 1617, and his No. 112 (originally Baldwin's) probably also passed through Jaggard's hands, as it was afterwards used by T. Cotes, Isaac Jaggard's successor.

? ROBERTS (J.) to PURFOOT (T.).
1599-1605
Device No. 136, used by James Roberts in 1599, appears in 1605 in a book which has Purfoot's device No. 344 on the title. It seems unlikely that it should have ever been in the hands of Purfoot, and possibly the book was a joint production of the two men.

? ROBERTS (J.) to WRIGHT (J.) or WINDET (J.).
See Wolfe (J.) to Roberts (J.).

ROBINSON (R.) to BRADOCK (R.). 1597-8
Robert Robinson died in or about 1597, and his widow married Richard Bradock, who took over his business and printing materials. We find Bradock using Robinson's device No. 207 in 1598, and No. 202 in 1607. Device No. 280, which he used in 1598, may perhaps also have passed through Robinson's hands.

ROSS (J.) to WALDEGRAVE (R.). 1590
John Ross, printer in Edinburgh, died in 1580. One of his devices, No. 189, may have been used in 1582 by Henry Charteris, but this seems very doubtful. Robert Waldegrave, who had been obliged to leave England in 1589, arrived in Edinburgh at the end of that year or early in 1590, and in the latter year was appointed King's Printer. He probably purchased some of Ross's materials from his widow or son, for we find him using Ross's devices, Nos. 187 and 189, in the year 1590 and later.

SCARLET (T.) to ROBINSON (R.). 1596-7
Thomas Scarlet died in 1596. His copyrights were transferred to Cuthbert Burby, and there seems some reason to think that his business was bought by Ralph Blower and George Shaw (*Dictionary I*, p. 236; Arber, iii. 702). We find, however, his device, No. 280, in the possession of R.R., presumably Robert Robinson, in 1597, and later in that of Richard Bradock, who married Robinson's widow.

SCOLAR (J.) to KYRFOTH (C.). 1518-19
The Oxford printer, John Scolar, ceased to work there in 1518. He appears to have been immediately succeeded by Charles Kyrfoth, who worked at the same address and in the single book which he produced, dated 5 Feb. 1519, used Scolar's device, No. 43.

SERES (W.) to DENHAM (H.). ? 1577
William Seres continued to print until about 1577, but in 1574 made over his patent for certain books to Henry Denham. Part of his materials probably passed to

Denham at the same time. He used them at first as Seres's assign, and in later books as his own. See compartment No. 148.

SERLE (R.) to CHARLEWOOD (J.). 1566-78
Richard Serle is last heard of in 1566, when he was working at the Half Eagle and Key in Fleet Lane. In 1578 John Charlewood was printing at the same sign in Barbican, and we may conjecture that he obtained possession of Serle's device, No. 136, on account of its representing his sign. I can discover no other connection between the two men.

SHORT (P.) to ALLDE (E.).   1599-1615
One compartment, originally Bynneman's, No. 230, used in 1595-9 by Short, seems in 1615 to have been in the possession of Edward Allde.

SHORT (P.) to LOWNES (H.).   1604
Peter Short, who, with Richard Yardley, had succeeded to the business of Henry Denham, died in 1603. His widow carried on his business for a short time, and then in 1604 married Humphrey Lownes, to whom most of Short's devices passed. He is found using three of these, Nos. 118, 148, 278, in 1604, and later Nos. 119, 211, 335, 366. Compartments Nos. 149 and 231 probably also reached Lownes through Short, but have not been found in Short's publications. Device 150 and the Walsingham ornament, No. 296, probably passed through Lownes' hands, but are not known to have been used by him.

SIBERCH (J.) to KAETZ (P.).
See Nos. 45, 57.

SIMMES (V.) to KINGSTON (F.).   ? 1607-9
Valentine Simmes printed until about 1622, but between 1607 and 1610 appears to have produced little or nothing. It is possible that at this time he was in difficulties, as he frequently was, and the passing of an insignificant ornament of his, No. 332, to Felix Kingston in the years c. 1603-9 may be thus explained.

SIMSON (G.) [to READ (R.)] to ELD (G.).
1600-4
Gabriel Simson died in or before August 1600, and in the following year his widow married Richard Read, a printer, who succeeded to Simson's business. Read died two or three years later, and in 1604 she married another printer, George Eld, to whom the business then passed. Device No. 308, used by Simson in 1597, is used by Eld in 1606, and another, No. 320, used by Simson in 1600, was in Eld's possession in 1607.

SMITH (R.) to WOOD (W.).   1595-9
Nothing is heard of Richard Smith after 1595, but his business perhaps passed into the hands of William Wood, who used his device No. 312, in 1599, and No. 331, which bears Smith's initials, though it is not known to have been used by him, in 1601.

SNODHAM (T.) to HARPER (T.).   1625-9
Thomas Snodham died in the autumn of 1625, his widow only surviving him for a few months. His printing materials appear to have been bought by George Wood and William Lee (*Dictionary I*, p. 299; Arber, iii. 703). About this time Wood had some dealings with Thomas Harper, which became the subject of litigation. According to Mr. Plomer (*Dictionary II*, p. 91), Harper

bought the business formerly Snodham's from George Wood and William Lee in 1634, but it seems that he may have had possession of it earlier, for in 1629 he used Snodham's device No. 227.

SNOWDON (G.) to OKES (N.).　　？1607

George and Lionel Snowdon, who appear to have taken over John Harrison III's printing business by 1606, transferred it to Nicholas Okes in 1608. Possibly, however, Okes was already in possession of it, for Harrison's device No. 334 was used by him in 1607. Device No. 316, which had been used by G. Snowdon in 1606, was used by Okes in 1608 (?) and 1622.

STAFFORD (S.) to PURSLOWE (G.).　？1614

There is some mystery about the later years of Simon Stafford's career. Sir John Lambe states in one place that George Purslowe bought Stafford's business in 1614, and in a list of printers dated 1615 Stafford's name does not appear. On the other hand he seems to have been printing in 1624-6, and according to another statement of Lambe, Purslowe succeeded him about 1630. Mr. Plomer regards the latter statement as the more probable (*Dictionary I*, p. 255), but Stafford seems to have transferred his device No. 281 to Purslowe between 1609 and 1617, which accords with the former. It is possible that Stafford went out of business for a time, and later returned and worked in some form of partnership with Purslowe.

STANSBY (W.) to BISHOP (R.).　　1634

William Stansby died in 1638 or early in 1639, and in March 1638/9 his widow assigned his copyrights to Richard Bishop (Arber, iv. 458-60). According to Mr. Plomer, however, Bishop bought Stansby's business in 1634 for £700 (*Dictionary II*, p. 25; Arber, iii. 701). The transfer of printing material must have taken place in 1634-8, see No. 282. Bishop also uses Stansby's Nos. 292 and 393 in 1640.

SUTTON (H.) to PURFOOT (T.).　*c.* 1562-81

Henry Sutton continued to print until 1563. Thomas Purfoot seems to have begun printing about 1562, though he had apparently been trading as a stationer for many years before. A border, No. 108, which had originally been Whitchurch's, then Wayland's, had apparently come into Sutton's possession, and part of it had been used by him in 1560. The whole border is used by T. Purfoot about 1581, but when he obtained it is unknown.

TOTTELL (R.) to DENHAM (H.).　　？1586

Richard Tottell is said to have been succeeded by his apprentice John Jaggard in or about 1593. In the last few years of his life, however, he printed comparatively little, and he may have got rid of some of his material. We find Henry Denham using his compartment No. 147 in 1586.

TOTTELL (R.) to GREENE (L.) or LEGGE (C.).　　　　　1554-1607

Part of a compartment, No. 91, originally R. Grafton's and used by Tottell in 1554 is found in a book printed for L. Greene at Cambridge in 1607, probably by C. Legge who had another piece of the compartment in 1613. It has not been noticed between 1554 and 1607, so we cannot say how it came into Legge's possession.

182

TREVERIS (P.) to BOURMAN (N.). 1532-40
The last book in which Peter Treveris' name appears was one printed for him by W. Rastell in 1532. He seems to have ceased to print in 1531, and may then have dispersed his material. A border-piece of his, No. 48, formerly Pepwell's, is found in use by Nicholas Bourman c. 1540.

TURNER (W.) to HALL (H.). 1644
William Turner died in 1644 and was succeeded as Printer to the University of Oxford by Henry Hall, who had been one of his apprentices. Devices No. 407 and 427 were used by Hall in 1644.

VAUTROLLIER (T.) to VAUTROLLIER (JACQUELIN) to FIELD (R.). 1588-9
Thomas Vautrollier, printer in London, 1562-84, 1586-7, and in Edinburgh 1584-6, died in July 1587. He bequeathed part of his printing material to his son Manasses, who seems however to have traded only as a stationer and bookbinder. The printing business passed to Vautrollier's widow Jacquelin, who used one of his devices, No. 192, in 1588. Within a twelvemonth of her husband's death she married his apprentice, Richard Field, to whom the business then passed. Field used Vautrollier's devices Nos. 164, 170, 179, 192, 210, 222, 246; and No. 233 also probably passed through his hands, as it is afterwards used by his successor George Miller.

WALDEGRAVE (R.) to ALLDE (E.). ? 1604
On the death of Robert Waldegrave in 1603 or 1604 some of his materials passed to East, and some (that left at Edinburgh) to Finlason. One small device, however, representing a fleur-de-lis, No. 270, used in a book stated to be printed by him, without indication of place, in 1603, is afterwards found in the possession of Edward Allde. It may originally have been Wolfe's (see Wolfe to Waldegrave).

WALDEGRAVE (R.) to BLOWER (R.).
See Wolfe (J.) to Blower (R.).

WALDEGRAVE (R.) to EAST (T.). ? 1604
When Robert Waldegrave threw in his lot with the Martin Marprelate group, and left London in May 1588 in order to act as their printer, he evidently took part of his printing material with him. Probably, however, some of it remained in London, for two devices of his, Nos. 83 and 227, do not seem to occur between the date of his disappearance from London and his return in 1603. Waldegrave died before the end of March 1604, and of these two devices one, No. 227, is found in the possession of Thomas East in 1606 (or ? 1603), and both were afterwards owned by East's successor, Snodham.

WALDEGRAVE (R.) to FINLASON (T.).
? 1604
Having printed at Edinburgh since 1590, Waldegrave returned to London in 1603, where he died a few months later. He seems to have left most of his printing materials in Edinburgh, and they were perhaps transferred in 1604 by his widow to Thomas Finlason at the same time as she transferred his patents. We find Finlason using Waldegrave's devices, Nos. 187 and 189, originally Ross's, in 1612 and 1620 respectively.

WALLEY (J.) to CHARLEWOOD (J.).
? 1582-3
John Walley printed until 1585, dying

in the following year. An ornament of his, No. 183, is found in a book printed by John Charlewood as the assign of Tottell in 1583, but as it has Walley's mark it is possible that it was used in consequence of some partnership arrangement, and had not become Charlewood's property.

WARD (R.) to JEFFES (A.).   c. 1595

Roger Ward is last heard of as a printer in 1595, when he was discovered to have set up a secret press in the Temple. In December 1595 a press and type of Abel Jeffes was seized for printing 'lewd ballads and things very offensive,' and he was imprisoned for a while. Perhaps on coming out of prison he purchased some of Ward's material to make good the loss of his own, for in 1596 we find him using Ward's device, No. 238.

WATKINS (R.) to DAWSON (T.).

See Watkins (R.) to White (W.).

WATKINS (R.) to WHITE (W.).   c. 1598

Richard Watkins apparently ceased to print in 1598, when he was reduced to poor circumstances. Device No. 188 passed to William White and was used by him in 1600. Compartments Nos. 181 and 182 seem to have passed either to him or to Thomas Dawson. Device No. 165, originally Jugge's, used by White in 1599, may have come to him through Watkins (see Jugge to Watkins).

WAYLAND (J.) to DAY (J.), SUTTON (H.) and BYNNEMAN (H.)   ? 1557

John Wayland died in 1556 or 1557 leaving ' desperate debts.' It is not known what became of his printing materials, which seem to have been dispersed. A com-

partment, No. 116, originally Day's, which was used in books printed about 1557 and bearing Wayland's name, later returned to Day. Part of a border (No. 108) originally Whitchurch's, and used by Wayland in 1554, seems in 1560 to have been in the hands of Henry Sutton. Lastly, device No. 99, also Whitchurch's, which perhaps passed through the hands of Wayland though it has not been found in work bearing his name, was from 1576 to 1579 in the possession of Henry Bynneman.

WAYLAND (J.) to PURFOOT (T.).

See Sutton (H.) to Purfoot (T.).

WAYLAND (J.) to TOTTELL (R.).

See Grafton (R.) to Wayland (J.).

WHITCHURCH (E.) to BYNNEMAN (H.).
1546-76

Device No. 99, used by Whitchurch in 1546 had come by 1576 into the possession of Bynneman. See Wayland to Day, etc.

WHITCHURCH (E.) to CAWOOD (E.) and JUGGE (R.).   ? 1564

Whitchurch's material probably passed to John Wayland in 1553 (see Whitchurch to Wayland), but one compartment, No. 109, appears to have passed to Cawood and Jugge, and later to John Kingston. It is, however, possible that it was merely lent to these printers by its owner, whoever he may have been.

WHITCHURCH (E.) to POWELL (W.).
1545-52

Some time before 1552, Edward Whitchurch, who had succeeded Byddell at

184

Wynkyn de Worde's house in 1545 (see Byddell to Whitchurch), seems to have made over a portion of the old material to William Powell who is found using one of de Worde's border-pieces, No. 50, in that year.

WHITCHURCH (E.) to WAYLAND (J.). 1553

Edward Whitchurch, being excluded from the general pardon proclaimed at the beginning of Mary's reign, was obliged to leave his shop at the Sun in Fleet Street. He seems to have been succeeded there by John Wayland at the end of 1553. Wayland used Whitchurch's compartment No. 108 in 1554, and No. 99 perhaps also passed through his hands.

WHITE (W.) to WHITE (J.) to MATHEWES (A.). 1623

The name of William White seems to occur for the last time in Greene's *Farewell to Folly*, 1617. He was succeeded by his son John, who apparently made no use of his devices. In 1623 John White made over certain rights to Augustine Mathewes and is said to have transferred his printing-house to him in 1624. It seems possible that the transfer took place somewhat earlier, for we find Mathewes using W. White's device, No. 188 (formerly R. Watkins') in 1623. Further, device No. 238, which had belonged to Jeffes, was used by Mathewes in 1622. It seems not unlikely that this also came to him through the Whites (see Jeffes to Mathewes), though it is not known to have been used by them.

WILLIAMSON (W.) to LEGATE (J.). ? 1574–? 1617

William Williamson seems only to have printed from 1571 to 1574, after which date he disappears. Some of his copyrights were transferred to Charlewood, but it is not known what became of his printing material. A device, No. 166, eventually fell into the hands of John Legate I (?) and II.

WINDET (J.) to STANSBY (W.). 1611

John Windet continued in business until 1611, when he assigned over his copyrights and apparently sold all his printing materials to William Stansby. Stansby used Windet's devices Nos. 282 and 292 in 1611, and later Nos. 208, 237, 243, 323.

? WOLFE (J.) to ALLDE (E.). 1599

John Wolfe's device No. 310 is found in 1599 and 1600 in books apparently printed by Edward Allde, and later passed to Elizabeth Allde. It is possible that it was never Wolfe's at all, and that the book bearing his name in which it appears in 1599 was really printed by Allde for him.

WOLFE (J.) to BLOWER (R.). ? 1601

John Wolfe died in 1601, and his printing business and stock were transferred to Adam Islip. His devices seem, however, to have been dispersed. One of them, No. 298, is found in the hands of Ralph Blower, and two others, Nos. 216 and 249, passed to a certain R.B., who may have been Blower, though this cannot be regarded as certain. In the case of No. 249 there is the difficulty that the device appears in a book purporting to have been printed by Waldegrave at Edinburgh in 1603 (see Wolfe to Waldegrave). It is not impossible that all three devices may have passed to Blower through Waldegrave, but the matter is obscure.

WOLFE (J.) to ISLIP (A.).   ? 1594

John Wolfe on his death in 1601 was succeeded by Adam Islip who bought his printing-house, type, and implements (Arber, iii. 700). It is possible, however, that there was some relation between these men at an earlier date, for in 1593-4 Wolfe apparently transferred to Islip his device No. 226, and before 1598 his No. 251. It is probable also that No. 263, used by Islip in 1602, was originally Wolfe's, but this may of course have come to Islip with the business. Islip's use of a fleur-de-lis, No 268, at a time when Wolfe was using a very similar one, No. 269, and their use of the two blocks of No. 251, are perhaps also indications of a connection between the two men.

? WOLFE (J.) to ROBERTS (J.).   1601-6

One of John Wolfe's devices, No. 294, is found in 1606 in a book without printer's name which also contains device No. 283. As that device was in the possession of William Jaggard in 1615, and had originally belonged to Richard Jones, we might guess that it had passed from Roberts to Jaggard in 1606. No. 294 is, however, used in 1607 by one I. W. The only printers with these initials at work in 1606 seem to have been John Windet and John Wright. Windet had succeeded Wolfe as printer to the City of London, and another device of Wolfe's, No. 252, may possibly have passed through his hands, as it is afterwards used by his successor, W. Stansby; but it is not easy to see how No. 283 could have been in his possession, or for that matter, in Wright's, in 1606. The simplest explanation is perhaps that No. 294, as well as 283, was in Roberts' hands in 1606, and that on the business being taken over by Jaggard he disposed of No. 294 to one of the two printers whose initials it bore. Of the two, Wright seems the most probable, as he had just commenced printing and had no device of his own.

? WOLFE (J.) to WALDEGRAVE (R.).   1601-3

Device No. 249 seems to have passed from John Wolfe to Robert Waldegrave. It appears in a book stated to have been printed by him at Edinburgh in 1603, but it is somewhat improbable that the device would make its way to Edinburgh, and it is perhaps more likely that the book was really printed in London, either by or for Waldegrave. Another device, No. 270, used in a book stated to be printed by Waldegrave in 1603, without indication of place, is very similar to one used by John Wolfe, No. 269, and may also have come from him. If so, Waldegrave may, on his return to London in 1603, have purchased these devices from Adam Islip, who is said to have bought Wolfe's printing materials on his death in 1601.

? WOLFE (J.) to WINDET (J.).   ? 1601

In 1593 John Wolfe was appointed printer to the City of London in succession to Hugh Singleton. On his death in 1601 he was succeeded in this office by John Windet, but his stock and other business passed to Islip. We find an I. W. using a block of Wolfe's, No. 294, in 1607, but it seems doubtful if this is Windet (see Wolfe to Roberts). If it is, he may perhaps also have owned No. 252, which is afterwards found in the possession of his successor, Stansby.

WOLFE (R.) to WOLFE (JOAN) to BYNNE-
MAN (H.).   1573, 1574-5
Reyner Wolfe died in 1573. His wife
Joan carried on his business for about a
year, using his device No. 118 in 1574.
On her death in that year a large part of
Wolfe's printing material came into the
hands of Henry Bynneman. He used
Wolfe's two serpent devices, Nos. 118, 119,
in 1575 and 1577, and one of his Tree of
Charity devices, No. 97, in 1575.

WOOD (W.) to MATHEWES (A.). 1602-24
Nothing is heard of William Wood after
1602. One of his devices, No. 312, was in
the hands of Augustine Mathewes in 1624,
but it is impossible to say how or when he
obtained it.

WORDE (W. DE) to BYDDELL (J.).   1535
Wynkyn de Worde is believed to have
died early in 1535, his business at the Sun
being carried on by his executors and
former assistants, John Byddell and James
Gaver, to whom presumably all his devices
passed. Byddell, who had previously been
engaged in business at another address, and
had several devices of his own, seems only
once to have used one of de Worde's
(No. 46), which is found in a book printed
by him in 1535, when he was dwelling at
the sign of the Sun, *i.e.*, presumably after
de Worde's death. De Worde's device No.
25, and border-piece No. 50, probably also
passed through Byddell's hands.

WYER (R.) to COLWELL (T.).   1560
Robert Wyer retired from business in
1556, in which year he is said to have been
succeeded by one Nicholas Wyer (Plomer,
R. Wyer, p. 2). In 1560 the printing-
house came into the hands of Thomas Colwell, who used Wyer's device, No. 68,
from about 1565.

WYKES (H.) to NEWBERY (R.).   *c.* 1571
Henry Wykes was one of Thomas
Berthelet's apprentices, and after his master's
death in 1555 appears to have continued to
occupy Berthelet's house jointly with Berthelet's nephew, Thomas Powell, and to have
printed there from *c.* 1557. Berthelet's
sign of Lucrece had passed to Powell, and
Wykes used that of the Black Elephant or
Oliphaunt. In 1563 Ralph Newbery was
also dwelling in Berthelet's house, having
apparently succeeded Powell there, and
when Wykes ceased to print in 1571, he
perhaps took over his materials. He is found
using Wykes' device No. 153 in 1574 (?)
and 1577.

YETSWEIRT (C.) to YETSWEIRT (J.).
See Denham (H.) to Yetsweirt (C.).

YETSWEIRT (J.) to WIGHT (T.) or NOR-
TON (B.).
See Denham (H.) to Yetsweirt (C.).

YOUNG (R.) to ANDERSON (G.).   ? 1637-8
Robert Young, who had been appointed
King's Printer in Scotland in 1632, seems
to have given up his Edinburgh business in
1637 or 1638, and to have sold his materials
to George Anderson, who began to print
there in the former year. Finlason's (originally Ross's) devices Nos. 187, 189, used
by Anderson in 1638, probably reached
him through Young; and Finlason's ornament No. 358, used in 1640 by Bryson,
probably also passed through his hands.

YOUNG (R.) to LEGATE (J.) II.　? 1632
A combination device, No. 335, originally used by Peter Short in the *Works of Josephus*, 1602, seems to have been transferred by Lownes or Young with the copyright of the book to John Legate II, by whom it is used in editions of 1632 and 1640 for A. Hebb.

REVERSED LIST OF TRANSFERS

INTENDED TO AID IN THE SEARCH FOR THE PERSON FROM WHOM A PRINTER IS LIKELY TO HAVE OBTAINED MATERIAL

Allde (E.) from Gubbin (T.).
   „   from Short (P.).
   „   from Waldegrave (R.).
   „   from Wolfe (J.).
Allde (Eliz.) from Allde (E.).
Alsop (B.) from Creede (T.).
Anderson (G.) from Young (R.).

Badger (R.) from Field (R.).
   „   from Miller (G.).
Badger (T.) from Badger (R.).
Barker (R.) from Barker (C.).
Beale (J.) from Bradock (R.).
Bill (J.) from Barker (R.).
Bishop (G.) from Barker (C.).
Bishop (R.) from Stansby (W.).
Blower (R.) from Waldegrave (R.).
   „   from Wolfe (J.).
Bourman (N.) from Hertford (J.).
     „   from Treveris (P.).
Bradock (R.) from Robinson (R.).
Bryson (R.) from Anderson (G.).
Buck (T.) from Newbery (R.).
Buck (T. and J.) from Legge (C.).
Byddell (J.) from de Worde (W.).
Bynneman (H.) from England (N.).
     „   from Wayland (J.).
     „   from Whitchurch (E.).
     „   from Wolfe (Joan) from
   Wolfe (R.).

Caly (R.) from Grafton (R.).
Cawood (J.) from Whitchurch (E.).
Charlewood (J.) from Baldwin (W.).
     „   from Serle (R.).
     „   from Walley (J.).
Charteris (R.) from Charteris (H.).
Colwell (T.) from Wyer (R.).
Copland (W.) from Copland (R.).
Cotes (R.) from Cotes (T.).
Cotes (T.) from Jaggard (I.) from Jaggard (W.).

Daniel (R.) from Buck (T. and J.).
   „   from Newbery (R.).
Dawson (J.) II from Dawson (M.) from Dawson (J.) I.
Dawson (T.) from Watkins (R.).
Day (J.) from Gibson (T.).
   „   from Wayland (J.).
Day (R.) from Day (J.).
Denham (H.) from Bynneman (H.).
     „   from King (J.),
     „   from Seres (W.).
     „   from Tottell (R.).

East (T.) from Waldegrave (R.).
Eld (G.) from Read (R.) from Simson (G.).

Field (R.) from Vautrollier (T.).

Finlason (T.) from Arbuthnet (A.).
　　　　" from Waldegrave (R.).
Fletcher (M.) from Eld (G.).
Franckton (J.) from Kearney (W.).

Gibson (T.) from Rastell (W.).
Greene (L.) from Tottell (R.).
Griffin (A.) from Haviland (J.).
Griffin (E.) I from Bradwood (M.).
Griffin (E.) II from Griffin (A.).
　　　　" from Haviland (J.).

Hall (H.) from Turner (W.).
Harper (T.) from Snodham (T.).
Hart (A.) from Charteris (R.).
Haviland (J.) from Griffin (E.) I.
Hearne (R.) from Islip (A.).
Howe (W.) from Hall (R.).

Islip (A.) from Wolfe (J.).
Islip (S.) from Hearne (R.) from Islip (A.).

Jackson (H.) from Colwell (T.).
Jaggard (W.) from Denham (H.).
　　" from Jones (R.).
　　" from Powell (T.).
　　" from Roberts (J.).
Jeffes (A.) from Ward (R.).
Jones (R.) from Charlewood (J.).
　　" from Danter (J.).
Jones (W.) from Barley (W.).
　　" from Blower (R.).
Jugge (R.) from Whitchurch (E.).

King (J.) from Middleton (W.).
　　" from Petit (T.).
Kingston (F.) from Orwin (J.) from Orwin (T.).
Kingston (F.) from Simmes (V.).
Kyrfoth (C.) from Scolar (J.).

Legate (J.) I from Williamson (J.).

Legate (J.) II from Bradock (R.).
　　" from Legate (J.) I.
　　" from Lownes (H.).
　　" from Young (R.).
Legge (C.) from Tottell (R.).
Lichfield (J.) from Barnes (J.).
Lichfield (L.) from Lichfield (J.).
Lownes (H.) from Short (P.).

Marshe (T.) from King (J.).
Mathewes (A.) from Barley (W.).
　　" from Blower (R.).
　　" from Jeffes (A.).
　　" from Jones (W.).
　　" from White (J.) from White (W.).
Mathewes (A.) from Wood (W.).
Maunsell (A.) from Jugge (R.).
Middleton (H.) from Marshe (T.).
　　" from Newbery (R.).
Middleton (W.) from Petit (T.).
Miller (A.) from Miller (G.).
Miller (G.) from Badger (R.).
　　" from Field (R.).

Newbery (R.) from Barker (C.).
　　" from Middleton (H.).
　　" from Wykes (H.).
Norton (B.) from Barker (R.).
　　" from Norton (W.).
　　" from Yetsweirt (J.) from Yetsweirt (C.).
Okes (J.) from Okes (N.).
Okes (N.) from Harrison (J.).
　　" from Middleton (H.).
　　" from Snowdon (G.).
Orwin (T.) from Marshe (T.).
Oulton (R.) from Allde (Eliz.).

Parsons (M.) from Mathewes (A.).
Pepwell (H.) from Jacobi (H.).
Powell (W.) from Byddell (J.).

189

Powell (W.) from Middleton (W.).
     ,,   from Whitchurch (E.).
Purfoot (T.) from Roberts (J.).
     ,,   from Sutton (H.).
     ,,   from Wayland (J.).
Purslowe (E.) from Purslowe (G.).
Purslowe (G.) from Stafford (S.).

Read (R.) from Simson (G.).
Redman (E.) from Redman (R.).
Redman (R.) from Pynson (R.).
Reynes (J.) from Gibson (T.).
Roberts (J.) from Charlewood (J.).
     ,,   from Jones (R.).
     ,,   from Wolfe (J.).
Robinson (R.) from Middleton (H.).
     ,,   from Scarlet (T.).

Serle (R.) from Hall (R.).
Short (P.) from Denham (H.).
Simmes (V.) from Howe (W.).
Smith (H.) from Gibson (T.).
     ,,   from Reynes (J.).
Snodham (T.) from East (T.).
Snowdon (G.) from Harrison (J.) III.
Stafford (S.) from Danter (J.).
     ,,   from Jones (R.).
Stansby (W.) from Windet (J.).
Sutton (H.) from Wayland (J.).

Tottell (R.) from Caly (R.) from Grafton
    (R.).

Tottell (R.) from Wayland (J.).
Treveris (P.) from Pepwell (H.).

W. (T.) from Norton (J.).
Waldegrave (R.) from Day (J.).
     ,,   from Ross (R.).
     ,,   from Wolfe (J.).
Watkins (R.) from Jugge (J.) from
    Jugge (R.).
Wayland (J.) from Day (J.).
     ,,   from Grafton (R.).
     ,,   from Whitchurch (E.).
Whitchurch (E.) from Byddell (J.)
White (W.) from Jugge (R).
     ,,   from Watkins (R.).
Wight (T.) from Yetsweirt (J.) from Yets-
    weirt (C.).
Wilson (W.) from Okes (J.).
Windet (J.) from Day (J).
     ,,   from Roberts (J.).
     ,,   from Wolfe (J.).
Wolfe (J.) from Kearney (W.).
Wood (W.) from Smith (R.).
Worde (W. de) from Caxton (W.).
Wright (J.) from Roberts (J.).

Yardley (R.) from Denham (H).
Yetsweirt (C. and J.) from Denham (H.).
Young (R.) from Finlason (T.).
     ,,   from Lownes (H.).

FACSIMILES

Imperfect at lower left-hand corner

1a

1b

2

3

4

5

6

7

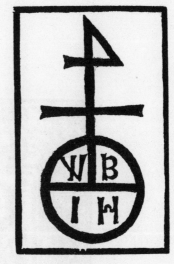

8α

8β

8γ

9a

9b

10a

11

10b

12

13

Guillam.

14 & 15

16

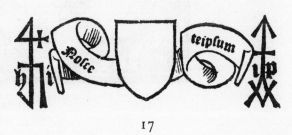

17

b

18a

18β

22

21

23a

23b

23c

24

25

Julyan Notary

26 (& 28)

27

28

29

30

c

31β

31α

32

33

34α

34β

Reduced from 250 × 182 mm.

35

37

36

38 & 39

40

41

42

43

44

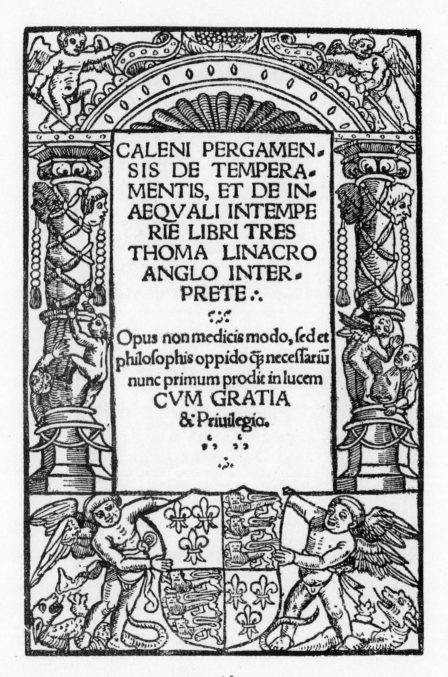

CALENI PERGAMEN-
SIS DE TEMPERA-
MENTIS, ET DE IN-
AEQVALI INTEMPE
RIE LIBRI TRES
THOMA LINACRO
ANGLO INTER-
PRETE ∴

Opus non medicis modo, sed et
philosophis oppido q̃ necessariũ
nunc primum prodit in lucem
CVM GRATIA
& Priuilegio.

45

d

46β

46α

47

48

49

50

51

53

52

54

55

Richard Fakes

56

57

58

59α

59β

PETRVS · TREVERIS

60

Reduced from 239 × 157 mm.

61

CRegistrum
omniũ bʒeuium
tam oʒiginaliũ
ꝗ̃ iudicia-
lium.

✠

LONDINI.
☞Apud Guilielmum, Rastell.

1531

☞CVM PRIVILEGIO.

63

64

65

66

67α

68 & 69

67β

70

71α

71β

72

73

74α

74β

75

76

77

78

79

80

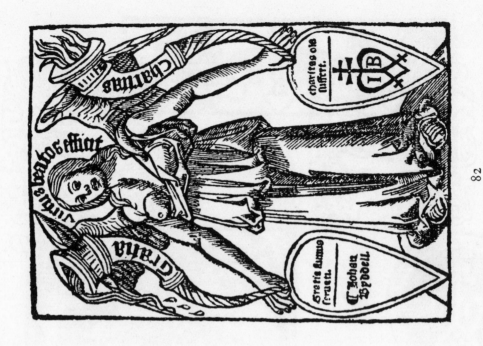

83α

83β

84α

84β

f

85

86

87

88

Judyth.

89

90

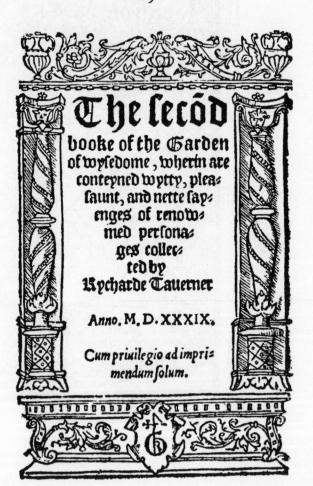

The lecōd booke of the Garden of wyſedome, wherin are conteyned wytty, pleaſaunt, and nette ſayenges of renowmed perſonages collected by Rycharde Tauerner

Anno. M. D. XXXIX.

Cum priuilegio ad imprimendum ſolum.

91

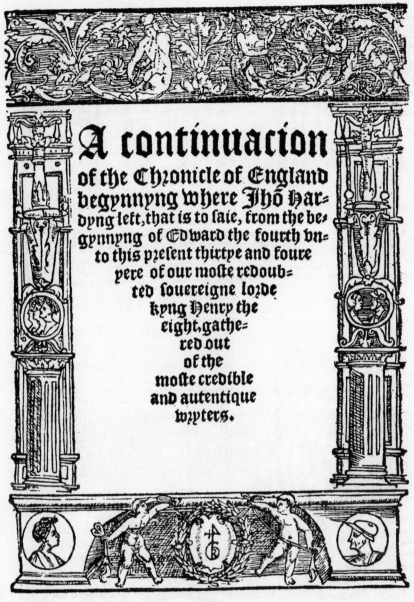

A continuacion

of the Chronicle of England
begynnyng where Jhō Har-
dyng left, that is to saie, from the begynnyng of Edward the fourth vn-
to this present thirtye and foure
yere of our moste redoub-
ted souereigne lorde
kyng Henry the
eight, gathe-
red out
of the
moste credible
and autentique
wryters.

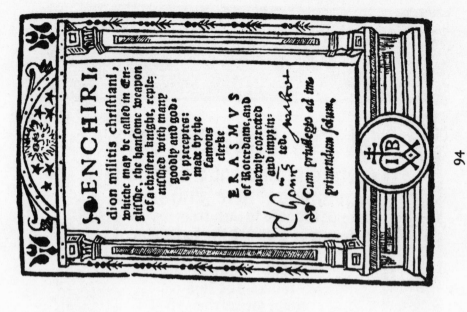

94

93

95

96

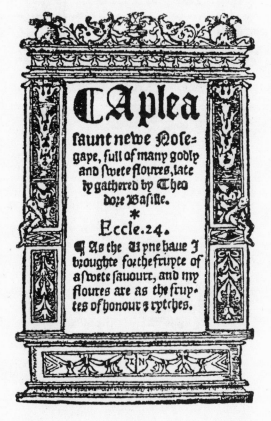

98

97

99

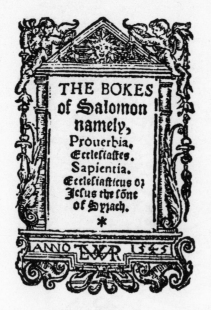

THE BOKES
of Salomon
namely,
Prouerbia.
Ecclesiastes.
Sapientia.
Ecclesiasticus oʒ
Jesus the sóne
of Syʒach.

ANNO E.W.R 1545

100

THE PRI:
mer set foʒth by þ kin:
ges maiestie and his
Cleargy, and none other
to be vsed through out
his domini:
ous.

M. D. XLV.

101

102

103

g

Certayne
Sermons, o₂ Homi
lies , appoynted by the
kynges Maiestie , to be
declared and redde, by all
Persones , Uycars , o₂
Curates, euery Sõ-
day in their Chur-
ches, where they
haue Cure.

ANNO, 1547.

108

107

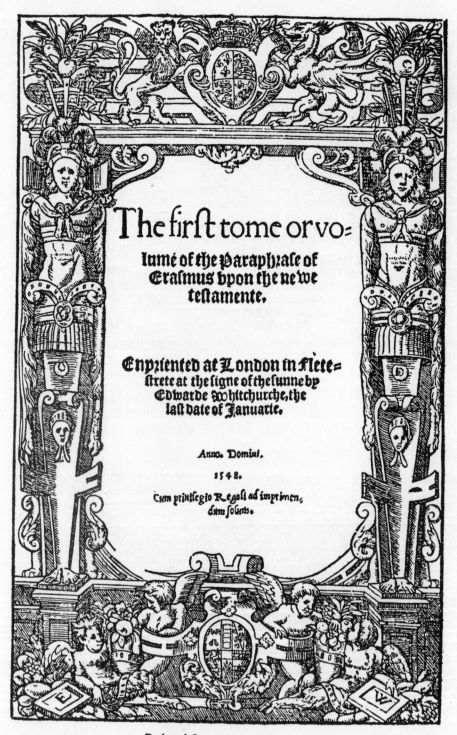

The first tome or vo=
lume of the Paraphrale of
Erafmus vpon the newe
teftamente.

Enpzinted at London in Flete=
ftrete at the figne of the funne by
Edwarde Whitchurche, the
laft date of Januarie.

Anno. Domini.
1548.

Cum priuilegio Regali ad imprimen,
dum folum.

Reduced from 231 × 145 mm.

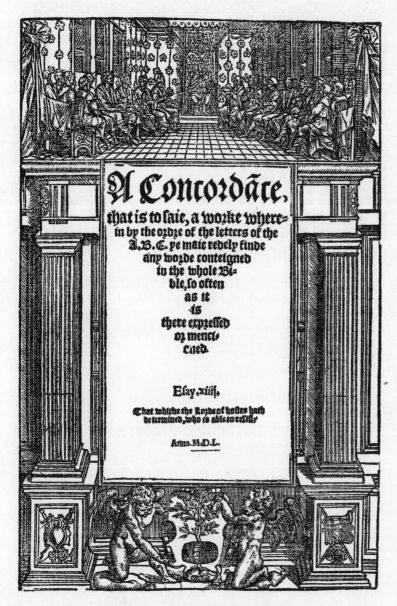

A Concordāce,
that is to saie, a worke where=
in by the ordre of the letters of the
A.B.C. ye maie redely finde
any worde conteigned
in the whole Bi=
ble, so often
as it
is
there expressed
or menci-
oned.

Esay .xliii.

That whiche the Lorde of hostes hath
determined, who is able to eslu?

Anno.M.D.L.

Reduced from 210 × 136 mm.

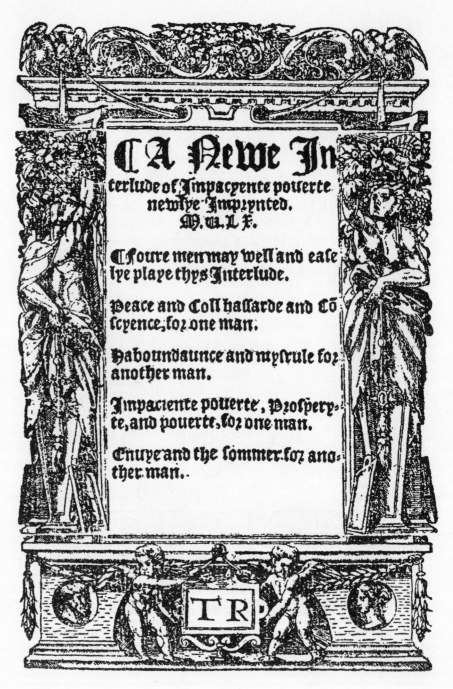

¶A Newe Interlude of Impacyente pouerte
newlye Imprynted.
M. vi. L. X.

¶foure men may well and easelye playe thys Interlude.

Peace and Coll hassarde and Cōscyence, for one man.

Haboundaunce and mysrule for another man.

Impaciente pouerte, Prosperyte, and pouerte, for one man.

Enuye and the sommer, for another man.

III

112α

112β

113

114

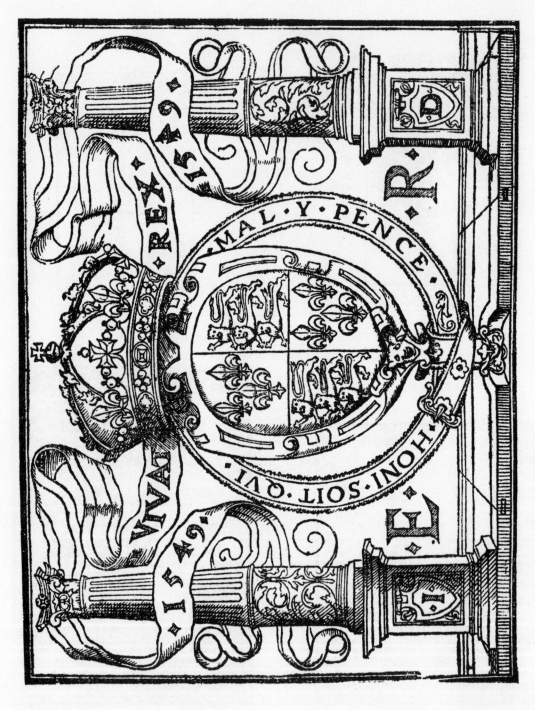

Reduced from 252 × 144 mm.

116

117

NVM.   XXI.

118

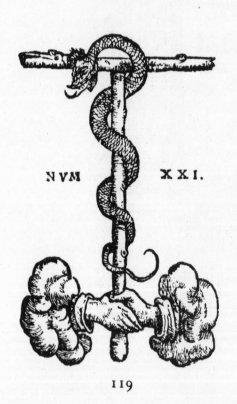

NVM   XXI.

119

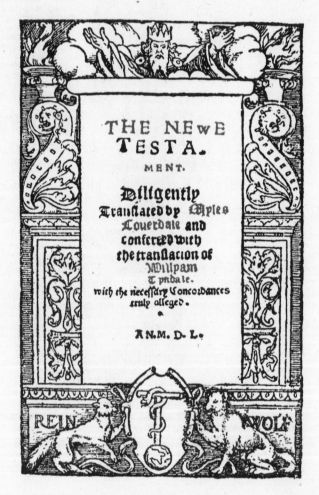

THE NEwE
TESTA.
MENT.

Diligently
Translated by Myles
Couerdale and
conferred with
the translation of
William
Tyndale.
with the necessary Concordances
truly alleged.

AN. M. D. L.

REIN   WOLF

120

121

122

123

124

126

GOD IS

MY HELPER.

127

125α

125β

128

129

¶ The sec:
pter of diuision.
Whych hathe euer bene
per the chefest vndoet of
any Regionor Citie, set
forth after the Auctours
old copy / by I. S.
Anno. M.D.L.
IX.the xiii.of
May.
(*)

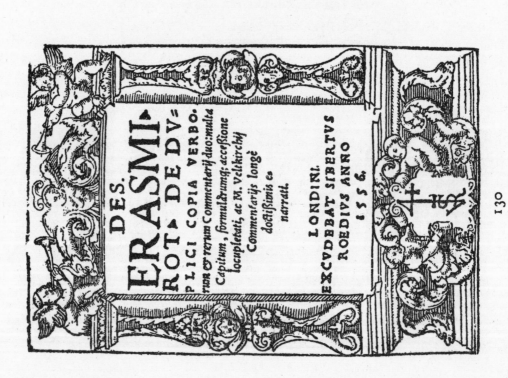

DES.
ERASMI
ROT. DE DV
PLICI COPIA VERBO
rum & rerum Commentarij duo: multa
Capitum, formularumq; accessione
locupletati, ac M. Velkirchij
Commentarijs longè
doctiʃʃimis ea
narrati.

LONDINI.
EXCVDEBAT SIBERTVS
ROEDIVS ANNO
1556.

An Anſwere in
defence of the truth.
Againſte the
Apologie
of
Priuate
Maſſe

LONDINI
Menſ.Nouēb.
1562.

133

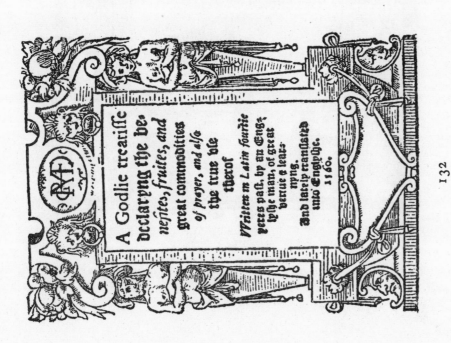

A Godlie treatiſe
declaryng the be-
neſites, fruites, and
great commodities
of prayer, and alſo
the true vſe
therof
Written in Latin fourtie
yeers paſt, by an Eng-
lyſhe man, of great
vertue & lear-
nyng.
And lately translated
into Englyſhe.
1560.

132

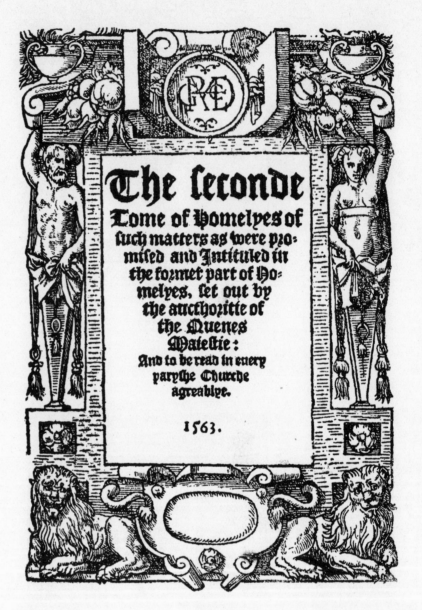

The seconde
Tome of Homelyes of
such matters as were pro-
mised and Intituled in
the former part of Ho-
melyes, set out by
the aucthoritie of
the Quenes
Maiestie:
And to be read in euery
paryshe Churche
agreablye.

1563.

134

135

136

137

138

¶ Aggeus and Abdias Prophetes, the one corrected, the other newly added, and both at large declared.

The earnest loue that I beare to thy house hath eaten me, Psal. lxix. Ioan. ii.

Phinees hath tourned awaye my anger because he was moued with loue of me, Num. xxv.

Imprinted at London by Wylliam Seres. 1562.

¶ How and whither a Chrysten man ought to flye the horryble Plague of the Pestilence.

A Sermon out of the Psalme. Qui habitat in adiutorio altissimi.

¶ Translated out of hye Almaine into Englishe.

¶ Imprinted at London, by Leonarde Askell.

141

142

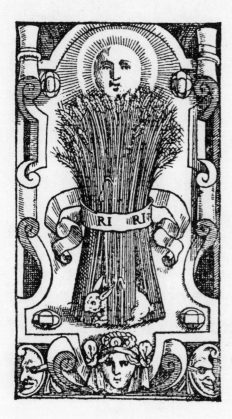

143

144α

144β

LIEFE IS DEATHE AND DEATH IS LIEFE · ÆTATIS SVÆ XXXX · 1562 · I·D

145

¶ Loue is pacient and courteous, enuieth not, doth not
frowardly, is not puft vp, dealeth not dishonestly, seeketh not her owne, is not
prouoked to anger, thinketh not euill, &c. suffereth all thin-
ges, beleueth all things, hopeth all things, endureth all things, &c. 1. Cor. 13

Reduced from 300 × 180 mm.

147

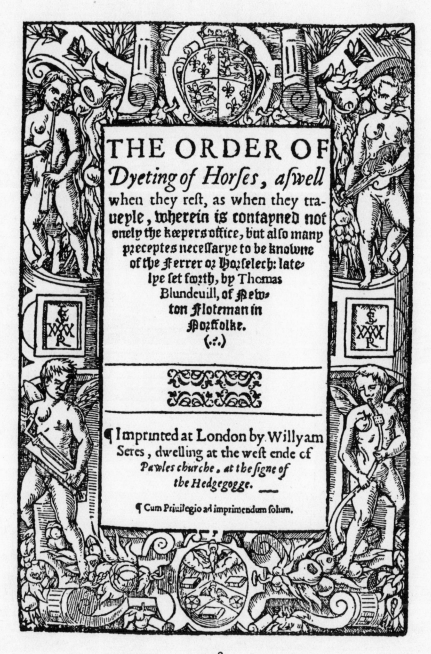

THE ORDER OF

Dyeting of Horses, aſwell
when they reſt, as when they tra-
ueyle, wherein is contayned not
onely the kœpers office, but also many
præceptes neceſſarye to be knowne
of the Ferrer oꝛ Hoꝛſelech: late-
lye ſet foꝛth, by Thomas
Blundeuill, of New-
ton Floteman in
Noꝛffolke.
(∴)

⁋ Imprinted at London by Willyam
Seres, dwelling at the weſt ende of
*Pawles churche, at the ſigne of
the Hedgegogge.*

⁋ Cum Priuilegio ad imprimendum ſolum.

149

150

151

152

153α

153β

CERTAINE
Tragicall Discourses
writtten oute of Frenche
and Latin, by Geffraie
Fenton, no lesse profitable
then pleasaunt, and of like
necessitye to al degrees
that take pleasure
in antiquityes or
foreine reap=
portes.

Mon heur viendra.

Imprinted at London in Flete=
strete nere to Saint Dunstons
Churche by Thomas
Marshe.

Anno Domini.
1567.

155

R, **I,**

156

157

158

159

160

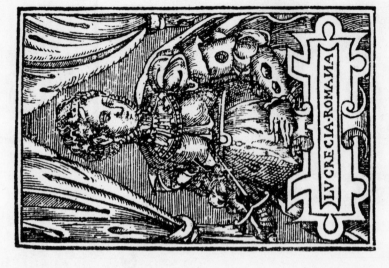

161

Reduced from 263 × 182 mm.

163

164

165

166

167

CICERO.
Historia est testis temporum, lux veritatis,
vitae memoria, magistra vitae, nuncia ve-
tustatis.

❡HISTORIA BRE-
uis Thomæ Walsingham,
ab Edwardo primo, ad
Henricum quintum.

LONDINI
Excusum apud Henricum
Binneman Typographum.
sub insigno Syrenis.

ANNO DOMINI
1574.

Reduced from 254 × 158 mm.

170

169

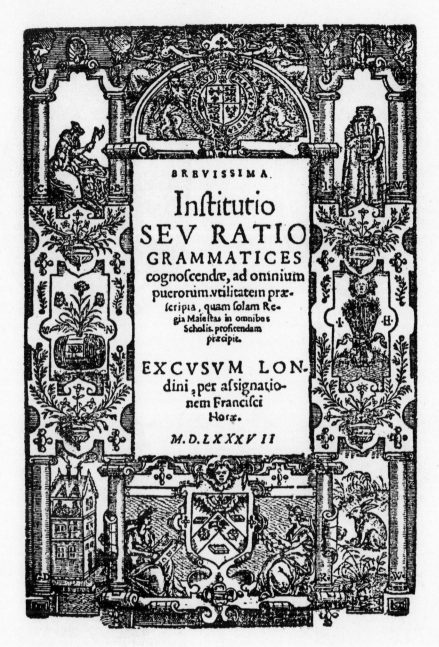

BREVISSIMA.

Institutio
SEV RATIO
GRAMMATICES
cognoscendæ, ad omnium
puerorum. vtilitatem præ-
scripta, quam solam Re-
gia Maiestas in omnibus
Scholis. proficendam
præcipit.

EXCVSVM LON-
dini, per assignatio-
nem Francisci
Horæ.

M. D. LXXXVII

171

172

173

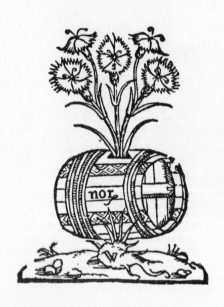

174

175

177

176

178

179

180

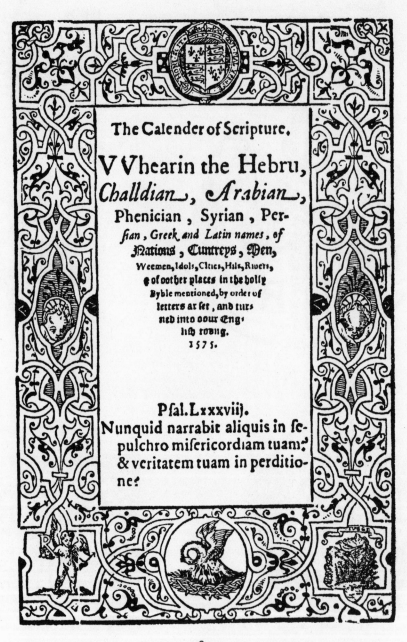

The Calender of Scripture.

VVhearin the Hebru,
Challdian, *Arabian*,
Phenician, Syrian, Per-
fian, *Greek* and *Latin names*, of
Nations, Cuntreys, Men,
Weemen, Idols, Cities, Hils, Rivers,
& of oother places in the holly
Byble mentioned, by order of
letters ar set, and tur-
ned into oour Eng-
lish toung.
1575.

Pſal. Lxxxviij.
Nunquid narrabit aliquis in ſe-
pulchro miſericordiam tuam?
& veritatem tuam in perditio-
ne?

¶ The seconde part of
the Byble, conteyning
these bookes.

The booke of Iosuah.
The booke of Iudges.
The booke of Ruth.
The fyrst booke of Samuel.
The second booke of Samuel.
The thirde booke of the Kinges.
The fourth booke of the Kinges.
The first booke of the Chronicles.
The second booke of the Chronicles.
The first booke of Esdras.
The second booke of Esdras.
The booke of Esther.
The booke of Iob.

OMNE · BONV · SVPERNÆ

183

184

185

186

I. R.

187

188α

188β

I O R

189

190

191

192

193

194

195

Cy ensu-
ont certeyne Ca-
ſes Reportes per
Edmunde Plowden vn
Apprentice de le commen ley,
puis le primer imprimier
de ſes Commentaries,
& ore a le ſeconde
imprimter de
les dits
Commentaries a
ceo addes.
(.*.)

Oueſque vn Table en fine de ceſt
Lieur des toutez les principall
caſes, cibien en le diſt primier
Lieur des Commentaries, come
de les caſes icy de nouel addes,
iammes deuaunt imprimie.

Cum Priuilegio.
Anno. 1579.

R   T

Reduced from 225 × 142 mm.

196

m

197

198

199

200

201

Imperfect at upper right-hand corner.

202α

202β

202γ

203

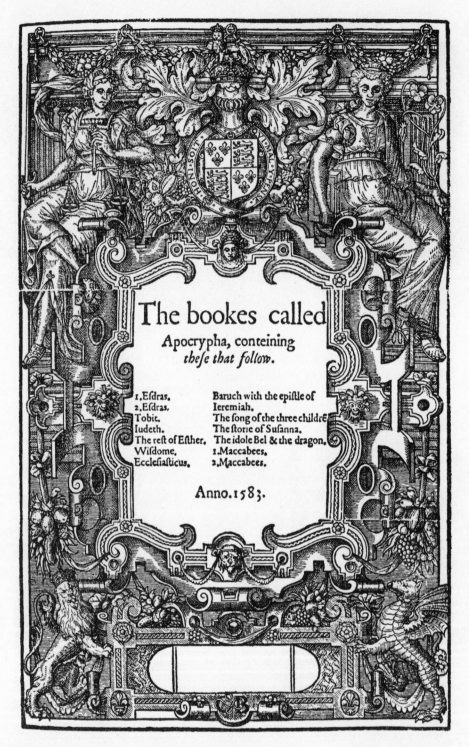

The bookes called Apocrypha, conteining *these that follow.*

1. Esdras.	Baruch with the epistle of
2. Esdras.	Ieremiah.
Tobit.	The song of the three childrẽ
Iudeth.	The storie of Susanna.
The rest of Esther.	The idole Bel & the dragon.
Wisdome.	1. Maccabees.
Ecclesiasticus.	2. Maccabees.

Anno. 1583.

Reduced from 301 × 190 mm.

205

206

207

208

209

210

212

211

213

214

215

216

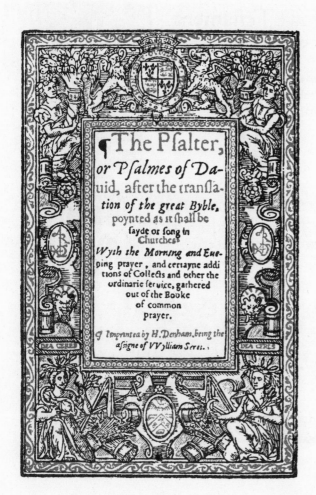

218

217

219

THE
Newe Teſtament
of our Lord Ieſus
Chriſt,

Conferred diligently with the Greeke,
and beſt approued tranſlations in
diuers languages.

Imprinted at London by
Chriſtopher Barker, printer
to the Queenes Maieſtie,
1579.

Cum gratia & priuilegio.

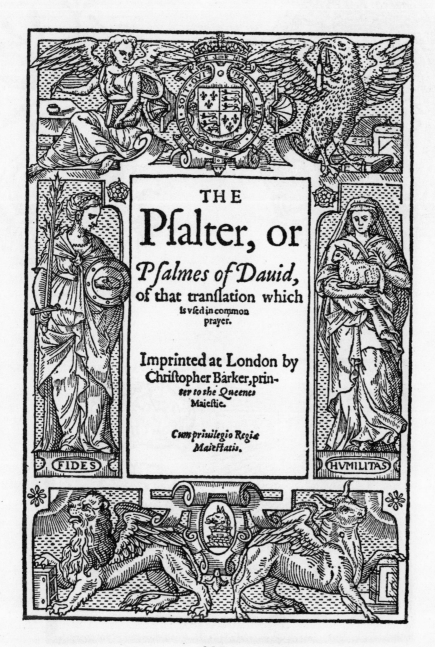

THE
Pfalter, or
Pfalmes of Dauid,
of that tranflation which
is vfed in common
prayer.

Imprinted at London by
Chriftopher Barker, prin-
ter to the Queenes
Maieftie.

Cum priuilegio Regiæ
Maieftatis.

FIDES

HVMILITAS

222

223

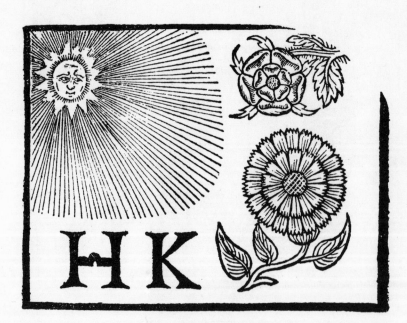

Imperfect at upper right-hand corner

224

225

226

228

227

229

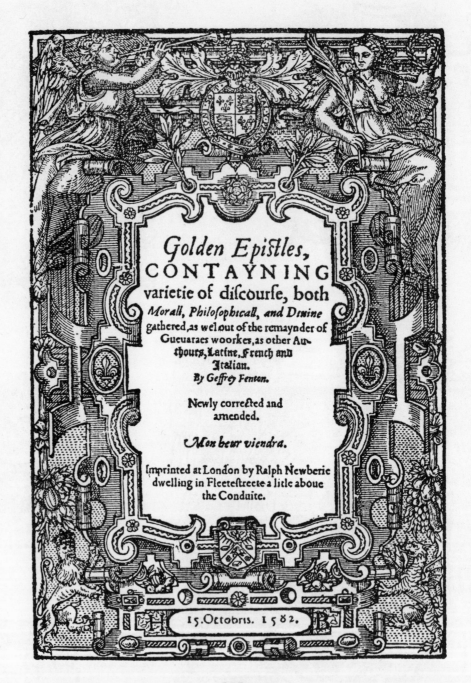

Golden Epistles,
CONTAYNING
varietie of difcourfe, both
Morall, Philofophicall, and Diuine
gathered, as wel out of the remaynder of
Gueuaraes woorkes, as other Au-
thours, Latine, French and
Italian.
By Geffrey Fenton.

Newly corrected and
amended.

Mon heur viendra.

Imprinted at London by Ralph Newberie
dwelling in Fleeteftreete a litle aboue
the Conduite.

15. Octobris. 1582.

230

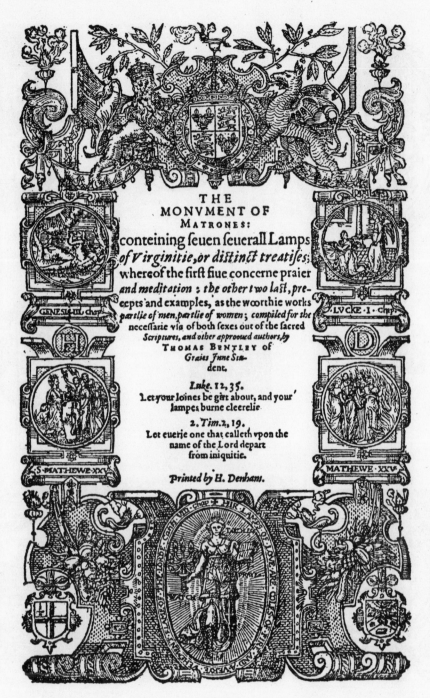

THE
MONVMENT OF
MATRONES:
conteining seuen seuerall Lamps
of Virginitie, or distinct treatises;
whereof the first fiue concerne praier
and meditation : the other two last, precepts and examples, as the woorthie works
partlie of men, partlie of women; compiled for the
necessarie vse of both sexes out of the sacred
Scriptures, and other approoued authors, by
THOMAS BENTLEY of
Graies Inne Stu-
dent.

Luke. 12, 35.
Let your loines be girt about, and your
lampes burne cleerelie.

2. Tim. 2, 19.
Let euerie one that calleth vpon the
name of the Lord depart
from iniquitie.

Printed by H. Denham.

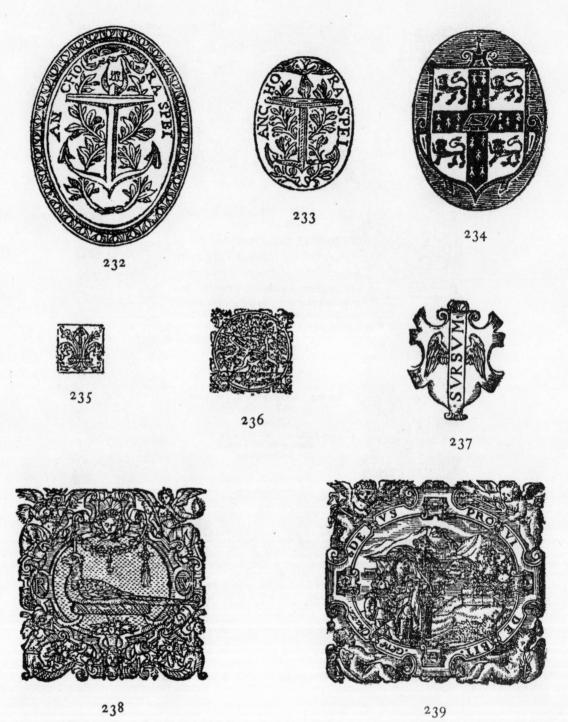

232

233

234

235

236

237

238

239

240

241

242

243

244

245

246

245*

247

248

249α

249β

250

251

252

253

254

o

A
BOOKE OF
CHRISTIAN
Exercife, appertay-
ning to *Refolution*, that
is, fhewing how that wee
fhould refolue our felues to
beenne Chriftians in
deed: by R.P.

Perufed by E D M.
BVNNY.

*Heb.*13.8.
Iefus Chrift yefterday
and to day, and the
fame for euer.

Imprinted at London.
1598.

256

THE
SICKE MANS
Salue,
Wherein all faithfull chriftians may learne both howe
to behaue themfelues pati
ently and thankefullie in the
time of fickneffe, and alfo.ver-
tuouflie to difpofe their tem-
porall goods, and finallie to
prepare themfelues
gladly and god-
lic to die.

Made by Thomas Beacon.
LONDON
Printed by Peter Short, for
the affignes of K. Day.
1594.

255

257

258

259

260

261

262

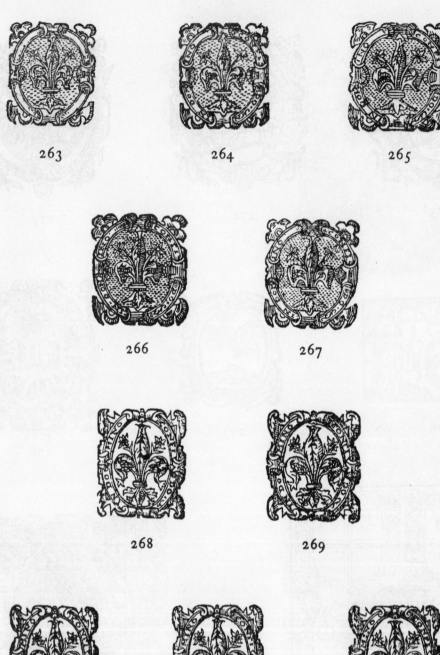

263   264   265

266   267

268   269

270   271   272

273

274

275

276

277

278

279

280

281

282

283

285

284

286

287

Imperfect

288

289

290

291

292

293

294

295

296

297

298

299

300

301

302

303

304

305

p

306

307

308

309

310

311

312

313

314

315

316

317

318

319

320

321

322

323

324

326

327

325

328

329

330

331

332   333

334

335

336

337

338

339

SALVS VITÆ.

340

341

342

343

344

345

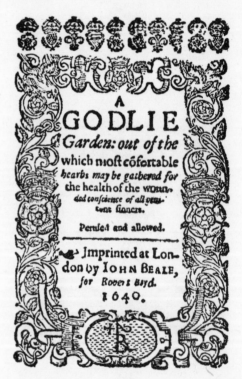

346

347

348

349

350

351

352

353

354

355

356

357

358

359

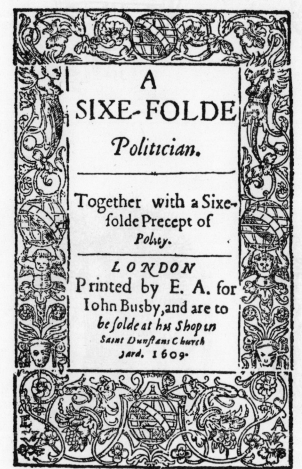

A
SIXE-FOLDE
Politician.

Together with a Sixe-
folde Precept of
Policy.

LONDON
Printed by E. A. for
Iohn Busby, and are to
be folde at his Shop in
Saint Dunstans Church
Iard. 1609.

360

361

362

363

364

365

366   367

368

369

370

371

372

373

374

375

376

377

378

379

380

381

382

r

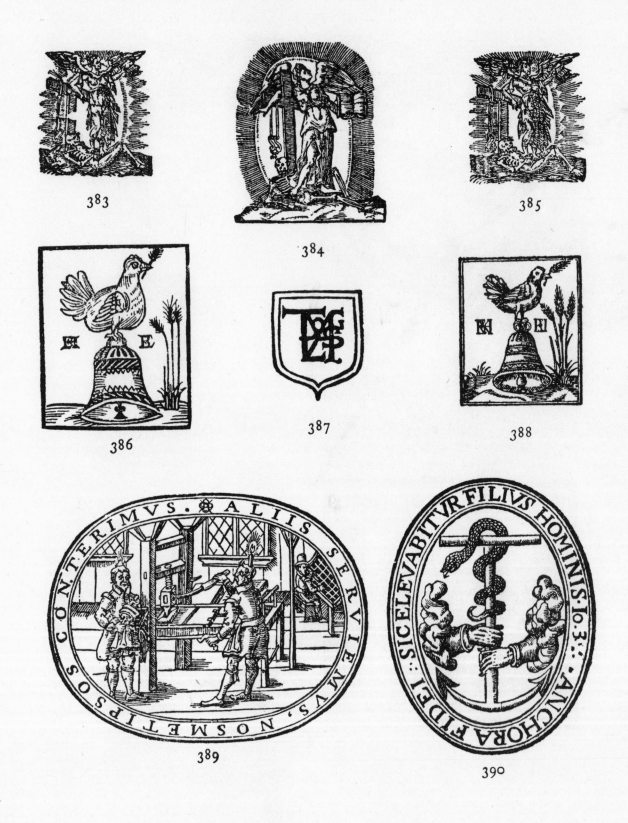

383

384

385

386

387

388

389

390

391

394

392

393

395

396

397

398

399

400

401

402

403

404

405

406

407

408

409

410

411

412

413

414

415

416α

416β

417

418

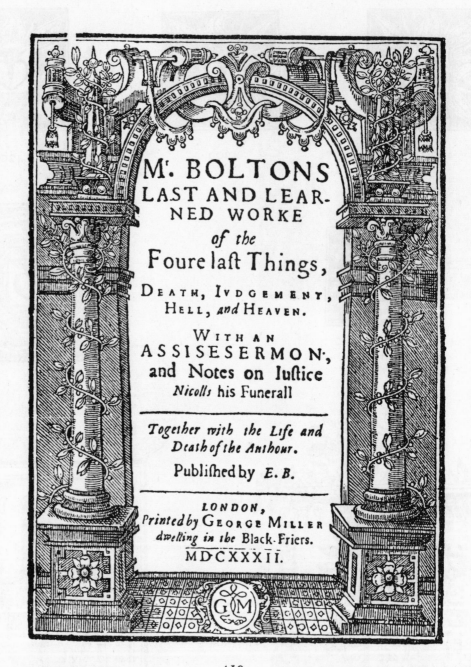

Mᵣ. BOLTONS
LAST AND LEAR-
NED WORKE
of the
Foure laſt Things,
Dᴇᴀᴛʜ, Iᴠᴅɢᴇᴍᴇɴᴛ,
Hᴇʟʟ, *and* Hᴇᴀᴠᴇɴ.

Wɪᴛʜ ᴀɴ
ASSISESERMON,
and Notes on Iuſtice
Nicolls his Funerall

*Together with the Life and
Death of the Authour.*
Publiſhed by *E. B.*

LONDON,
Printed by Gᴇᴏʀɢᴇ Mɪʟʟᴇʀ
dwelling in the Black-Friers.
MDCXXXII.

420a

420b

420c

421

422

423

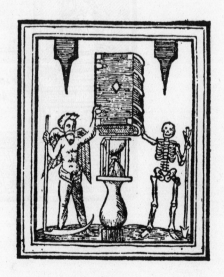

424

425

426

427

428

INDEXES

I. DEVICES AND COMPARTMENTS ACCORDING TO SIZE.

II. PRINTERS, BOOKSELLERS, ETC.

III. MOTTOES AND INSCRIPTIONS.

IV. INITIALS OF DESIGNERS OR ENGRAVERS.

V. DEVICES AND COMPARTMENTS ACCORDING TO SUBJECT.

INDEX OF DEVICES AND COMPARTMENTS
ACCORDING TO SIZE

THE following index of measurements will, I think, prove the most convenient way of finding the devices and compartments here dealt with, and, what is equally important, of making sure whether a device sought for is included or not. It should, however, be remembered that the size of a print varies somewhat according to the dampness of the paper at the time of printing, and therefore if a device is not found at the measurements expected, it should be sought for some distance above and below them.[1] As explained in the note following the introduction, the measurements given are in most cases a rough average of those of a number of prints and are not necessarily those of the particular print selected for reproduction. The height is in all cases given first, and the measurements (in millimetres) are those of an enclosing rectangle.

Comp. = compartment or border. App. = Appendix (pp. 160-2).

Bracketed numbers refer to blocks cut down from their original size, to parts of compartments, or to devices mentioned in the text but not reproduced.

7 × 12. Monogram, 364.	21 × 67. Hornblowers, 295.
9 × 59. Walley's mark, 183.	21 × 108. Caxton's mark, 50.
11 × 6.5. Cawood's mark, 126.	22 × 74. Grafton's mark (91).
11 × 10.5. Crowned rose, 332.	22 × 85. J. Skot's initials, 54.
11.5 × 12. Swan, 303.	22 × 109. Pepwell's mark, 48.
11.5 × 60.5. Wyer's mark, 69.	22.5 × 108. J. Skot's initials, 51.
12.5 × 17.5. Monogram of G. F., 15.	23 × 13.5. Crowned rose, 333.
14.5 × 14. Tun and mark, 127.	23 × 23. Three cranes, 236.
15 × 14. Fleur-de-lis, 381.	24 × 24. Tun and mark, 250.
16 × 15.5. Fleur-de-lis, 235.	24 × 106. Caxton's mark, 49.
17 × 18. Two heads, 365.	24 × 112.5. Tiger's head, 323.
19 × 49. Tiger's head, 296.	24.5 × 72. Marks, H.I., I.P., 17.
19 × 68. Tiger's head, 212.	25 × 41. Ram and goat, 103.
20 × 89. A and heart, 377.	25 × 42. Shield, two keys, 373.
21 × 28. Horse's head, App. 7.	25 × 93. Henry Pepwell, 47.

[1] The difference in size between the smallest and largest print from a block may amount to five or six per cent., and in some cases, especially when the block is cracked, may be considerably more. The easiest way of using this index is probably to start with the approximate *height* of the print, and then to run the eye up and down the column of figures indicating *breadth* until a measurement is found corresponding with the one sought.

25.5 × 24. Fleur-de-lis (251).
26 × 26. Sun in glory, 395.
26 × 89. Copland's mark, 77.
26 × 94. J. Skot's monogram, 76.
27 × 19. Sparke's mark, 406.
27 × 26. Fleur-de-lis, 251.
27 × 27. Factotum of flames, 421.
27 × 89. Mylner's mark, 39.
27.5 × 36.5. Mars in car, 177.
27.5 × 39. S.P.Q.R., 276.
28 × 24. Fleur-de-lis, 263.
28 × 26. Angel with shield, 426.
28 × 82. Petit's mark (86).
28.5 × 25. Fleur-de-lis, 264.
29 × 25. Fleur-de-lis, 268, 270, 271.
29 × 25.5. Cambridge arms, 399.
29 × 27.5. Fleur-de-lis, 265.
29 × 31. Tiger's head, 184.
29 × 50. Man and tree, 311.
29 × 70. Sun, stars, etc. (25).
29 × 145. Two fat boys, I.D., 152.
29.5 × 25.5. Fleur-de-lis, 267, 272.
29.5 × 26. Fleur-de-lis, 269.
29.5 × 26.5. Fleur-de-lis, 266.
29.5 × 48.5. Man and tree, 310.
30 × 25. Monogram, 387.
30.5 × 26.5. Good Shepherd, 207.
31 × 35. Woman's head (193).
31 × 43.5. Resurrection, 124.
31 × 87. Open book, 347.
31.5 × 26. Oxford arms, 336.
31.5 × 28. Mark of J. Reynes, 55.
31.5 × 29. Griffin, 246.
31.5 × 29. Eagle and young, 277.
32 × 25. Woman, sun, cup, 416.
32 × 47. Caxton's mark, 11.
32.5 × 32.5. Factotum of lily, 420.
33 × 27. Shield with wings, 237.
33 × 27. Gilly-flower (320).
33 × 27. Oxford arms, 338.
33 × 30. Mask and A. H., 379.
33.5 × 19. Crowned rose, 400.

33.5 × 30. Clenched fist, 357, 359.
33.5 × 36.5. Owl, snakes, M.B., 380.
34 × 31. Protestant angel, 383.
34 × 32. Clasped hands, 372.
34 × 34. Hind (Hatton's crest), 229.
34 × 34. Boy with weight, 393.
34 × 48. Byddell's mark, 79.
34 × 50. Two boys, 141.
34 × 60.5. Crowned thistle, 418.
34.5 × 28. Hand and star, 260.
34.5 × 29.5. Anchor, 210.
35 × 29.5. Griffin, 339.
35 × 32. Protestant angel, 385.
35 × 35. Woman's head, 193.
35 × 39. Lamb, 371.
35.5 × 26.5. Anchor, 233.
35.5 × 33. Gilly-flower, 320.
35.5 × 35.5. Oxford arms, 427.
36 × 28. Flower-vase, sun, 290.
36 × 34. Clasped hands, F. K., 397.
36 × 34.5. Crowned falcon, 401.
36 × 36. Star, 150.
36 × 45. Compasses, 411.
36 × 46. Caxton's mark, 27.
36 × 53.5. Sea-goats, 249.
36.5 × 30. Pelican, 165.
36.5 × 36. Mermaid, 248.
36.5 × 37. Justice and bushel, 313.
36.5 × 37. Burning heart, 392.
37 × 35. Three lilies, 217.
37 × 37. Lion's face, H. M., 215.
37.5 × 37.5. Mermaid, 259.
38 × 24. Fleur-de-lis, 258.
38 × 35. Griffin, 144*.
38 × 37. Time and Truth, 331.
38 × 38. Byddell's mark, 78.
38 × 46. Griffin, 157.
38.5 × 32. Feathers (354).
38.5 × 47. Griffin (144).
39 × 20. Crowned rose, 396.
39 × 27. Phoenix and satyrs, 252.
39 × 29. Plant, 156.
39 × 33. Hen, rye, bell, 388.

39 × 35. Altar with R. Y., 404.
39 × 37. Tree in storm, 302.
39 × 39. Old man, 282.
39 × 39. Finlason's mark, 358.
39.5 × 20. Crowned harp, 398.
39.5 × 34. Opportunity, 281.
40 × 31.5. Notary's mark, 13.
40 × 39. Bird and 'wick,' 368.
40 × 43. Caxton's mark, 2.
40.5 × 35. Open book, 278.
40.5 × 36. Time, 425.
41 × 32. Fame, App. 5.
41 × 35. Swan, 227.
41 × 35. Rose, gilly-flower, 283.
41 × 36. Two-headed eagle, 361.
41 × 36. Griffin's head, arms, 374.
41 × 45. Palm tree, 428.
41.5 × 32.5. Man barking logs, 190.
41.5 × 72.5. Scroll with I. R., 40.
42 × 26. Pegasus, 316, 317.
42 × 27. Pegasus, 318.
42 × 32. Fleur-de-lis, 216.
42 × 36. Dragon-car, 188.
42 × 37.5. Phoenix and satyrs, 254.
42 × 42. Factotum of rose, 422.
42.5 × 34.5. Anchor, 164.
42.5 × 58. Sun in glory (99).
43 × 39. Clasped hands and caduceus, 273.
43 × 49. Griffin, 144.
43.5 × 43.5. Geneva arms, 136.
43.5 × 43.5. Griffin, 262.
43.5 × 59. Sun in glory, 99.
44 × 30.5. Tun and mark, 198.
44 × 38.5. Two-headed eagle, 362.
44 × 39. Clasped hands, caduceus, 274.
44 × 39. Compasses, 334.
44 × 41. Saint, hare, rye, sun, 275.
44 × 54. Boy with weight, 142.
44.5 × 26. Woman, sun, cup, 326.
44.5 × 34.5. Woman, sun, cup, 327.
44.5 × 43. Pynson's initials (32).
45 × 29.5. Boys and tree, 97.
45 × 34. Two figures, 344.

45 × 39. Ox on bridge, 289.
45 × 40. Candle, 412.
45 × 43. Judith, 89.
45 × 44.5. Winged skull, globe, 341.
46 × 44.5. Men and mirror, 337.
46.5 × 46.5. Circle in triangle, 369.
47 × 34.5. Cherub's head, 219.
47.5 × 49. Three cranes, 241.
48 × 36. Cambridge arms, 234.
48 × 37. Rose and pomegranate, 135.
48 × 40. Hare, rye, sun, 319.
48 × 41. Hen, rye, bell, 386.
48 × 48. Mars, 180.
48.5 × 47. Phoenix, 297.
49 × 37. Feathers, 354.
49 × 37.5. Pynson's monogram (3).
49 × 42. Protestant angel, 384.
49 × 43. Oxford arms, 408.
49 × 45. Crest: wyvern, 199.
49 × 45. Crowned eagle, 409.
49 × 50. Woman's head, 179.
49.5 × 50.5. Head and A. H., 378.
49.5 × 65.5. Kingfisher, 321.
50 × 38. Arms of R. Day, 245.
50 × 40.5. Truth scourged, 299.
50 × 42. Woman and book, 187.
50 × 42. Hester's monogram, App. 4.
50.5 × 43. Pynson's initials, 32.
51 × 37.5. Pynson's monogram (3).
51 × 40. Pynson's monogram, 3.
51 × 42. Griffin, 284.
51 × 45. Flower and sun, 315.
51 × 47. Daw, sun, gardener, 201.
51 × 51. Pheasant, 238.
52 × 45.5. St. John (67).
52 × 46. Vase, hare, rye, sun, 286.
52 × 47. Mercury on globe, 382.
52 × 52. Landscape and coronet, 291.
52.5 × 43. Man and tree, 349.
53 × 39. Man and tree, 351.
53 × 40. Faques' initials, 56.
53 × 41. Man and tree, 348.
53 × 42. Man and tree, 350.

53 × 45. St. John, 70.
53 × 47. Men planting, 352.
53 × 53.5. Death's head, 304.
54 × 45. Clock, 342.
54 × 48. Open book, 300.
54 × 53. Eagle and young, 280.
54.5 × 49. Fleur-de-lis, 415.
55 × 43. Mermaid, 155.
55 × 45. Pavior, 345.
55 × 58. St. John (67).
55.5 × 47. Anchor, 195.
55.5 × 60. Abraham and Isaac, 239.
56 × 38. Brazen serpent, 118.
56 × 46. Armorial bearings, 322.
56 × 48. Oxford arms, 407.
56 × 50. Time and Truth, 186.
56 × 56. St. John (70).
56.5 × 36. Caduceus, book, dove, 112.
57 × 46. Notary's mark, 28.
57 × 48. Black horse, 206.
57 × 48. Clasped hands, F. K., 403.
57 × 52.5. Man praying, 308.
57 × 62. St. John (67).
57.5 × 48.5. Anchor, 192.
58 × 145. Sill-piece, Cawood's mark, 129.
58.5 × 40.5. Tun and tree, 88.
58.5 × 44.5. Anchor, 232.
58.5 × 46.5. Altar with R. Y., 405.
58.5 × 58. Time and Truth, 312.
59 × 50. Rake, hay-fork, scythe, 305.
59 × 53.5. Pelican, 123.
59.5 × 54. Mercury's hat, caduceus, 293.
60 × 48. Fleur-de-lis, 294.
60 × 48.5. Phoenix and arms, 417.
60 × 49. Siberch's mark, 58.
60 × 50. Winged serpent, 340.
60 × 54. Ling and honeysuckle, 301.
60 × 55. Marks, F.E., G.B., 7.
60 × 67. Fleur-de-lis, 298.
60.5 × 54. Truth, Calumny, Time, 306.
60.5 × 56. Fortune, 167.
60.5 × 60.5. Arms, bell, etc., 279.
61 × 46. Anchor, skull, child's head, 287.

61 × 48. Bird and 'wick,' 376.
61 × 49. Old man, two birds, 292.
61 × 53. Tiger's head, lamb, 191.
61 × 56.5. Hand and star, 257.
61.5 × 53. Tree, two women, 410.
62 × 55. Good Shepherd (202).
62.5 × 53. Angel, 172.
62.5 × 67.5. Caxton's mark, 10.
63 × 45. Heart in fire, 83.
63 × 51. Lion and anchor, 240.
63 × 52. Two women, 307.
63 × 53. Time, Death, Book, 424.
63.5 × 46.5. The Trinity, 33.
63.5 × 48. Woman, sun, cup, 325.
64 × 48. Shield, three roses, 63.
64 × 50. Hester's monogram, App. 4.
64 × 54. Jove and eagle, 367.
64 × 55. Good Shepherd, 202.
65 × 45. St. John, 72.
65 × 45. Wheatsheaf, 356.
65 (?) × 54. Ox on bridge, 288.
66 × 51. Pelican (125).
66 × 53.5. Woman and horses, 138.
67 × 39. Boys and tree, 96.
67 × 43. Mark with I. N., etc., 8.
67 × 44. St. George, 64.
67 × 48. Barker's arms, 213.
67 × 51.5. Lucretia, 173.
67 × 55. Pelican, 225.
67 × 55. Hare, rye, sun, 343.
67 × 58. Sun, 159.
67 × 66. Arms of R. Day, 245*.
67 × 70. Arms of Aberdeen, 394.
67 × 89.5. Printing-press, 389.
68 × 49. Tun and tree, 95.
68 × 54. Armorial bearings, 244.
68 × 59. Wrist with snake, 355.
68 × 94. Caxton's mark, 42.
69 × 52. Star in oval, 214.
69 × 53. Tun with 'nor,' 174.
69 × 92. Caxton's mark, 23.
70 × 60. Boy on dolphin, 166.
71 × 59. Anchor, 222.

71 × 61. Candle, 413.
71 × 67. Cock on wood-pile, 247.
71.5 × 53.5. Mermaid, 149.
71.5 × 53.5. Anchor and snake, 366.
72 × 51.5. Hooded hawk, 163.
72 × 52.5. Comp., Jugge's monogram, 137.
72 × 58. Seton's rebus, 261.
72 × 58. Summits of Parnassus, 328.
72.5 × 61. St. John, 68.
73 × 56. Stationers' arms, 353.
73 × 60. Pynson's monogram (9).
73 × 60. Clasped hands, F. K., 402.
73 × 62. Phoenix, 203.
73.5 × 57. Anchor and snake, 390.
73.5 × 75. R. S. or N. B. in circle, 84.
74 × 48. Sheep and plant, 223.
74 × 49. Comp., Whitchurch's monogram, 100.
74 × 50. Middleton's mark, 102.
74 × 57.5. Tun with 'nor,' 175.
74 × 59.5. Dolphin and anchor, 414.
74 × 61.5. Arms of J. Day, 200.
74 × 70. Bird-headed pillar, scales, etc., 309.
74 × 77. Gnomon, App. 6.
74.5 × 63.5. Pope, cardinals, etc., 391.
75 × 60. Pynson's monogram, 41.
75 × 63. St. George, 117.
75 × 63.5. St. John (67).
77 × 53. The Trinity, 34.
77 × 101. Sun, H. K., 224.
77 × 104. Finlason's mark, 363.
77.5 × 53.5. Royal arms, 57.
77.5 × 64. Caxton's mark, 24.
78 × 57. Palm and serpents, 226.
78 × 70. Sun, 90.
78 × 96. Rose garland, 71.
79 × 63. Arms: horses' heads, 209.
79 × 70. Caxton's mark (30).
79 × 72. Caxton's mark, 30.
80 × 62. Shield, bear, ass, 38.
80 × 67. Bankes' mark, 66.
80 × 68. Caxton's mark, 12.
80.5 × 62. Time, 243.

81 × 61. Star, 211.
81.5 × 68.5. Old man, 205.
82 × 61.5. Fleur-de-lis, 242.
82 × 62. Griffin, 158.
82 × 62.5. Hand and touchstone, 113.
82.5 × 70. Tiger's head, lamb, 194.
85 × 38.5. Arms of St. Albans, 4.
85 × 59. Comp., R. B.'s mark, 346.
85 × 71. Christ, 208.
85.5 × 64.5. Andrewe's mark, 74.
86 × 61. Bell and A. I., 253.
86 × 68. Burning bush, 197.
87 × 66. Anchor and foliage, 423.
88 × 63.5. St. John, 67.
89 × 55. Brazen serpent, 119.
89 × 62. Seven sciences, 122.
91 × 70. Caxton's mark, 25.
91 × 91. Good Shepherd, 153.
92 × 78. Mailed hand and sword, 314.
92.5 × 91. Good Shepherd (153).
93 × 69.5. St. Nicholas, 5.
93 × 77. Hand and star, 121.
94 × 70. Caxton's mark, 46.
94 × 73.5. Oxford arms, 285.
95 × 70. Rose garland, 73.
96 × 72. Woman and book, 189.
96 × 87. Sun and clouds, 375.
97 × 64. Lucretia, 161.
97 × 66. Shield, T. D., 65.
97 × 71. Woman, sun, cup, 329.
97 × 72. Skot's monogram, 75.
97 × 86.5. Skot's mark or monogram, 59.
99 × 67. Tun and tree, 114.
99 × 70. Anchor and serpent, 176.
100 × 71. Maiden's head, R. F., 31.
101 × 56. Hare, rye, sun, 143.
101.5 × 97. Oxford arms, 43.
102 × 63. Comp., Grafton's mark, 105.
103 × 72. Merman and mermaid, 37.
103 × 73. The Trinity, 16.
103 × 74. Shield with W. C., 29.
103 × 77. Copland's mark, 36.
103 × 85. Caxton's mark, 21.

103 × 89. Caxton's mark, 19.
103 × 90. Caxton's mark, 20.
104.5 × 63. Comp., Middleton's mark, 106.
105 × 66. Comp. with I. N., 98.
106.5 × 68.5. Middleton's mark, 93.
107 × 55. Triangles, 14.
107 × 75. Comp., birds, etc. (26).
107 × 76. Comp., Jugge's monogram, 132.
107 × 78. Men and skeleton, 128.
107 × 81. Windmill, 22.
108 × 67. Comp., Whitchurch's monogram, 101.
108 × 75. Anchor, 170.
109.5 × 69. Comp., Byddell's mark, 94.
110 × 71. Comp., Seres' monogram, 139.
110 × 77. Lucretia, 80.
110.5 × 62. Woman and beasts, 107.
111 × 62. Comp. with H. D., 256.
111 × 72.5. Comp., Purfoot's mark, 140.
111 × 80.5. Lucretia, 151.
111 × 85. Pelican, 125, 228.
111.5 × 77. Our Lady of Pity, 82.
112 × 93. Pynson's monogram, 9.
113 × 80. The Trinity, 52.
114 × 79. Boys and tree, 146.
115 × 94. Pynson's monogram, 6.
116 × 76. Comp. with I. A., 160.
117.5 × 83. Shield with P. T., 60.
118 × 81. Comp., Byddell's mark, 85.
119 × 74. Comp., Grafton's mark, 91.
119 × 75. Comp., Denham's mark, 218.
119 × 79. Comp. with I. M., I. N., 81.
119 × 82. Comp., Pynson's monogram, 53.
120 × 77. Comp. with O. R., 131.
120 × 78. Comp. with rebuses, 169.
120 × 110.5. Combination device, 335.
121 × 73. Comp. with tiger's head, 185.
121 × 77. Comp. with fox and wolf, 120.
122 × 116. Comp. with devices, 370.
123 × 74.5. Comp. with H. D., 255.
123 × 75.5. Comp. with E. A., 360.
124 × 83.5. Comp., Roedius' mark, 130.
125 × 80. Comp. with Lucretia, 133.

125 × 96. Pliny's *Historia*, 330.
127 × 95. Boys and tree (146).
127 × 126. Frame, History of Rome, 324.
130 × 82. Comp., Petit's mark, 86.
130 × 106.5. Caxton's mark, 1.
137 × 176. Royal arms with I. D., 115.
140 × 97. Comp. of birds, I.N., 26.
140 × 100. Arms of W. Marshall, 87.
143 × 89. Comp., Whitchurch's monogram, 108.
147 × 104. Tun and tree, 104.
148 × 98. Armorial bearings, 18.
148 × 98. Pynson's monogram, 44.
149 × 102. Comp., Jugge's monogram, 134.
155 × 110. Comp., Grafton's mark, 92.
157 × 106. Comp. with tiger's head, 221.
158 × 106.5. Comp. with nightingale, 182.
162 × 104. Comp. with pelican, 181.
163 × 107. Comp. with rebuses, 171.
164 × 107. Comp., Seres' monogram, 148.
167 × 115. Comp. with G. M., 419.
168 × 110. Comp. with Royal Arms, 45.
168 × 117. Comp. with Grammatica and Rhetorica (205).
169 × 114. Comp. with H. B., 230.
170 × 120. Comp. with C. B., 220.
172 × 113. Comp. with T. M., 154.
174 × 116. Comp. with T. R., 111.
177 × 107. Comp. with H. D., 231.
178 × 132. Portrait of J. Day, 145.
198 × 142. Comp. with W. R., 62.
210 × 136. Comp., King in Council, 110.
211 × 157. St. George and Dragon, 61.
225 × 142. Comp. with R. T., 196.
231 × 145. Comp. with E. W., 109.
239 × 157. St. George and Dragon, 61.
250 × 182. Arms of R. Pynson, 35.
252 × 144. Comp. with Day's motto, 116.
254 × 158. Comp. with mermaid, 168.
263 × 182. Comp. with bee-hive, 162.
300 × 180. Comp. with R. T., 147.
301 × 190. Comp. with C. B., 204.

INDEX OF PRINTERS, BOOKSELLERS, ETC.

THIS index is intended to include the names of all owners, or possible owners, of the devices and compartments dealt with. It therefore gives all those whose names appear in small capitals in the body of the work, but it does not include other names appearing in an imprint in which one name is in small capitals, for such persons must be presumed to have no connection with the device. On the other hand, in the case of imprints in which no name is given in small capitals (*i.e.*, when the owner of the device used in the book is unknown or is not mentioned in the imprint), *all* names in the imprint are included, as any of the persons named *may* have owned the device.

References in heavy type are to names of probable owners, *i.e.*, generally those in small capitals in the text. References in ordinary type are to other names occurring in imprints. Thus all the devices which can *with probability* be assigned to any particular printer or bookseller should be found by turning up the references in heavy type alone.

Bracketed references are to possible owners whose names do not occur in the imprints and to certain other persons incidentally mentioned.

When the names signified by initials may be regarded as certain, references are given under the names alone.

The dates given are, with a few exceptions, taken from the *Century* and the two *Dictionaries*, and are intended to give the approximate period during which the printer or bookseller was at work. They have no reference to the dates at which he used the devices. The place of business is always London unless otherwise stated.

Pr. = printer; bk. = bookseller, stationer, or publisher.

ADAMS, T., (1591-1620) bk., 166, 181, 182, 259, 283, (291).

AGGAS, E., (1576-1616) bk., 199.

ALLDE, E., (1584-1628) pr., 230, 270, 284, 290, (310), 360.

ALLDE, ELIZ., (1628-40) bk. and pr., 290, 310.

ALLDE, J., (1555-82) pr., 160.

ALLOT, R., (1625-35) bk., 410.

ALSOP, B., (1616-50) pr., 314, 339.

ANDERSON, G., (1637-8) pr. at Edinburgh, (1638-47) at Glasgow, 187, 189, (358).

ANDREWE, L., (1527-30) pr., (45), 74.

'Antoniello degli Antonielli, Heredi d'' (= J. Wolfe), 226.

'Anversa,' 242.

ARBUTHNET, A., (1576-85) pr. at Edinburgh, 225, 228.

ASPLEY, W., (1598-1640) bk., 354.

B., J., 280.

B., R., 202, 207, 216, 249, 265.

BADGER, R., (1602-42) pr., 170, 195, 222, 265, 410, 417.

BADGER, T., (1639-46) pr., (417).

BALDWIN, W., (1549) pr., 112.

BALLARD, H., (1597-1608) pr., 322.

BANKES, R., (1523-8, 1539-45) pr., 66, 91.

BANKWORTH, R., (1594-1612) bk., 91.

BARBIER, J., (1496-8) pr., 8.

BARKER, C., (1569-99) bk. and pr., (169), (171), 184, 185, 190, 191, 193, 194, 204, 212, 213, 220, 221, 248.

BARKER, C., Deputies of, (1588-99) pr., 204, 220, 221, 248, 300.

BARKER, R., (1589-1645) pr., 193, 204, 220, 221, 248, 293, 300, 347.

BARLEY, W., (1591-1614) bk. and pr., 304, 322.

BARNES, J., (1573-1616) pr. at Oxford, 285, 336, (338).

BARRENGER, W., (1600-22) bk., 215.

BARRETT, W., (1607-24) bk., 320.

BARREVELT, G., (1494-5) bk., 7.

BARTLET, J., (1619-37) bk., 373, 404, 405.

BASSANDYNE, T., (1564-77) pr. at Edinburgh, 176, 178.

BEALE, J., (1612-41) pr., 168, 346, 374.

BEE, C., (1636-72) bk., 168.

BELL, H., (1606-38) bk., 386, 388.

BERTHELET, T., (1520-55) pr., 80.

BEST, R., (1640-53) bk., 215.

Bibliopolarum, Officina. *See* Stationers, Company of.

BILL, J., (1604-30) pr. and bk., 162, 193, 204, 220, 221, 248, 293, 300, 306, 348, 349, 351, 352, 354, 365, 382, 393, 396, 410.

BISHOP, G., (1562-1611) bk. and pr., 153, 168, 182, 185, 236, 239, 246, 248, 293, 300, 306.

BISHOP, R., (1631-53) pr., 282, 292, 393.

BLACKMORE, E., (1618-58) bk., 227.

BLADEN, W., (1612-42) bk., 391.

BLOUNT, E., (1594-1632) bk., 293.

BLOWER, R., (1595-1613) pr., ?216, ?249, 298.

BOLER, J., (1626-35) bk., 266.

BOLLIFANT, E., (1584-1602) pr., 239, 293, 306, 352.

BONHAM, W., (1520-57) bk., 92.

BOSTOCK, R., (1629-58) bk., 417.

BOURMAN, N., (1539-60) pr., 48, 84.

BOURNE, N., (1601-57) bk., 304, (373), 383.

BOURNE, R., (1586-93) pr., 251.

BOUVIER, F., (1583-1618) bk., 223.

BOVER. *See* BOUVIER.

BRADOCK, R., (1581-1615) pr., ?202, 207, 280, 346.

BRADWOOD, M., (1584-1618) pr., (1610-15) pr. at Eton, (293), (347), 354, (380).

BRETTON, W., (1506-10) bk., 18.

BREWSTER, E., (1621-47) bk., 168, 263.

Britain's Burse, 252.

BRYSON, R., (1637-45) bk. and pr. at Edinburgh, 358.

BUCK, J., (1625-68) pr. at Cambridge, 327, 399. *See* Cambridge, Univ. Printers.

BUCK, T., (1625-70) pr. at Cambridge, 240, 327, 399, 416. *See* Cambridge, Univ. Printers.

BUDGE, J., (1606-25) bk., 252, 359.

BURBY, C., (1592-1607) bk., 297, 340, 352.

BURTON, F., (1603-17) bk., 364.

BUSHELL, T., (1599-1617) bk., 313.

BUTLER, J., (1529-35) pr., 72.

BUTLER, W., sen., (1614-25) bk., or jun., (1615-19) bk., 357.

BUTTER, N., (1605-64) bk., 136, 207, 259, 294, 316, 318, 375, 425.

BYDDELL, J., (1533-45) bk. and pr., (25), 46, (50), 78, 79, 82, 85, 94.

BYNNEMAN, H., (1566-83) pr., 97, 99, 118, 119, 134, 138, 148, 149, 155, 168, 185, 203, 229, 230.

C., I. (? = J. Cheke), 108.

CALY, R., (1553-8) pr., (91), 92, 105.

Cambridge, University Printers, 264, ?326, 327, 416.

CAWOOD, J., (1541-72) pr., 109, 123, 126, 129, 132.

CAXTON, W., (1476-91) pr., 1.

CHARLEWOOD, J., (?1554-93), 112, 136, 183.

CHARLTON. *See* CHORLTON.

CHARTERIS, H., (1568-99) bk. and pr. at Edinburgh, 189, 307.

CHARTERIS, R., (1599-1610) pr. at Edinburgh, 307.

CHEPMAN, W., (1508-10) pr., 29.

CHORLTON, G., (1603-14) bk., 294.

COKE, W., (1632-41) bk., 404.

COLWELL, T., (1561-75) pr., 68.

Company of Stationers. *See* Stationers.

COOKE, T., (1577-99) bk., 237.

COPLAND, R., (*c.* 1514-*c.* 1548) pr., 36, 71, 73, 77.

COPLAND, W., (*c.* 1548-68) pr., 71.

COTES, R., (1635-52) pr., 283.

COTES, T., (1620-41) pr., 112, 136, 283.

COTTON, W., (1602-9) bk., 207.

CREEDE, T., (1593-1617) pr., 299, 314, 339.

CROOKE, A., (1630-74) bk., 251, 304.

CURTIS, L., (1677-90) bk., 226.

DABBE, or TAB, H., (1539-48) bk., 89.

DANIEL, R., (1627-66) pr. and bk. in London and Cambridge, 240, 264, 327, 416, 428.

DANTER, J., (1589-99) pr., 281, 295.

DAVIDSON, T., (1540-1) pr. in Edinburgh, 65.

DAVIS, R., (1646-88) bk. at Oxford, 427.

DAWLMAN, R., (1627-59) bk., 259, 296, 413.

DAWSON, E., (1609-36) bk., 373.

DAWSON, J., senior, (1613-34) pr., 414.

DAWSON, J., junior, (1637-48) pr., 414.

DAWSON, M., (1635-6) pr., (414).

DAWSON, T., (1568-1620) pr., 181, (182), 201, 236, 241, 306.

DAY, J., (1546-84) pr., 83, 115, 116, 124, 128, 145, 152, 200, 208, App. 3.

DAY, R., (1578-84) pr., 217.

DAY, R., Assigns of, 116, 245, 245*.

DENHAM, H., (1560-89) pr., 86, 104, 116, (118), (119), 138, 147, 148, (149), 150, 162, (168), 211, 214, 215, 218, 230, 231, 239, (255), (256).

DEWE, T., (1621-5) bk., 238.

DEWES, G., (1560-91) pr. and bk., 154, 167, (169), (171).

DEXTER, R., (1590-1603) bk., 257, 260, 334.

DISLE, H., (1576-80) bk., 172.

DOWNES, B., (1618-36) bk., 402.

DOWNES, T., (1609-58) bk., 373.

DRAWATER, J., (1593-7) bk., 277.

DRING, T., (1649-68) bk., 426.

Dublin, Soc. of Stat., 398.

DUNMORE, J., (1665-79) bk., 195.

E., G., 369.

EAST, T., (1567-1609) pr., (83), 177, 206, 209, 227, 305.

EDGAR, E., (1600-13) bk., 354.

EDWARDES, G., (? 1624-33) bk., 412.

EGMONT, F., (1493-1502) bk., 7.

ELD, G., (1604-24) pr., 308, 320, ? 369, 375.

ENDHOVEN. *See* RUREMOND.

ENGLAND, N., (1558-68) bk., 138.

ESTIENNE. *See* STEPHANUS.

Eton, in Collegio Regali, 293, 347, 380.

FAQUES, R., (1509-30) pr., 31, 56.

FAQUES, W., (1504-8) pr., 14, 15.

FAWCETT. *See* FORCET.

FERBRAND, W., (1598-1609) bk., 249, 284, 310.

FIELD, R., (1579-1624) pr., 164, 170, 179, 192, 210, 222, (233), 246.

FINLASON, T., (1597-1628) pr. at Edinburgh, 187, 189, 225, 358, 363.

FISHER, T., (1600-2) bk., 321.

FLASKET, J., (1594-1613) bk., 356.

FLESHER. *See* FLETCHER.

FLETCHER, J., (1652-67) pr., 308.

FLETCHER, M., (1611-64) pr., 137, 259, 308, 320, 356, 375, 413, 425.

FLOWER, F., Assigns of, 169, 171

FORCET, T., (1621-43) pr., 261.

FRANCKTON, J., (1600-? 1618) pr. at Dublin, 219.

G., E., 272, 392.

GARDINER, T., (1576-7) pr., 201.

GAULTIER, T., (1550-3) pr., 108.

GAVER, J., (1539-45) bk., 90.

GIBBS, G., (1613-33) bk., 415.

GIBSON, T., (1535-9) pr., 62, 83.

'Giolito, G., de' Ferrari,' 252.

GODFRAY, T., (1532-5) pr., App. 2.

GOES, H., (1509) pr., at York, App. 1.

GOWGHE or GOUGH, J., (1526-43) bk., 98.

GRAFTON, R., (1534-73) pr., 88, 91, 92, 95, 104, 105, 110, 114, 122.

GREENE, L., (1606-30) pr. at Cambridge, 91.

GRIFFIN, A., (1634-43) pr., 306, 392, 409.

GRIFFIN, E., I, (1613-21) pr., ? 272, 293, (306), 354, 380, 390, 392.

GRIFFIN, E., II, (1638-52) pr., 306, 392, 409, 420, 422.

GRISMOND, J., (1618-38) bk., 238, 249, 392.

GROVE, F., (1623-61) bk., 137.

GRYFFYTH, W., (1552-c. 1571) pr., 87, 144, 144*, 157, 158.

GUBBIN, or GUBBINS, T., (1587-1629) bk., 262, 284.

H., I., 8, 391.

HACKET, T., (1560-90) pr., 139.

HAEGHEN, G. van der, (1527-36) pr. at Antwerp, 57.

HALL, H., (1637-? 1679) pr. at Oxford, 407, 427.

HALL, R., (1560-3) pr., 136, 142.

HALL, W., (1598-1614) pr., (346).

HARDIE, J., (1594-1609) bk., 283, 294.

HARFORD, R., (1629-51) bk., 383.

HARPER, T., (1614-56) pr., 227, 300.

HARRISON, J., I-IV, (1564-1639) bk. and pr., 86, (169), (171), 239, 275, 286, 316, 319, 334, ? 343.

HARRISON, R., (1561-2) pr., 143.

HART, A., (1587-1621) bk. and pr. at Edinburgh, (307), 377, 378, 379, 384.

HART, A., Heirs of, (1621-39) pr. at Edinburgh, 307, 377.

HATFIELD, A., (1584-1612) pr., 162, 293, 306, 354.

HAUKYNS, J., (1530) pr., 44.

HAVILAND, J., (1613-38) pr., 293, 306, 390, ? 391, 392, 409, 420, 421, 422.

HAVILAND, T., (? 1582-1619) pr., (346), 361.

HEARNE, R., (1632-46) pr., 251, (263).

HEBB, A., (1625-48) bk., 335.

HELME, J., (1607-16) bk., 369.

HERRINGMAN, H., (1653-93) bk., 263.

HERTFORD, J., (1534-9) pr. at St. Albans, (84).

HESTER, J., (1591) apothecary, App. 4.

HILL, W., (1548-9) pr., 111.

HODGETS, J., (1601-25) bk., 382.

HOWE, W., (1565-90) pr., 142.

HUGGINS, T., (1609-36) bk. at Oxford, 400.

HUNT, J., (1594-1613) bk., 310.

HUVIN, J., (1496-7) bk., (8).

I., A., 412.

I., S., 263.

I., W., 212, 248.

ISLIP, A., (1591-1640) pr., 168, 226, 251, 263, 268, 309, 324, 330, 340, 347, 352, 412.

ISLIP, SUSAN, (1641-61) pr., ? 263.

J., W., 304.

JACKSON, H., (1576-1616) pr., 68.

JACKSON, J., (1584-96) pr., 239, 293.

JACKSON, ROGER, (1601-25) bk., 280, 391.

JACOBI, H., (1505-14) bk. at London and Oxford, 17, 34.

JAGGARD, I., (1613-27) pr., (112), (283).

JAGGARD, W., (1594-1623) pr. and bk., 86, (112), 133, 136, 283, 355, 370.

JEFFES, A., (1584-99) pr., 238, 253, 279, 287.

JONES, R., (1564-1602) pr. and bk., 136, 156, 273, 283, ?295.

JONES, T., (1600-37) bk., 212.

JONES, W., (?1601-?1642) pr., 298, 389, 423. *See* W. J.

JUGGE, JOAN, (1577-88) pr., 123.

JUGGE, R., (1547-77) pr., 101, 109, 123, 125, (132), 134, (137), 165, (181), 182.

KAETZ, P., (1523-5) pr., (45), 57, 63.

KEARNEY, W., (?1573-97) pr., 219, 258.

KING J., (1555-61) pr., 86, 111.

KINGSTON, J., (1553-84) pr., 92, 109, 110. 138, 159, 197.

KINGSTON, F., (1597-1651) pr., 167, 180, 273, 274, 315, 328, 332, 397, 402, 403.

KIRKHAM, H., (1570-93) bk., 224.

KIRTON, J., (1638-46) bk., ?405.

KNIGHT, C., (1594-1629) bk., 215, 230, 316.

KYRFOTH, C., (1519) pr. at Oxford, 43.

LANGLEY, T., (1615-35) bk., 387.

LAW, M., (1595-1629) bk., 251, 361.

LEAKE, W., (1592-1633) bk., 341.

LECOMTE, N., (1494-8) pr., 5.

LEE, W., senior, (?1621-52) bk., 311.

LEE, W., junior, (1672) bk., 263.

LEGATE, J., I, (1586-1620) pr. at Cambridge and London, ?166, 259, 276, 325, 326, 329.

LEGATE, J., II, (1620-58) pr. at Cambridge and London, 166, 202, 259, 325, 326, 329, 335.

LEGGE, C., (1606-c. 1629) pr. at Cambridge, 91, 252, 264, 399.

LICHFIELD, J., (1605-35) pr. at Oxford, 285, 336, 408.

LICHFIELD, L., (1635-57) pr. at Oxford, 285, 336, 408.

LING, N., (1580-1607) bk., 301.

LOBLEY, M., (1531-67) bk., 108.

LOWNES, H., (1587-1629) bk. and pr., 118, 119, 148, 149, 211, 231, 278, (296), 335, 353, 366, 373, 404.

LOWNES, M., (1591-1625) bk., 167, 231, 310, 316, 353, 373.

LOWNES, R., (1640-75) bk., 426.

LOWNES, T., ?IV, (1621-7) bk., 278.

LYNNE, W., (1547-50) bk., 103.

M., A., 392.

M., G., 383.

MAB, R., (1610-42) bk., 202.

MACHAM, J., (1615-26) bk., 392.

MACHAM, S., I, (1608-15) bk., 354.

MAN, T., senior, (1576-1625) bk., 216, 316, 340.

MARRIOTT, J., (1616-57) bk., 212, 238, 392.

MARSHALL, W., (1535) publisher, 87.

MARSHE, T., (1554-87) pr., 106, 111, 129, 154, 167, 180.

MATHEWES, A., (1619-53) pr., 188, 238, 249, 304, 312, 392.

MATTS, E., (1597-1613) bk., 320.

MAUNSELL, A., (1576-1604) bk., 125.

MAYLER, J., (1539-45) pr., 98.

MEARNE, S., (1655-83) bk., 112.

MEIGHEN, R., (1615-41) bk., 339.

MEREDITH, C., (1629-53) bk., 210.

MIDDLETON, H., (1567-87) pr., 111, 153, 202, 207, 215.

MIDDLETON, W., (1551-7) pr., 86, 93, 102, 106.

MILBORNE or MILBOURNE, R., (1618-41) bk., 210, 278, 356, 380, 391.

MILLER, A., (1646-53) pr., 164, 233, 246.

MILLER, G., (1601-46) pr., **164**, **168**, **170**, **179**, **192**, **195**, (**210**), **222**, **233**, **246**, ? **383**, **412**, **419**.

MILLINGTON, T., (1593-1603) bk., **302**.

MORE, J., Assigns of, (1629-61) pr., **231**, **404**, **405**.

MORLEY, T., (1598-? 1604) patentee for music-books, **305**, **322**.

MYLLAR, A., (1503-8) bk. and pr. at Edinburgh, **22**.

MYLNER, U., (1513-6) pr. and bk. at York, **38**, **39**.

N., I., **238**.

N., T., (**149**).

NEWBERY, R., (1560-1607) bk., **153**, **185**, **202**, **203**, **230**, **239**, **240**, **248**, **293**, **300**.

NORTON, B., (1594-1635) pr. and bk., **168**, **174**, **204**, **220**, **221**, **248**, **300**, **308**, **349**, **352**.

NORTON, J., (1586-1612) bk. and ? pr., **162**, **192**, **274**, **293**, **306**, **347**, **348**, **352**, App. **5**.

NORTON, J., senior, Heirs of, **351**.

NORTON, J., junior, (1621-45) pr., ? **238**, **251**, **267**, **381**, **396**.

NORTON, R., (1637-62) bk. and pr., **296**.

NORTON, W., (? 1557-93) bk., (**169**), (**171**), **174**, **175**, **293**.

NOTARY, J., (1496-1520) pr., **8**, **13**, **26**, **28**.

OKES, J., (1636-44) pr., **381**.

OKES, N., (1606-39) pr., **168**, **182**, **215**, **251**, **316**, **334**, **367**, **381**.

ORWIN, T., (1587-93) pr., **154**, (**167**), **130**, **254**, **273**.

ORWIN, Widow, (1593-7) pr., **273**.

OULTON or OLTON, R., (1633-43) pr., **290**, ? **405**.

OXENBRIDGE, J., (1589-1600) bk., **288**, **289**, (**291**).

P., T., **411**.

PAINE, T., (1630-? 1650) pr., ? **411**.

PARKER, J., (1617-48) bk., **182**.

PARSONS, M., (1607-40) pr., **304**, **312**.

PARTRIDGE, J., (1623-49) bk., **395**.

PAVIER, T., (1600-25) bk., **202**, **345**, **357**.

PELGRIM, J., (1504-8) bk., **17**.

PEPWELL, H., (1518-41) pr. and bk., **34**, **47**, **48**, **52**.

PERRY, H., (1626-45) bk., **238**.

PETIT, T., (1536-54) pr., **86**. *See* **111**.

PICKERING, E. *See* REDMAN, R., Widow of.

PIETERSEN VAN MIDDELBURCH, H., (1536) pr. at Antwerp, **45**.

POLLARD, R., (1655-9) bk., **426**.

PONSONBY, W., (1571-1603) bk., **118**, **296**.

PORTER, J., senior, (1587-1607) bk., **251**.

PORTER, J., (? 1576-1608) bk. at Cambridge, **259**.

POWELL, T., (1556-63) pr., **133**.

POWELL, W., (1547-68) pr., **50**, **101**, **106**, **117**.

PURFOOT, T., senior, (1546-? 1615) bk. and pr., **108**, ? **136**, **140**, **151**, **161**, **173**, **344**.

PURFOOT, T., II, (1591-1640) pr., ? **411**.

PURSLOWE, Eliz., (1633-46) pr., **311**, ? **405**.

PURSLOWE, G., (1614-32) pr. and bk., **281**, **306**, **311**, **372**.

PYNSON, R., (1492-1530) pr., **3**, **6**, **9**, **32**, **35**, **41**, **44**, **53**.

R., I., App. **6**.

R., R., **280**.

RABAN, E., (1620-58) pr. at Edinburgh, St. Andrews, and Aberdeen, **394**, **418**.

RASTELL, J., (*c.* 1515-36) pr., **37**, **40**.

RASTELL, W., (1530-4) pr., **62**.

RAWORTH, J., (1638-45) pr., **311**, App. **7**.

RAYNALD, T., (1540-? 1555) pr., **111**.

READ, R., (1601-3) pr., (**308**), (**320**).

REDMAN, R., (1523-44) pr., **3**, **41**, **44**, **64**, **81**.

REDMAN, R., Widow of, **3**.

REYNES, J., (1523-44) bk., **48**, **55**, **61**, **62**.

RIDDELL, W., (1552-60) pr., 116.

RIME, J., (1599-1600) bk., 342.

ROBERTS, J., (1569-1615) bk. and pr., 112, 136, ?256, (283), (294), App. 6.

ROBINSON, R., (1583-97) pr., 202, 207, 244, ?280.

ROEDIUS, S., (1556) pr., 130.

ROGERS, O., (1555-66) pr., 131.

'Roma,' 249.

'Rome, Castle of S. Angell,' 127.

ROSS, J., (1574-80) pr. at Edinburgh, 187, 189.

ROUNTHWAITE, R., (1618-28) bk., 348.

ROWBOTHAM, J., (1559-80) bk., 135.

RUREMOND or ENDHOVEN, C., (1523-31) pr. at Antwerp, 63.

RUREMOND, H. VAN, (1525) pr. and bk. at Antwerp and London, 57.

S., I., 411.

S., P., 296.

S., T., 391.

Saint Albans, 4.

SCARLET, T., (1590-6) pr. and bk., 277, 280.

SCOLAR, J., (1517-18) pr. at Oxford, 43.

SCOLOKER, A., (1547-9) pr. at Ipswich and London, 113.

SERES, W., (1546-77) pr., 106, 134, 139, 148, 215.

SERLE, R., (1563-6) ? bk., 136, (142).

'Sermartelli, B.,' 252.

SETON, G., (1577-1608) bk., 261.

SHEFFARD, W., (1621-30) bk., 401, 402.

SHORT, P., (1589-1603) pr., 118, 119, 148, (149), (150), 211, 214, 230, (231), 255, 278, 296, 335, (366).

SIBERCH, J., (1520-2) pr. at Cambridge, 45, 57, 58.

SIMMES, V., (1585-? 1622) pr., 142, 303, 332, 333.

SIMSON, G., (1583-1600) pr., 182, 308, 320.

SINGLETON, H., (1548-93) pr., 127, 198, 250.

SKOT, J., (1521-37) pr., 51, 54, 59, 75, 76.

SMETHWICK, J., (1597-1640) pr., 368, 376.

SMITH, H., (1545-6) pr., 62.

SMITH, R., (1567-95) bk., 186, 312, (331), App. 6.

SNODHAM, T., (1603-25) pr., 83, 227, 365, ?391.

SNOWDON, G., (1606-8) pr., 316, (334).

SPARKE, M., (1616-53) bk., 283, 406, 424.

SPENCER, J., (1617-80) bk. See 411.

STAFFORD, S., (1596-1626) pr., 281, 295.

STANSBY, W., (1597-1639) pr. and bk., 208, 237, 243, 252, 282, 292, 323, 359, 393.

Stationers, Company of, 116, 148, 168, 208, 230, 268, 283, 347, 367, 371, 372, 373, 382, 383, 385, 393, 396, 402. See Dublin.

Stationers, Company of, Printing-House of, 268, 347, 350, 353, 371, 380, 397.

STEPHANUS, A., (1618-64) pr. at Paris, 278.

STEPHENS, P., (1622-70) bk., 210.

STEVENAGE, R., abbot, (84).

'Stoer, J.,' 393.

SUTTON, H., (1552-63) pr., 92, 108, 139, 141.

T., W. See TURNER, W.

TAB, H. See DABBE, H.

THOMAS, T., (1583-8) pr. at Cambridge, 234.

THORPE, T., (1603-25) bk., 142, 304.

TOTTELL, R., (1552-91) pr., 91, 104, 105, 108, 109, 110, 121, 129, 147, 183, 196.

TOY, H., (1560-78) bk., 104, 138.

TOY, J., (1531) pr., 59.

TREVERIS, P., (1522-32) pr., 48, 60.

Trinity, Sign of the, 16, 17, 18, 33, 34.

TURNER, W., (1624-43) pr. at Oxford, 86, 285, 400, 407, 427.

VAUTROLLIER, J., (1588-9) pr., 192.

VAUTROLLIER, T., (1562-87) pr. in London and Edinburgh, 164, 169, 170, 179, 192, 210, 219, 222, 232, 233, 246.
VINCENT, G., (1595-1629) bk., 182.

W., I., (149), 294.
W., J., 226.
W., R., 188.
W., T., (? T. Warren), 267.
WALBANCKE, M., (1618-67) bk., 404.
WALDEGRAVE, R., (1578-89, ? 1603-4) pr. in London, (1589-1603) at Edinburgh, 83, 187, 189, 227, 249, 270.
WALKLEY, T., (1619-58) bk., 269, 272, 316.
WALLEY, J., (1546-85) pr., 108, 123, 183.
WARD, R., (1577-95) pr., 238.
WARREN, T., (? 1638-? 1661) bk. and pr., ? 405. See T. W.
WATERSON, S., (1584-1634) bk., ? 256, 280, 317, 352.
WATKINS, R., (1561-98) pr., 134, (165), (169), (171), 181, 182, ? 188.
WAYLAND, J., (1537-? 1557) pr., (99), 108, 110, 116.
WELBY, W., (1604-18) bk., 227.
WHITAKER, R., (1619-48) bk., 311, 356, 396.
WHITCHURCH, E., (1540-60) pr., 25, (50), 99, 100, 101, 107, 108, 109.
WHITE, E., ? senior, (1577-1612) bk., 343.
WHITE, J., (? 1613-24) pr., (188), (238).
WHITE, W., (1577-? 1617) bk., 165, 182, 188, (238), 362.

WIGHT, J., (1551-89) bk., 138, (169), (171), 205.
WIGHT, T., (1580-1608) bk., 168.
WILLIAMSON, W., (1571-4) pr. and bk., 159, 166.
WILSON, W., (1640-65) pr., 381.
WINDET, J., (1584-1611) pr., 116, 125, 208, 237, 243, 271, 282, 292, ? 294, 323, 337.
WISE, A., (1589-1603) bk., 222.
WOLFE, J., (1579-1601) pr., 216, 226, 235, 242, (249), 251, 258, 261, 269, 294, 298, 310.
WOLFE, R., (1542-73) pr., 96, 97, 118, 119, 120, 146, 163.
WOLFE, R., Widow of (1573-4) pr., 118, (119).
WOOD, W., (1598-1602) bk., 312, 331.
WOODCOCK, T., (1570-94) bk., 153, 247.
WORDE, W. DE, (1491-1535) pr., 1, 2, 10, 11, 12, 19, 20, 21, 23, 24, 25, 27, 30, 42, 46, 49, 50.
WRIGHT, J., senior, (1605-58), ? 294, 409.
WRIGHT, J., junior, (1634-67) bk., 395.
WYER, RI., (1548-50) pr., 67.
WYER, RO., (c. 1529-60) pr., 67, 68, 69, 70.
WYKES, H., (1557-71) pr., 153.

YARDLEY, R., (1589-97) pr., 118, 148, 214.
YETSWEIRT, C., (1594-5) patentee, 168.
YETSWEIRT, J., (1595-7) patentee, 168.
YOUNG, R., (1625-43) pr. in London, (? 1632-8) at Edinburgh, 119, 150, (187), (189), 231, 266, 296, 363, 373, 401, 404, 405.

INDEX OF MOTTOES AND INSCRIPTIONS

THE mottoes of the royal arms are omitted, as are also simple names of objects represented, and such inscriptions as 'Academia Oxoniensis.'

A Barker if ye will, etc., 190.
Aliis serviemus, nosmetipsos conterimus, 389.
Anchora Fidei, 390.
Anchora Spei, 164, 170, 192, 195, 210, 222, 232, 233.
Arise, for it is day, 116.
Armipotenti Angliae, 138.
Auspicante Deo, 296.
Aut nunc aut nunquam, 281.

Behold your glory, 337.
Be thankful to God, 370.
Bon accord, 394.
By wisdom Peace, by Peace Plenty, 273, 274.

Cantabo Jehovae quia benefecit mihi, 247.
Cerva charissima et gratissimus hinnulus, 229.
Charitas, 97.
Christus, 83.
Christus lucrum, etc., 408.
Cogita mori, 123.
Confidite, vici mundum, etc., 208.
Contrahit avaritia bellum, 314, 359.

Dat esse manus, superesse Minerva, 300.
Dela mia morte eterna vita i vivo, 252, 254.
Depressa resurgo, 428.

Désir n'a repos, 240.
Deum cole, 307.
Deus imperat astris, 257, 260.
Deus in aeternum, 322.
Deus providebit, 239, 404, 405.
Doctrina parit virtutem, 347.
Dominus dedit, dominus abstulit, 84.
Dum spero, fero, 275, 319.
Dum tempus habemus offeremur donum, 172.

Etsi mors indies accelerat, 128.
Et usque ad nubes veritas tua, 278, 335.
Ex avaritia bellum, 357.
Ex igne resurgit virtus, 417.

Fide iustus vivet, 404, 405.
Floreat in aeternum, 423.
For thou shalt labour, 282, 292.
Fructibus eorum cognoscetis eos, 88.

Give God the glory now and evermore, 157.
God is my helper, 127, 198, 227, 250.
God save the Queen, 279.
Granted by her Majesty, prohibited to be counterfeited, 426.

Hanc aciem sola retundit virtus, 425.
Heb Ddieu heb ddim, 283.
Her lamps of love are coals of fire, 231.

Hinc lucem et pocula sacra, 325, 326, 327, 329, 416.
His suffulta durant, 307.
Horum charitas, 83.

Ich dien, 105, 354.
I live to die, I die to live, 341.
Il vostro malignare non giova nulla, 226.
Immortality is gotten by the study of letters, 166.
Immota, 391.
In aeternum floreat, 423.
In Domino confido, 5, 264-72, 298.
Invidia. See Sibi.
Iustitia regat, 40.

Labore et constantia, 288, 289, 334, 411.
Liefe is deathe and death is liefe, 145.
Love and live, 112.
Love is patient and courteous, etc., 146.
Love keepeth the law, etc., 123, 125, 225, 228.

Μακροκοσμος, μικροκοσμος. Pingit utrumque tibi Plinius, 330.
Marcantia reale, 291.
Melior est patiens . . . Melius est modicum, etc., 14.
Melius est nomen bonum, etc., 36.
Mieulx vault mourir en vertu que vivre en honête, 206, 209.
Mihi vita Christus, 200.
Mollia cum duris, 393.
Motos soleo componere fluctus, 321.

Ne moy reproues sauns cause, 147.
Ne quid nimis, 112.
Noli altum sapere, 310, 311, 348-51.
Non altum peto, 368, 376.
Non cercami fuori, 369.
Non licet exiguis, 315.

Non plus, 304.
Non solo pane vivet homo, 243.
Nosce teipsum, 17, 112.

Omne bonum supernae, 182.
Omnia tempus habent, 149.
Os homini sublime dedit, 150, 211, 214, 335.

Parnasso et Apolline digna, 328.
Pater non est filius, etc., 16, 33.
Periit et inventa est, 153, 202, 207.
Ponderibus sonitum, 342.
Post funera virtus vivet tamen, 128.
Post tenebras lux, 136, 370.
Praelucendo pereo, 412, 413.
Praise the Lord with harp and song, 253.
Princeps subditorum incolumitatem procurans, 414.
Pro lege, rege, et grege, 123, 125, 225, 228.
Prudentia, 355.

Quibus respublica conservetur, 309.
Qui peut atendre alaventure tout vient aponit [sic], 75.

Sacrifizio agnello salvazione mundo, 371.
Salus vitae, 340.
Sapientiae et felicitatis, 285, 336, 338, 407, 408, 427.
Sapientia pacem, pax opulentiam, 397, 402, 403.
Sed adhuc mea messis in herba est, 305.
Semper eadem, 252, 254, 297.
Sibi et aliis venenum invidia, 261.
Sic Augustinus dissipabit, 375.
Sic crede, 277, 280.
Sic elevabitur filius hominis, 390.
Sic omni tempore verno, 410.
Sic semper ero, 249.
Sicut lilium inter spinas, 217.
Sol oriens mundo, 99.
Sub hac patienter vivit ovis, 223.

Such as I make such will I take, 313.
Sursum, 237.
Suscipite insitum verbum, 95, 104, 114.
Suum cuique, 307.

Tam robur, tam robor, ni-colis arbor Iovis,
367.
Tempore patet occulta veritas, 186, 312,
331.
Tenebras lux forte sequetur, 163.
Thou shalt labour for (Peace, Plenty), 282,
292.
Thou shalt labour till thou return to dust,
345.
Tigre reo animale, etc., 191, 194.

Ubique floret, 242.

Verbum Dei, 113.
Verbum Dei manet in aeternum, 243.
Veritas filia Temporis, 306.
Veritas liberabit, Bonitas regnabit, 43.
Versutus celat scientiam, 122.
Vincet tandem veritas, 187, 189.
Viressit [sic] vulnere veritas, 299.
Virtus beatos efficit, 82.
Vivat rex, 115.
Vivet tamen post funera virtus, 128.

Welcome the wight that bringeth such light,
205.

INDEX OF INITIALS OF DESIGNERS OR ENGRAVERS

A., 123, 125a, 129, 225, 228.
B., E., 152.
B., G., 242.
B., R., 169, 171.
D., I., (?) 128.

D., W., (149).
G., T., 173, 182.
S., (?) 174.
T., C., 169, 171.
V. L., A., 225, 228.

INDEX OF DEVICES AND COMPARTMENTS ACCORDING TO SUBJECTS REPRESENTED

THE Royal Arms, the Arms of the Stationers' Company, and those of London occur in many devices and compartments, and are therefore only indexed when they form the main part of a design.

Initials are only indexed when the design might most conveniently be described as one containing the initials in question.

Numbers in square brackets indicate compartments or borders.

Armorial bearings, initials, marks, monograms, and rebuses should be sought under the general headings.

A and heart, 377.

Abraham and Isaac, 239.

Alcione (kingfisher), 321.

Altar with R. Y., 404, 405.

Anchors: with *Anchora Spei*, 164, 170, 192, 195, 210, 222, 232, 233; with *Floreat in Aeternum*, 423; anchor and dolphin, 414; —— and lion, 240; —— serpent and hands, 176, 178, 366, 390; —— skull, child's head, etc., 287.

Angel with heart and cross, 172; —— with rose and E. R., 426.

Armorial bearings: Aberdeen, 394; Arbuthnet, 225, 228; Badger, 417; Barker, 213; Beale, 374; Bretton (?), 18; Burghley, [162]; Cambridge University, 234, 399; Catherine Parr, [109]; Cumberland, Earl of, 199; Davidson, 65; J. Day, 200; R. Day, 245, 245*; Drapers' Company, 135, [185]; East, 206, 209; Geneva, 136, [370]; Hatton, 229; Marshall, 87; Oxford University, 43, 285, 336, 338, 407, 408, 427: Pynson, 35; Royal Arms, [45], 57, 115; Saint Albans, 4; Seton, 261; Stationers' Company, 353; Walsingham, [185], *and see* Tiger's Head: Westminster, 355.

Armorial bearings (not identified): (?) a battle-axe, 410; five fusils conjoined in fess, etc., 322; fretty, a martlet for diff., 244; lion on anchor, 240; (?) open book and sword, 347; wyvern's head, two keys, 373.

Barrel. *See* Tun.

Beehive, [162].

Bell and A. I., 253, 279.

Biblical scenes, H. D., [231], [256].

Bird and 'wick,' 368, 376.

Bird-headed pillar, etc., 309.

Birds, butterflies, I. N., [26].

Book, open, with glory from clouds, 278, 300, [335]; —— and sword, 347.

Boy on dolphin, 166; —— waking another, [116]; —— with wings and weight, 142, 393.

Boys and I. D., 152; —— throwing at tree, 96, 97, 146; four, playing musical instruments, [148]; two naked, 141.

Brazen Serpent. *See* Serpent.

Bush, Burning, 197.

Caduceus, with serpents, book, and dove, 112; —— Mercury's hat, cornucopias, 293; —— owl and M. B., 380. *See* Clasped hands.

Candle, Burning, 412, 413.

Chariot, 177, 188.

Cherub's Head, 219.

Charity, Tree of, 96, 97, 146.

Christ Triumphant, 208.

Circle in triangle, 369.

Clasped hands, caduceus, cornucopias, 273, 274; —— —— —— with F. K., 397, 402, 403; —— and rope, 372.

Clock, 342.

Cock on woodpile, 247.

Combination devices: Geneva arms and Jaggard's mark, [370]; open book, star, and Short's monogram, [335].

Compasses, 334, 411.

Cranes, Three, 236, 241.

Daniel in the wilderness, 308.

David and Goliath, H. D., [256].

Death's head. *See* Skull.

Demeter (?), 188.

Dolphin and anchor, 414. *See* Boy.

Dragon car, 188.

Eagle and young, 277, 280; crowned eagle, 409; two-headed eagle, 361, 362. *See* Half Eagle.

Edward VI in Council [110].

England, Genius of, 138.

Evangelists, Ensigns of the Four, 16, 33, [221].

Faith and Humility, [221]; Faith triumphant over Death (?), 383-5.

Falcon, crowned, 401.

Fame (?), Athena, and tree, 410; Fame and Victory, H. B., [230].

Feathers, Prince of Wales's, 354.

Fides et Humilitas, [221].

Fist, clenched, 357, 359; mailed, with sword, 314.

Flames (factotum), 421.

Fleur-de-lis, 216, 235, 242, 251, 258, 263-72, 294, 298, 381, 415, (420).

Flower-vase and sun, 286, 290, 343.

Fortune on globe, 167.

Fox and wolf, [120].

Gardener, daw and sun, 201. *See* Men planting.

George, St., and dragon, 61, 64, 117.

Gillyflower with G. S., 320: —— with rose, etc., 283.

Good Shepherd, The, 153, 202, 207.

Griffin, 144, 157, 158, 262; —— on stone, or book, over ball with wings, 246, 339; —— segreant, 144*, 284; griffin's head, 374.

Half eagle and key, 136, [370]; half rose and half pomegranate, 135.

Hand and star, 121, 257, 260. *See* Clasped hands; Fist; Wrist.

Hare, [169], [171]; —— rye, sun, 143, [169], [171], 275, 286, 319, 343.

Harp, crowned, 398.

Hawk, Hooded, 163; 'hawk and small bird,' *see* Eagle and young.

Heart, Burning, 392, 420, 421, 422; —— purged in fire, 83; —— and A, 377.

Heads, Two, joined at back, 365.

Hen, rye, bell, 386, 388.

Hind (Hatton's crest), 229.

Honeysuckle and Ling, 301.

Hornblowers, I. D., 295.

Horse, Black, 206, 209.

213

Initials: E. A., [360]; I. A.,[160]; C. B., [204], [220]; H. B., [230]; N. B., 84β; H. D., [231], [255], [256]; R. F. and D., 56; W. L., 103; G. M., [419]; I. M., [81]; T. M., 167; I. N., [26], [81], [98]; T. Pf., [140]; I. R., 135; O. R.,[131]; T. R.,[111]; W. R., [62]; I. S., 51, 54; R. S., 84α; P. T., 60; R. T., [147], [196]; E. W., [109].

John, St., the Evangelist, 67, 68, 70, 72.
Jove with oaks, 367.
Judith, 89.
Justice striking a bushel, 313; —— and Mercy (?), [204], [220]; —— and Religion, 307.

Keys, Two, 373.
King in Council, [110].
Kingfisher, 321.

Lamb, 371. *See* Sheep.
Landscape and coronet, 291.
Lily (factotum), 420; three lilies on one stalk, 217.
Ling and honeysuckle, 301.
Lion's head, H. M., 215.
Lucrece, 80, [133], 151, 161, 173.

Maiden's head, 31.
Mailed hand and sword, 314.
Man (? Mars) armed, 180; —— in chariot, 177; man barking logs, 169, 171, 190; man and woman, T. P., 344; old man praying, 308: —— —— with doves, 282, 292; —— ——, *Scientia*, [169], [171], 205; —— —— and tree, 310, 311, 348-51. *See* Men.
Marks (often with monogram): L. Andrewe, 74; R. Badger, 417; R. Bankes, 66; G. Barrevelt, 7; R. Bradock, [346]; J. Byddell, 78, 79, 82, [85], [94]; J. Ca-

wood, 126, 129; W. Caxton, 1, 2, 10-12, 19-21, 23-5, 27, 30, 42, 46, 49, 50; R. Copland, 36, 71, 73, 77; H. Denham, [218]; H. Disle, 172; F. Egmont, 7; T. Finlason, 358, 363; R. Grafton, [91], [92], 95, 104, [105], 114, 122; W. Gryffyth, 144: H. Jacobi, 17, 34; W. Jaggard, [370]; P. Kaetz, 63; N. Lecomte, 5; W. Middleton, 93, 102, [106]; A. Myllar, 22; U. Mylner, 39; J. Notary, 8, 13, 28; J. Pelgrim, 17; H. Pepwell, 47, 48, 52; T. Petit, [86]; T. Purfoot, [140]; J. Reynes, 55, 61; S. Roedius, [130], J. Skot, 59α; J. Siberch, 58; H. Singleton, 127, 198, 250; M. Sparke, 406; J. Walley, 183; R. Wyer, 69.
Mars. *See* Man armed.
Mask and A. H., 379.
Men dicing in garret, [169], [171]; —— planting and watering, 352; —— and skeleton, 128; —— mirror, Death, 337.
Mercury on globe, 382.
Mermaid, 149, 155, [168]; two-tailed, 248, 259; merman and mermaid, 37.
Mill and miller, 22; mill and sun, 38.
Monograms: H. Bell, 386, 388; T. Burton, 364; H. Bynneman, 149, 155; W. Chepman, 29; R. Copland, 71, 73; T. Creed, 314; H. Denham, [218]; W. Faques, 15; A. Islip, 330; R. Jugge, 123, 125, [132], [134], [137]; T. Langley, 387; T. Marshe, [154], 180; R. Pynson, 3, 6, 9, 32, 41, 44, [53]; J. Rastell, 37, 40; W. Seres, [139], [148]; P. Short, [335]; J. Skot, 59β, 75, 76; R. Tottell, 121; E. Whitchurch, [100], [101], [108]; W. Williamson, 166; R. Wolfe, 163.
Moses and David, H. D., [255].

Nicholas, St., and three children, 5.
Nightingale in bush, [181], [182].

Occasio, 281.
Old Man. *See* Man.
Opportunity, 281.
Owl, snakes and M.B., 380.
Ox on bridge, 288, 289.

Palm tree, 428; —— with toads and serpents, 226.
Parnassus, Summits of, 328.
Pavior, 345.
Peace and Plenty, 282, 292,? 344.
Pegasus, 316-18.
Pelican in her piety, 123, 125, [137], 165, [181], 225, 228.
Peter and Paul, Sts., 276.
Pheasant, 238.
Pheons, Three, 65.
Phœnix, 203, 297, 417; —— and satyrs, 252, 254.
Pity, Our Lady of, 82.
Plant with R. I., 156.
Pliny's *Historia Naturalis*, 330.
Pope, cardinal, bishop, etc., 391.
Portraits: J. Day, 145; J. Wight (?), [169], [171], 205.
Prince of Wales's feathers, 354.
Printing-press, 389.
Protestant angel, 383-5.
Prudence and Justice, 123, 125*a*, 225, 228.

Rake, hay-fork, scythe, 305.
Ram and goat, 103.
Rebus: of Barker, [169], [171], 190: Henry Bell, 386, 388; Dawson, 201; Day [116]; Garrat Dewes, [169], [171]; Gardiner, 201; Grafton, 88, 95, 104, [110], 114; Harrison, 143, [169], [171], 275, 286, 319, 343; Abel Jeffes, 253, 279; Jugge, [181], [182]; Middleton, 93, 102, [106]; William Norton, [169], [171], 174, 175; Oxenbridge, 288, 289; Seton, 261; Singleton, 127, 198, 250; Watkins, [169],

[171]; Wight, [169], [171], 205; Reyner Wolfe, [120].
Rebuses, Comp. with six, [169], [171].
Resurrection, The, 124, 208.
Right hand and star, 257, 260.
Rome, History of, [324].
Rose, 420; (factotum), 422; crowned rose, 332, 333, 396, 400; three roses, 63. *See* Half rose.
Rose-garland, 71, 73.

Sciences, The Seven, 122.
Sea-goats, 249.
Serpent, The Brazen, 118, 119, [120]; winged serpent, 340. *See* Caduceus; Anchor; Wrist.
Sheaf. *See* Hare, rye; Wheatsheaf.
Sheep, and *Virgula Divina*, 223; the Lost Sheep, 153, 202, 207.
Shield with maiden's head, 31; with mill and sun, 38; with S.P.Q.R., 276; with wings and *Sursum*, 237; comp. with two shields at top, [62].
Skull, hour-glass, etc., 304; —— book, globe, 341.
Smew and 'wick,' 368, 376.
Spheres, E. A., [360].
Star, 150, [335]; —— with H. D., 211, 214. *See* Hand and Star.
Sun, 49, 99, [100], [101], [108], 395; —— and clouds, 375; —— and winds, 90; with I. M. S. W., 159; with sunflower, rose, H. K., 224. *See* Flower-vase; Hare, rye; Woman.
Sun, moon, and stars, 12, 19-21, 23-5, 27, 30, 37, 42, 46.
Sunflower, sun, night (?), 315.
Swan, 227, 303.

Thistle, crowned, with E. R., 418.
Three cranes, 236, 241.
Tiger's Head, 184, [185], 212, [221], 296, 323; —— and lamb, 191, 194.

Time, 243; —— reaping, 425; —— and Truth, 186, 312, 331; ——, Death and Book, 424; ——, Truth and Calumny, 306.

Touchstone with *Verbum Dei*, 113.

Tree, and two female figures, 410; —— in storm, 302. *See* Boys; Man.

Triangles interlaced, 14. *See* Circle.

Trinity, The, 16, 33, 34, 52.

Triptolemus (?), 188.

Truth scourged, 299. *See* Time.

Tun (Middleton's rebus), 93, 102, [106]; (Singleton's rebus), 127, 198, 250; —— and graft, or tree, 88, 95, 104, [110], 114; —— and 'nor,' 169, 171, 174, 175; —— in sea, 261.

Virtues, Seven, [85].

Wheatsheaf, 356.

Wild Men (as supporters), 29, 60, 65.

Woman, and horses, 138; —— clothed with the sun, 107; —— with book and candle, 187, 189; —— with sun and cup, 325, 326, 327, 329, 416; woman's head, 179, 193, 378.

Women, Two (Justice and Religion), 307; women and tree, 410.

Woodwoses. *See* Wild Men.

Wrist and snake, 355.

Wyvern, 199; wyvern's head, 373.